Acclaim for Lesley Blanch's

# The WILDER SHORES of LOVE

"Lesley Blanch had the engaging idea of making a portrait gallery of four nineteenth-century European women whose lives are woven into the history of North Africa and the Near East. A fabulous quartet . . . who out-dared the heroines of romantic novels, lived lustily and swayed the course of empire."
—*New York Times Book Review*

"Four seething but most enjoyable studies in headlong nonconformity. The subjects are nineteenth-century European women who were similarly possessed by imperative drives—neurotic, atavistic, or sexual—toward the desert East."
—*The New Yorker*

"Love, wanderlust, faraway places—all that Romance implies—make up this delicious book about four European women who preferred life in the Levant to the confines of 'civilization.' Ideal reading."    —*Washington Post Book World*

"Four unusual women form the subject of these lighthearted biographical studies. They were rebels who broke away from western restraints in order to share an uninhibited life. . . . A sophisticated, witty book."    —*Times Literary Supplement*

"A splendid quartet of biographies. . . . They were women of character, style and spirit who all wrote lusty footnotes to history. It is as engrossing a literary trip through the exotic East as I have taken. Extraordinary."    —*San Jose Mercury News*

# *The*
# WILDER SHORES
# *of* LOVE

# The
# WILDER SHORES
## of LOVE

## LESLEY BLANCH

CARROLL & GRAF PUBLISHERS
NEW YORK

THE WILDER SHORES OF LOVE

Carroll & Graf Publishers
An Imprint of Avalon Publishing Group Incorporated
161 William Street, 16th Floor
New York, NY 10038

First Carroll & Graf trade paperback edition 1983
Second Carroll & Graf trade paperback edition 1996
Third Carroll & Graf trade paperback edition 2002

Published by arrangement with Simon & Schuster

Library of Congress Cataloging-in-Publication Data is available.

ISBN: 0-7867-1030-6

Printed in the United States of America
Distributed by Publishers Group West

# ACKNOWLEDGMENTS

I wɪsʜ ᴛᴏ acknowledge with gratitude the generosity of all those people who have placed their valuable time and knowledge at my disposal. My thanks are especially due to General Catroux, for "talking Sahara" on the subject of Isabelle Eberhardt. To Major Hartley-Clarke, for permission to quote from his collection of Burton manuscripts and correspondence. To Mr. Peter de Hunt, for the loan of unpublished Burton material. To Mr. John Hilliard, for permission to reproduce one of his photographs of North Africa. To Mrs. Osyth Leeston, for her patience in dealing with the manuscript in all its stages. To Monsieur André Dermenghen, Director of the Bibliothéque du Gouvernement Général of Algiers. To Canon Gibney of St. Mary Magdalene's Church, Mortlake. To the Librarian and staff of the Foreign Office Library, and that of the Public Records Office. To the Director and Trustees of the Camberwell Public Library, for permission to reproduce photographs from Lady Burton's estate, now in their possession. To the Chief Librarian and the Director of the Kensington Public Library, for permission to study the Burton library and private papers. To the Curator of Leighton House, for permission to reproduce drawings from Sir Frederick Leighton's sketchbooks. To Mr. Cox, late of the London Library, for his recollections of Sir Richard Burton. To the staff of the many libraries where I worked while writing this book: in particular, the Sorbonne, the Bibliothéque National and the Library of Ste Geneviève. To the New York Society Library where I am greatly indebted to Miss Helen Ruskill, the Public Library of the City of New York, and that of Columbia University. I wish to acknowledge my debt to E. M. Oddie's biography of Lady Ellenborough, published in 1936, and also Mr. B. Morton's book on Aimée Dubucq de Rivery, published in 1923, both of which provided much valuable material. Lastly, I wish to thank Professor Louis Massignon for his indulgent encouragement and interest, when this book was only a shadowy project scrawled on the back of an envelope.

# CONTENTS

Love and Love always read from the same book, but not always from the same page.

Richard Garnett,
*de Flagello Myrteo*

# INTRODUCTION

THE FOUR women who form the subject of this book might be described as northern shadows flitting across a southern landscape. All of them belonged to the West, to the fast-graying climate of nineteenth-century Europe, where the twentieth-century disintegration of women, as such, was already foreshadowed. Yet although of widely different natures, backgrounds and origins, my subjects all had this in common —each found, in the East, those glowing horizons of emotion and daring which were, for them, now vanishing from the West, to be replaced by "careers" *tout-court*. Each of them, in her own way, used love as a means of individual expression, of liberation and fulfillment within that radiant periphery.

There have been many women, particularly Englishwomen, who have been enthralled by the Oriental legend; who have followed the beckoning Eastern star wherever it led. On great voyages or little trips; as travelers or tourists; as eccentrics such as Lady Hester Stanhope, or Orientalists such as Gertrude Bell or Freya Stark. But the women I have chosen are less intellectual; they are women whose achievements remained on a purely emotional plane, and who, for all their daring, saw the East from an entirely personal or subjective viewpoint.

Aimée Dubucq de Rivery, the gentle, inexperienced convent girl, in violent contrast to Isabelle Eberhardt, the chaotic Slav, mystic and voluptuary; Jane Digby, the wealthy, raffish divorcée, loving so many yet always retaining a curious innocence, a romantic idealism; Isabel Arundell, the impoverished Victorian miss, loving with single-minded fury, biding her time, stifled in conventional living. All of them responded to a similar inward impulse to which the East offered fulfillment.

All these women were realists of romance who broke with their century's dream, to live it, robustly. At that moment, romantic living, if embraced at all, was interpreted in terms of sighs and renunciations. La Dame aux Camelias coughing out her lungs behind a lace-edged handkerchief. Chopin's music, played by Liszt, its strains floating out over the misty lakeside gardens of Como to mingle with the bells of some forgotten convent. Charlotte Stieglitz committing suicide, hoping, thus, to provide artistic stimulus for her second-rate husband. It was a pallid way of life, and between its negations and the alternative Victorian gentilities and pruderies, which gained, year by year, life, living—loving—was muffled, and womanhood itself became a scandalous secret. Between the coughing poets and the social and sociological taboos, it required great daring to snatch at the underlying richness which the East still promised.

It was a time when the West was suddenly aware of the romantic aspects of the East. In the eighteenth century it had been seen as a fabulous backdrop; a stage setting for Mozart's *L'Enlèvement du Serail*, all toppling turbans and giddy goings-on in key with the elegant salons of Versailles or the Hofburg where it was first applauded. But even such tinkling echoes had died away by the time the nineteenth century dawned and Byron's verses were intoxicating an avid public. Now another, more sultry East was seen, although treated with an equal subjectivity. Mock heroics gave place to savage grandeurs. Travelers such as Prince Pückler Muskau returned with tales of chivalresque Arabs and the splendors of Oriental hospitality. Far away, across the steppes Pushkin luxuriated in the exoticism of Crimean legends and was to be followed by Lermontov, writing of Caucasian warriors. Presently, jeweled scimitars adorned even the most prosaic country houses and the "Mameluke's Valse" lay open on every pianoforte. But Ingres and Delacroix were covering huge canvases with voluptuous scenes where beneath the expanses of exoticism and local color, the most disturbing realities of flesh and blood were apparent.

And some women, such as my four subjects, must have been aware of this, even subconsciously. Instinctively they must have sensed the contracting horizons of their age and seen the cold light of reason spreading like a gray streak across the blue. It was to spread over the whole sky. Yet the romantic mirage could still be translated into reality, could still be lived—elsewhere. They turned Eastward trustingly.

However, it must be admitted that in the turning they still expected and retained a degree of freedom unknown to Eastern women. Purdah, the veil . . . these things they swept aside. Isabel Eberhardt avoided the question by dressing as a man. Lady Ellenborough retained financial independence and was accordingly accepted even more unquestioningly by her husband's tribe. Aimée Dubucq de Rivery, although for some years compelled to live entirely on Eastern terms, finally obtained her own. Of all four, it was perhaps Isabel Arundell, the brisk, the managing, the Anglo-Saxon, who most nearly approximated to the traditional pattern of Oriental wifely submission. But all four of them, as I remarked before, seemed to sense in their passivity far larger opportunities of self-expression as women, than any left to their Western sisters.

Perhaps, too, this very passivity offered something which was vanishing from the West, something to which they were all subconsciously drawn. Repose: the Eastern climate of contemplation, of *Kef*, of nothingness, brought to its quintessential state of voluptuous, animal stillness was a state wholly alien to the West. Even leisure, an entirely different thing, was vanishing. From afar, a mighty whirring could be heard approaching: it was the roar and clatter of a million mechanical devices gaining momentum, forming into an overwhelming uproar of ingenuity and efficiency: speed and action for their own sake. This onslaught was to hammer at Western mankind until there were nerves, but no senses left.

*Kef*, contemplation, gilded opium pills and the drowsy peace of senses lulled by satiety . . . these things the East still offered, and some, if not all of my subjects, were, I believe, aware of this. In the East, there was still "world enough and time" to be *women*.

If we consider the least free of all, Aimée Dubucq de Rivery, a convent girl captured by corsairs and flung into the harem of the Grand Turk, we see that even in the Seraglio, as a slave, she had considerably more freedom to be essentially a woman than many women now enmeshed in the complex mechanism of our economic civilization.

In writing of romantic women who turned toward the East, it might be asked why I have not included Lady Hester Stanhope, the archetype, or doyenne of this band. But to me she does not qualify, since she was not so much seeking fulfillment as a woman, as seeking escape from her own nature; she craved power rather than love. To me she always remains a puppet, strutting grandiosely, forever posturing before an alien landscape she persisted in regarding as her backcloth.

My subjects are of softer clay.

Take the case of Jane Digby, Lady Ellenborough, who, for all her birth and beauty, sweetness and allure, still came to grief, to what seemed the end, to romantic bankruptcy in her forties. This was the point of disillusion at which she, too, turned Eastward. To love fully, with complete abandon (but ever with great style), she smashed all the taboos of her time; her conduct was at best eccentric, at worst, scandalous. Hers was a life lived entirely against the rules, reasons and warnings: and it was triumphantly happy.

I have chosen Isabel Burton because she is the supreme example of a woman who lived and had her being entirely through love. Her life story is one of the greatest adventure stories, too, because she loved Burton of Arabia, one of the greatest adventurers of his age. She was a Victorian woman, an impassioned Catholic, with all the prejudices and conformisms those two states imply; yet she married a heretic, one of the most unorthodox, defiant social outlaws. She was never to accompany him on those desperate ventures which made his life so astonishing. But such is the power of love that she lived them all by proxy. Through loving him she entered Mecca, explored Africa, penetrated Harar. . . . Thus she achieved a greater degree of liberation, knew more of achievement and the East, and came closer to the heart of adventure than perhaps any other woman of her day.

Lastly, I chose Isabelle Eberhardt as being the embodiment of a period of transition, from that age when women looked for fulfillment in love, to the moment when they hoped to find it through an equality of work, aims and means. She is a haunting figure, this Russian-born girl who went into the desert dressed as a man, with shaven head, to live among the Arabs as one of them. Her slow disintegration and disillusion stands out prophetically at the turn of the century, as a first manifestation of what was later to grow into this, our age of anxiety.

The mistake made by Isabelle Eberhardt, and by so many other women who followed, was to believe she could go as a man, into a man's world, and thus live more fully. But she remained forever *en travesti*. The disguise was only skin deep. Beneath, she remains submissive, gentle, generous, and men exploited her cruelly. She is the forerunner of many characters in contemporary fiction, that nihilistic, neurotic and disillusioned flotsam.

She is, too, first symbol of the disintegrating West. And this brings me back to my beginning; each of these four women found some, if not all of her fulfillment, as a *woman,* along wilder Eastern shores.

# ·I·

# ISABEL BURTON

*A Two-Headed Profile*

From the beginning she had known what she wanted, and proceeded single-minded, with the force of a steam engine, towards her goal. There was never a moment's doubt or regret. She wanted the East; and from the moment she set eyes on Richard Burton, with his dark Arabic face, his "questing panther eyes," he was, for her, that lodestar East, the embodiment of all her longings. Man and land were identified. He was one of the world's greatest travelers, an Orientalist without equal, who wore the green turban of the Hadj as his right: besides Burckhardt he was the only European, at that time, to have penetrated Mecca as a pilgrim; to have attained the inner sanctuary and seen what few other infidels had lived to recount. He spoke twenty-eight languages (one of them pornography, it was unkindly said) and many obscure Oriental dialects, but he always averred that Arabic was his native tongue. His travels in the East had created a stir in England, then unaccustomed to the cheap easy voyages inaugurated later by Mr. Cook. His books had been Isabel's constant reading since her youth. She had followed his legendary adventures step by step, and so, when at last they met, he had become the personification of an ideal—a hemisphere. "I have *got* to live with him night and day *for all my life*," she wrote to her mother, when after ten years of passionate longing and frustration, parental sanction was still withheld. "I wish I were a man," she went on. "If I were, I would be Richard Burton; but, being only a woman, I would be Richard Burton's wife." Isabel Arundell's emphasis had an obsessive force. She had to have him—in life—in death.

They were a strange pair for any age: in their own, they were particularly odd. But most people recognized their absolute dependence on each other, in spite of offhand posturings on Burton's part. They were elective affinities, "one soul in two bodies," never far apart in life or death, as Hagar the Gypsy foretold. Burton, who rocked Victorian England by the pre-Freudian tone of his writings on the East, and whose brilliant and cynical mind was a jumble of hard facts and woolly mysticisms, always maintained that psychologically speaking he was a broken twin, and that she was the shattered, or missing fragment. Throughout their lives they seemed to be united by a series of curiously predestined, or coincidental happenings. There were waking and sleeping visions, telepathic conversations, presentiments and strange chance encounters that fitted so neatly into the web of predestination and prayer which Isabel delighted to spin. She was an ardent Catholic, but superstitious too, and given, in her later years, to psychic research, which like her belief in a soul for the animals she loved, caused black looks from her Church. He was a loudly self-proclaimed agnostic, but his superstitions and mystical nature kept him alternating between bouts of Sūfism (he was a Master Sūfi) and a sort of left-handed Catholicism. His true religion (and perhaps, his love for Isabel) was the only thing about which he had any *pudeur*. He delighted in mocking all ecclesiastical hypocrisies, high and low; he disliked religious manifestations as much as cant, and appeared to most people as a swaggering iconoclast. Yet he was very emotional, and used to sob, on the rare occasions he attended Mass, Isabel records in her journal. When her brother died, Burton gave her five pounds for a Mass to be said for the dead man. Though this, like so many of Isabel's statements, might be interpreted two ways. Her proselytizing zeal was such that Burton may well have been buying himself some peace and quiet. Still, this would be the cynic's view, and not mine.

The more I study this odd couple, the more I perceive their tragic grandeur. He was a desert eagle in a cage, brought low largely by a tactless manner—an insistence in both word and deed of that principle *Honor, not Honors* which he took as his device, and which so impressed General Gordon that he never failed to quote it, as a heading, in his correspondence with Burton. In his public life Burton almost invariably did right—but did it in the wrong way, a fatal reverse of the more worldly method of doing the wrong thing in the right way.

As to Isabel, she "nothing petty did or mean"; though often maddening, no doubt, she emerges from the tangle of contradictory memoirs, letters and journals as a great woman; overwhelming, but loving, loyal, courageous and generous, with a sense of humor (not, however, applied to Richard, whom she described as her Earthly God and King). Both were tragic and comic figures. Together they found much happiness: yet together their life had the doomed inevitability of a Greek drama. Loving with her all-encompassing greed, she destroyed him; and he, trapped and tamed by her affections, destroyed himself. In the development of their strange relationship, we see that the West overcame the East. Indeed, Isabel acted towards Burton very much as England was then acting towards the East. She colonized him. To Burton's East, she became the managing West, civilizing, refining, elevating, protecting, suppressing. . . . And her burning of his journal was the ultimate gesture of conquest, the final suppression of any posthumous independence. It was a last assertion of personal domination over her empire. In the margin of Queen Victoria's reign, a more intimate, but no less glorious conquest was consummated.

If, in this profile of Isabel Burton, I am thought to give too much place to her husband, it must be remembered that her whole life and being was bound up in his: he was her all. His every action, every thought came to have a bearing on her life and character. At first, it was a girlish passion; it grew into love, a merging of one being into another, until, at last, to write of the Burtons apart would be impossible. What the Victorian woman could not achieve herself she sometimes achieved by proxy, by *loving*: all the adventures and dreams and aspirations; the failures, too, for no man ever fails in the eyes of his love. After all, as one French writer has said, "*It is enough to love a man, to have him accomplish, for you, all the conquests he has failed to make; to have him fulfill, for you, a purpose for which he himself has known only failure.*" Isabel lived through her husband, and summed up her whole life's attitude when she chose the epitaph for her tomb, placed beside his, in the bizarre marble tent where he is buried at Mortlake:

". . . *Isabel, his wife.*" It was enough. Life could have offered her no greater crown.

*       *       *

Isabel Arundell was born on March 20, 1831, at 4 Great Cumberland Place, which was then not tainted by the proximity of commercial Oxford Street. It was a sober and elegant residential quarter of London, suited to the Arundell family, who though by no means rich, belonged to the once puissant Catholic nobility of England. The Arundells run through the history of England from the time of William the Conqueror: but always when they jockeyed for position it was with an eye on Rome. They were courtiers, statesmen, patriots—but first of all Catholics. Isabel's father had no particular property to sustain him, and turned to trade, dividing his time between a wine-merchant's establishment in London and a wing of Wardour Castle, lent him to accommodate his burgeoning family by his rich cousin, Isabel's godfather, Lord Arundell. Her childhood was rosily innocent, full of country delights, bird's-nesting, following the hounds on a fat pony, visiting the sick cottagers, wearing a Red Riding Hood cloak, a basket of goodies on her arm. Christmas tree parties for the tenants, dispensing the mysterious and much prized Victorian "flannels"; pet dogs, pet lambs, pets everywhere, little brothers and sisters gamboling in the June hay, and over all, the temperate English sunshine.

In London, there were more worldly delights: rides in the Park, in the family carriages, the coachmen and footmen in dark green and gold liveries; life lived upstairs, in the fifth-floor nursery world of a London childhood, barred windows through which the lamplighter could be glimpsed on his rounds; little narrow basket grates, where muffins could be toasted, flight after flight of stairs, up which the three nursemaids toiled, bringing wholesome food or coals or hot water; and ruling over all, the mighty head nurse, old Nanny, who shepherded her starched charges downstairs to the drawing room every day at six o'clock, for a sort of ceremonial parental levee.

For a few years before Isabel and her sisters were to make their debut in London society—"The Season" being a sort of ritual marriage market to which every parent then subscribed anxiously—the Arundells found it expedient to withdraw altogether from London, in order to husband their resources for the decisive season. They retreated to Essex, and Isabel's memoirs paint a nostalgic picture of Furze, the pretty, unpretentious old house that was her home. There, she ran wild, in the woods, as in the library. At Furze she first began groping towards her lodestar East. In the woods, she found the Gypsy encampments, and spent her days among them, drawn irresistibly towards the dark, free Romany people. In them, she found those first echoes of the exotic, the East, which was to be her life's obsession. In the library she discovered *Tancred*; and Disraeli's strange Oriental conte remained a lifetime companion, a bedside book, and one which, with her Bible, went with her everywhere, even in the desert, in her saddle pocket. "I almost knew it by heart, so that when I came to the Lebanon . . . when I found myself in a Bedouin camp or among the Maronite and Druze strongholds, . . . nothing surprised me. . . ."

She was going through the "difficult" stage; she was obstinate, secretive and overweight. "I liked to slope off to my own den, moping there for hours." She confided to her journal her apparently hopeless craving for "Gypsies, Bedouin Arabs and everything *Eastern and mystic; and especially a wild and lawless life.*" Poor Mrs. Arundell. She began to have premonitory twinges over Isabel's first season. So important to make a good first impression: second seasons, besides being a double outlay, lowered the starting price, so to speak. . . . Thus Mrs. Arundell, discussing her daughter's sporting chances like a thoroughbred filly. Mr. Arundell was easygoing, and more interested in fox hunting. He relied comfortably on his noble relatives, such as the Duchess of Norfolk, to launch Isabel on the social flood tide, which was, in fact, what happened. Isabel's first season was brilliant. Her debut was at Almack's, and she was greatly in demand among the eligible young gentlemen who were not insensible to her charms and birth. An Arundell, a Junoesque blonde, went far to mitigate the awful fact that she had no dowry. Isabel received much gratifying notice, which she treated with indifference. In vain did her mother and aunts try persuasion, threats and tears. Miss Isabel, "Puss" to the family, had other ideas. To the

Gypsies she had become "Daisy," *persona grata* in their camps and caves hidden in the Essex woods. One of them, Hagar Burton, a self-styled Romany princess, had cast Isabel's horoscope as a farewell present. She wrote it out for her in Romany characters. Isabel could not read it, but she learned it by heart, treasured it, believed in it implicitly and shaped her life accordingly.

"You will cross the sea, and be in the same town with your Destiny and know it not. Every obstacle will rise up against you, and such a combination of circumstances that it will require all your courage, energy and intelligence to meet them. . . . You will bear the name of our tribe, and be right proud of it. You will be as we are, but far greater than we. Your life is all wandering, changes and adventure. One soul in two bodies in life or death, never long apart. Show this to the man you take for your husband. . . . Hagar Burton."

But such a document, redolent of wood smoke and all the mystery of an outlaw race would not have been any more acceptable to the *jeunesse dorée* of the London ballrooms than this *jeunesse dorée* was to Isabel. She kept her secret, and went on waltzing dutifully while remaining obviously detached from the scene. Presently the season came to an end and with it the Arundell family's first hopes for Isabel's future. Until next year, then, they must retrench. They sailed for Boulogne, at that time the haunt of impoverished English society, both select and shady. The two sets never met. There were fast streets and respectable promenades. The Arundells moved among the slow set in unimpeachable dullness. It was the first time Isabel had been abroad. She had the English arrogance of her age and birth. "Abroad" was of course not identified with the legendary, longed-for East. "Abroad" was merely the rest of Western Europe that was not English, a wretched place, full of foreigners and bad food. Isabel's journal dismisses the French *cuisine de famille* as "dinners which would have been scarcely served up in my father's kennel at home. . . ." She was still a long way from that state of tourist bliss in which later she was to live beside Burton in the Syrian desert, often in conditions of sharp discomfort, but which she was to describe as "holy, solemn and wild."

In Boulogne, Isabel and her sisters were strictly dragooned by Mrs.

Arundell, but even so they learned to smoke their father's cigars. "People used to say, 'What makes those Arundell girls so pale? They must dance too much.' Alas, poor things! it was just the want of these innocent recreations that drove us to so dark a deed," she says in her memoirs.

The family remained in Boulogne for two years, years of economy and a good deal of idling. Walks along the jetty with Mama. Needlework in the salon, or a covert eyeing of the fast set, glimpsed shopping in the Grande Rue. These were the carefree families of retired half-pay officers, Indian Army grass widows, or rakish young men of good family, "generally with something shady about money hanging over them," says Isabel, a note of longing creeping in. The daily pattern must have been stifling to such a girl, who burned for "a wild, lawless life"; still craved to be "different" . . . to reach that remote and unattainable East. But Hagar's horoscope still brought her hope . . . meanwhile, there was *Tancred*, and Papa's cigars, and her journal. She had confided to its pages her ideal man—the mysterious unknown lover who would one day materialize, and with whom she would justify Hagar's prophecy of "one soul in two bodies." Once again, she knew exactly what she wanted: "My ideal is about six feet in height; he has not an ounce of fat on him; he has broad and muscular shoulders, a powerful, deep chest; he is a Hercules of manly strength. He has black hair, a brown complexion, a clever forehead, sagacious eyebrows, large, black, wondrous eyes—those strange eyes you dare not take yours from off them—with long lashes. He is a soldier and a *man*; he is accustomed to command and to be obeyed. . . . His religion is like my own, free, liberal, and generous-minded. . . . He is only not a fidgety, strait-laced or mistaken-conscienced man on any subject; he is one of those strong men who lead, the mastermind who governs. . . ." Here is the romantic beau ideal of every novelette, a pre-Ouida guardsman, with an added virility in keeping with Isabel's vitality. . . . "Such a man only will I wed. I love this myth of my girlhood—for myth it is—next to God; and I look to the Star that Hagar the Gypsy said was the Star of my destiny, the Morning Star, which is the place I allot to my earthly God, because the ideal seems too high for this planet . . . and may never be found here. . . ."

9

Having thus disposed of her future, for good or ill, there was nothing for it but to return to the hateful present. But one day all was changed: walking on the Ramparts with her sister she came face to face with her Destiny—and, remarkably, recognized it as such. Here is her description: "One day . . . the vision of my awaking brain came towards us. He was five feet eleven inches in height, very broad, thin, and muscular; he had very dark hair; black, clearly defined eyebrows; a brown weatherbeaten complexion; straight *Arab* features; a determined-looking mouth and chin nearly covered by an enormous black mustache. I have since heard a clever friend say that 'he had the brow of a god and the jaw of a devil.' [Would Swinburne have recognized himself so temperately described as 'a clever friend,' one wonders?] But the most remarkable part of his appearance was two large black flashing eyes with long lashes, that pierced one through and through. He had a fierce, proud, melancholy expression; and when he smiled, he smiled as though it hurt him, and looked with impatient contempt at things generally. He was dressed in a black, short, shaggy coat, and shouldered a short thick stick, as if he were on guard."

Compare this catalogue of masculine charms with the paragon she had already described so minutely in her journal two years earlier, and it will be seen that the man she saw before her now was indeed its embodiment. He advanced towards her, a sort of darkling Heathcliff, indescribably alluring to the Victorian miss. "He looked at me as though he read me through and through in a moment. [Oh! to think of it, after all those myopic prigs at Almack's!] I was completely magnetized, and when we had got a little distance away, I turned to my sister and whispered to her, *That man will marry me.*'"

This swarthy stranger, this diabolic, was none other than Richard Burton, and that they were met together to fulfill the magic of the Gypsy's prediction was something Isabel never doubted. Next day, of course, they met again, at the same place. Of course, he followed the young ladies, and producing a piece of chalk scrawled his overture. *May I speak to you?* leaving the chalk on the wall; "so I took up the chalk," says Isabel, "and wrote back *No; mother will be angry*; and mother found it, and was angry; and after that we were stricter prisoners than ever."

To Isabel the encounter had come like some divine revelation: it was the justification of all her romantic longings. This ideal man, this dream lover, this wild and lawless Arab creature existed—he lived and breathed the same air—and he had noticed her, too! A week or so later the revelation was completed by an introduction. With a violent shock, Isabel heard his name, and the whole force of Hagar Burton's prophecy returned. " . . . You will cross the sea, and be in the same town with your Destiny and know it not. . . . *You will bear the name of our tribe, and be right proud of it.* . . ." She goes on, "I could think of no more at the moment. But I stole a look at him, and met his Gypsy eyes—those eyes which looked you through, glazed over, and saw something behind; the only man I have ever seen, not a Gypsy, with that peculiarity."

As the days went by, Isabel was in a frenzy of love, "grew red and pale, hot and cold, dizzy and faint. . . ." Her exasperated parents, unaware of the true nature of her complaint, sent for the doctor, who diagnosed indigestion and physicked her accordingly. But Isabel was always practical. She threw the pills on the fire, and though still fretting, remained confident in the Gypsy, her Destiny and her Morning Star, and concentrated on hours of prayer and a thorough reading of everything Burton had written at that time. "One day an exception was made to our dull rule of life. My cousin gave a tea party and dance, and the great majority flocked in, and there was Richard like a star among the rushlights! That was a night of nights; he waltzed with me once, and spoke to me several times, and I kept my sash where he put his arm round my waist to waltz, and my gloves, which his hands had clasped. I never wore them again."

\*     \*     \*

Now began a four-years period of longings and hopes deferred. The Arundells returned to London, and Isabel left Boulogne without seeing Burton again. Soon afterwards, he left for his daring pilgrimage to

Mecca. Isabel resumed the old social round and continued refusing advantageous suitors. She was now of age, very sure of herself and her love for Burton. The journal received a flood tide of confidences on the subject. "Shall I never be at rest with him to love and understand me, to tell every thought and feeling in far different scenes from there? Under canvas before Rangoon," she adds, wildly; and striking a more mystical note continues, "If Richard and I never marry, God will cause us to meet in the next world; we cannot be parted; we belong to each other." There was no stopping her, now, though the awful inaction, the necessity of being a ladylike stay-at-home in the narrow confines of the Victorian household appalled her. She was, without realizing it, as much in love with the adventurous life as the adventurer. There are frequent references to Richard's enviable vagabondage, and how well suited she would be to such a life. "A dry crust, privations, pain, danger for him I love . . . there is something in some women that seems born for the knapsack. . . ." It must have been particularly frustrating for her that there were now such frequent references to Richard Burton's daring travels; while she, his soul-mate, continued the treadmill of womanly restraint in Montague Place. "I believe my sister and I have now as much excitement and change as most girls, and yet I find everything slow. I long to rush round the world in an express; I feel as if I shall go mad if I remain at home."

She was sorely tried. No sooner had Burton achieved his pilgrimage to Mecca than he disappeared into India. His book on Mecca had made him famous overnight, but he did not come back to be lionized. Isabel prayed and hoped, and gloried in his fame, but pined too, behind that façade of buxom young womanhood which was so misleading. She appeared a tall, strong, auburn-haired creature with a high color, a large bust and soulful blue eyes. There is a portrait of her in girlhood, showing a rather heavy-chinned, ovoid face, the nose beaky with breeding, the compressed lips those of a prim miss rather than the passionate woman she was. Yet the general opinion was unanimous. She was beautiful to some, handsome to all; "exquisitely dressed," "fascinating," "radiant," "elegant" were some of the adjectives applied to her in contemporary memoirs. But it is sadly evident that she was not photogenic.

From India, Burton was off on another wild venture; Isabel read with pride and terror that he was heading an expedition to Harar in Abyssinia. Like Mecca, no white man had dared to enter it. But Burton succeeded, disguised as an Arab merchant. He always had a weakness for disguise, and indeed many of his moods and poses might be said to be another aspect of this craving. His love of mockery, of shocking, of presenting himself in a demoniacal light was all part of the mania for travesty. In the West it did him harm. Victorian England recoiled from his apparent lawlessness and swashbuckling. But in the East it bore rich fruits. His command of half a dozen dialects, imposed on perfect Persian, Hindustani, Arabic or whatever nationality he chose to impersonate, along with a complete identification, in both appearance and mental approach, was often his salvation in a tight corner.

His own adventures were as picturesque as anything in *The Thousand Nights and a Night* which he was later to translate. In his account, in the *Pilgrimage to Meccah*, one of the greatest of all travel books, we find, beside the dry facts he recounts so dispassionately, a lesser narrative thread full of gusto and Oriental slyness, which must have been most disquieting for Isabel. We read of drinking bouts in place of duels, to settle disagreements; of an incident where Burton outdrank and outwrestled an Albanian Captain of Irregulars in riotous post-Ramadan celebrations; of his most successful masquerade, that of a Persian peddler, who thus gained entry into all the harems; or as a physician, also most welcome to the ladies, one whose potions and philters had, besides other miraculous properties, cured some ebony slave girls of the fatal habit of snoring. Their prices had risen overnight, and he became *persona grata* at the slave traders' headquarters.

But he could not linger forever in the teeming *souks* he loved. One day, having bought the shroud that every pilgrim carries with him on the desert crossing, Burton rode out towards Mecca, under "a sky terrible in its stainless beauty and the splendors of a pitiless blinding glare." Around him licked the simoon "like a lion with flaming breath; it was a dread land where the bursting of a water-skin or the pricking of a camel's hoof would be a certain death of torture in this haggard land infested with wild beasts and wilder men. . . ." Oh! how Isabel longed to share the dangers with him, how she hung on his words, transported in ecstasies of love and envy. . . . "Born for the knapsack"? Of course she was!

*       *       *

At this point, let us look at the facts, besides the romantic aura with which not only Isabel, but the general public, now surrounded the name of Richard Burton, whose reputation either as "demigod" or "that blackguard Burton" was as ambiguous as his nature itself. His family was wellborn and impoverished, with a mixed strain of ancestry, part Irish, part Scottish and part French, a bastard of Louis XIV being a forbear. There was no acknowledged trace of Oriental or Gypsy blood, although Burton is an English tribal name. Moreover, Gypsies always claimed him as their own, wherever he went. "What are you doing in that black coat?" they would ask, and others might have asked it too, seeing this arresting creature tricked out by Savile Row. "Why don't you join us, and become our king?" was their usual greeting. They, at least, recognized his stature. No condemnation or official damping-down, here. Arabs, too, never questioned his affinity. It is possible that, somewhere far back, an unknown Arab ancestor accounted for his unmistakably Eastern cast of countenance and characteristics. Only atavism explains such a pronounced throwback. Theophile Gautier, who was himself of Andalusian and Moorish stock, held such theories. "There is a reason for that fantasy of nature," he says, "which causes an Arab to be born in Paris, or a Greek in Auvergne. The mysterious voice of blood, which is silent for generations, or only utters a confused murmur, speaks, at rare intervals, a more intelligible language. In the general confusion race claims its own, and some forgotten ancestor asserts his rights. . . . The great migrations from the tablelands of India, the descents of the northern races, the Roman and Arab invasions have all left their marks. Instincts which appear bizarre have sprung from these confused memories, these echoes of a distant country. . . . Hence . . . the impulses that cause man to leave his luxurious life to bury himself in the Steppes, the desert, the Pampas, the Sahara. He goes to seek his brothers."

Apart from all such theories, there was the fact of Burton's physical appearance. "I have often wondered," wrote Ouida, the novelist, in her brilliant memorial essay, "where Burton got his Oriental physiognomy, his un-English accent, his wonderfully picturesque and Asiatic appearance. . . . He had a dramatic and imposing presence: the disfigurement of modern attire could not destroy the distinction, and the Oriental cast of his appearance and his features." In particular, it was his Gypsy eyes which were remarked, though the famous description might apply to Arab eyes, too. *"Those eyes which looked through, glazed over, and saw something behind."* Everyone who knew him remarked them. They were the "questing panther eyes" which impressed the little Harold Nicolson. "Eyes of a tiger, voice of an angel." Swinburne spoke of "the look of unspeakable horror in those eyes which gave him at times an almost unearthly appearance." They were "the sullen eyes of a stinging serpent," according to Arthur Symons, whose opulent style found a worthy subject here. He goes on to say Burton was "Arab in his cheek bones and gypsy in his terrible magnetic eyes . . . he had a deeply bronzed complexion, a determined mouth, half-hidden by a black mustache which hung down in a peculiar fashion on both sides of his chin. This peculiarity I have often seen in men of the wandering tribes of Spain and Hungary. Burton's face," he continues, "has no actual beauty in it. It reveals a tremendous animalism, an air of repressed ferocity, a devilish fascination. There is an almost tortured magnificence in this huge head, tragic and painful, with its mouth that aches with desire, with those dilated nostrils that drink in I know not what strange perfumes. . . ." From these descriptions of Burton by his contemporaries we see why Isabel was in such a state. We see, too, why Mrs. Arundell was to be so adamant. Whatever Burton might have promised as a lover, he cannot have inspired confidence as a son-in-law.

\*      \*      \*

Richard Francis Burton was born in Hertfordshire in 1821. His father, Colonel Joseph Netterville Burton, was a handsome Irishman; his mother, a homely English girl. His maternal grandfather had wished to leave him his fortune of half a million pounds; but Burton's mother, who seems to have had an overriding affection for her half brother, a ne'er-do-well lawyer, declined the proposed legacy for her baby son, insisting that it go to the half brother. Nevertheless, her father decided to settle things in his own way without dictation, and calling his carriage, drove to the lawyers to make his will. Stepping out he dropped dead of heart disease. Thus the little Richard was cheated of his legacy. It was the first of many instances of ill luck which always snatched good fortune from him unexpectedly.

Very young, he was accustomed to a vagabond life. The family shuttled backwards and forwards between England and the Continent, seeking economy and a cure for the half-pay Colonel's asthma. Richard, the eldest, Edward, his brother, and their sister Maria were *enfants terribles*. They had little regular education, but learned a great deal about life from their freedom in such forcing-houses as Naples. The boys gained an early mastery over both the foils and pistols. They were partial to dueling; and rode, smoked, gambled, and experimented with all the available forms of profligacy. They were too much for a series of unfortunate tutors, and at nineteen Richard was dispatched to Oxford, Edward going to Cambridge. Divided, it was felt, they might be more amenable. Richard did not shine at Trinity. The restraints irked him. He loathed the damp, the bad food and the ever tolling bells. His adolescent companions were dull. "I have fallen among grocers." Nevertheless he read twelve hours a day, and wished to study Arabic, but was balked by the Regius Professor of Arabic, who avoided the issue by saying his business was to teach a class, and not an individual. As no class could be mustered, either for Arabic or Hindustani, Burton had to rely on himself: he invented a system which, he claimed, enabled him to master, if not perfect, a language in two months: though no doubt he had, besides his mysterious Arab heritage, and a predilection for Eastern tongues, a fabulous linguistic ability.

It was not getting him anywhere at Oxford, however, where his pronunciation of Latin in the Italian, and Greek in the ancient manner, exasperated the Dons. His father refused his pleas to be transferred into the Army. Richard was to take Holy Orders, said the Colonel, and the matter was closed. Richard reopened it by deciding to be sent down.

It did not take long. Now his father had to listen to reason. A commission in a crack regiment being beyond their means, the Burtons settled him into the Indian Army. He joined the John Company's Indian Force, crammed Hindustani, and sailed for Bombay as an ensign, in June, 1842.

The India he first encountered proved almost as frustrating as Oxford. The Afghan war had ended just before his boat docked. There was no active service. The stagnation and petty daily life of the compound appalled him, as it had appalled another remarkable young officer John Nicholson, 'Nikal Seyn,' who had already become a legend in the Punjab. Without any campaign, there was only one path to promotion—a staff appointment. For that, influence or languages were needed. Burton was never a moderate man; it was always all or nothing. During the next few years he mastered Persian, Punjabi, Pushtu, Sindhi, Maruthi and as many more dialects. He was greedy for knowledge; for experience, too. India opened before him, not only as a picturesque landscape to be admired, but as a whole way of life, to be lived. At that time, few white women joined their husbands. The *bibi*, or white wife, was a great rarity; but the *bubu*, or native wife, was an accepted institution. Like all the others, Burton acquired one—but, unlike the other young officers, he experienced a whole range of Indian life. He did not content himself with its domestic aspects alone. The *bubu* was only one of the many chains by which he grappled the Orient to him. Presently his studies with the religious savants were recognized, and he was permitted to wear the Brahmanical Thread of the thrice-born. All the East he could find, sacred or profane, was absorbed. From his native mistresses, Eastern erotica. From his Sepoy troops, tricks of wrestling, Indian sword and lance thrusts, and their command of the small tricky horses that danced and swerved in a manner calculated to unseat all but native riders. He learned to overcome his horror of serpents, and to handle and charm them. Now he began his first essays in those disguises which were later to bring him such extraordinary adventures.

Dressed as a Balochi, he went into the hills with the tribesmen to study falconry. Next he went as assistant to the officer conducting a survey of Scinde. Captain Scott was a nephew of Sir Walter, and appreciated Burton's qualifications. He enabled Burton to penetrate further into the unknown life around him, acting as a Secret Service agent. It was a dangerous game. He grew his hair and beard, stained himself even darker, and disappeared, to live among the tribes, unsuspected, sometimes passing as a Pathan, a Persian, or a Ját—the aboriginal Indian Gypsy. His favorite character was Mirza Abdullah, a half-Arab, half-Persian peddler. The mixture accounted for any imperfections of accent. By day, transformed into a street vendor, he would sit, apparently dozing, in the bazaars . . . listening, watching, noting. . . . By night, he would quit the British tents, to slip away into the darkness, emerging, soon after, metamorphosed once more. The Mirza was a loquacious character, always chattering, drawing out his listeners, giving specially generous measure to the fair sex, who as a source of news were particularly rewarding. He learned much. Long, long before the Mutiny, he had been told of its planning and passed on the warning to the authorities, who of course did nothing about it.

Burton was always a verbose writer, undisciplined and inexhaustible. His scientifically detached accounts of the anthropological, geographical and physiological aspects of his travels totaled eighty or more volumes at his death. He had considerable medical knowledge, and recounts the most surprising facts with professional exactitude. There is no saying what will come next. Peculiarities of Swahili sex life, damp, jungle climates, where the "sexual requirements of the passive sex exceed those of the active sex." (Nymphomania was ever one of his pet subjects.) Tabus and magic: urinary and genital maladies, along with venereal disease in Lanzabas, methods of castration: exsection of the ovaries as a Malthusian measure much practiced by Australians (as he called the Aboriginals); the erotic urges of apes, circumcision and rape, besides statistics on rainfall, or the behavior of a cornered hippo—Captain Burton's books, it will be seen, were not always parlor reading.

If much of his subject matter was highly colored, his style was singularly colorless. With him, *le style n'est pas l'homme*. All he records is interesting—so are his reactions, the workings of his mind: but his actual writing is second-rate—the only ordinary thing about him, and he gives a flat account of a life which must have blazed with color and drama.

There was one romantic episode which he never forgot. A high-bred Persian beauty returned his love. There were stolen meetings in the jasmin-scented moonlight. Like Leila and Mahjnoun they loved passionately. Burton was faced with the problem of his false position: but before he could come to a decision, his jetty-eyed ghazelle was dead. Had she lived, it is possible that the world would never have heard of Burton the Explorer—he might have found, in her, the final inducement to go native. After her death Burton was desolate. His sister, Lady Stistead, says that he could never afterwards speak of this lost love without overwhelming grief. But then she was likely to have piled on the tragic aspects of the affair out of a wish to minimize Isabel's place in his affections.

At this time Major General Sir Charles Napier, the conqueror of Scinde was setting about the pacification of the country, and although fired by the noblest intentions, plunging from one blunder to another. Among his more resounding reforms was that of abolishing various native customs such as Badli, that of the rich criminal's right to purchase a poor man who would suffer the death penalty for him. When Napier hanged the true criminal, local opinion rose to boiling point. And when, on the other hand, he revoked the aggrieved husband's traditional right to hang an unfaithful wife, even greater uproar broke loose. The ladies were enchanted by such a clement measure: soon their freedom became excessive; to such a point, that while their husbands raged, a deputation of prostitutes from Hyderabad demanded to see Sir Charles, complaining that the married women (or amateurs) were now taking the bread out of their mouths.

Napier soon realized the rare qualities of young Lieutenant Burton and employed him as his official interpreter. Presently he began entrusting him with confidential missions. One was particularly dangerous; he was to vanish from the Mess, and make his way, disguised, into the stews of Scinde. He was to observe and report on various sexual practices of which the Government thought it best to be well informed. It is likely that Napier agreed with Burton's theory that pederasts are grouped climatically rather than racially, and that in India, British troops might tend to adopt *Le Vice;* just as, in North Africa, during the French occupation, under Louis Philippe, Arab customs so affected the French regiments that the Marquis de Boissy complained of *un effrayable débordement péderastique*. In India there was every encouragement; the brothels had few women, and they were far more expensive than boys. When, later, Burton wrote the footnotes and "Terminal Essay" to his *Thousand Nights and a Night,* he had some curious things to say of the indirect effects of Persian pederasty on the British conquest of India. He speaks of Afghan and Persian tastes, and how their neglect of their women brought disastrous results. The Afghans, he says, were commercial travelers on a large scale; each caravan was accompanied by numbers of boys, *kuch isafari,* 'traveling wives'; the boys were dressed as women, henna'd, painted and adorned. They rode luxuriously in the camel litters while their 'husbands' trudged alongside. "The Afghan women were perpetually mortified by marital pederasty," says Burton, and goes on to claim that one of the causes of the general rising at Kabul in 1841, when Macnaghten, Burnes and other British officers were butchered, was due to the frantic wave of debauchery which broke out among the neglected Afghan wives. And again, in 1856 during the unfortunate campaign of Sir James Outram's Bombay Army "there was a formal outburst of the harems, and even women of princely birth could not be kept out of the officers' quarters."

For one of Burton's insatiable anthropological interests, it was an assignment of the greatest value, though most of his later biographers can scarcely bring themselves to touch on the episode. . . . "He descended into the unspeakable haunts of the Persian vice," says one. . . . "It was as repulsive a task as ever was given an officer and a gentleman," says another.

Burton had seen most things, even in his twenties. Moreover, it is clear, in light of his "Terminal Essay," that he had accepted all the variations of Eastern life. He was the least effeminate of men—but his face with 'that terrible air of animalism' which so impressed Symons, seems to indicate a sensuality which must have taken much to assuage, and which probably only found its match among Eastern voluptuaries.

When, after four months' absence, Burton returned with a detailed report, he stipulated this should not be generally circulated; that it should remain in the custody of the chief who had ordered it. Unfortunately, Napier was recalled soon after, the report was overlooked, and lay in the files from where it was unearthed, with disastrous results for Burton, by Napier's successors. Its infamy was immediately identified with Burton. He became the John Company's anathema. All hopes of promotion evaporated. Small-fry lieutenants fresh from home were advanced over his head. It was a bitter pill. He shrugged it off, flung himself into Moslem theology, and became a Master Sūfi; but his rancor deepened when he remained in a permanent state of disgrace with the authorities.

The society of his fellow officers having become odious, Burton experimented with forming a monkey vocabulary. He set up house with forty monkeys of all kinds, to study their language. He allotted them various roles, and had his doctor, his chaplain, his valet and aide-de-camp. It was a mimic simian world which must have exasperated the regiment upon which it was modeled. One particularly silky pretty little ape Burton called his wife, putting pearls in her ears, and seating her by his side at the long table where each monkey had its own plate, and was waited on ceremoniously by the servants. Burton found them vastly entertaining, and succeeded in distinguishing around sixty definite words, and establishing a sort of conversation with them. Unfortunately, his notes, and the vocabulary, were lost in the warehouse fire where so many of his Oriental treasures, priceless Indian and Persian manuscripts and a huge collection of costumes perished.

These simian distractions could not blot out for long the futility of Burton's life in the Army. When, on the grounds of "unsuitability" he was barred from the Mooltan campaign (some malicious underling having pinned his Scinde report to his application for active service) and dapper juniors who barely lisped in Hindustani were sent, Burton broke down. A violent bout of fever left him half dead. His few friends bundled his stretcher onto the next boat for home. Seven years of loyal service, brilliant initiative and an incomparable knowledge of Indian affairs had led nowhere. "The dwarfish demon called Interest had, as usual, won the fight," he wrote bitterly: it was the first of many such battles which Burton was always to lose.

But men of Burton's kidney do not die of disappointment at twenty-seven. The process is slow, imperceptible at first, only gaining a hold after several repetitions. We have a parallel, perhaps, in T. E. Lawrence. Repeated injustices and disappointments killed Burton the explorer at forty-five—but the man lingered on till past seventy. Now, returned from the first disillusion of his Indian career, he recovered slowly, and began writing his books on the country. Presently the old obsession took hold again. He had always wished to visit the world's great religious citadels: forbidden cities held an irresistible allure. He would explore Africa, cross China to Thibet, make a pilgrimage to Mecca. . . . As his leave had still some time to run, he left for Boulogne with his family, where he spent much of his time at the *Salle d'armes* run by Constantine, the celebrated *maître d'armes*, a coveted title Burton now won for his superb fencing and the various technical new systems of cuts and thrusts he had developed.

The meeting with his Destiny, in the shape of Miss Isabel Arundell, appears to have made no particular impression on him at the time. Why should it? He was her destiny—her Mecca—but *his* Mecca was other-wise—*his* Destiny, the East. Although there is no doubt he loved Isabel, and never, save for his Persian ghazelle, contemplated marrying anyone else, yet he was not, at heart, a man who depended greatly on personal relationships. According to H. J. Tedder, the Librarian of the Athenaeum Club, where Burton was to spend so much time later, writing his books, he was a compound of Benedictine monk, Crusader and Buccaneer—a thoroughly unsatisfactory trio, from the wifely view-point. So after the first intriguing encounter with the bread-and-butter miss, as Isabel must have appeared, he dismissed her from mind. He was not to know of the Gypsies' prediction, nor of the gloves and the sash folded away so reverently. He had not the slightest idea, then, of the strength of Isabel's passion and determination.

Now came his supreme adventure, which was to place him among the immortals, those whose names are forever symbols of imaginative dar-ing and achievement. Marco Polo of China, Columbus of America,

Livingstone of Africa, Burton of Mecca. Mecca! the secret city of Islam, holy of holies, eight days' march across the torrid Arabian desert, where no infidel could enter, and live. His proposition to penetrate Mecca, and explore the unknown wastes of Central Arabia was accepted by the Royal Geographical Society, and the East India Company were finally won over to granting a rather grudging year's leave. Since Burton knew his life was at stake, death being the least of the horrors reserved for any infidel dog discovered among the Faithful, it would be wiser to assume his Moslem self before quitting London. Therefore, his clothes, possessions, and very identity were all left behind at the house of a friend, the one person who was in his confidence. Overnight, Richard Burton was swallowed up in the rank autumnal fogs, and there emerged another man, of another race and creed, an Afghan Moslem, bound for Cairo. We have Burton's own account of this remarkable adventure in detail; how he set about perfecting his religious rituals, his dialects and disguises, for he intended to pass from one character to another as soon as he was absorbed into the Eastern panorama. All he set out to do he did, except that, for reasons too involved to recount here, he abandoned his secondary, or commercial scheme of inquiring into a possible market for horses, to be opened up between Central Arabia and India, where the breed was becoming poor. He had enough on his hands without embarking on hazardous business deals in the Arabian wastes. After a fabulous series of adventures which he recounts with gusto, he penetrated the Holy City. But where his predecessor, Burckhardt, had panicked, Burton remained detached in the hour of greatest danger. Surrounded by fanatics who would have killed him hideously had they suspected, he managed to conceal paper and pencil, and even make some rough notes of the Ka'abah, the Moslem Holy Grail. His true achievement was this—he made the pilgrimage as an *initiate*, as a Moslem among Moslems, in a spirit of both reverence and inquiry. Later, when his book, *A Pilgrimage to El Medinah and Meccah*, won him world fame, no Arab voice was ever raised against the exploit, for his piety and erudition were accepted. He was a Master Sūfi; one of the Faithful, a master Dervish too; and now, as one who had made the Pilgrimage, a Hadji. The green turban was won.

Many years later, Doughty, who made the same pilgrimage undisguised, had some very caustic things to say about the benefits of disguise. But as Isabel pointed out airily when, as a widow, she wrote her husband's life, Richard did not go *disguised*. He simply *became* a Moslem—he was no longer Burton, as an Arab—he was Burton the Arab. This identification with every aspect of Moslem life and faith, a sort of duality, is constantly seen in Burton's character. He notes it casually, throughout his books: "I was too much of an Arab to weary of the endless preparations for forming a caravan," he writes; or again "Arabic is my native tongue." Even his attitude towards women, to marriage, and Isabel, is profoundly Oriental.

At home Isabel lived only for news of him. She pored over his books, read and re-read *Falconry in the Valley of the Indus, The Játs of Scinde,* or *A Complete System of Bayonet Exercise,* and surprised polite gatherings by her apparently unsolicited testimonials for these unlikely works. She followed with pride every scrap of information as to his doings. Since the pilgrimage he had come into the limelight. She prayed he would return to England to lecture. "Pray! Pray!" is a perpetual self-admonishment in her journal. Faith, we are told, is only love in the form of aspiration. She needed all her faith, for soon she learned that Richard had gone back to rejoin his regiment in Bombay, after finishing his book on Mecca in Egypt. " . . . instead of coming here, he has gone to Bombay. . . . I glory in his glory," she writes in her journal, "but I am alone and unloved . . . is there no hope for me? Is there no pity for so much love?"

By his return to Bombay at that crucial moment, Burton showed, as so often, that disastrous disregard for worldly considerations, that ill timing, which was to cost him all the high rewards he should have won. Instead of launching himself on the flood tide of enthusiasm with which England waited to receive him, instead of capitalizing his success, he threw it away and returned to the small Indian Army world where he was still "Ruffian Dick, the White Nigger." That he chose to linger in Cairo is more understandable when we remember that long before he contemplated translating *The Thousand Nights and a Night,* he had been passionately interested in the sources of Arabic legend and literature. He must have heard many of those fabulous Nights as told by the seductive storyteller of Baghdad. But the tales had originated in Cairo, in the fourteenth century, where they had been written in the vernacular, in the debased Arabic peculiar to the Mamelukes for whom they were designed. Then, too, he had become affiliated with an order of Dervishes, whose society must have offered exceptional attractions to such an Orientalist.

Whilst in Egypt, he had also completed his epic poem *The Kasidah or Lay of the Higher Law* which contains, in the idiom of the East, much that was perplexing the West at that moment: problems of determinism and philosophic and mystic questions which later, Isabel was to describe as "the most exquisite gem of Oriental poetry that I have ever heard or imagined, nor do I believe it has its equal either from the pen of Hafiz, Saadi, Shakespeare, Milton, Swinburne or any other." Since this perfervid judgment was written in her widowhood, after thirty years of marriage, it will be seen that custom had never staled the bliss of being Richard's wife.

Back in Bombay, Burton's wanderlust was still unappeased. He cast about for further expeditions. Harar, in Abyssinian Somaliland, had the reputation for being another impregnable citadel. No white man had ever entered it and lived. Thirty travelers had failed. It was a center of the East African slave trade as well as a seat of Moslem culture, it was said. Sinister and mysterious legends abounded. Burton was raring to go. It had considerable strategic importance since Berberah, the chief port, was the best harbor on the western side of the Indian Ocean. The East India Company eyed it with interest; but their enthusiasm for Burton's project was mixed with typical caution. They granted him leave, but no funds. The Government, too, favored the scheme from afar, but afforded no official protection.

Then, as later, Burton was not to be discouraged by lack of adequate funds; he would go without, paying what he could himself. After a series of intrigues and setbacks, Burton, accompanied by three lieutenants of the Bombay Army, Stroyan, Speke and Herne, seconded to his service, set off for Harar in 1855. The account of this daring expedition can be read in *First Footsteps in East Africa*.

Looking back, from this age of specialization, we see that Burton belonged to the age of Tudor appetites, of gargantuan plurality. In our time, one man flies the Atlantic; another becomes the world's boxing champion. Another climbs Mount Everest, writes a best seller, or achieves fame as a scientist. But Burton possessed a multiplicity of genius. He was the foremost Orientalist of his day; the first to reach Mecca as a Moslem; the first to reach Harar; the explorer of the Great Lake region; one of the finest fencers, one of the world's outstanding linguists; an unequaled Oriental scholar, a poet, and the author of the greatest version of the Arabian Nights; he was, besides, a doctor in all but his degrees; a man of scientific bent, whose theories, although naïvely expounded, foreshadowed those of Freud and Jung.

The expedition to Harar began well enough. Disguised as a Moslem merchant Burton achieved his goal, entered the impregnable fastness, was received by the Emir, a sinister character, took a number of notes, and left in triumph to rejoin his companions who had waited at the base camp. But they were ambushed and a fearful battle ensued, with three hundred and fifty savage Somalis attacking the tiny camp. Stroyan was killed, and while the Somalis dipped their ostrich plumes in his blood, Speke and Burton, both badly wounded, hacked their way out with their swords. Burton's jaw and palate were transfixed by a lance: he carried the great scars down his cheek till his death. But at the Court of Enquiry there was censure rather than glory, and once more Richard returned to England ill and under a cloud. Still, he had seen what he had seen. There was material for another book.

However, when the details of his exploit—in reality more of an achievement than the pilgrimage to Mecca—reached England he was once more famous. It is impossible for us today, surfeited as we are on travel films and easy voyages, to realize the degree of interest with which Victorian England followed travelers and explorers. Much of the world was still strange, unknown and unmapped. Australia was six months away; and not *bien vu*. America was the wildest west, and where there were no Indians, there were Mormons. Tea came from China, but no one went there. India—the India of the East India Company, that is—was better known, and mistakenly accepted as settled.

But Africa was still the dark continent, mysterious and uncharted. It contained savages and gold and diamonds, and perhaps, the legendary Mountains of the Moon. Missionaries and geographers alike gave lectures with lantern slides, and the public followed the lecturer's pointer with rapt attention. To be an explorer, in the nineteenth century, commanded reverential interest. As a profession, it held all the prestige and mystery which now surrounds atomic scientists. Figures such as Burton, Livingstone or Du Chaillu were regarded by the young with the same enthusiasm now reserved for Spacemen.

It was an age of great exploration and geographical research. Barth had returned from the Sahara. Duveyrier wrote of the mysterious Touaregs; de Lesseps was opening up the Suez Canal zone, while Dr. Rae discovered virgin tracks in the Arctic. Arminius Vambéry returned from his Asiatic wanderings to find England made much of him. He was besieged by questioners, from the Foreign Office to the Manchester cotton manufacturers. It was a flattering surprise to the Hungarian Orientalist.

\* \* \*

The dramatic accounts of Burton's latest exploit and the attack had been a nightmare to Isabel. "Pray! Pray!" There was so much to pray for: Richard's safety, Richard's recognition and rewards, above all, Richard's return, and the way to effect a meeting. But when he did return, it was to find his thunders stolen by the Crimean War which swamped any personal exploits however sensational. For a while he languished at Bath, writing an account of his adventures, badgering the Government to suppress slavery and annex Somaliland, but getting nowhere. Presently he succeeded in obtaining an appointment to General Beatson's Horse, and left for the Crimea, hoping to see active service at long last. But he was detailed, instead, to organize a force of Bashi-Bazouks. These undisciplined Balkan mercenaries were the despair of their English officers. Burton was the perfect man for such a task. He set about licking the Bashi-Bazouks into shape largely by teaching them the use of the sword, cavalry charges, and discouraging their propensity for dueling among themselves, a pistol in one hand, a glass of *raki* in the other, the first to drink down the *raki* being the first to draw. It was a picturesque habit, but reduced their ranks alarmingly. Before Burton could see service on the field, however, Kars fell, a political maneuver rather than a military operation. Burton was disgusted, and said so loudly, in the wrong places. Soon after he was recalled to London to give evidence in General Beatson's lawsuit against his detractors.

Isabel breathed again. She had been trying to force herself on Miss Florence Nightingale, as a means of reaching the Crimea, and Richard, but Miss Nightingale had not been helpful: Isabel was too young and inexperienced, she regretted, politely. This was particularly frustrating, since the Crimea was accessible to so many women who did not crave adventure greatly. The Crimean campaign was the last of those chivalresque wars which retained a certain social aspect about them, with camp followers, *vivandières* and such. The wives and families of the officers often traveled out to set up house behind the lines. Some girls even went out to marry their fiancés and spend a martial honeymoon. But that was not to be Isabel's portion. Balked at every turn, she flung all her frustrated forces into a period of social work among fallen women in the London slums, thus bearing out Burton's pre-Freudian interpretation of the average woman's attraction for nursing, for *ministering* as a form of thwarted or frustrated sexual instinct. "Seeing the host of women who find a morbid pleasure in attending the maimed and dying, I must think that it is a tribute paid to sexuality by those who object [or cannot obtain?] to the ordinary means." Really! nothing was sacred to that dreadful Captain Burton! He even sought to destroy that inviolate Victorian myth, the Ministering Angel.

There were dark days when echoes of Richard's activities among the Circassian harems of the Bosphorus reached London. Still, there were lighter moments too. On the race course at Ascot, in June, 1856, among the crowds and carriages, the tumblers, bookies and touts of the unchanging scene that Frith's *Derby Day* has immortalized, Isabel encountered Hagar Burton once more. The sybil of the Essex woods had not forgotten. "'Are you Daisy Burton?' was her first question. I shook my head. 'Would to God I were!'" (Oh! what was Richard up to on the

Bosphorus?) "Her face lit up. 'Patience! it is just coming. . . .'" At this point they were separated by the crowds, and were never to meet again. But two months later, Circassians or no, Richard had proposed.

\*     \*     \*

One sultry August day when Isabel and her sister Blanche were walking in the Botanical Gardens, Richard Burton crossed their path again. He recognized them on sight, and it was as if, at long last, the world had righted itself. For an intoxicating fortnight there were daily meetings. He discovered Isabel knew all his books and every step of his travels. Her large moon-face was by turns worshiping and indignant, and envious, as his story unfolded. She asked him to explain *Tancred* and hung on his words. What man could resist? Certainly not Burton, at that moment so lonely and frustrated. He asked her to marry him. "Was it not foretold?" wrote Isabel complacently. "Do not give me your answer now," said Burton, "because it will mean a very serious step for you—no less than giving up your people and all you are used to, and living the sort of life that Lady Hester Stanhope led. I see the capabilities in you," he added enigmatically; thinking perhaps of her possibilities as an appendage to the caravan. "Men who marry according to Christian law [with one wife, as opposed to the Moslem plurality] cannot be too careful," he observed, about this time. Isabel was unaware, or indifferent to any such shades; he had proposed! "It was just as if the moon had tumbled down and said, 'You have cried for me so long I have come.' But he, who did not know of my long love, thought I was thinking worldly thoughts, and said, 'Forgive me; I ought not to have asked so much.' At last I found voice and said, 'I don't *want* to think it over—I have been thinking it over for five years . . . and I would rather have a crust and a tent with you than be queen of all the world; and so I say now, Yes, *yes*, YES!'"

That glimpse of paradise had to suffice Isabel for another long period of waiting, however, for very soon afterwards Burton sailed for Africa, this time to discover the sources of the Nile. How Isabel must have loathed the Dark Continent. There was nothing she could do about it as with a rival of flesh and blood. Her diary records a curious episode, at this moment: Richard was sailing while their engagement was still a secret; he did not tell her the exact date of his departure, for he had a horror of farewells. (Isabel's force of emotion may have made him quail, too.) At any rate, she was at the theater, when she thought she saw him across the house, in another box. He stared at her, but did not come when she beckoned. That night she dreamed he stood beside her bed. "Good-bye, my poor child. My time is up, and I have gone," the vision said. "But do not grieve. I shall be back in less than three years, and I am your Destiny. Good-bye."

"He pointed to the clock, and it was two. He held up a letter and looked at me with those Gypsy eyes, and put the letter on the table, and said in the same way, 'That is for your sister—not for you.' "

Isabel spent the rest of the night in convulsions of grief. At eight o'clock next morning the letter she had seen in her dreams arrived. It was addressed to her sister: inside, there was one for Isabel. "Richard had found it too painful to part from me, and thought we should suffer less that way: he begged Blanche to break it gently to me, and to give me the letter which assured me we should be reunited in 1859. . . . He had received some secret information which caused him to leave England at once and quietly, lest he should be detained as witness at a forthcoming military trial. He had left his lodgings in London at ten-thirty the preceding evening (when I saw him in the theater) and sailed at two o'clock from Southampton (when I saw him in my room)." Isabel goes on to say that she believes a certain sympathy, or means of psychic communication exists between persons who are attuned, or have close affinities. Not that any such reflections were of much consolation with Richard sailing off and accepting their three-year separation so philosophically. She hung his letter round her neck in a little bag, and went back to praying monotonously.

Although she obviously luxuriated in her pining state, one must agree it was a great waste of the last years of her youth. She was now twenty-eight, a ripe age, at that time. "I love and am loved, and so strike a balance in favor of existence," she philosophizes. "Whatever harshness the future may bring, *he has loved me,* and my future is bound up in him with all consequences. My jealous heart spurns all compromise: it must have its purpose or break. . . ." She fretted over the dangers that beset him: so many unknown dangers. . . . But her heart was comparatively calm on the score of possible feminine rivals. Darkest Africa, she felt, offered no serious challenge on that score. And she was sustained by Hagar Burton's prophecy, slowly but surely fulfilling itself. "One soul in two bodies, never far apart, in life or death." Oh! it was inexpressibly beautiful! She *must* have faith in her Star—the Morning Star that Hagar had said was her own. "I believe that we often meet in spirit, and often look at the same star." She must have faith in her destiny, in this world and the next. "There is another life if I lose this." Richard would yet be hers, here—or there. Was it not foretold?

It was a bitter-sweet pleasure to hear him discussed widely. People spoke of him with bated breath: to go and search for the source of the Nile, then, was comparable to some sound barrier experiment today. Burton's personality was beginning to be felt in London, and wild stories were circulated by those many to whom he was antipathetic. There was that unfortunate occasion when he had tossed a scalp across the dinner table to his hostess who had asked him to bring her a souvenir of his travels. He *would* defend cannibalism, too.

As a rule he was indifferent to the gossip: indeed, one of his lifelong pleasures was to *épater le bourgeois*. He was always scrupulous to hide the man behind the devil. But the story that while in Turkey he had been discovered in a harem and suffered the traditional penalty infuriated him. In this he showed a thoroughly conventional reaction; male vanity is ever sensitive on this point. And Isabel, we suppose, was not in a position to contradict the story: at any rate, she appears to have remained silent, for once not springing loudly to his defense.

She had discovered his secret yearning for fame—Ambition, she calls it. She shared his yearnings. "I knew he was great in the literary world, men's society, clubs and the Royal Geographical Society. But I wished him to be great in the world of fashion. . . . I also knew that if a man gets talked about in the right kind of way, in handfuls of the best society, here and there, his fame quickly spreads." Mixing a shrewd worldly sense with her devout mysticism, she now launched into that lifelong campaign of proselytizing for Richard. It was a campaign that was to assume gigantic proportions: years later, it was due to her efforts alone that Burton was vindicated after his ignominious recall from the Consulate at Damascus. Many people, the Foreign Office first, grew to dread Mrs. Burton's zeal.

To one mid-Victorian child, Isabel's proselytizing impressed itself forever. The little Laura Haine Friswell recalled visits where Isabel, now Mrs. Burton, "a stylishly dressed woman, my childish idea of a Princess . . . came and talked for whole days at a time, and it was all about Dear Richard and the Government. . . . Mrs. Burton's stream of eloquence never seemed exhausted." "Richard was a Fairy Prince, and Government was an Ogre." Which was how Isabel always saw it, too.

But while she was still Miss Arundell she had to be circumspect. She had not yet arrived at even the fiancée's proprietary rights. Neither her family nor the public was to know of the engagement, yet, least of all her mother, who regarded Burton as an undesirable atheist.

Richard was proving a poor correspondent: months went by with no news. In January, 1857, Isabel read in the papers that he had left Bombay for Zanzibar. It would be unreasonable to expect letters from darkest Africa, still—it should not impede her flow: they were to be kept in touch by her diary-form letters, she decided, and writing them at night, she would post them off next day into the blue.

Neither she, nor the life she lived, was typically Victorian—she had much more independence and freedom than was general. When her sister and brother-in-law set out on a sort of protracted European honeymoon, Isabel accompanied them. They wandered about, the newlyweds mooning over each other, Isabel mooning over her love. Every vista conjured thoughts of Richard. He was beside her on the Alps—in a gondola . . . "In Nice my windows looked out over a little garden where the African tree is, and the sea beyond, and beyond that again, Africa—and Richard." She traveled with a portrait of Richard in Arab costume; and a Monsieur Pernay, a passing acquaintance, seeing it hung over the piano in their lodgings, was so overcome by the romantic situation that he composed a *valse*, there and then, called *Richard in the Desert,* and said he would like to compose a libretto too. The beauties of Europe were all seen in relation to Richard. Pisa was where he had been at school; she mounted the Leaning Tower and found his name carved on the stone, marveled, and carved her own, beside it.

In Geneva there were more worldly delights, a ball, fêtes, and the *Corps Diplomatique* in attendance. A wealthy American widower proposed and offered his three hundred thousand dollars' worth of California gold. "But there is only one man in the world who could be master of such a spirit as mine. People may love (as it is called) a thousand times, but the real *feu sacré* only burns once in one's life. . . . Love is the one bright vision Heaven sends us in this wild, desolate, busy, selfish earth to cheer us on to the goal." For Isabel, *Arabian* Richard was the real goal. Even heavenly prospects paled beside the earthly paradise he promised. There were still no letters from Africa, though other suitors continued pressing. At Geneva, a Russian general, who seems to have had all the excessive qualities of his race, became very attentive. He was loaded with decorations and titles, had a large family and nine châteaux. He had first glimpsed Isabel as she knelt in prayer before the Madonna, in Genoa. How could he know she was praying to become Mrs. Richard Burton? With boyish ardor he followed her to Geneva, arrived at her hotel and at last obtained the next-door room, from where he bombarded her with flowers, and regularly spaced violin serenades from 6 A.M. till midnight. But Isabel was not to be tempted. She had sterner matters to occupy her mind. Dressed in thick boots, and red petticoats for safety (that they might be easily seen at a distance) she and her sister went mountaineering. An explorer's future wife must take mountains in her stride. There were storms and mishaps with alpenstocks, but Isabel, learning to toughen up, made light of it all. Reaching a high plateau where nature was particularly sublime, she plunges into a hypothetical choice: Richard, chained to the plateau in expiation of his sins for a hundred years or an earthly throne, elsewhere, *without* him? There is no hesitation. "A throne would be exile *without* him; an exile with him, home!" Later, when the evening star came out in the pale sky and the glow-worms shone like brilliants in the grass, "I thought of Richard in that faraway swamp in Central Africa, and a voiceless prayer rose to my lips. I wonder if he too is thinking of me at this time? And as I thought, an angelic whisper knocked at my heart and murmured 'Yes.' "

Rheumatic fever was the result of these twilight maunderings and after a severe illness, cured, it seems, by Kirschwasser, Isabel decided to go home ahead of the honeymooners. En route, her first journey alone, she lost luggage and money, and was in a third-class compartment with an unfortunate gentleman who had a fit. This was splendid emergency training for an explorer's wife. Isabel showed her resourcefulness, and poured a whole bottle of sweet spirits of nitre (her fever cure) down his throat as he lay writhing on the floor; covering his distorted face with her black silk scarf, she squeezed herself into the furthest corner of the compartment and tried to think of other things . . . of Richard, no doubt.

\*     \*     \*

Meantime, in the remote African hinterland Burton's expedition hacked its way slowly onwards. Although the Royal Geographical Society had persuaded the Government to back the expedition, most of the funds and supplies had not arrived on time; it was just one of the many setbacks which dogged Burton now, and which mounted to an accumulative tragedy. They were traversing virgin country. Only one man before them, a French officer named Marzan, had attempted the journey; he had been murdered at the start. Burton succeeded; his party reached the great lake, Tanganyika, and his exploration was the base upon which the subsequent journeys of Livingstone, Stanley and others were made. It is always held that Stanley traveled with one book—the Bible: but in reality he also carried Burton's book. As late as the First World War, Burton's findings were still considered as the most reliable. The fact that Speke, his companion, subsequently returned to England ahead of Burton, and tricked him so ignobly, by claiming full credit for both discoveries and leadership, clouded the proper appreciation of Burton's achievement. But the truth emerged, at last, and Burton's reputation was vindicated—years too late. There were so many tragic and embittering episodes in Burton's life that it is comforting to know that, however much he was put aside, discredited and slandered, at least he savored the living of those wonderful years of achievement. *Not the fruit of experience, but experience itself is the end,* said Pater. Burton failed, or, more exactly, was robbed of the fruits. But no one could rob him of those years of action. His travels were the breath of life to him—every hardship was gladly accepted. Isabel was one of many sacrificial offerings on the altar of adventure. She must never get in the way, or cling. To "pay, pack and follow," his much-quoted dictum, was the task she assumed, as his wife. But now, she must wait; once more, she must have faith. Burton describes departure—the act of leaving, as "one of the gladdest moments of human life. . . . Man feels once more happy, fresh dawns the morn of life. . . ." There speaks the escapist; but traveler and escapist have much in common.

The Great Lake expedition was proving more than had been bargained for. Burton suffered twenty-one bouts of fever; Speke went down with the ghastly Kichyomachyoma, or Little Irons, which appears to be a mixture of hydrophobia, epilepsy and delirium tremens. There were fearful dangers, animal, vegetable, climatic and human. Speke was proving "jealous and difficult." He spoke none of the African languages, practically no Arabic, and very little Hindustani. His attitude towards both African and Arabs was one of arrogance, acquired, perhaps, from the Anglo-Indians of John Company.

On February thirteenth the expedition reached its objective. Through the close matted vegetation they saw a streak of light. "Look! Master, look!" cried the Arab guide, "behold the great water!" Before them lay a vast shimmering stretch—it was the lake of Tanganyika, which Burton maintained to be the headwaters of the Nile. On their return journey, Speke was detailed to go north and visit the lake now known as Victoria Nyanza, to report on its size and the ethnography of the region. Burton stayed behind at the base, Kazeh, working up their notes and scientific data, an exactitude quite beyond Speke's abilities. Speke found the new lake far larger than he had expected, and claimed it was in fact the true source of the Nile. Neither Burton nor

Speke had any certainty for their respective claims, but they disputed fiercely. Speke, being far less expert than Burton, went largely by guesswork. His theory that the lake was linked with the Nile subsequently proved to be correct; he also mapped a noble range, "The Mountains of the Moon," which did not, in fact, exist. But now he became arrogant and held a grievance against Burton for disputing his theories. Burton nursed him patiently through another bout of fever, and they reached Zanzibar in March, 1859, on apparently good terms. Now, once again, Burton showed that foolish procrastination which cost him so dearly.

Speke, always so worldly wise, sailed for England at once, but Burton, mortally tired, entered the hospital to rest and prepare his notes. It was a fatal delay. When at last he reached England, two months later, he found that in spite of Speke's good-by promise to do nothing about reporting their findings till Burton rejoined him, he had, in fact, lost no time in making off to the Royal Geographical Society, claiming the discovery of the Nile sources as his own, and cashing in on the general enthusiasm, maneuvered to be nominated as head of a new expedition, *without* Burton. Speke had stolen all the glory, delivered the lectures, and become the hero of the hour. Once again Burton faced disillusion, poverty and neglect, made doubly bitter by the knowledge that it was the treachery of a companion and friend.

We can imagine Isabel's emotions during Speke's lionization: she had no news of Burton, and grew desperate when she heard rumors that Burton was remaining in Zanzibar and would again leave for the interior without returning home. Whatever Hagar and the Morning Star might promise, she could bear no more: she would retreat from the world and become a nun. But at this crucial moment she received a letter from Africa. Six lines of indifferent verse, no signature, nothing besides, but they changed the world.

To Isabel, she read:

> *That brow which rose before my sight*
> *As on the palmers' holy shrine;*
> *Those eyes—my life was in their light;*

*Those lips my sacramental wine;*
*That voice whose flow was wont to seem*
*The music of an exile's dream.*

"I knew, then," says Isabel, "that it was going to be all right." A few days later she read in the paper that Captain Richard Burton was on his way home. Her impulse was to run, "lest after all I have suffered and longed for, I should have to bear more." While she was still undecided, there was another example of what she liked to think of as their "predestined" meetings.

"On May 22," writes Isabel, "I chanced to call on a friend. I was told she was out . . . but asked if I would wait. I said 'Yes.' In a few minutes another ring came to the door, and another visitor was also asked to wait. A voice that thrilled me through and through came up the stairs, saying 'I want Miss Arundell's address.' The door opened . . . and judge of my feelings when I saw Richard! For an instant we both stood dazed . . . we rushed into each other's arms. I cannot attempt to describe the joy of that moment." They were overcome. Isabel describes her state as being "absolute content, such as I fancy people must feel in the first few moments after the soul has quitted the body." Burton, who had landed only the day before, was a wraith of the adventurer who had swaggered along the Ramparts eight years before. His twenty-one bouts of fever had left him partially paralyzed and blind. "He was a skeleton figure, his yellow skin hanging in bags, his eyes protruding, and his lips drawn away from his teeth," writes Isabel, in transports of love and pity. Together the lovers tottered downstairs and out to a passing cab, where locked in one another's arms they drove about the streets, heedless of all else. "When we were a little recovered, we mutually drew each other's pictures from our respective pockets at the same moment, to show how carefully we had always kept them."

They met every day now, and Isabel used to convey him "almost fainting, to our house, or a friend's who allowed and encouraged our meeting." Alas, Mrs. Arundell was adamant when marriage was discussed. Richard Burton was not a Roman Catholic—not even a Mohammedan, some said. He had suffered under the new Indian Army reductions, he had no fortune, and a very sinister reputation. In short, a thoroughly unsuitable match for her darling girl. Isabel was strangely docile, and would not go against her mother, so there, for the present, the matter stood. Perhaps Burton breathed easier for the respite. He was in love with Isabel, in his own fashion, but possibly, like so many men, he preferred his loved one as the girl he left behind him.

Isabel, with the true Victorian woman's passion for nursing, was now in her element cherishing her earthly god. Richard needed her: she was restoring him to life and hope—and love. "Never did I feel the strength of my love as then. He returned poorer and dispirited by official rows and every species of annoyance; but he was still 'my earthly God and King,' and I could have knelt at his feet and worshiped him. I used to like to sit and look at him and think, *'You are mine,* and there is no man on earth the least like you.'"

Such an attitude must have been wonderfully restorative.

\*          \*          \*

Had she known that another parting was in store for her, Isabel might have been less anxious to restore Richard to perfect health. As it was, he was scarcely recovered before he had gone again—this time to cross America and visit the Mormons. His *City of the Saints* tells with a good deal of irony his impressions of Brigham Young and his ways, his cocktails, or "little nips," and his wives. After Africa, even Indian country seemed tame, though Burton took the precaution of shaving his head, to discourage any possible scalpers en route. (Burton's niece, Miss Stisted, writing of her uncle's Mormon voyage, says, in a tone of European astonishment: ". . . nothing but water was drunk, except when some peculiar person preferred to wash down his pork with *milk,* a truly horrible mixture; but the meal ended with a glass of whisky served in the bedroom, there being no bar." By which it would seem Burton lived, then, much as Midwest 'motel' travelers do today.)

Just as Burton had worn Arab costume on his Mecca journey, so now he donned the black frock coat and glossy top hat of a Mormon elder, not perhaps his most convincing disguise. And once again he left London stealthily, unable to face Isabel's grief. Once more, Isabel was overcome by a premonition which was subsequently proved correct. A tightening of the heart—a sudden certainty that Richard had gone—and half an hour later, his farewell letter. He would be away nine months, he said, and when he returned she must choose between him and her mother. If she had not the courage to risk the marriage, he would return to India, and they would meet no more. "I was to think it over for nine months," says Isabel, who had now been doing nothing else for nine years.

She spent the next few months in active preparation for the marriage she so ardently desired. She retreated to the country, on the pretext of a change of air, and set about acquiring all the practical knowledge that would equip her for her new life, wherever it might lead her, and under whatever material conditions. She learned to milk the cows, groom and care for the horses and ride astride. Poultry, gardens, cooking, washing, fishing—nothing was to be left to chance. Back in London she sought out a celebrated fencer, and demanded he take her as a pupil. "What for?" he asked, bewildered by the sight of Isabel, her crinoline tucked up, lunging and riposting with savage concentration. "So that I can defend Richard when he is attacked," was the reply.

While she was in the country, Isabel also decided to tackle her mother once again on the question of marriage. A prodigiously long letter was dispatched, stating Isabel's views in no uncertain terms: "The moment I saw his brigand-daredevil look I set him up as an idol and determined that he was the only man I would ever marry. . . . But when I came home one day in ecstasy and told you that I had found the Man and the Life I longed for, and that nothing would turn me, and that all other men were his inferiors, what did you answer me? That he was the *only* man you would never consent to my marrying; that you would rather see me in my coffin. Did you know that you were flying in the face of God? Did you know it was my Destiny?" She goes on to list Burton's qualities: "Look at his military services—India and the Crimea! Look at his writings, his travels, his poetry, his languages and dialects! Now Mezzofanti [the great prelate and linguist] is dead, he stands first in Europe: he is the best horseman, swordsman and pistol shot. . . . He has been presented with the gold medal, and is a F.R.G.S., and you must see in the newspapers of his glory and fame, and public thanks, where he is called 'the Crichton of the day,' 'one of the Paladins of the Age,' 'the most interesting figure of the nineteenth century,'" she adds, rising to a crescendo of pride. On a more intimate diminuendo she goes on: "He is lovable in every way; . . . every thought, word or deed is that of a thorough gentleman (I wish I could say the same for all our own acquaintances or relations)." Next, some sharp words about breeding and family pride: "I believe that our proudest record will be our alliance with Richard Burton . . . and I wonder you do not see the magnitude of the position offered me. . . ." Now comes her famous phrase: *"I wish I were a man. If I were, I would be Richard Burton; but being only a woman, I would be Richard Burton's wife."* More pages, on religion and finance. Here Isabel had no defenses. Burton was practically penniless. Although his father had left him fifteen thousand pounds a few years back, this had been swallowed up in the costly subsidies Burton's explorations always required. Back to the attack, Isabel scores heavily on social matters. "You have said you do not know who he is— that you do not meet him anywhere. I don't like to hear you say the first, because it makes you out illiterate, and you know how clever you are; but as to your not meeting him, considering the particular sort of society whom you seek for your daughters, you are not likely to meet there, because it bores him, and is quite out of his line. He is a world-wide man, and his life, and talents, open every door to him . . . he is a great man all over the East, in literary circles in London, and in great parties where you and I would be part of the crowd, he would be remarkable as a star. . . ." And so on—underlinings and exclamation points, cajolery, pleas and threats too, for Isabel knew it was her last chance.

No doubt the letter prostrated Mrs. Arundell by its length, as much as its force. There is no record of her reply, but she seems to have remained obdurate. Both mother and daughter were, in Burton's words, gifted with the noble firmness of mules.

*       *       *

Since Richard remained a bad correspondent, there was no news of him from Salt Lake City, "The Pinchbeck Zion" as he called it, either; but Isabel had perfect faith in his return, since he had himself announced it. At Christmas, she was one of a family house party with her cousins in the north. It must have been the sort of scene that John Leech drew so often in Punch. The great open fireplace, round which ringleted and crinolined ladies netted silk purses, the gentlemen lingered over their port, and the snow piled up outside the heavily curtained windows, while the waits caroled lustily in the porch. God Rest Ye Merry, Gentlemen! Isabel was seated at the piano, accompanying some drawing-room warbler. The music was propped up on a folded copy of *The Times*, when suddenly her eye fell on an announcement that Captain Richard Burton had arrived in London from America. O! Rapture! O! Terror! Why had he not written? She must rush south at once. She could scarcely finish the song, and sat up all night in her room, packing and concocting feverish plans to get herself summoned by a telegram. To be cut off in a Yorkshire snowdrift was child's play, to Isabel. She duly arranged telegrams, transport to the nearest station (nine miles in a blizzard) and reached London without any of her family being the wiser.

Richard, she found, was in a truculent mood. He had waited four years, he said, now she must choose between him and her mother. "Is your answer ready?" he asked. "I said 'Quite. I marry you this day three weeks, let who will say nay!'" It will be seen that in moments of deep emotion Isabel's language always acquired a portentous Biblical ring.

While Mr. Arundell was acquiescent, Mrs. Arundell was stony as ever. Isabel confided in Cardinal Wiseman, who undertook to arrange the affair. The Cardinal saw Burton, and stipulated that Isabel must continue the practice of her religion freely, that any children should be brought up in the Catholic faith, and that the marriage should take place in the Catholic Church, to all of which Burton agreed. The Cardinal was amused by his vehemence. "Practice her religion, indeed! I should rather think she *shall*! A man without a religion may be excused, but a woman without a religion is not the woman for me." The Cardinal obtained a special dispensation from Rome, and it was decided that since Mrs. Arundell was ill, and likely to take the whole matter very hard, the marriage should be without her knowledge and unattended by any of the family.

During the ensuing three weeks, Isabel prepared herself with all the solemnity of a novice entering Holy Orders. She made religious preparation, received the Sacraments and wrote in her devotional book various reflections upon her future life, the principal features being her parents' blessing, a son, money earned by "literature," doing a great deal of good, and a lot of traveling. In the fashion of her age, she also wrote out a lengthy self-memorandum, Rules for My Guidance as a Wife, by which we see that she set herself a grueling standard. She was to be wife, mother, nurse, secretary, traveling companion, confidant and mistress. Her views on the latter role are explicit. "Never refuse him anything he asks. Observe a certain amount of reserve and delicacy before him. Keep up the honeymoon romance whether at home *or in the desert*. At the same time do not make prudish bothers, which only disgust and are not true modesty." Perhaps she sensed that in view of Richard's past, she would be up against very high standards of delight. She was to be elegant, *soignée*; the home, snug; she must improve and educate herself in every way, keep pace with the times, with him, "work up his interests with the world, whether for publishing or for appointments. Let him feel, when he has to go away, that he leaves a second self in charge of his affairs at home." Rule X says: "Never permit anyone to speak disrespectfully of him before you; and if anyone does, no matter how difficult, leave the room. Never permit anyone to tell you anything about him, especially of his conduct with regard to other women . . . always keep his heart up when he has made a failure."

Rule XVII admonishes her to "keep everything going, and let nothing ever be at a standstill; nothing would weary him like stagnation." Only in Rule XIII, "Do not bother him with religious talk," did she sometimes fall short of her standards. It was a brave program, and for the most part it was to be bravely fulfilled.

*       *       *

On Tuesday, January 22, 1861, Isabel achieved the sum total of her earthly desires, and became Burton's wife. In the raw early morning she left her parents' home on the pretext of joining friends in the country. Farther down the road the cab waited, loaded with the cumbersome portmanteau and carpetbags of the time. Isabel said good-by to her unsuspecting mother and father, and superstitious as ever, seeking for symbols and portents, she decided that if they blessed her it should be taken as a sign. "Good-by, child, God bless you!" they said, and Isabel was too overcome to reply: tearing herself away she clung to the lintel of the door, sobbing and kissing it. But those were the only tears and kisses of this outwardly arid ceremony. Burton regarded weddings as "barbarous and indelicate exhibitions," and wished for no display. Besides, he had to be particularly on his guard, taking such a step, that the demonic mask did not slip. Isabel tells us that she wore a fawn-colored silk crinoline, a black lace cloak and a white bonnet, a toilette she excuses as being rather unbridal, though no doubt she looked elegant, as this is always how she struck her contemporaries. She drove to the Bavarian Catholic Church in Warwick Street, where Burton was waiting on the steps, puffing a large cigar and evincing the classic signs of nervousness. After the ceremony there was a small luncheon at the house of some old friends, in the course of which the host, Dr. Bird, chaffing Burton on his adventures, asked him how he had felt when he killed a man. "Quite jolly, doctor, how do you?" was the much-quoted reply. Beginning as he meant to go on, that is, riding roughshod over Isabel, Burton decreed there should be no fuss, nothing exceptional to mark the day. "Let us pretend," he said, "that we have been married a couple of years." And beginning as she, too, meant to go on, in Oriental submission, Isabel agreed. What did it matter to her, now? She was Mrs. Richard Burton. No celebration could mean more. The ten years of prayer and hope deferred had been realized at last. Perhaps she had not imagined it quite so prosaic– perhaps she had visualized a desert honeymoon, in black tents, with Richard in a burnous, and the limpid twilight lit by the evening star, shining down upon their transports.

Instead, they walked off together into the foggy London winter twilight. Burton had rooms in St. James's. "We had very few pounds to bless ourselves with, but were as happy as it is given to any mortals out of heaven to be," says Isabel in her memoirs. That evening an unsuspecting friend called, to find Isabel installed. Burton pressed him to join them in a cigar: Isabel, no doubt remembering her Rules for My Guidance as a Wife, warmly seconded the invitation, and all three settled down to their cheroots. Still, in spite of Burton's deliberately offhand manner, behind the little-boy swagger, he was, in his odd way, in love with Isabel: as much as such an egotist could love, that is. The day after the marriage, Burton wrote to his father-in-law; a letter which Isabel rightly described as beautiful and characteristic:

St. James'

Jan. 23, 1861

My dear Father

I have committed a highway robbery by marrying your daughter Isabel at Warwick Street Chapel, and before the registrar—the details she is writing to her mother.

It only remains for me to say that I have no ties or liaisons of any kind, that the marriage was perfectly "legal and respectable." I want no money with Isabel; I can work, and it will be my care that Time shall bring you nothing to regret.

I am
Yours sincerely
Richard F. Burton

There is no doubt that Burton needed her, for she represented protection, warmth, and seemed a sort of reflection, or projection of himself in more practical, or worldly terms. At first, her powerful family connections may have dazzled him. She could be both a buffer and a spearhead in the Western world he never learned to conquer. If only he could have approached London, and the Government in particular, with the same instinctive tact and initiative he showed in his dealings with desert or jungle strongholds.

Theirs had been a romantic, if protracted, courtship, and for thirty-one years Isabel saw to it that their marriage remained, outwardly, at any rate, one of love and harmony. Ouida, who came to know them well, and who, for all her hyperbole as a novelist, was a remarkably shrewd woman, described Burton as looking like Othello and living like the Three Musketeers. At her celebrated Langham Hotel soirées, where she queened it over London's most distinguished men, Isabel Burton was the only woman guest. Isabel and Ouida had certain interests in common: kindness to dumb animals, strong cigars, and a conviction that Burton was a demigod.

"I have undertaken a very peculiar man," Isabel noted, with truth, in the early days of her marriage. At once, she set about fighting his battles. There was family opposition to overcome, first of all. Her mother had remained in ignorance of the wedding for some weeks, but heard of it in a roundabout way. An officious family friend hastened to tell her that Isabel had been seen *going into bachelor chambers in St. James's*, to Victorian England, a fate worse than death. Mrs. Arundell, in agonies of maternal anxiety, telegraphed her husband, then away on business; he replied, SHE IS MARRIED TO DICK BURTON AND THANK GOD FOR IT. But Mrs. Arundell was not convinced, and is reported to have protested, to her dying day, "Dick Burton is no relative of mine." However, outward appearances had to be maintained, and Isabel brought her husband in triumph to a family reunion. It was proceeding icily enough until Isabel's little brother was banished for some lapse in table manners. But Burton interceded: "Oh! Mother, not on my first night at home!" he said, and even Mrs. Arundell melted at such diplomacy. Then there were Burton's own relatives, who were not so easily won. His sister, Maria, who as a beauty had been known as the Moss Rose, was now the wife of General Sir Henry Stisted. The family were as staunchly Anglican as the Arundells were Papist. To the Stisteds, Isabel always remained "that woman." Her militant Catholicism enraged them. They had not been consulted, or indeed informed of the marriage until too late to interfere, a fact they could not forgive. . . . When Lady Stisted's daughter Georgina wrote the prissy and venomous account of her uncle's life, some thirty years later, rather in the manner of a (Low) church-mouse nibbling at a lion, she says of the marriage: "This step surprised both friends and relatives—those who knew him best were perfectly aware that it surprised *him* most of all."

Money was the next battle, for there was only Richard's army half-pay: that too, was soon to be discontinued, since the John Company found, at last, a technical loophole by which they could escape any further commitments towards their stormy petrel. Isabel flung herself into the *beau monde* for which she always had so great a weakness and from which she intended to wrest advancement for Richard. There was a dazzling social round—dinner parties and receptions. Lord Palmerston gave a party for her, on her marriage, and she was presented at Court by Lady Russell. And here a rather pathetic little incident illustrates, once again, Burton's curiously ingrained need to hide behind a mask of coldness and indifference. Only very much later, under her gentle influence, does he seem to have dropped this pose, or sadistic indulgence, and to have realized how much it hurt her, or perhaps, how much the expression of his love meant to her. On the occasion of her presentation she was leaving for the Drawing Room, and went to show herself off to him in all the traditional splendors of train and ostrich plumes. Burton, maintaining the satanic myth, looked her over with his usual impassive gaze and said nothing. Poor Isabel, feeling crushed, was turning to leave, when she overheard him say to her mother, *"Cette jeune femme n'a rien à craindre."* We do not know why Burton addressed his relatives in French, but at any rate, Isabel went off to the Palace glowing.

\*       \*       \*

After a season of hard social work and fishing in high places, all that could be obtained for England's greatest explorer and Orientalist was an obscure Consular post at San Fernando Po, on the west coast of Africa. It was an appalling climate, and known as the Foreign Office grave. No white woman could live there—the Burtons must accept the post and be separated, or starve, it seemed. Hoping it would be a steppingstone to better things, Burton accepted. In August he sailed from Liverpool. Isabel was determined to be disciplined, but the parting unnerved both of them. For once, Burton allowed his emotions to appear, most gratifyingly, and was scarcely consoled by the prospect of studying the gorillas at first hand. Du Chaillu's recent findings had made sensational reading; and it will be remembered the simian world had fascinated him years before, in India. Darwinism, too, was making the monkey an object of vital or even family interest to Victorian England just then.

Isabel moved back to live with her parents, and entered on a period of strict economy. She continued as Richard's unofficial publicity agent, and now he had entrusted her with the task of putting his latest book to press. *The City of the Saints,* his Mormon reportage, was a sad disappointment to the public, who had been longing for highly colored revelations. Since polygamy was one of Burton's lifelong crusades, and he often expounded his theories on the place which the "Hetæra, or plurality-wife" should occupy in civilized living, and the part she could play in banishing his anathema, the old maid, the book had a certain shock appeal, especially in relation to his recent marriage. But sales were disappointing.

After sixteen weary months of separation, Isabel could bear it no more. Once again she went to the Foreign Office, where she burst into tears on a distinguished black-coated shoulder. It had a magic effect. Richard was spirited home on leave, and they spent a happy Christmas together, going from one country house party to the next. Richard's reports of life at San Fernando Po were discouraging. It was even worse than its reputation. "They sent me there hoping I'd die," he said, "but I intend to live—to spite 'em." Isabel attributed the Government's coldness largely to Richard's too loudly expressed views on polygamy. In a letter to a friend she wrote, "They [the ogre Government] are making a complete Aunt Sally of the poor fellow, and he can't stand up for himself. You and Mrs. F. will say he deserves it for his polygamous opinions, but he married only *one* wife and he is a *domestic* man at home, and a *homesick* man away!" Poor dear Richard—poor dear Isabel! What a problem he was for both of them. He could not be fitted into any really acceptable mold, either official or domestic: he could not be bottled—he always emerged in a clap of thunder, a puff of sulphurous smoke—the Arabian Nights djinn.

All too soon his leave was up, and Isabel could not be placated; she was, as she said, neither maid nor wife, nor widow. Richard conceded she should go with him as far as Madeira, where they would stay together for a while, before he went on to the Foreign Office grave, and she back to London. This was Isabel's first journey with her husband —her first taste of the life she had longed for with almost as much passion as for the man. True, Madeira was not really an unexplored or savage waste, even in the sixties, nor was it Tancred's beloved desert— but still, it was semitropical. Isabel was overjoyed to be leaving "matter-of-fact old England where one *can't* get into a difficulty" (though it might be remarked that throughout his life Burton had only to land there to be involved in official troubles). They climbed a mountain, and slept beneath the stars, and at last Isabel saw Richard in what she considered a proper setting—in wild country—(though not the desert) and by the light of the campfire.

The next two years were spent between long periods of separation and short reunions at Madeira. Both fretted. Burton loathed his post, but performed his duties with military precision, imposing discipline and a respect for his office upon even the most slipshod traders. Bored, he fell back on liquor, while Isabel tried the numbing effects of social life. Neither was consoled. During this time, however, Burton was given one interesting assignment, for the Foreign Office dispatched him to report on and make overtures to the King of Dahomey. Isabel was fired with the idea of accompanying him, and introducing a softening Christian influence by means of lantern slides, but this was discountenanced by both Richard and the Foreign Office. Burton's subsequent book *A Mission to Gelele, King of Dahomey,* did not follow the precedent of most Government reports; indeed it would make advanced reading for those reared on the Kinsey Report. It is an absorbing anthropological treatise. But from the viewpoint of the Victorian public, sadly unsuitable for general reading, what with its pre-Freudian approach to the psychology of Amazons, its specific data on aphrodisiacs, Catamites, prostitution, methods of abortion, and such disagreeable spectacles as confinements and decapitation dances. In spite of the Amazon troops being sworn to chastity, there were occasions when "as many as one hundred and fifty were all found to be pregnant—so difficult is chastity in the tropics." Isabel, still languishing at home, and editing the report, found it very disturbing. Her wifely patience was at the breaking point when she learned that one of these Amazons had been attached to Richard as his *aide-de-camp*. . . . She had fevered visions of a beautiful female warrior, decked out in plumes and daggers, galloping by Richard's side, down jungle paths leading towards indescribable delights. It was no comfort to fall back on the poem with which Richard had dedicated his recent book *Wanderings in West Africa*.

> *Oh, I could live with thee in the wildwood*
> *Where human foot hath never worn a way;*
> *With thee, my city and my solitude,*
> *Light of my night, sweet rest from cares by day.*

. . . Someone else was with him in the wildwood now. She was not to be appeased, until Richard sent her a sketch of his Amazon Chieftainess, a squatting, ferocious figure of repellent aspect.

In 1864, during Burton's leave spent in England, he was at last provoked by Speke's bragging, to have it out publicly. The platform of the British Association at Bath was to be their meeting place. They had not met since their parting at Zanzibar; and since then Speke's veracity had begun to be challenged. His capacities, like his personality, it had become evident, were very inferior to Burton's. The Council and a distinguished scientific gathering were present. Burton, with Isabel beside him, took his place on the platform: he had brought a number of notes, and was in a restive, pugnacious mood. At long last he had the chance to vindicate himself—to fight it out with Speke, publicly. But the time passed, and there was no sign of Speke. Suddenly a messenger arrived—a paper was handed to Burton, who grew deadly pale, and left the hall. Speke had killed himself out shooting. Whether it was an accident or suicide was never decided. He was of a moody, depressive nature, and was said to have first plunged into exploration because he set so little value on life. Isabel believed that overcome with remorse, he had taken his life rather than face Burton and public ignominy.

*     *     *

The rest of Burton's leave was spent in the usual strict round of pleasure for business: they must see, and be seen, Isabel maintained—they would get nowhere by skulking economically. There were more big house parties, more amusing Bohemian friends—the young George du Maurier and Dante Gabriel Rossetti, Swinburne and Charles Bradlaugh, with his dangerous spiritualistic experiments: these were particularly fascinating to the Burtons, who dabbled in mesmerism, Isabel always being Richard's victim, and compelled to accept, very unwillingly, the state of trance to which he could quickly reduce her, and from which he would induce her to talk without reserve, on past, present or future. Indeed there had been ugly scenes over Richard wanting to mesmerize some other woman (he preferred the blue-eyed and yellow-haired type) and for once we have an independent account of the Burton menage in furious combat. *The Amberly Papers* include entries from the journal of Lady Russell during January, 1865, when the Burtons were her guests, and mesmerism was the rock upon which the whole house-party split after a great deal of nocturnal door-slamming.

At last the string-pulling and social treadmills bore fruit; Burton was appointed to Santos, in Brazil, a post where Isabel might also go. Still not the desert; still no nearer to Tancred and the lodestar East! Isabel concealed her frustrations and made the best of things, as usual. They made their farewell rounds, and were given a dinner of honor by the Anthropological Society. Isabel packed up, started learning Portuguese, and with great foresight of prevailing insect conditions in Brazil, took a pair of iron bedsteads along. At Lisbon three-inch cockroaches seethed about the floor of their room. Isabel was caught off her guard, but Burton was brutal. "I suppose you think you look very pretty standing on that chair and howling at those innocent creatures," he growled. Isabel's reaction was typical: she stopped screaming and reflected that of course he was right; if she had to live in a country full of such creatures, and worse, she had better pull herself together. She got down among them, and started lashing out with a slipper. In two hours she had a bag of ninety-seven, and had conquered her queasiness. On arrival in Brazil, she found that Portuguese fauna had been a mere sugary bagatelle. Now there were spiders as big as crabs. In the matter of tropical diseases it seems to have ranked with darkest Africa; there were slaves, too, often maintained in conditions of the utmost savagery. It was the South America of which we get a glimpse in Gauguin's memories of his childhood: a steamy, brilliant landscape, where gaudy parakeets flashed through the rubbery vegetation, a dissolute society smoked huge cheroots, and drank brandy for breakfast, and no one condemned the habit of chaining a mad slave to the rooftop as a sort of domestic pet, or clown.

Isabel became acclimatized painfully. There was cholera, and the less dramatic but agonizing local boils "so close you could not put a pin between them"; Isabel battled through the boils on frequent draughts of stout; she unpacked her fifty-nine trunks, set her house in order, and gave her first dinner party successfully. The Emperor found the new Consul and his wife a great addition to the country; once again Burton's wonderful conversation held his audience spellbound. But chic Brazilians looked askance at Isabel wading barefooted in the streams, bottling snakes, painting and furbishing up a ruined chapel, or accompanying Richard on expeditions to the virgin interior. He taught her to fence; there were gymnastics, and cold baths, and Mass, and market, "helping Richard with Literature" (his writing was always in capitals to her) or working on the wearisome pages of the Foreign Office reports she was always so loyal and dutiful in copying out for him. "Thirty-two pages on Cotton Report—one hundred and twenty-five Geographic Report—eighty pages General Trade Report—this for Lord Stanley, so I do it cheerfully," she wrote home. But it was really for *Richard,* so of course it was a labor of love. It was unjust that later she was accused of interference, and a power complex, when she occasionally referred to "my Foreign Office reports."

Both Burton and his wife were wasted in small-fry Consulate posts. Fortunately, in Rio, they were appreciated not only by the Emperor, but by the British Minister too; they were signaled out for attentions which aroused violent jealousy among other, less privileged consular personnel. Burton was accused of being disagreeable, haughty, unconventional and eccentric. Isabel was said to be ridiculously "*grande dame*" for her modest rank. But neither of them depended on protocol shadings for their stature. They were exceptional personalities in their own right; *hors concours*. Except for Damascus, they were never given a worthy post. It was a deliberate policy and both of them knew this: it accounts for much of Isabel's social touchiness—her determination not to be put down below what her own breeding, and her husband's achievements, deserved. It accounts, too, for the raging sense of frustration and bitterness which was gradually to overcome Burton's original initiative and strength.

About now, a note of sadness creeps into Isabel's letters home. We sense an immense loneliness behind the courage with which she always faced life, whatever the conditions. It was said of her that if she were to find herself in a coal hole, she would set about arranging it to the best advantage. Richard was going through a particularly trying phase. The explorer was dying hard, strangulating in office tape. He would cut loose, and disappear for weeks at a time, returning as bitter and restless as when he left. It was she who held everything together and kept up the façade both with the Foreign Office, who were constantly making the most awkward inquiries, and the local society, who were equally curious. There were few diversions for Isabel. "The ladies are namby-pamby," she wrote: and so they seem to have been, for they took exception, as improper, to four puny English railway clerks rowing at the Regatta in jerseys. Writing home, in a rare burst of exasperation engendered by her life of pinching, scrimping and bravado in the face of local snobbishness, "I often think a *parvenue,* or half-bred woman would burst if she had to do as I do . . . keeping up appearances, lancing boils, coping with insects, with Richard, with everything. . . ." And again: "I do hate Santos. The climate is beastly, the people fluffy. The stinks, the vermin, the food, the niggers are all of a piece. There are no walks [at home or abroad Walks are the eternal Anglo-Saxon panacea]; if you go one way you sink knee-deep in mangrove swamps; another, you are covered with sandflies. . . ."

Even local dances, where the Brazilians spun round with the frenzies of Hungarians at their *czardas*, were denied to Isabel, until she took to going alone, for Richard would have none of them. He preferred to sup with the Capuchin monks, discussing metaphysics and astronomy. He was studying mathematics; and his new telescope was a great pleasure, keeping him good-humored through many long starry tropic nights. But he was in a bad way: frustrations had wrecked his nerves; his iron physique began to crack, too: he had abused it for twenty years. He continued his disappearances into the pampas, or the mountains, or the virgin forests, and Isabel learned to solace herself by solitary minor expeditions. Even to such an intrepid woman as she, there were lurking terrors which spoiled the simplest pleasures. Huge hairy spiders, deadly snakes, and so much leprosy that she dared not sleep in a bed at an inn, but lay on the ground, or in her own hammock. She was forming the pattern of her life as Richard Burton's wife. Perhaps no other man could have given her so much—but certainly no other woman could have given him so much loyalty, or have been content to live so much in the margin of another's life. She was learning, now, to be self-sufficient, to manage, unobtrusively, the practical side of both their lives; to rough it both physically and emotionally. Loving so greatly must have been a lonely, isolating experience. It required suppleness too. She had to combine the plastic, shadowlike devotion of the Oriental woman, which does not come naturally to an Anglo-Saxon, with an independence, a fighting spirit seldom found basically, in woman, and certainly not in most Victorian women.

However, Isabel had made up her mind. "I intend to make myself content here," she writes characteristically from the wilds of São Paulo to a friend in Rio, a Mr. Tootal who appears to have been her means of keeping in touch with the world. She asks him to send her some music— "any of those gay little Andalusian songs, bull fights, *contrabandrista* or gypsy things. . . . I am spoony on anything Spanish and have got a guitar and castanets." Poor brave, deluded, determined Isabel, twanging her guitar, snapping her castanets at fate. . . . Meanwhile Burton was writing to another friend, "Don't speak much of it but I am off into the interior when I get my June mail. The journey will occupy at least eight months." From his point of view this was an excellent arrange-

ment leaving plenty of time for Isabel to cope with all the correspondence, letters, Foreign Office affairs, or publishers' proofs in his absence:
it gave him, too, the agreeable feeling of having deserted her, even if
only temporarily. So loving a nature must have been an especial pleasure
for him to torment.

In the autumn of 1867, Burton exceeded all bounds of vagrancy. For
more than four months there had been no news from him, no news of
his whereabouts since he had set off to paddle down the São Francisco.
Isabel had been dealing as best she could with Consular matters (fortunately not of a very exigent nature) and was distracted with anxiety.
No word of this dreadful time ever sounded through her memoirs, or,
miraculously, reached the Foreign Office, who we must suppose had no
inkling of the true state of affairs. It was in the comic tradition of a
nineteenth-century satiric farce, worthy of Gogol's *Government Inspec-
tor*; comings and goings, impersonations, hoodwinkings, ostrich blind-
ness and maneuvers in which everyone conspires to preserve the illusion
that nothing unusual is happening. Isabel played her part with an exag-
gerated nonchalance, and sat up half the night keeping abreast with official papers. "My reports"—just a little extra copying she was doing, to
while away the tedium, while Richard took a nap—this was her attitude.
It may have deceived the Foreign Office; after all, they were a long way
off, and Santos seldom in their minds; but it did not deceive the inhabitants of Santos. They shrugged it off. Crazy English. So Isabel went
on holding the fort, her head high.

There are glimpses of this time of stress in her letters home, and indirectly, in the memoirs of Wilfred Scawen Blunt, the poet and traveler, who ran into Burton in Buenos Aires, where he was consorting with
the Tichborne claimant, or Arthur Orton, the butcher from Wagga-
Wagga, whose claims to the Tichborne titles and fortune gripped London in the seventies, and were the occasion of fierce legal battles, in
which Burton was called as a witness. He gave evidence so diametrically
opposed to his earlier opinions, as expressed in letters, that we are
tempted to believe he was coerced, perhaps by some threat of expos-
ure. He must have had many incidents in his life which it was
more politic to forget: he may have been either blackmailed or bribed

by promises of some splendid new post by the all-powerful Tichborne family, who, besides being related to both Isabel and the Arundells, were prepared to go to any lengths to obtain the verdict they wished (as in the ruthless persecution of Father Meyrick); and yet such a supposition is against Burton's basic integrity, though Isabel, with his preferment in view, would have stopped at nothing. Wilfred Scawen Blunt describes the Claimant as "a mountain of flesh, of no very refined clay"; and Burton, as "a grim being to be with at the end of his second bottle, with a gaucho's *navaja* handy." At forty-eight, Blunt thought him already a broken man; physically, a husk. "Burton was at that time at the lowest point, I fancy, of his whole career," wrote Blunt. "His dress and appearance were those suggesting a released convict. He reminded me by turns of a black leopard, caged but unforgiving; and again, with that close-cut poll and iron frame, of that wonderful creation of Balzac's, the *ex-gallerien* Vautrin, hiding his grim identity under an abbé's cassock. He wore, habitually, a rusty black coat with a crumpled black stock, his throat destitute of collar, a costume which his muscular frame and immense chest made singularly and incongruously hideous. Above it a countenance the most sinister I have ever seen, dark, cruel, treacherous, with eyes like a wild beast." But he added: "Even the ferocity of his countenance gave place at times to more agreeable expressions, and I can just understand the infatuated fancy of his wife that in spite of his ugliness he was the most beautiful man alive."

This interlude in Burton's official life was never even hinted at in any of the subsequent biographies. "Journeys to the interior," said Isabel, loyal as ever. Poor Isabel! All she had asked from heaven was to be Richard Burton's wife—but had she reckoned, when she took him for better or worse, to find him, her earthly god and king, a piece of barely human wreckage—"a black leopard, caged but unforgiving"? This is only one of the many episodes in Burton's life of which we shall never know the truth. When after his death, Isabel burned the manuscript of *The Scented Garden*, she also burned all his private papers, including his journals and notes. We shall never know the key to his veiled, unassessed personality. How had he, for instance, picked up with the Tichborne claimant? What was he doing rotting in Rio? How did he come to be wearing a greasy tattered black frock coat? It hardly seems likely he would have chosen such a garment, even if in its pristine state, as suitable for his canoe voyage down the São Paulo. Or are we to infer that whatever the climate of Brazil, the frock coat was *de rigueur* for Her Majesty's consuls, and Burton had been, perhaps, overpowered by a sudden tempestuous wanderlust, rushing out of his office to embark there and then? This is only one of the many fascinating speculations which every aspect of Burton's character arouses.

During the months of Burton's disappearance, Isabel had become increasingly anxious. At last she went down to the coast and stayed there, meeting the few steamers that put in from Bahia. But there was no sight of Burton. She feared the worst: he must be ill, or taken prisoner for his money. "He always *would* carry gigantic sums in his pockets hanging half out," she wrote home, planning to go and look for him up-country. "I am not afraid of anything except the wild Indians, fever, ague, and vicious fish which can be easily avoided: there are no other dangers." While waiting, she was encountering sharks, when bathing in the boiling surf. "I shall feel rather shy of the water in future," she adds offhandedly.

Just as she was preparing to set out on a rescue expedition, Burton reeled off the only tramp steamer she had not met for weeks, and was unreasonably offended that she had not come aboard to meet him. Isabel realized his condition and acted with great discretion, whipping him off to the country before scandal could start. But a few weeks later Burton collapsed with an obscure and agonizing liver complaint, the result of the climate and his late excesses. For some while he lay delirious, and screaming. Isabel nursed him devotedly. "In this country if you are well, all right; but the moment you are ailing, lie down and die, for it is no use trying to live," she wrote home. "I kept Richard alive by never taking my eyes off him for eight weeks. . . ." Burton mended slowly. But he was a wreck. "He looks about sixty. I'm afraid his lungs will never be quite right again." In another letter: "I tried to go out in the garden yesterday, but nearly fainted and had to come back. *Don't mention my fatigue or health in writing back.*" How she loved him! How she loved nursing him! He was all hers, now. The world had lost a great explorer, but she had found her husband. "He has given up his expeditions," she wrote home, thankfully; prematurely, too.

Still, the old ways died hard: the explorer lingered on. Even in his delirium, Burton was planning another voyage down the River Plata, to Paraguay. As soon as he was convalescent, he flung a fresh bombshell on the exhausted Isabel. He would resign. He detested the post, it was a dead end. He would apply for six months' sick leave, and go across the Andes to Chile and Peru, taking in the war then raging in Paraguay en route. Isabel could not dissuade him from either project. It was decided she must return to England before him, see another book through the press, and do what she could to find him a better post. Although Isabel feared for Burton's health and felt bitterly the dissolution of what had been, however erratic, the only real home they had established together, she made no complaints. Perhaps she knew, now, that his health was shattered, that he would never again stray very far afield, and that it was only the wraith of the traveler, who set out on the echo of a voyage.

\*       \*       \*

Back in London good fortune awaited them. It was like a fairy tale reward for Isabel's years of endeavor and trial. At last—the East! Her machinations obtained one of the plum posts: Damascus, and a salary of one thousand pounds a year. A great Orientalist like Burton had everything to give to such an appointment. And everything to gain, too; Isabel must have felt an enormous relief, that at last he would be in a country where there would be no more rotting in swamps, no more craving for suicidal journeys into the limbo, and where every aspect of the land and the life was a challenge to his knowledge. He would be among his beloved Arabs once more; well handled, the post could lead to Morocco or Constantinople . . . vistas of paradise. They trod on air. All the same, Isabel took lessons in revolver shooting, and the cleaning and management of guns. She had no intention of making polite picnics on the edge of the desert.

Yet even in that radiant moment clouds were gathering unperceived;

they were no bigger than a man's hand, but they were part of those shadows which were always to fall, always to come between Burton and fulfillment. There were strong objections to his appointment from various quarters, based chiefly on religious grounds: a man of such loudly proclaimed agnosticism was scarcely suitable for the Holy Land. He was not called Ruffian Dick for nothing, said others. Burton had been given the post by Lord Stanley, who believed he would be the right man in the right place: but the pattern of Burton's ill-timing continued, even indirectly. No sooner was the appointment made, than the Government fell. The new Foreign Secretary, Lord Clarendon, was hostile to Burton, and listened to his many enemies. He told Burton frankly that he considered the appointment ill-advised, and was only prevailed upon to let matters stand after Burton had undertaken to be specially prudent and vigilant, regarding his private inclinations, perhaps. Thus Burton started out under a cloud, and when later, events precipitated his recall, he was never able to clear himself of the prejudices which had accumulated against him. That was to become Isabel's crusade; but when she had won her husband's vindication at last, it was too late to matter much, either way.

\*       \*       \*

In the summer of 1869 Burton started out ahead once more, this time by way of Vichy, in company with Swinburne, and Isabel was left to wind up their affairs. "This sort of thing," she says cheerfully, "is what Shakespeare meant when he spoke of 'chronicling small beer.' Husbands are uncomfortable without Chronicle—though they never see the *petit détail* going on, and like to keep up the pleasant illusion that it is done by magic." Isabel's small beer gradually assumed a gigantic range. Paying and packing for Burton—and following him, was a life's work in itself. There was his uncontrollable spate of books to edit and see through the press: his tangled business affairs to be sorted, and the ever-vital necessity of championing and publicizing him too. But now, all seemed golden—the paradisaical vistas beckoned; it was Tancred's East at last! She left England in December, armed with her total fortune, some three hundred pounds which was subsequently stolen, a pony chaise, which proved to be useless on Syrian tracks, innumerable boxes and the "magpie trunk," a huge crate painted half black, half white, for distinction's sake, and in which Burton stored many of his manuscripts. There were also five adored dogs. She was one of those Englishwomen who always collect a menagerie round them. One of Burton's pet names for her was Zoo: another, Puss.

It was her initiation to the East, the consummation of her longings. "My destination was Damascus, the dream of my childhood. I should follow the footsteps of Lady Mary Wortley Montagu, Lady Hester Stanhope, and the Princesse de la Tour d'Auvergne, that trio of famous European women who lived of their own choice a thoroughly Eastern life, and of whom I looked to make a fourth. I am to live among Bedouin Arab chiefs: I shall smell the desert air; I shall have tents, horses, weapons, and be free. . . . Fortunately my husband has had the same mind from his youth." At last, it had all come true, all she had prayed for, longed for, and all that Hagar had foreseen. . . . Tancred's East and Richard's arms!

\* \* \*

*"O Damascus! though old as history itself, thou art fresh as the breath of spring, blooming as thine own rosebud, as fragrant as thine own roses, as fragrant as thine own orange-flower, O Damascus, Pearl of the East!"*

If Isabel swam in bliss, Burton for a while seemed reborn. Once again he was in the East he adored and to which he belonged, fundamentally. He was among the people he understood and craved. "He was the sole example," says Isabel, "of one not born a Moslem, who having performed the Hadj, could live with Moslems in perfect friendship after. They considered him *persona grata*—something more civilized than the common run of Franks—they called him Hadji Abdullah, and treated him as one of themselves." The Burtons found a house outside the city, at the Kurd hill village of Salahíyyeh; it was beautiful and simple; cascades of roses and vines adorned the walls. A fountain splashed in the arcaded courtyard: there was a mosque, adjoining their house, and the muezzin's haunting call to prayer was wafted through the windows with the mountain breeze. Soon, there were twelve horses in the stables, a rather spoiled and troublesome Arab staff, and an enormous collection of most unsuitable but taking pets, ranging from leopards to lambs. Isabel's tender heart went out to all the starved pathetic animals of the East. As she had taken in, housed and fed the outcast poor of Brazil ("my poor") so she now opened her doors to any animal she could protect ("my pets"), and Burton was entirely in agreement. In this instance there were none of the acrimonious disputes which had arisen whenever he discovered Isabel's poor idling away in the cellars, waxing fat on her bounty, in Brazil. And then there were the sick. Isabel shared the Victorian woman's passion for concocting experimental draughts, for poulticing, and generally ministering. It appears to have occupied an obsessive place in their make-up. Burton opined it was the expression of a subconscious desire for power, for domination (and certainly, the dominant, free twentieth-century career women show little inclination toward nursing, either as a career, or as a hobby). Even George Sand, that most tempestuous of romantics, was swept by the ministering instinct. To her lover, Alfred de Musset, whom she had abandoned in Venice, she writes "Oh, who will nurse you now that I have gone . . . *and whom shall I nurse?*" (The italics are mine.) It is the cry of the age, a profound need.

The Burtons flung themselves into the life of Damascus with abandon, boldly inaugurating receptions at which every creed and race and class were welcomed, a startling innovation which worked well. There were days and nights spent riding across the desert, exploring the country, visiting the desert Sheiks, the ruins of Palmyra, or the churches of Jerusalem. There were overtones of Turkish politics, undertones of Levantine intrigue, and all the ritual and grace of households such as that of the Emir Abd El Kadir, the celebrated old Algerian warrior, now freed from his years of exile in France, and living in princely state in Damascus. He had been a legendary figure, holding at bay half a dozen great French generals and several princes of the blood; when at last he was vanquished, he was treated with chivalresque generosity, and was often to be seen in Paris, riding haughty and aloof across the Place de la Concorde, surrounded by his Algerian guards in their flowing white burnouses. In 1857, Louis Napoleon gave him his liberty, and an income of four thousand pounds a year, upon which he was living, in Damascus, when the Burtons knew him. With the years he had become the staunch ally of France; after his defense of the Christian Maronites, in 1860, the French gave him the Grand Cross of the Legion d'Honneur. When, during the Franco-Prussian War, he heard of his son's plans to attack the French in Algeria—a stab in the back to a harassed nation, he sent furious messages and threats, forbidding any movement against the country which had been, for twenty-five years, his generous friend.

Lord Redesdale recalls being taken to see him by Burton. They followed the usual squalid passages which bloomed suddenly into a sun-splashed courtyard of voluptuous beauty, with fountains and oleanders. The great Emir, a majestic figure in white robes, was then sixty-four, but his beard and eyebrows were blackened, and his cheeks faintly rouged, though this, in the Orient, was no sign of effeminacy. Abd El Kadir was poring over a huge book; he was studying Magic, but broke off to serve them the ceremonial glasses of tea. Lord Redesdale enjoyed the visit as an excursion into the exotic—but to Burton, it was home, and to Isabel it was Heaven.

There were other visitors from England—Lord Leighton arrived and made sketches of the charming house at Salahíyyeh, its ocher walls blazing under the blue and cloudless skies. Burton was absorbed into Arab life, the honored guest of savants and simple Arabs alike, who were as quick to appreciate the intellect of Her Majesty's new Consul, as to recognize his integrity. Very soon, it was seen he was not to be bribed, or led, and he was feared or respected, or disliked, accordingly. But first, all was calm, in the lovely unhurried tempo of the East.

At dusk, when the great gates of the city clanged shut, and the moon swam high and dazzling overhead, there were long night of talks, "wonderful talk" sighed Isabel, remembering it still on her deathbed. Nights when Abd El Kadir and Lady Ellenborough (Jane Digby El Mezrab of whom I write elsewhere, now married to her Mezrabi Sheik) would loll beside the Burtons on the cushion-spread roof terraces, talking, talking, always of the East, its beliefs and legends, its past glories, and its future. It is probable that Burton obtained from Jane Digby El Mezrab many of the psychological, sexual and historic aspects of harem life which he later incorporated in his notes to *The Thousand Nights and a Night*. Even when he passed as a physician in Cairo, or when he dallied in the arms of his Persian houri, he could not have come by such jealously guarded secrets. Isabel, who was learning Arabic, hung on their words, dispensing coffee, replenishing the *narghilyés*. "Our life was holy, solemn, wild," she wrote later.

Wild it was, compared to conventional diplomatic standards. Burton had returned to his old ways of disguise too, often wandering unsuspected, in the bazaars and mosques. He remains an enigmatic figure; we do not know how much of his life was spent this way, nor how much he was influenced, perhaps unconsciously, by his return to the East. Did he begin, imperceptibly, at first, perhaps, to go native? It would have been, after all, more in the nature of the return of the native, for he was more at home in the East than in the West, and this may have been known, ultimately, to the Foreign Office; if so, it is a probable explanation of their obstinate refusal to appoint him, after his recall from Damascus, to any other Oriental post. Meanwhile, at Salahíyyeh, Burton would choose his various disguises, and disappear discreetly from the house, to merge into the teeming life of the city, where no doubt he learned and did much that was hidden from the rest of his diplomatic colleagues.

Sometimes Isabel, also in Oriental dress, but not, as she fondly believed, in disguise, would also descend into Damascus, savoring various aspects of Eastern life. Although only forty, she seems now to have lost most of her looks, to have become rather matronly, though the life she led was not, and had never been, either staid or static. When voyaging in the desert she wore Syrian men's clothes, baggy trousers and burnous, being accepted everywhere, she says, as Richard's son. With her florid coloring, and ample proportions, we feel she cannot always have been accepted unquestioningly.

It would seem that their personal relationship had now shifted to another key. The lovers had given place to the friends—they were inseparable comrades, or as Burton himself said, like elder and younger brothers: what Isabel the single-minded, the passionately loving, thought of this metamorphosis is not known. Richard on any terms would be better than no Richard. Besides, he was her Mission: in her devotional book she notes: "I am to bear *all* joyfully, as an atonement to save Richard. . . . let me not think my lot is to be exempt from trials. . . . I must take difficulties and pain with courage and even with avidity. As I asked ardently for this Mission—none other than to be Richard's wife—let me not forget to ask as ardently for grace to carry it out." In this ambiguous state of spiritual and physical love she began and continued her married life. She was the stuff of martyrs; only a martyr's zeal could have submitted to some of her domestic trials.

Although Isabel was briskly Anglo-Saxon, and never shared the dark torments of the flesh known to Isabelle Eberhardt, nor yet those lusty and divergent appetites so much enjoyed by Lady Ellenborough, she shows, throughout her life, a truly passionate and overwhelming love for Richard Burton, a love which was not basically maternal, however much life forced her into that role. But had there ever been a real response from him? Had there ever been, hidden away behind the offhand manner, those burning desires which Isabel must have sensed in Burton when she first encountered him on the Ramparts, and which his face, for all its air of ferocious animalism, came to belie? He was not perhaps *au fond* a sensualist—or only for a very few years, during his unfettered life in India. Perhaps those years had been too demanding. Later, he seems to have chosen to canalize his emotions, first, in the violent activities and dangers of exploration, and later still, in the abstract or theoretical *voluptés* of his exotic literature. Between them, there cannot have been much time left over for Isabel, the woman.

That there were no children was something she at first regretted. Later she wrote: "We thought it better so. . . . Everything that happens to us is always for the best," she adds with perfect submission and faith. In her middle age, writing to a friend she said: "Yes, I have twelve nephews and nieces, five boys and seven girls . . . quite enough. Thank God we have none." For Isabel the robust, the ardent, the Orientally disposed wife, who had once shared the Eastern longing for a son, to arrive at last at this conclusion seems proof of the overwhelming strain daily life with Richard had imposed. It shows how the manifold burdens had at last distorted her views upon even such a question.

Ouida opined that Isabel could never have shared Richard, even with his child, she was too possessively in love. But Burton, says Ouida, regretted their childless state. He loved children and was too much of an egoist not to want his own. Burton's views elude us, on this point, as on so many others, vanished forever in the widow's bonfire. Burton wrote little about himself: Isabel presented to the world only what she saw, or chose to see, so that with the destruction of his journals, only the outward shell, the myth of this strange man, remains. There are interpretations of his nature which can be made in the light of his *Terminal Essay*—but such inferences would have been utterly incomprehensible and repugnant to Victorian England. Even today we are too close to Burton to write of him without reserve. He appears to have been caged as much by his century as his nationality. It was a lost battle, to reconcile himself, his profoundly Eastern tastes, to the life he came to lead. "A leopard, caged but unforgiving . . ." "The desert eagle in his cage. . . ." In his later days, his eyes stare out from the faded photographs, raging, bold eyes; sullen, too. "I have tamed Richard a little," wrote Isabel, cruelly loving. But did she ever come to realize how far she, the Foreign Office, and all Victorian England were from the real Richard? When Burton turned away from the East he deliberately detached himself. Once that step had been made, once the West had been chosen, his marriage to Isabel brought him the best he could hope from that alien way. Burton the Arab had been sacrificed to Burton the Englishman, but not—as Isabel's detractors would have it—to Burton the husband. That state was quite incidental.

Perhaps this accounts for the trajectory, the sharp, descending curve of his life, his curiously muffled quality, when, after his return from Africa and the Great Lake Expedition, the man, in all his force, was never again to emerge. The real man seemed no longer there: he had been left behind, in the East, to which he belonged. Why, we shall never know. But alas! the puppet had memories. It was as the prisoner of this brooding *Doppelgänger* that Burton lived out the rest of his ill-fated life. No one, nothing, not even Damascus would ever put him right again. "That look of inexpressible horror"—was it not that of a man who looks inwards and finds emptiness? A man who had watched his true self turn aside and fade into the faraway desert horizons? And now, when in, but not of, the beloved Arab world once more, he knew he had made the choice: it was only a masquerade he played out in Damascus; a brief curtain call, a final bow before the blow fell, before his enemies struck, and he was recalled in ignominy.

In Damascus, Isabel reached her zenith. The two years of their life there were something she most treasured, next to her love for Richard. She was lit by their afterglow for the rest of her life; everywhere else seemed an exile. When people asked her if she had liked it, and why, she was both indignant and inarticulate before such tepidity. Like it! Syria was under her skin, as it had always been in her heart. It had been her earthly fulfillment of paradise. But as always, besides her emotionalism, she showed sound practical sense. Every opportunity to proselytize was seized: she was as naïve, as ingenuous as a child. There were always ways to turn the subject to her cause. Catholicism, cruelty to animals, cruelty to Richard—nothing was allowed to stop the flow. When she was not bombarding the newspapers, the Royal Geographical Society or the Foreign Office with telegrams, letters and personal visits (happily for her adversaries, the telephone was not yet in use), she found other ways to continue the fight. In her preface to Burton's book, *The Highlands of Brazil,* she cunningly established the Catholic point of view on his *cheval de bataille*—polygamy—while firmly pointing out (expressly to clear him) his personally monogamous habits. In the same book, his vivid account of a Catholic priest's attempts to seduce a peasant girl could not be tampered with; Isabel burned with indignation but did not dare suppress the passage. In her book *The Inner Life of Syria,* she contrived to work in whole chapters of a biographical or missionary nature, all cunningly calculated to direct public attention to Richard's worth, or the injustice and ingratitude displayed towards him by lesser mortals. At this time she was writing regularly, but anonymously, for the *Levant Herald,* published in Constantinople, and as always singing Burton's praises with indiscreet fervor. She was very resourceful. In her books she could have it all her own way. There were no interruptions, no arguments. They were her paper pulpit. So, Chapter XXVII is devoted entirely to visionary subjects which have a soundly materialistic core. Since this chapter is particularly typical of the unblushing way she worked, whether indirectly, or in her official visits to wilting civil servants, or at influential dinner tables, it is perhaps worth quoting at length.

She starts the unsuspecting reader off by her tourist's expedition to the caves of Magharat el Kotn, undertaken in a state of exhaustion brought about by Lenten fasting. Looking down on Jerusalem, far below, she falls asleep. "*I dreamt a dream*—perhaps I ought not to detail it, but an inner voice bids me to do so." She is off, the first of the press agents. A superior Guardian Angel whisks her to the Throne of Grace where a remarkable dialogue ensues. Jehovah grants her an Easter favor. Getting the best of both worlds, Isabel asks to remain in heaven, her husband with her. Jehovah seems pleased, and offers to grant her another wish.

It needs no more. Isabel sets about reforming the dream world, *particularly the dream Foreign Office,* with a view to obtaining proper recognition for Richard. Another angel is detailed to accompany Isabel on her reformatory tour. She next sets about contriving a series of crystal and golden thrones, and as she was always strongly imperialistic she has soon settled Queen Victoria on one, as Queen of all the world. (We feel she shows great restraint not to install Richard as Consort.) The Royal Family are grouped round on slightly lower thrones. "I then retired and looked at my handiwork," says Isabel, rather in the manner of a parish worker decking the altar for Harvest Festival. But she perceives the Koh-i-noor glittering in the regalia: that will never do. She has long, and publicly, voiced her distrust of this ill-omened trophy. So she firmly removes it, replacing it by a Star, provided by the Guardian Angel. "The Queen looked at me severely, for she could not see the Spiritual Star. 'Why have you robbed my crown of its brightest ornament?' she asks." Isabel explains her case against the Koh-i-noor, how it always brings ruin and decay to its possessors. But the Queen is not amused. She changes the conversation and says severely, "For whom is that Throne and Imperial Scepter far above mine?" (We tremble, lest Isabel forget herself so far as to say they are for Richard.) But they are for the Prince of Wales, from whom Isabel expects great things. The Queen is, of course, appeased; but still eyes the Koh-i-noor, and asks, "What are you going to do with it?" "Madam," I replied, "I am going to keep it as a present for Your Majesty's most powerful rival!" By which we see that Isabel sometimes allows sycophantic considerations to overcome Christian principles.

The dream now assumes a more realistic tone, and after an energetic tour of England, where Isabel slaps various religious denominations into place, she advances the Conservative party, but shows no patience towards an idle, vaporing aristocracy. She passes all sorts of strict laws against cruelty to animals and vivisection, has some sharp words to say on the police, on temperance societies and feminist movements. Having passed to England's foreign policy, still with great restraint keeping off Richard's theories regarding the East, she lets fly at Mrs. Grundy, always Isabel's *bête noire*, the more so since she was Richard's deadliest enemy. She is described as "an objectionable old person who talked hashed Bible with a nasal twang and rubbed her hands complacently." We see, sometimes, as in these dream accounts of Mrs. Grundy and the Queen, that Isabel had the true novelist's eye for character and dialogue.

This might be all right for Grundys, but not for the Foreign Office attitude towards Richard. Something more concrete is needed here. Isabel has so far held back, but now closes in to the attack. "Having done all we could for England, we now returned to London" (and of course, the Queen). Her Majesty, like the Almighty, also wishes to confer some mark of lasting favor upon Isabel. This is obviously what Isabel has been angling for—to what she has led the reader so cunningly along the mazes of her dream. Taking a deep breath, she goes direct to her grievance— her Cause, and certain, no doubt, of the Royal views on doting wives, commends Richard to the Royal care. "Madam," she says, "he is a man unlike everybody else. . . . I am not worthy to tie the latchet of his shoe. He has toiled every hour and every minute for thirty-two years, distinguishing himself in every possible way. . . . The others are as nothing to him." (Here we feel the Queen may have frowned, sensing a possible slight on the Prince Consort and Mr. Disraeli.) But Isabel is warming to her subject. "Yet others are at the top of the ladder of fortune and honor, whilst by some strange fate, he alone—a very king amongst them—has *never* been advanced, never received an honor. . . ." The eulogies rise to a paean of worship and praise.

The Queen is much moved, and replies, "Tell me all the public career of your husband." What an opening! Isabel seizes it, plunging into a minutely detailed account of Richard's entire life. Dream or no, nothing is overlooked. The flood tide of indignation overflows twelve pages of small print, till the point where Her Majesty manages to get in a word, and asks how this grievous state came about. Isabel is off again. Humbug stands abashed before this demigod! He lives sixty years before his time! Alas! His upright nature finds but little favor in England. The Queen is much affected, and asks Isabel what she considers Burton's rightful position in the world. Of course, Isabel has it all pat. Envoy Extraordinary and Minister Plenipotentiary to some Eastern Court, and K.C.B.; likewise to be restored to honorary rank in the Army. . . .

The dream Queen, of course, grants the dream favors, and Isabel departs in peace, her Mission accomplished. Still—just one more parting shot at the Foreign Office, via the Vatican. Before this remarkable dream closes, Isabel and her Guardian Angel float off to Rome to visit the Pope, where a most gratifying audience takes place. The Angel guides Isabel through all the intricacies of social ritual in these unusual circumstances. The Pope does not have to be told things, like the Queen. He comes straight to the point: He sends his special blessing to Richard "as one of God's elect." Amongst other things he says, "My daughter, why do you afflict yourself at seeing your noble husband passed over in regard to worldly honors? . . . Look at your husband, and then look at the people who *do* get these honors and places, and cease to repine. It is not the will of God, for your husband is *far greater* than any of these, and He has great designs, in proportion, in store for him. . . . Take this as a sign: In the very place where Jesus said 'No man is a prophet in his own country,' the people shall treat your husband as they treated

Jesus." On this prophetic, but not altogether reassuring note, we will leave Isabel the dreamer, still unassuaged in her search for Richard's earthly recognition.

*       *       *

Burton, as it was remarked earlier, soon established a reputation for incorruptibility, which, in the East, is a rare and fearful virtue. His enemies multiplied; their ranks closed in, imperceptibly at first, for they were playing a waiting game. Turkish officials were enraged by Burton's curt refusals of their bribes; Moslem fanatics suspected Isabel of proselytizing for the Catholic Church. The Jewish money lenders and financiers fumed at Burton's unfavorable reports to the Foreign Office on their high rates of interest which extorted cruel sums from the Arabs. The English residents and visitors found their Consul decidedly eccentric; his lady, too. The missionaries detested Burton's loudly proclaimed agnosticism: they found him unsympathetic to their dreams of converting the Faithful. They complained he spent hours in the Mosques which would have been more suitably employed at the Bible Society. They remembered how Burton had been known as Ruffian Dick, how he claimed to be proud of his Royal bastard descent, how he bragged he had committed every sin in the Decalogue, and called the Bible a whited sepulcher. Burton's bravado was coming home to roost.

Now although Burton had always maintained a *pudeur* regarding his real religious beliefs, which, as Isabel said, were probably part Sūfi, part Catholic, he could never hide the state of emotion to which all sincere religious manifestations reduced him. "He always sobbed at Mass," says Isabel happily, luxuriating in the fact that the colorless restraints of Low Church ways left him unmoved. But his dislike of most missionaries and their religious cant amounted to loathing. He was particularly hostile to their hypocrisies, so typical of mid-Victorian England—"the only country where I never feel at home," he once remarked. He enjoyed baiting the Bible bangers, and could not show, towards them, any of the sympathy he showed towards even the most fanatic Moslem sects, such as the Assaioui, or the howling Dervishes, to whose ranks he had been admitted long ago in Cairo.

69

*They eat and drink and scheme and plod*
*They go to Church on Sunday*
*And many are afraid of God*
*And more of Mrs. Grundy. . . .*

The exasperating words would boom out in Burton's deep, beautiful voice, as he strolled in the gardens, below the open windows where official gatherings sat round talking "hashed Bible," planning Sunday school treats for the Bedouin babies.

Isabel's marked preference for everything Arab was considered as unsuitable and incomprehensible by the Western society of Damascus. The East had indeed proved a heady draught. She began to fancy herself as a reincarnation of Lady Hester Stanhope, the heroine of her youth. Not only did she adopt Arab dress wherever possible, but while Burton slipped off, disguised, into the life of the *souks*, Isabel spent voluptuous hours in the Turkish baths, or stayed for days at a time in the harems. Sometimes she was persuaded to entertain the inmates by wearing her most décolleté gown, and describing in detail her coming-out ball at Almack's. The harem thought low necks and waltzes very dashing. Sometimes she was invited to be the guest of honor at wedding or circumcision celebrations, where as a special mark of esteem she would be asked to hold the victim steady for the knife, a proceeding she accepted in the gratified manner of a godparent holding the baby at the christening.

Every day she was drawn further into the East. She wanted no more of the West, except her Faith, which she stoutly proclaimed, and was accused, not without some truth, of wholesale proselytizing. Other, more vicious, less just rumors had it that if Burton did not accept bribes, she did, and was festooned with diamonds and other illicitly acquired valuables. Both of them were so absorbed by their new life that European visitors, save a few old friends, or any really distinguished personages, either social lions or the archaeologically inclined, were not encouraged. But the proximity to Jerusalem and the Holy Land implied a steady stream of callers. Little trips to the Holy Sepulcher were becoming fashionable, and about this time the more intrepid of Mr. Cook's tourists were being shepherded on Holy Tours. In 1871, Isabel records that a hundred and eighty swarmed over Syria, making for Jerusalem. In such masses, they were safe from plundering Arabs: the Arabs regarded them quite outside the general run. *"Hum Kukiyjeh,"* they said contemptuously. "They are not travelers—they are Cookii."

Isabel had a special weakness for one compatriot, however. The Honorable Jane Digby El Mezrab was not only the daughter of a noble lord, but she was the wife of a Bedouin Sheik, too, and shared the Burtons' profound love of all things Arabic. Though it must be admitted Isabel could not stomach the marked duskiness of Jane's husband. "The contact with that black skin I could *not* understand . . . that made me shudder," she notes in her journal. Whether she would have overcome such a basic aspect of racial prejudice, had she reached the lodestar East alone and unattached, as Jane Digby El Mezrab had done, we cannot tell. Although she had craved it since childhood, it had long since come to be identified in her mind with Richard. The East around her was seen subjectively as Richard's East—Richard's desert—the proper background to his dramatic personality and legendary exploits.

Julian the Apostate called Damascus the Eye of the East. Isabel was profoundly conscious of its beauty, its mystery; the "Solemn Mystery, the Romantic Halo of Oriental Existence" was something she loved and savored every moment of her brief time there. She plunged into a grueling round of sightseeing, combined with desert outings and those ceremonial visits to the Bedouin tribes, which both Burton the Arab and Burton the Consul delighted to make. Dressed as an Arab boy, her riding habit bundled into baggy trousers, with a make-weight dagger or two, she accompanied Burton in the humble manner of a page waiting on his knight. She attended to the horses, supervised the setting up of their camp, organized their dragomans with military precision, and then, saluting, seated herself at a respectful distance from the group of Bedouin nobles and dignitaries gathered under the black goat-haired tents.

How she loved re-creating the scenes of Richard's greatness! Richard in Arab robes once more, indistinguishable (but for his superlative good looks) from the Arabs around him. Richard as a prince among them, talking with them, eating with them, quoting Arabic poets to them, praying with them, observing their rituals—one of them, once more—*and she there too,* living this crystallization of all her dreams. As they jogged homewards towards Damascus, and the melancholy cry of the muezzin pierced the evening calm, Burton would go into one of the village mosques, and Isabel would wait outside with the horses, and remember that beneath all his voluminous Bedouin robes, and the camel's-hair *aba,* or cloak, he still wore the miraculous medallion of the Virgin which she had given him before he set out to find the sources of the Nile. No doubt she prayed, too: a paean of praise, that all she had prayed for, all that Hagar the Gypsy had foretold, had come to pass. For Isabel, religion and the supernatural were always inextricably confused.

But even apart from the double spell of Richard and the East, she was enraptured by every aspect of Oriental life. The color, the climate ("not a breath of air stirring, we felt like the curled up leaves of a book"), the people, their customs, music and food; the landscape, the pastoral life and the swarming city; the noise, and the stillness, too. Often at night, she tells us, when Burton was absent on one of his sorties in disguise, she would sit by the window, looking out across the valley slopes to the far distant mountains, rapt, "listening to the stillness." "O! how shall I tear the East out of my heart?" was her desperate cry, when, later, she followed her husband in his exile and disgrace.

There cannot, however, have been much time for listening to the stillness. Isabel's daily round was formidable. Sometimes she described their lives as "solemn, holy and wild"; at other times, as "peaceful, useful and happy." Keeping up with Burton's exigencies may have been happy and useful, but peaceful it was not. Besides Isabel's devotional pilgrimages, Old and New Testament in hand, there were archaeological expeditions full of dangerous incidents in the brigand-infested desert: the sort of incidents that would have put most women to bed for weeks afterwards with nervous prostration and shock; but not Isabel. This was "the wild and lawless life" of her childhood's craving. Even classifying human remains for Burton's archaeological outings assumed a daring quality. The Vicomte de Perrochel, then traveling across Syria, found her calm in the face of excavations quite extraordinary. "One sees clearly, Madame," he said, "that you are English. A French woman would have fainted, or at least had an hysterical seizure . . . you are so calm and practical, you might be classifying *colifichets,* and not human remains. I must admit," he added, "that this attitude repels me; I would prefer to see a little more sensitivity. . . ."

Winter and summer, visitors streamed through the Consulate, all expecting to be entertained, fed, and conducted on tours of the city. Isabel was prone to regard both Abd El Kadir and Jane Digby El Mezrab as fair game for her sightseers. Once her enthusiasm overreached itself, and she conducted one of Jane's own relatives (by her unfortunate first marriage) to the Mezrab establishment. Since Jane was sensitive on the point of being exploited as a matrimonial peep show, and her first marriage was four husbands away from her present state of bliss, a slight coldness sprang up between the two ladies. Isabel's enemies did not allow the story to languish: it was fuel to their fires. Besides, there were stranger stories that Isabel, who was officially accompanied on her walks abroad by four scarlet-coated *Kavass,* or Consular servants, allowed them to slash a way for her through the streets with horsewhips. Another inexplicable story is told by Lord Redesdale, who remembered her entering a mosque to show him the architecture, and on finding an Arab at prayer, ordered him to move: when he did not comply, Isabel set on him with her riding crop. It is hard to dispute an eyewitness account, but the incident does not seem in keeping with the rest of Isabel's reverence for Richard's East; though it is just possible that Isabel's pinkness and plumpness may have proved inflammatory to some of the more audacious Arabs, and this was her forthright way of discouraging their sly pinchings and oglings.

At their home, the Burtons kept open house once a week; the calls began at daybreak and went on till midnight. Every race and creed were jumbled, but the atmosphere was generally genial. Sometimes Isabel's feminist determination to instil courtesy *à l'Européenne* into the Arab noblemen caused little misunderstandings. When she placed the wives in chairs, and expected the husbands to pass them cakes, or cups of coffee, she was violating every sacred tradition of the Islamic home. "Pray don't teach our women what they don't know," was the parting shot from one outraged Arab, flinging out in dudgeon, followed by his scuttling ladies. And Isabel's triumph at obtaining the innovation of Arab women visitors was short-lived. However, there were Burton's Divans, all-male soirees, at which she presided, preening. No other women were ever present, she tells us. "The privilege was accorded me on account of my husband who is with the Moslems as if he were one of themselves." Besides these Islamic excursions, there were the tidal waves of Victorian correspondence which beat backwards and forwards between Europe and the Near East, and which Isabel sustained tirelessly. There were the journals and notes she was accumulating for her book; there was secretarial work for Richard and Consulate affairs too (here, as in Brazil, she was sometimes left to hold the fort alone). There was the house, the servants, her menagerie of pets, ever-increasing, but kept in check by their unfortunate habit of eating each other. Then there were the horses, twelve of them, and the perpetual battle she waged with the grooms trying to impose her own standards of horse-grooming and care. Besides her pets, there were her poor, and also her sick. Her daring curative draughts always filled Burton with apprehension, for she was slapdash in her pharmaceutical methods. When there was a cholera epidemic and nature proved too strong, or her draughts too weak, and the sufferers died, Isabel often had the satisfaction of baptizing them in a little flask of holy water she always carried.

Then there were extensive rereadings of the Bible, in the light of their expeditions. Arabic lessons, too. Isabel battled on, refusing to be discouraged beside Burton's stature as a linguist, just as her bounce, her optimism, refused to accept her inability to write. Indeed, by her sheer vitality and exuberant sense of wonder, she often conveys more sense of places, of atmosphere, than Burton, with his cut-and-dried exactitudes, which were his sole strength, until he flung the glittering bombshell of *The Thousand Nights and a Night*.

While Burton tried to maintain a scrupulous detachment in his dealings with the Moslems, it was impossible for him to conceal his preference for them over the Jews or Christians. Even so, he made enemies, thick and fast. His integrity, as much as his fatal weakness for meddling in local administration, had made an arch-enemy of the Turkish Governor General, the Wali Rashid Pasha, a scoundrel whose power at that time was absolute, but who had, besides, the Eastern voluptuary's delight in dallying on the eve of revenge. This made him appear complacent of Burton's actions long after he had decided to remove him, and was even planning his assassination. Although Disraeli's *Tancred* opines that Arabs are but Jews on horseback, this view was not shared by the Burtons. She saw Arabs through a special *optique:* he disliked Jews as a race; indeed his book, *The Jew and Islam,* is a farrago of unbalanced nonsense. Now, his instinctive mistrust of the Jews was fostered by their ruthless exploitation of the Syrian Arabs. Jewish usurers, many of them under British protection, were charging as much as sixty per cent, and then trying to make Burton enforce payments from the ruined Arabs. "I found these things done in the name of England," wrote Burton, outraged. He threw them out in a body, and reported the whole scandal to his Government, urging them to support his measures. But the bankers of Syria, powerful throughout the Near East, were allied to other, more powerful international financiers. They lost no time forming into a sinister opposition, and letters posted energetically between Syria and the big banking houses of Western Europe. Meanwhile Burton went on his way, pursuing what he believed to be right. Presently he arrested two Jewish boys for chalking crosses on the city walls. His summary action was explained by his knowledge that such crosses were often the sign for an outbreak of Christian persecution. With the hideous memories of the 1860 massacres still fresh, he was taking no chances, and removed, as a temporary measure, the British papers of the Jewish families for whom the two boys worked. His action was high-handed; but Burton knew the East, knew the tinder-box climate of racial prejudice in such a mixed city as Damascus, and it is possible that he averted another disaster. But it is certain, in so doing, he roused the hostility of every Jew between London and the Levant.

While they were complaining singly, and in masses, to the Foreign Office, that H. M. Consul in Damascus was a Jew-baiting pro-Arab, and his wife a fanatic Jesuit, he next succeeded in alienating the Druzes, by fining them heavily for their attack on two English missionaries traveling across their territory. This exasperated not only the Consul General in Beyrout, who refused to enforce the fine, but also the Turkish authorities, headed by the Wali, who now complained to the Foreign Office that Burton was exceeding his authority. Having lost the sympathy of the Moslems, by defending the missionaries, he now succeeded in enraging the missionaries. His passion for blind justice, it will be seen, was not compatible with his Consular duties. He next alienated a missionary from Beyrout. The Reverend Mentor Mott and his wife Augusta (the Superintendent of British Syrian Schools) were a forbidding pair. He had considerable influence among ecclesiastical circles in England, and was on very good terms with Burton's jealous superior, the Consul General at Beyrout, who was at once torpid and waspish. The Reverend and Mrs. Mott's methods of proselytizing were provoking, to say the least; Burton warned them that tact was of more value than tracts: the Moslems were becoming dangerously restive under the Motts' interference: at last Burton ordered them to leave Damascus and go back to the calmer climate of Beyrout. "Do you want to be killed?" roared the exasperated Burton, thinking, no doubt, far more of the general bloodshed which might ensue. "I should glory in martyrdom!" replied the reverend gentleman. When it was explained that all the other Christian inhabitants might not share this view, he took himself off, angry and brooding. Balked of his martyr's crown, he lost no time in stirring up trouble, and sent malign reports to London, in which he charged Burton with obstructive anti-Christian behavior.

Yet Burton's defense of the Moslems, here, did nothing to endear him to the Wali, who continued to regard him as a dangerous meddler. And perhaps he was. With the best intentions in the world he was busy once more, doing the right thing the wrong way. His manner, never social or conciliatory in official dealings, infuriated the Consul General more, day by day. There was no peace! Burton had now succeeded in alienating his own superior; the Moslems (the Turkish authorities, that is, for to the Arab masses he remained a hero), the Jews and the missionaries, who did not turn the other cheek, being far too busy complaining to their bishops at home. The Victorian age had brought the simultaneous worship of God and Mammon to a fine art; it was a comfortable achievement, and those who held the reins had no wish to see it disrupted. Bishops and bankers alike now began to pester the Foreign Office for Burton's recall. What was such a savage atheist (and married to a dangerous Papist!) doing in the British Consulate? Oh! the pity of it all! The Foreign Office pursed its lips and sent for Burton's explanations, which might be best summed up by his motto, *Honor, not Honors.*

Since Isabel, too, managed to put up so many backs in her own right, and has so often been held responsible for her husband's recall, I dwell at length on the chain of incidents which led up to his dismissal. It is easy to say, as Burton's niece Georgina Stisted did when she wrote her uncle's life story, that it was Isabel, alone, who broke his career. Nothing she says on this score convinces her readers, who are merely left with the over-all impression of family feuds; above all, the raging jealousy the Stisted family felt for Isabel, who as much as any person could be said to possess Burton, possessed him, to the exclusion of his own relatives. But this was something Miss Stisted could never forgive. After Isabel's death she hurried to malign her. It is significant that in her own copy of *Abeokuta* (the book Burton wrote while in San Fernando Po, and which Isabel saw through the press in London), she chose to distort his dedication. Burton had written:

*To my best friend, my wife, these pages are lovingly inscribed.*

But Miss Stisted's copy has deeply scored brackets round the words "my best friend" and "lovingly." *Added by Isabel Burton!* is written below in her handwriting. A less biased account of Burton's recall can be read in the Government Blue Book published in 1871; *The Case of Capt. Burton, late H. B. M. Consul at Damascus* shows conclusively that only Burton's weakness for impartial justice and meddling brought about the disaster. It will be seen that although Isabel was often tactless, and too loud in her religious beliefs, and appallingly sure of her right to doctor, or baptize, she was no more than a bit player in the whole tragedy. If anything, her loyal support, her constant engineering of influential friends and relations at home, did much to postpone it. In the final incident, the Shazli affair, as we shall see, Isabel was involved to the extent of offering to stand sponsor to two thousand Moslem converts to

Catholicism: but Burton alone was responsible for his strange proposals to the Foreign Office.

In the meantime, there had been yet one more disagreeable incident: this time with the Greeks. The Burtons had been camping near Nazareth, not far from the Greek Orthodox Church. At dawn, a Copt was discovered trying to steal into Isabel's tent; for what purpose is not known. The dragoman ordered him to go; he became insolent, and threw stones. Angry, the dragoman set about him with sticks. Ordinarily, this sort of fracas would have come to nothing. Unfortunately, at that moment a large number of Greeks came out of church, and wished to aid the Copt. Burton and Charles Tyrwhitt Drake, hearing the uproar, came out and tried to calm the Greeks. They were pelted with enormous stones and pieces of rock. A rich and respectable Greek called out, "Kill them all, I'll pay the blood money!" One of Burton's grooms shouted back, "Shame! This is the English Consul of Damascus." Another Greek cried, "So much the worse for him. . . ." Isabel records that she dressed hurriedly and watched Burton standing calm, refusing to be provoked, though stones hit him right and left. She rushed out to bring him his six-shot revolvers, but he waved her back. "So I kept near enough to carry him off if he were badly wounded, and put the revolvers in my belt, meaning to have twelve lives for his, if he were killed." And so she would have; where Richard was concerned, Isabel always meant business; a lioness, defending her mate, her cub, her all. When things got desperate, the Greek mob closing in, and three of the dragomens badly hurt, Burton pulled a revolver from his servant's belt and fired a shot into the air. Isabel dashed off to summon help from a nearby camp of English and American travelers. When the Greeks saw the reinforcements arrive they fled. Later, says Isabel, it transpired that Greek ill-feeling "had originated with the Greek Orthodox Bishop of Nazareth, who had snatched away a synagogue and cemetery from British-protected Jews, against which arbitrary proceeding Richard had once strongly protested." Once again his actions in the interests of justice had turned against him. The incident was grossly distorted by the Greeks, who, bent on justifying themselves, sent their own version, signed and sealed by their Bishop, to Constantinople, Beyrout, and the whole Levant. Presently a distorted version telegraphed by the Wali, via the Porte, reached London, unhappily before Burton's official statement. For once, Isabel's flowing pen seems to have delayed, while Burton showed, again, his fatal tendency to procrastination. It was a matter he should have reported at once, and in his own light. In brooding silence the Foreign Office filed the new complaints; noted that H. M. Consul had been stoned—was there ever smoke without fire?—and sat back coldly awaiting the end, which was, to them, now only a matter of weeks.

Meanwhile, back at Salahíyyeh the Burtons went on their own highly colored road to ruin. A bossy pair, they were nicknamed the Emperor and Empress of Damascus, a title which did not altogether displease them. When the Shazli affair broke over Syria it was the Burtons, rather than the Shazlis, who became the focal point of all the trouble. The Shazlis were a religious sect, Moslems who were not, however, passive in their acceptance of the Prophet. Like Burton, they were forever casting round for a more convincing belief. Their mystical Sūfi tenets and rituals had interested Burton for some while. He used to attend their meetings in disguise, a fact which did not escape the Wali's spies, who considered him a dangerous political agitator. During one of these gatherings, a Shazli, in a state of religious ecstasy, claimed to have seen the vision of a venerable man who bade the seekers after truth follow him along the true path to heaven. Soon this venerable man was identified as Fra Emmanuel Forner, a Spanish monk from a monastery nearby, and Isabel's father confessor into the bargain. Isabel was enraptured, claimed a miracle, and besides showering the Shazlis with crucifixes and rosaries, offered to stand sponsor to two thousand converts. Burton, as always, spellbound by mysterious or legendary occurrences, spent much time among the Shazlis, observing their religious transports. He was convinced of their absolute sincerity. He and Isabel talked of nothing else: Burton seems to have felt that perhaps—who knows?—at long last the true religion might be revealed to him too. After all, Saul of Tarsus had, in this very land, been converted to Christianity; was he, Burton the agnostic—the Arab—about to witness some new advent, a triumph of the Cross over the Crescent? Thus, reveling in drama and dogma, he was so carried away by it all that he proposed to the

Foreign Office the Government should sponsor his scheme for purchasing a tract of land on which the Shazlis could settle, there to enjoy the free practice of their new religion. We do not know why Burton, a professed nonbeliever, non-Catholic, felt himself empowered to act for the Shazlis; his zeal would have been more in keeping with an emissary from the Vatican; however, he was perhaps merely sensing the persecutions which were presently to be the Shazlis' lot. And Burton always championed the persecuted, whether Jew, Gentile or Moslem. We do not know, either, what was the reaction of the Foreign Office, and in particular, that of Lord Granville, for the business of the Damascus Consulate had now become urgent; but they stayed their hand a little longer.

Syria was rocked by the Shazli conversion. The bazaars hummed with it; each religious sect or Damascus drawing-room faction read into it the evil they wished to attribute to the Burtons. The Jews and the missionaries saw their moment approaching; they redoubled their demands for Burton's recall. The Wali Rashid Pasha decided that the Shazli defection from Islam might spread, undermining his authority, and bringing dangerous political complications. Without more ado, he jailed large numbers of them, and confiscated their property. Burton countered by flying into one of his terrible rages, and just as he had thrown out, bodily, the Pasha's emissaries when they tried to load him down with bribes, just as he had denounced the usurers, or the missionaries, or the marauding Druzes, so now he denounced the Wali, and took it on himself to protect the Shazlis from persecution, in the name of H. M. Government. In principle, as always, Burton was right. In practice, he was wrong. He had acted courageously, according to his principles; but not diplomatically.

> *Do what thy manhood bids thee do*
> *From none but self expect applause;*
> *He noblest lives and noblest dies*
> *Who makes and keeps his self-made laws,*

he wrote in his poem, *The Kasidah*. It was a creed to which he held, throughout his life. It was one to which Isabel, too, aspired, however imperfectly. Her journals and devotional book always show the same struggle for grace—to be worthy—worthy of her God, of her husband.

\*　　　\*　　　\*

On August 16, 1871, the Foreign Office struck with viperish suddenness. Burton was recalled and superseded overnight, and without a word of warning or explanation. He and Isabel were at their summer quarters at Bludan in the Anti-Lebanon. The Foreign Office acting with a mixture of panic and malice, sent the new Consul to Damascus before informing Burton. News of his dismissal arrived together with his successor. A ragged messenger had trotted up on foot from Damascus "with a curt note from the Vice Consul of Beyrout, informing Richard that, on orders, he had arrived in Damascus the previous day, and had already taken charge of the Consulate."

The Burtons were stunned. Burton and a friend galloped down to Damascus at once. Isabel waited in an agony of suspense; a few hours later she received the much-quoted message, *"I am superseded. Pay, pack and follow."* She sat amid the ruins of her life. It was the expulsion from Eden. All that she had hoped and planned and desired had fallen to nothingness. If she wept for her own loss of the East, she overboiled with rage at the way Burton had been treated. The greatest Orientalist of his time, dismissed, like a clumsy housemaid! No warning, no explanation! When the news spread, the house was surrounded by Arabs, who walked up from the city, or Bedouins, who galloped in from the desert, to protest and grieve with her. Their laments rose from the black tents they pitched on the hill slopes all around. But behind everything, like a malevolent echo, Isabel heard the rejoicing of her enemies.

Most of the Arab nobles, and in particular, Abd El Kadir and Jane Digby El Mezrab stood beside her, but the Wali Rashid Pasha could hardly restrain his joy. There had been rumors, and Isabel herself speaks of attempts on Burton's life a little earlier, which were thought to have originated from the Wali. Sooner or later, one way or another, Burton was doomed to go. Several loyal Arab friends now came to Isabel and proposed to liquidate her enemies, if she would only give the word. A

Jew whom Burton had befriended offered to poison anyone she named; by which it will be seen that although the Burtons made enemies, they also made useful friends. Here, we sense the regret in Isabel's tone; regret that, as a Christian gentlewoman, she could not accept these tempting offers.

Isabel was never one to sit down under slights or injuries. But how could she fight all these seething Oriental intrigues single-handed, with Burton gone, betrayed by his own Government? She behaved with great restraint, bottling her grief and rage, concentrating on practical matters and biding her time until she could reach England and have it out with the Foreign Office. Both the Burtons believed firmly in some supernatural and benign force, rather than coincidence, which saw to it that anyone who did Richard a wrong always came to grief soon after. This sustained Isabel in moments of trial. Speke's untimely end was, to her, an example of this force at work. When, later, Rashid Pasha came to a bad end, it was just another, even more gratifying example. The Foreign Office, however, remained obstinately flourishing.

When Burton received his brutal recall, he left, on the minute. "He never looked behind him, nor packed up anything, but went straight away from Damascus, though it was the place where he had spent two of the happiest years of his life," says Isabel, who probably believed it had been for him, as for her, paradise. Twenty-four hours after he had gone, while Isabel was bracing herself to pay, pack and follow, and he had already reached Beyrout, where he was awaiting a boat, Isabel, in the Bludan, had one of her dream-visions. "Something pulled me by the arm. 'Why do you lie there? Your husband wants you. Get up and go to him!' said a Voice." She rushed to the stables, saddled her horse and galloped out into the night. She rode like one possessed; perhaps she was—possessed by the eternal craving for Richard. For five hours she galloped over rocks and through swamps, making for the diligence station at Shtora. It was a fearful ride, but Isabel was convinced of Divine aid, "another Presence was with me, beside me, and guarded my ways." At last she sighted the diligence on the point of leaving. She was too exhausted to shout, her horse was dead-beat, but they made a last spurt, and leaving her horse at the inn, she reeled into the coach. As they rumbled into Beyrout, she caught sight of Burton walking alone, as if dazed. He was a tragic figure. There were no friends, no servants, not even the customary Consulate *Kavass* to attend him. Eldridge, the British Consul General had cut him dead. "The jackals are always ready to slight the dead lion," says Isabel, the lioness. "But I was there, thank God! and he was so surprised and rejoiced when he greeted me. His whole face was illuminated. But he only said, 'Thank you. *Bon sang ne peut mentir!*' We had twenty-four hours to take comfort and counsel together, and it was well that I was with him," says Isabel, sounding once again that sonorous Biblical note always apparent in moments of stress.

The bitterness of that twenty-four hours was softened by the hospitality of the French Consul, who insisted they should stay with him. Isabel saw her husband aboard, and as the boat steamed out from the jetty, Burton's Arab servant, Habib, struggled through the crowd. He had come on foot, all the way from Damascus, to see his adored master once again and arrived ten minutes too late. He watched the boat dwindle into the blue, and then flung himself on the ground in transports of grief. Isabel returned to Damascus to complete the packing up, and was agreeably surprised to find so many people had rallied round. She found the house at Salahíyyeh, as in the Bludan, a center of nomad encampments; from all over Syria the Arabs had gathered to stand guard over the wife of the man they had loved and admired. Among the letters the Burtons cherished was one from the Sheik Medjuel El Mezrab (Jane Digby's husband), in the name of his tribe; another, from Abd El Kadir, in a similarly poetic strain, read, "You have left us the sweet perfume of charity and noble conduct in befriending the poor and supporting the weak, O wader of the seas of knowledge! O cistern of learning of our globe exalted above his age!"

The poetic tributes poured in from all over the desert, the various Sheiks speaking for their tribes: "The love of this your servant is too deep to be expressed by the pen, and it dates from the days when the disembodied souls met in hosts innumerable during the beginning of time" . . . "Oh, I was sorely grieved, and may Allah ruin the house of the man who caused your departure. . . . All creeds and denominations pray for your return to this land and curse the other man, hoping for his speedy ruin. Allah is merciful!" This, from Ahmed Musallim, Chief of the Great Mosque at Damascus, striking a militant note. No wonder the Consul General felt uneasy. The testimonies speak for themselves, and are both vindication and indictment. Burton was loved and honored by the Arabs as one of them; far too loved, far too honored to suit the Consul General, or the Wali, either.

It was a terrible time for Isabel. She liquidated their affairs, sold up the house and found good homes for her servants and menagerie. Those pets who could not be happily placed were shot, rather than left to the mercy of a country that showed none towards animals. After Richard, animals were always Isabel's dearest care, and even in this debacle she did not forget them. There were heartbreaks on all sides. Sometimes she paused in her packing and sorting to ride out, once again, over the landscape she loved. It was the land of her longing, and after only two years, she was exiled. . . . On the day of the sale she could not bear to see the last shell of her Eastern life go under the hammer; she went up on to the mountain, beyond the garden, "and gazed down on my Salahíyyeh in its sea of green and my pearl-like Damascus, and the desert . . . and watched the sunset on the mountains for the last time."

Arab popular feeling was now agitating for Burton's reinstatement: "O what have we done that he is taken from us?" they cried, tearing their beards, grief-stricken, on Isabel's doorstep. Prayers for Burton's return were chanted in the mosques, and a delegation wished to visit Queen Victoria in person to intercede for him. When Isabel rode down to Damascus for the last time, the plain of Zebedani shimmering in the September sun, she was accompanied by a huge train of followers. "Just outside the city gates I met Rashid Pasha driving in state with all his suite. He looked radiant and saluted me with much *empressement*. I did not salute him."

On September 13, always a date the superstitious Burtons dreaded, she left Damascus forever. Although greatly gratified by the Arab demonstrations, she thought it wiser to slip away as unobtrusively as possible, which disagrees with the popular estimate of her character as hysterical, vain, and irresponsible. Just before dawn, accompanied only by

Jane Digby El Mezrab, and Abd El Kadir, she rode through the city gates, where they bade her farewell. "Jane Digby rode a thoroughbred black Arab mare; as far as I could see anything in the moonlight, her large sorrowful blue eyes glistened with tears. . . ." It was a parting worthy of all Isabel's Eastern longings, all her sense of drama. The legendary Algerian warrior and the romantic English noblewoman, wife of the Bedouin Sheik, remained at the gates of the world's oldest city, saluting her as she turned her horse towards exile. *O! how shall I tear the East out of my heart?* She rode out of the East forever; only postcard glimpses, little tours, were to remain. But the West still held Richard, her embodiment of the Eastern myth.

\*　　　\*　　　\*

While Isabel was paying, packing and following, Burton was spending his time in gloomy immobility at Norwood with his sister, Lady Stisted, who was convinced it was all Isabel's fault. He took his recall stoically; fatalistically, too, making no effort to justify himself, or even see Lord Granville. The Foreign Office had done with him; very well, then, he had done with the Foreign Office. He busied himself in his writing and never spoke of Damascus. The transposition to a London suburb cannot have been stimulating, and the hushed sympathy of his relatives must have irked him, too. As soon as Isabel arrived he fled from them to her more tonic society. They lodged in a cheap London hotel. It was a somber time for Isabel, too. Eastern life was behind her; there were no prospects, no money. "Since Richard would not fight his own battles I fought them for him." The Foreign Office was her first objective. Refusing to take no for an answer, she swept through the various departments where she had many friends, rousing them to the attack, rallying press and public in her campaign for justice. She cornered Lord Granville, from whom she forced an official statement as to the reasons behind Burton's recall. She then compelled him to say he would reconsider the case. She was three months preparing her husband's defense, answering the charges point by point, until, theoretically, she carried the day. The Foreign Office, stung by the countercharges and public outcry, printed an account of the whole case: *Confidential Print*

*Respecting Consul Burton's Proceedings at Damascus, 1868-71.* It contains a mass of correspondence pertaining to the recall, from Arab chieftains, missionaries, eyewitnesses, Burton himself, and the Jews, addresses to the Chief Rabbi at London. It makes monumental reading: but one thing emerges. Burton in Damascus was very much better informed on the whole panorama of Syrian and Levantine politics than the Consul General, who, living in the margin, at Beyrout, relied entirely for his information on what his dragomans (all of whom were first influenced by the Wali) chose to disclose.

By way of conciliatory gesture, the Foreign Office presently offered some minor posts which both Burton and Isabel enjoyed refusing indignantly; still, it was a sort of reinstatement.

Isabel's next battle was with Burton himself. He showed an altogether Arab fatalism, a passivity which left him indifferent to any projects for another post. Isabel was very uneasy. Since she had found by experience it was difficult to argue with him, she wrote a long, persuasive and tonic letter which she tactfully put between the pages of a book he was reading. Although Burton did not stop skulking, she dragged him out, and they went about a good deal, being seen at many of the big house parties and dinners. Isabel did not hold with "the world forgetting by the world forgot." She believed the one to be the outcome of the other. There was a general feeling that Burton had been treated shabbily. Later, one outspoken partisan went so far as to say that the foolish and impudent slighting, by the English Government, of Burton and Matthew Arnold, the one in minor Consulates, the other in a school's inspectorship, made one long to impale Britannia on her own trident.

During all this time, the Burtons hid their financial difficulties bravely, but for such an improvident couple there were no savings on which to fall back; no means of living economically. On the way to Garswood, the home of Isabel's uncle, Lord Gerard, she dropped one of their last remaining fifteen golden sovereigns. It rolled through a chink in the railway carriage. Isabel sat on the floor, sobbing brokenheartedly; Burton knelt beside her, consoling her with exceptional tenderness. It was cold comfort—but still, comfort, during their trials, to learn that Rashid Pasha had fallen from favor: the Sublime Porte recalled

him "and the new administration of Syria incorporated most of the reforms which Richard had advocated." But no one remembered Burton,
either in Constantinople or London. At a moment when things were desperate, he was approached to survey some sulphur mines in Iceland for a
private enterprise. He accepted thankfully. But although it was travel
—escape—new horizons, the journey meant little to him. Glaciers and
geysers were not the landscape of his predilection. He took it as a means
of earning, rather than the personal adventure all his earlier expeditions
had been. Isabel did not envy him Iceland, although she always saw him
go with reluctance. She remained at home to continue her siege of the
Foreign Office. After ten months of relentless departmental badgering,
Lord Granville was brought to heel sufficiently to write, asking her if
she thought her husband would accept Trieste as a post. It is eloquent
of Isabel's dominance, that it was to her, rather than Burton, the Foreign Office addressed their offer. After Damascus it was a sad come-
down, but Isabel accepted. They were very near the end of their tether,
now. Trieste was a small commercial Consulate, with a salary of seven
hundred pounds a year. Charles Lever had held it before (Stendahl had
been nominated French representative there, too). It was considered a
sinecure, since the duties were negligible. There were no political or
religious complications, nor any of those Eastern snares so fatally attractive to both Isabel and Richard. And so the greatest Orientalist of his
age, "the desert lion," walked meekly into the cage.

Isabel grew to love Trieste, but Burton always hated it, as if, with a
sort of animal instinct, he sensed he would die there. In his diary for
December, 1883, he wrote, "This day eleven years I came here. *What a
shame!!!*" At first, both of them tried to believe it was in the nature of a
stopgap, before better things, before some post worthy of Burton's stature: Morocco, or Constantinople, perhaps. . . . They would not believe Burton's career was smashed. Thus the first sense of humiliation
was softened. Trieste was a town of threes, Isabel tells us. Three races,
Italian, Austrian and Slav. Three quarters, the old, the new, and the
port. Three winds, the icy *bora*, the stifling *sirocco*, and the *contraste*,
which contained the worst features of both. If the town lacked political
interest, it swarmed with drawing-room intrigue. The Slavs held aloof

from the rest; the Italians enjoyed resenting their Austrian rulers. But all the arch-snobs edged towards the Austrian Court and its protocol. A lot of the time was spent exchanging formal visits, wearing every available order, decoration and jewel. Commerce was in the hands of the Jews and Greeks. According to some, the Burtons lived in a third-rate apartment behind the railway station; according to others, an extraordinary straggling top-floor apartment of twenty-six rooms, commanding magnificent views of the Adriatic and the rocky villages of the Karso.

In any case, the Burtons knew what they were doing; "we live on the fourth floor because there isn't a fifth." They liked the air, light and quiet, and knew the steep stairs discouraged passing callers, time-wasting droppers-in. Both wrote: "Literature" was a great stand-by. Burton liked spartan surroundings and curtainless rooms, so that he could see the last of the twilight, the first break of day. He worked on ? number of large deal tables Isabel had designed for him, each one spread with a different book, translation or poem, each in different stages of completion. As he tired of one he would move over to another, rather in the manner of a tournament chess player engaged on many fronts. Isabel worked in a communicating room, wearing a *choga*, or Indian camel's-hair dressing gown, and smoking cap. Burton generally disliked music, particularly amateur singers, but if she sang sad songs in the minor key he would open his door and listen, remembering, perhaps, the siren songs of his vanished East.

The apartment was eloquent of their lives and interests. Cross and Crescent were jumbled together. There were Oriental divans and Persian prayer rugs, scimitars and *tchibouks* and inlaid coffee tables; crucifixes, holy relics, hundreds of photographs and souvenirs, palmy groves, tinseled altars and lacy bowers, beyond which the roof tops of Trieste were glimpsed. They maintained the same vigorous timetable as of old, rising at 4 A.M. to breakfast on tea and fruit. Then "Literature" until noon, when they strolled down to the town for an hour's exercise with the foils, or swimming, Isabel wearing an emancipated blue serge costume, and braving the sharks which frequented the Adriatic and often penetrated the nets designed to protect the bathers. Their fencing master, Reich, was considered one of the best broadswordsmen alive, Burton included. Isabel had learned to fence passably well, in her years of practice with Burton. Her nerves were steely; speaking of Reich, she writes, "He has frequently told me to stand steady, and he has made a *moulinet* at me; you could hear the sword swish in the air, and he has touched my face like a fly in the doing of it. Reich used to say he would not do it to any of his men pupils, for fear they would flinch, which would, of course, have cut their faces open; but he knew I should stand steady. I liked that." But then Isabel always stood steady, in the *salle d'armes*, in life. . . .

Burton paid his Vice Consul to delegate for him during his many absences, but when he was in Trieste, he was able to supervise most of the Consular work during an hour or two, each day, since the post was not an exigent one. Isabel says that he had "considerable leisure for Literature," though for her, with her enormously varied interests, the days were always too short; there were Italian and German lessons, reading, writing, looking after the poor, working for the Church or a local branch of the S.P.C.A., and a formidable social round. They reverted to their Damascus practice of keeping open house once a week, where every race, creed and kind of guest was welcomed. There was a visiting list of three hundred or more families, all of which had to be placated by protocolaire gestures—visiting cards, luncheons and such—duties which invariably fell to Isabel. "Our own little *clique intime*," she tells us, "was a mere sixty or seventy persons"; though no doubt fifty or sixty of these were Isabel's rather than Richard's, cronies. She was sociable by nature, though self-sufficient enough to support, as she had done in Brazil, long stretches of solitude. Sometimes Burton showed a really sadistic delight in outraging her *clique intime* with the most hair-raising remarks. These childish outbursts, curiously ineffectual but passionate little revolts, were most trying for Isabel, since so many of the *clique intime* had not, as yet, in spite of her tireless lectures, quite grasped how transcendental a genius they harbored in their midst. On one dreadful occasion Isabel was dispensing tea to a group of Trieste's aristocracy, when Burton stalked into the room and placed a manuscript among the *petits fours*. Something Captain Burton had just written? Might they take a peep? Isabel, who had excused his frequent absences on account of "Literature," assented graciously. Just a peep, then! The *clique intime* fell back before the title page, *A History of Farting*.

In Trieste, as everywhere else they lived, they soon found a retreat; somewhere to hide out from the pressure of seventy *intime* friends, no doubt. Instinctively, they turned eastwards. Opçina was a Slav village high in the stony wastes of the Karso. The mountains looked down on the feathery green Italianate setting of Trieste, but Opçina was already the Balkans—at once harsh and exotic. Over the mountains was Zagreb, with the first of the mosques and minarets of Eastern Europe . . . farther to the south lay the Albanian gorges, and Belgrade and Nish, with its tower of skulls, its traditions of violence, and the Turkish villages where the Slav peasants lived in perpetual Balkanic unrest. The Burtons were drawn, at once, towards its Oriental undertones. At Opçina they kept a few rooms in a primitive inn which straddled the pass. It was a bleak eyrie. They furnished it their own way, always kept some work on hand, and would retreat there for weeks at a time. Sometimes bands of matted-haired *tziganes* straggled up to the inn, their dancing bears lumbering after them. The *tziganes* were happy to find, in Burton, one who spoke their language and seemed one of them. They would sing and dance for him, and invite him to be their king. The wild dervish dances would go on far into the night, stamping and shrieking, their version of the Serbian *Kola,* and the *Kadjunjubek,* a sort of Turkish *danse du ventre,* which must have reminded Burton of other exotic dancers, in other, more exotic settings when he had lived among the Játs, or Indian gypsies. Isabel would watch, fascinated, as always, by anything which smacked of her beloved Orient, and Trieste and its waltzing salons were forgotten. . . . At first the local peasantry disapproved of Isabel's habit of coddling her favorite fox terrier. They scowled at its little sealskin winter jacket and were outraged by its curtained cot, where it slept in sheets, "like a Christian," they said. Both Isabel and Burton were prone to treat their pets like the children they did not have. But gradually, the peasants, and indeed, all sections of the population at Trieste, came to love Isabel and revere Burton, sensing his true greatness, and his hidden kindness. Animals, children and simple people were never deceived by the devil's mask.

Although shuttled into a siding, both geographically and politically, Burton saw things very clearly. Some of Disraeli's machinations are described as "a typical Dizzybody dodge for doing something shiny that's not wanted." Certain Anglo-Indians were dismissed as "The Junglees." On a visit to England, when staying with the Foreign Secretary, Lord Salisbury, at Hatfield House, the statesman asked Burton to think over the Eastern problem, Egypt in particular, and give him his considered opinion on a line of policy. Burton went upstairs to his room, but returned almost at once, handing Lord Salisbury a slip of paper. "You've been very quick making up your mind," remarked the statesman. He opened the paper: on it Burton had written the single word "Annex." He was for strict measures—"If only we govern like Men—not like Philanthropists and Humanitarians!" Taking the world on a long-term view, he saw the Slav as Europe's future race, just as he regarded the Chinese as the future race of the East. China armed, he said, would be a colossus. One day, Russia and China would meet face to face—Asia as the prize. . . . "I would make her [Russia] spread herself eastward as far as possible, instead of stopping her as you would," he wrote to Grattan Geary, "and when she meets China I should be safe."

He foresaw, too, the twentieth-century struggle between science and religion—a war to the death. With his friend and co-founder of the Kama-Shastra Society, Arbuthnot, he used to discuss the ultimate triumph of law and order; of logic over dogma, doctrine and the supernatural, or the age-old faith of Jew, Moslem and Christian. He foresaw a day when the police force would supersede the priesthood; at which Isabel would sigh: "If only Richard could be brought into the fold!" So amulets and holy medals were slipped into his pockets with renewed vigor; special Masses were ordered for the iconoclast, and with her confessor, in her private chapel, Isabel prayed on, indefatigably.

The Burtons had no intention of letting Trieste become too monotonous. There were frequent jaunts to Rome, or Venice, or Vienna. They had friends everywhere, and Isabel now discovered she was a Countess of the Holy Roman Empire by virtue of her family's long tradition of Papal allegiance. New visiting cards were engraved: *Mrs. Richard Burton, née Countess Isabel Arundell of Wardour,* was her chosen title, by which we must suppose the glitter of such rank had superseded the once all-desirable state of being Richard Burton's wife. Though perhaps it was in the nature of armor against the pin pricks of Austrian snobbery. The Foreign Office seems to have been aware of their long absences, but to have accepted it as a small price to pay for the satisfaction of having the Burtons off their hands, if not their conscience—and hamstrung too.

It had always been Burton's habit to pass over as much of his business as possible to Isabel; it was always she who wrestled with publishers, contracts, legal formalities, proofreading and such. He used to dispatch her to England whenever there was a new book to be launched. Isabel resented these separations, but always went obediently, following his closely written pages of instructions to the letter. To her, they were Holy Writ. The burdens which life, and Richard, put on Isabel multiplied ceaselessly. Writing from her father's country place where they were on holiday in October, 1878, she says, "I have a little share of the work: here is my program:

1. Learning assaying to be practically useful to Dick.

2. Attending to a small lawsuit.

3. Correcting proofs for a new book to come out in November.

4. Writing four large and fifteen short articles for magazines, and try to see all my relatives and friends. Visits.

5. Commissions and preparations for the expedition. [One of Burton's mining surveys]

6. Usual correspondence and reading. "I brought sixty-eight unanswered letters with me and I have done all but three. I have a big bazaar on hand for the animals, a big wedding (my cousin Tiny Gerard with Colonel Oliphant, a very bad match), then ten days' retreat at my Convent New Hall." Add to this the strain of moving house, or moving about, as often as Isabel did, and of surrounding Burton in whatever climate or circumstance with an ever-protective glow of love and forbearance, and we begin to gauge something of her will power and sense of dedication.

Her daily life in Trieste was further complicated by a deathbed charge which neither her religious nor social instincts could refuse.

Maria-Theresa, Contessa de Montelin, the ex-Queen of Spain, bequeathed her a pious guild she had formed, the Apostleship of Prayer. All Isabel's sense of generalship was called into play. Soon the membership increased to fifteen thousand and Isabel became the president, running it with clockwork efficiency. In spite of everything else, she managed to bring out her own book, *The Inner Life of Syria,* which enjoyed an instant success. When she arrived in London for the season (and some advance publicity for Richard) she was feted everywhere. So "Literature" *did* pay! She purred with gratification. Burton joined her on long leave, and in a rare state of indulgence and financial stability, asked her where she would like best to go for a trip—with him. "India," replied Isabel, who had always longed to visit the scenes of Burton's Eastern apprenticeship.

They were to sail from Trieste, and make a leisurely journey there by way of Boulogne, this being for Isabel a sentimental pilgrimage to the scene of their first, predestined meeting. Together, they went back to the Ramparts, Isabel now luxuriating in the realization of a dream come true. She was Richard Burton's wife—and he, Burton of Arabia, was leading her towards the lodestar Araby at last. Proceeding to Paris she found it terribly changed since the Franco-Prussian War: she speaks of the "sulkiness, silence and economy run mad, a rage for lucre and a lust for revenge. . . ." "The women even painted badly; and it is a sin to paint—badly." For all her athletic living, she never despised the aid of cosmetics, which in itself was considered *outré* in mid-Victorian England. (When banished from Syria, along with other Arabic habits, such as puffing at the *tchibouk,* they both continued to rim their eyes sootily with kohl, the Oriental and Western *maquillage* struggling oddly for supremacy on the plump pink planes of Isabel's face.)

"I am afraid I am one of the very few women who do not like Paris," she notes, complacently, as with a sigh of relief they headed East once more. Trieste—Port Said—Jeddah, the port of Mecca . . . *Richard's* East! When the yellowing-ivory silhouette of the Arabian towns rose out of the glassy sea they hung over the rail breathing the desert air hungrily. Isabel was determined to savor every moment of the Orient. She was reading Moore's *Veiled Prophet of Khorassan, Lallah Rookh,* and

*The Light of the Harím.* Each day, the ship took her further into that enchanted region made sacred to her by Burton's *Pilgrimage to El Medineh and Meccah.* She knew it by heart. Passing the tawny shores she recalled the legend of Abu Zulayman, patron saint of those seas, who sits watching over the safety of devout mariners, hidden in a cavern in the rocks, sustained by coffee brought him from Mecca, by green birds; the brew being prepared by ministering angels. Burton seemed withdrawn. Now it was Isabel's turn. It was *her* Pilgrimage, in search of *his* past.

At Jeddah, "the most lovely town I have ever seen," there was the thrilling moment of seeing the *very* Khan where Richard had lived as a pilgrim; the *very* minarets he had sketched in his book (he was an excellent draftsman) and the bliss of standing under it *with him,* to hear the call to prayer. There were desert expeditions, and visits to the Governor. Everyone was very civil. Burton's Mecca pilgrimage was well remembered in Jeddah; both the Turkish authorities and the fanatical Jeddáwis accepted him as one of them; but even so, and even twenty years later, it was impossible to consider another journey to Mecca, with Isabel. "It was not the time to show my blue eyes and broken Arabic on Holy Ground," she writes regretfully. So she had to console herself by riding through the Mecca Gate and gazing out across the Arabian desert towards the Ka'abah; "this had a great attraction for Richard," says Isabel, with masterly understatement. Sometimes she went with him to the bazaars, wandering in the ill-lit tunnels piled with merchandise, spices, perfumes, turquoises, pearls and slaves. They would watch the pilgrims' camels and all the paraphernalia of the scarlet and gold litters, plumed like Victorian hearses, in which the wealthy pilgrims traveled. Or the extraordinary jumble of races gathering for the Hadj, Turcomans, Persians, Kurds, Arabs and Bengali. "We felt happy in this atmosphere and the Arabic sounds so musical and so familiar. . . ." At last Isabel was living a chapter from Burton's own Arabic life . . . her life's envy. But Burton, so dutifully escorting Isabel on her outings, must have felt himself a revenant. In Arabia the shadow of his true self fell across his path once more. The shadow wore a burnous. *"All other life is living death, a world where none but phantoms dwell. . . ."* There, where once he had seen the green banners of the Prophet raised aloft, there was now only Isabel's parasol.

The voyage to Bombay on the *Calypso,* a pilgrim ship, was almost too much for even Isabel's Oriental enthusiasms. Eight hundred pilgrims, returning to India from Jeddah, were packed aboard in nightmare conditions. They died at the rate of two a day. "I can hardly express what I suffered during that fortnight's voyage on board the pilgrim ship. . . . Imagine eight hundred Moslems, ranging in point of color through every shade, from lemon or *café au lait* to black as ebony; races from every part of the world, covering every square inch of the deck . . . men, women and babies reeking of coconut oil. It was a voyage of horror. I shall never forget their unwashed bodies, their seasickness, their sores, the dead and the dying, their rags, and last but not least, their cookery. Except to cook or fetch water or kneel in prayer, none of them moved out of the small space or position which they assumed at the beginning of the voyage. Those who died did not die of disease so much as of privation and fatigue, hunger, thirst and opium. They died of vermin and misery. . . . I cannot eat my dinner if I see a dog looking wistfully at it. I therefore spent the whole day staggering about our rolling ship with sherbet and food and medicines, treating dysentery and fever.

"During my short snatches of sleep I dreamt of these horrors too. But it was terribly disheartening work, owing to their fanaticism. Many of them listened to me with more faith because I could recite their Bismillah and their 'call to prayer!'" We have no record of Burton's attitude towards the pilgrims. Did he puff a cheroot and pace the quarter-deck, aloof and westernized, fearing perhaps to fall again under the old spell? He left the cabin to sleep out under the stars; and Isabel tells us that instead of the customary nightshirt, he wore loose Oriental trousers called *pájhámas.* Isabel's maid found the voyage a great strain. She flatly refused to help her mistress with the afflicted pilgrims. "I have the nose of a princess; I cannot do such work," was her answer, perhaps understandably. But Isabel always made the best of things: one entry in her diary reads, "A charming day, and no one died. Have seen the prettiest sight possible late afternoon. Thousands of dolphins playing leapfrog under our bows, and keeping up with the ship."

At Aden the heat became infernal. A storm raged in the Red Sea, and some of the pilgrims fell overboard, but none of the others so much as prayed for them. It was Allah's will! Two Russians added to the general discomfort by getting crying drunk, and then fighting all over the first-class dinner table, below. But they settled down together quite cozily, after they had upset everybody else. Isabel was accused of having poisoned those pilgrims who had died. "Though there was still a crowd of sufferers who came to me daily, demanding I should wash, clean, anoint and tie up their feet which were covered with sores and worms." This was the East without varnish; Burton watched her ironically; but Isabel's forte was clinging to an ideal; she stuck it out. It was Richard's East; she wanted all of it.

India was everything she had hoped. Burton was on his best behavior —he seemed content to play cicerone, and show her all the sights, though sometimes, as in Syria, her relentless tourist zeal was too much even for him. She went to the *Tabút* or *Múharram,* a Moslem miracle play, alone, "because Richard had seen it before, and none of the other Europeans apparently cared to see it at all." She managed to get through the pullulating crowds and take her place among a shrieking, fanatic audience. "The religious emotion was intense and so contagious that although I could not understand a word, I found myself weeping with the rest." There were other, equally emotional occasions; a meeting with the Persian Mirza who had been Burton's *munshee,* or teacher, when he was in Bombay in 1848. Or the delights of Poona, dinner parties and a ball at Government House, which was Burton's official Anglo-Indian vindication, at long last. But at sunset "the wild but mournful sound of tom-tom and kettle, cymbal and reed suddenly struck up." Social politics faded; the Eastern mirage glowed again. "I could have shut my eyes and fancied myself in camp again in the desert, with the wild sword dances being performed by the Arabs." Isabel always had a preference for Arab over Hindu; always harked back to Syria the beloved. A visit to Golconda, on elephant-back, recalled Damascus. The Tombs of the Kings recalled the Tower Tombs of Palmyra.

But Burton? What did he remember, what did he struggle to forget? What memories of the adventurer assailed the tourist, now? The phantom of his Persian ghazelle, loved and lost so long ago; echoes of a faraway flute, or some unseen lover singing behind a lattice? That moment of blazing triumph when, Mecca attained, he stood before the black stone of the Ka'abah. Ghosts of the brawling, verminous crowd of beggars and bawds and hemp smokers among whom he lived in those first early days of the Eastern revelation. . . . Ghosts of his many disguises: when he crouched in the bazaars, watching, listening. . . . Ghosts of the ebony slave girls he cured of snoring, and the grateful slave owner who made him free of the whole harem. . . . Phantoms of landscape, of light and shade, of far horizons and shadowed alleys; of snake pits and veiled mysteries. Glittering, swaggering phantoms of youth and pride; a train of caparisoned ponies trotting through the valley of the Indus, riders and falcons and hooded cheetahs, all lit by the sunrise of his youth. Phantoms which clouded and marbled in his mind as, once again, he saw himself drowsed with hashish, sprawled on the deck of some Arabian *dhow*, anchored off a spice-sour port in the Red Sea. . . . Inertia, action, killings, lovings . . . all states of being, of life lived to the full . . . and now?

Presently the insatiable Isabel decreed another romantic pilgrimage, to Goa. "The place had a great attraction for Richard, and this was the third pilgrimage (or voyage, as he would have called it) he had made here since 1844," wrote Isabel, who was plainly hoping the Jesuit *ambiance* of Goa would bring about Richard's long-deferred conversion to Roman Catholicism, or, at any rate, some definite declaration of faith. Pray! Pray! . . . But her prayers remained unanswered; so she busied herself with what she describes mysteriously as "my work amongst the old Portuguese manuscripts," and a series of devout outings in the footsteps of St. Francis Xavier, whose sarcophagus, in all the gold and silver magnificence of Portuguese Baroque, Bom Jesus, is the center of the old city. The seventy-odd mile strip which was Portuguese India appalled Isabel by its poverty and desolation, its unhealthy vegetation and blistering heat. The jungle was creeping back over the ruined city, where there was nothing—no punkahs, no ice, no shade, no hope. It recalled that Arab city *"with impenetrable gates, still, without a voice or inhabitant; the owl hooting in its quarters and night-birds skimming in circles in its ruins, and the raven croaking in its great thoroughfares, as if bewailing those that had been there. . . ."* Still, there were picnics and fresh coconuts, monkeys, and haunting native music, influenced by the Portuguese *fados* they had heard and loved in Brazil. Isabel enjoyed it all, robustly.

One aspect of the East appalled her. She could never reconcile herself to the misery of the animals. There were horrors on all sides: Burton was always having to placate natives whom she had attacked. Several times she risked being locked up for assault. When she rounded on the driver for beating the ponies, Nip, her fox terrier, also turned ugly, and "not being allowed to bite the cruel coachmen, laid her head on my shoulder and went into hysterics; the tears actually ran down her cheeks, for she was extremely sensitive." Fortunately, Burton shared his wife's love of animals; they vied with each other in doting indulgence towards every pet.

The indomitable Isabel now founded an Indian branch of the S.P.C.A. and took faint comfort from being taken to see a hospital for sick animals, where the maimed and starving beasts lingered on, in accordance with the Hindu belief that all life is sacred. Isabel, never blindly Catholic, where animals were concerned, records that she admired the religion that believes in animals having a soul and a future. " . . . God is too just to create things, without any fault of their own, only for slow and constant torture, for death, and utter annihilation." It is evident that she had not encountered the ghastly Kali festivals of animal slaughter, which are another aspect of India's many religious manifestations. Perhaps Burton spared her; he must have known of them himself. But except for cock fights, he seems to have hated any forms of cruelty to animals. Where human beings were concerned, however, he was wonderfully tough. Cannibalism, capital punishment or execution by torture left him unmoved; "he would listen to descriptions of Chinese cruelty and Russian self-mutilation or American lynchings till the stars paled," says Frank Harris. . . . "Catholic in his admiration and liking for all greatness, it was the abnormalities and not the divinities of men that fascinated him." But Harris, like Isabel, tended to present Burton subjectively.

Apart from all the Indian horrors, there were other, less painful, wholly absorbing spectacles: ostrich races, snake charmers and jugglers. Or the Parsee Charnel House where large black vultures gorged on corpses of the smallpox and cholera epidemic then raging. (Suttee—the widows' sacrifice, was something Isabel could easily understand.) Then there was the hospitality of the Rajahs in their sumptuous palaces, the princes dripping with pearls and uncut rubies, and dispensing mutton cutlets for breakfast *à l'Anglaise,* in honor of their distinguished visitors, with everything served on jewel-studded gold plates. Sometimes there were forbidden peeps inside Brahmin temples, and a magnificent wedding ceremony for a little bride and bridegroom aged nine and ten, and Isabel, getting thoroughly overexcited by it all, records, rather bewilderingly, "they were actually theoretically married today." And in a tone of prophetic justification, writing of a celebrated old Anglo-Indian lady, Mrs. Hough, who had died a year or two before, and who used, in 1803, to dance with Sir Arthur Wellesley, as the Duke of Wellington was then, "the Editor of the Bombay paper regretted that before her death she burnt all her memoirs. . . . I dare say she knew why she burnt them; I dare say thousands of people's descendants have cause to bless her for it."

There was one memorable occasion; a *nautch,* "which I thought very stupid, for the girls did nothing but eat sweetmeats and occasionally ran forward and twirled round for a moment with a half-bold, semiconscious look; and only one was barely good-looking. Perhaps that is the *nautch* to dance before ladies," Isabel adds condescendingly, "but in Syria I remember they danced much better *without being shocking.*" One wonders what were Burton's thoughts, as he sat beside his wife, watching the *nautch* to dance before ladies. Did he remember his Persian ghazelle, and their nights in the jasmin-scented moonlight? Did he remember his adventures in the stews of Scinde? But this was Isabel's turn: he let her enjoy every moment of the treat-outing. If there were any backward glances, she did not notice them.

On the way home from Goa, there was a revealing incident. A small boat had to ferry them eight miles down river to the mouth of the bay, where the Bombay steamer was to pass; but they were late in starting.

The tides were against them, and when they reached the bay there was no sign of the ship, and they began to pitch dangerously in the open sea. They put into shore, to wait. Unlikely as it seems, everyone fell asleep, and did not see the ship's lights as it came into view. Nor did they hear its gun—a warning that it would leave within the hour. Isabel woke, uneasily, to see the lights of the ship apparently three miles or so out, and, according to a man on shore, just about to leave. Now although Isabel doted on the East, and wished nothing more than to stay there, with Richard, forever, it is typical of her energetic Anglo-Saxon nature, her sense of order and punctuality, that she could not let the boat go without her; she could not accept the excuse of another month or so, lost in the thickets of Goa. ( . . . *"Oh I could live with thee in the wild wood . . ."*) No: they had arranged to catch that boat, so catch it they must. She shook up the drowsy crew, urging them to unheard-of feats of speed and endurance. "I trembled lest the steamer should put further out to sea, and determined that no effort of mine should be spared to prevent it. Richard slept, or pretended to sleep, and so did some of the others." But then they had all eaten of the lotus, which Isabel's Orient never really included. And then, too, Burton's inertia was probably deliberate. *Inch'allah!* If it was written, they would miss the boat; he would do nothing to force fate. Besides, to remain in the wild wood with Isabel would not be the wild wood of his poetic image. And anyhow, it was giving him one of those enjoyable opportunities to torment her—to punish her for being there, in the boat, in his life, his heart! Just how bitterly he resented the fetters of his love we shall never know. Isabel's burning of the journals took care of that.

Now, briskly organizing, she set about rousing the crew. "I managed adroitly to be awkward with the boat hook, and occasionally to prick their shins." How much the boat *wálás* must have disliked the blond memsahib's prodding and fussing. . . . "Everybody except myself was behaving with Oriental calm, and leaving it to Kismet. It was no use doing anything to Richard," says Isabel, a certain exasperation in her tone. After an hour of fearful efforts, in high seas, they reached the ship; but the waves kept washing them away from the ladder; "no one had the energy to hold onto the rope, or hold the boat hook to keep us close, so at last I did it myself, Richard laughing all the while at their supineness, and my making myself so officious." (Laughing perhaps at Fate, now in the shape of Isabel, banishing him once more from the East; laughing with that ominous chill ring of his "like the rattle of a pebble across a frozen pond.") But Isabel remembered she had undertaken a very peculiar man: she never looked for the more reassuring, husbandly attributes: and when at long last they were forthcoming, love and warmth and tenderness, they were doubly sweet.

She paints a fearful picture of lashing waves and supine Moslems. "An English sailor threw me a rope. 'Thanks,' I cried, as I took advantage of an enormous wave to spring up on the ladder. 'I am the only man in the boat tonight,'" was her parting shot at the lubbers below. Not that Richard cared; not that the *wálás* understood. At this time Isabel was rising forty-five, decidedly matronly, her ample curves braced into the stays she always urged her voluptuous Syrian maid to wear too; with her curled golden bangs and heavily kohl-rimmed eyes, she must have been a remarkable sight, swarming up a rope ladder in the middle of the Indian Ocean. Whatever Burton thought of being dragged back to civilization, we shall never know. But the Indian trip ended on a lyrical note. At Suez they went ashore for one more expedition into the Arabian Desert; one last lingering backward glance. . . . It was a golden evening, the mountains and sands flowing together in the sunset. "The most romantic spot was a single tiny spring under an isolated palm tree, all alone on a little hillock of sand in the desert, far from all else. I said to Richard, 'That tree and that spring have been created for each other, like you and I.'" And Burton did not contradict her.

\*         \*         \*

Back in Trieste, Burton had taken one of his sudden unaccountable dislikes to their fourth-floor apartment in the town and they moved to an imposing *palazzo* embowered in tall trees, high on the hills. It was splendid but drafty; however, during the few months of the year they spent at home, they both enjoyed the gardens. Sometimes they were away for as much as a year at a time, forever wandering in search of change, of health, of life itself. But all of life that Burton valued was fading with his strength; and all of life that Isabel held dear was bound up in him. When someone remarked that life went very fast, Burton replied, "I find it goes *very* slow." Isabel began to watch him with a special, agonizing care. There was no prayer, no faith to meet the eventuality of Richard's death. Gradually she was finding their former pattern too strenuous. Reluctantly she gave up fencing and swimming. Both began to go from doctor to spa in search of health. Between whiles, there was Spiritualism. The occult had always exercised a fatal fascination over both of them, and Burton delivered several lectures on Indian supernaturalism and mystic practices. Isabel, although reproved by her Church, was partial to dabbling, and made various pronouncements on Eastern mystical manifestations. She was rather inclined to infer the East was her own special province; and having married Burton she felt herself especially suited to interpret it to less informed Westerners. The West, she said, was receiving "supernaturalism" wrong. Isabel the Catholic contrived to accept Isabel the spiritualist in a most ingenious fashion, " . . . nothing happens by luck or chance—but we are moved by our good and bad angels, and those who are in the habit of meditating arrive at a proficiency in knowing and understanding their calls."

So that was settled; she could go on receiving spirit messages, interesting herself in mediums and seances, and it could all be, really, a sort of Divine revelation. Thus Isabel, having her cake and eating it. Poor Isabel! There were so few pleasures left now; money worries gnawed. There was no denying Burton was failing; and at last she had discovered why none of the cures did her any good. She had a malignant growth: but she went on hiding it from Burton. Had she undergone the operation her doctors advised, the disease might have been arrested: but to do that would have been to worry Richard, to leave him, to fail him . . . she preferred to go on as she was. When General Gordon, the Governor General of the Soudan, Darfur and Equatorial Provinces, asked Burton to accept the governor-generalship of Darfur, Burton refused curtly. "I could not serve under you, nor you under me." Isabel regretted that this last door to the East was slammed, but whatever Burton did was always right, in her eyes. "I am glad to say there was only *one* will in the house, and that was *his* . . . I like that. I was only too lucky to have met my master; I hate a house where the woman is at the helm," she wrote in retrospect.

1883 was a bad year. Burton had returned from his last glimpse of Eastern adventure. It had been an abortive dash, made at the request of the Government, to trace his friend Professor Palmer, the Oriental scholar, who had been sent to parley with the restive Arab chieftains, and had been betrayed and murdered, somewhere in the Sinai desert. Burton must have felt, bitterly, the comparison with other triumphant sorties of the past. Isabel missed him cruelly. She fretted, fearing his health was not equal to the strain; and as always, she envied him the East. She wrote to a friend: "I am as you may think, fearfully sad. I have been nowhere. I neither visit nor receive, nor go out. Men drink when they are sad, women fly into company; but I must fight the battle with my own heart. Learn to live alone and work, and when I have conquered I will allow myself to see something of my friends." Worn out with the battles of daily life, she went into retreat at the Convent della Osolini at Gorizia. In her devotional book she writes: "In retreat at last. I have so long felt the need of one. My life seems to be like an express train, every day bringing fresh things which *must* be done." (Thirty years earlier she had written, "I long to rush round the world in an express!" But life with Richard had forced the pace remorselessly, since then.) "I am goaded on by time and circumstances, and God, my first beginning and last end, is always put off, thrust out of the way, to make place for the unimportant, and gets served last and badly. This cannot continue. What friend would have such long-enduring patience with me? None! Certainly less a king! far less a husband! . . . I am here, my God, according to Thy command: Thou and I, I and Thou, face to face in the silence."

Isabel had scarcely obtained a degree of serenity when Burton returned. He was dispirited and embittered, needing all her understanding. Palmer was dead, and Burton had been practically dismissed from the scene by Sir Charles Warren, a martinet whom the Government had sent to supersede Burton—their customary technique. It was his last sight of the desert, and he knew it. *"All other life is living death, a world where none but phantoms dwell. A breath, a wind, a sound, a voice, a tinkling of the camel-bell. . . ."*

The shadows gathered fast, now. All their old friends were dying. When news of Abd El Kadir's death reached them Burton was stricken. For eight months he was bedridden with a succession of ailments, heart, liver and gout. Isabel nursed him with her customary devotion, sleeping on a mattress on the floor beside him. She never spoke of her own health. There were so many other cares. Their finances worsened month by month. But as soon as Burton was better, they resumed the old, restless, expensive life of travel. Anything—*anything* rather than the cage; for Burton, the humiliation of being caged; for Isabel, the anguish of seeing him, this paladin and prince of men, "the desert lion, dying of the cage" as Frank Harris put it. So there were trips to Styria to study the local arsenic-eaters; Venice, Rome, Florence, Switzerland, the Riviera; dashes to Vienna, where Isabel reveled in receptions at the Hofburg; in Germany, the *Nibelung* cycle in its entirety was most distracting. In London there was *The Mikado*; at Oberammergau, the Passion Play. Portrait sittings with Professor Herkomer; meetings of the S.P.C.A., and a vain attempt on Isabel's part to interest the Vatican in her humane work. Journalism, giving lectures, being given dinners of honor (one dinner in particular, when Isabel records that Mrs. Gladstone said: "I don't know what it is; I cannot get Mr. Gladstone away this evening," and Isabel replied, "I think I know what it is; he has got hold of my husband. . . ."). Isabel, as everyone else, knew that when he chose, Burton could be an incomparable conversationalist. Mme. Nicastro, who as Daisy Letchford had known the Burtons well at Trieste, recalls "that wonderful man, Sir Richard Burton, with the eyes of a tiger and the voice of an angel . . . from his lips would come forth such enchanting conversation—such a wonderful flow of words and so marvelous in sound that often I have closed my eyes and listened to him, fancying thus, that some learned angel had descended from Heaven unto Earth." There is, however, another version of Burton's meeting with Gladstone which does not tally with Isabel's, but also has the ring of truth. Burton was talking to the old statesman in his usual vehement fashion, when a hurriedly scrawled note was passed to him. It read: *"Please do not contradict Mr. Gladstone. No one ever does."*

During all their comings and goings they contrived to write. "Literature" took them out of themselves. Sometimes it brought in a little much-needed money. Isabel's book *A.E.I.—Arabia, Egypt and India*—followed up the success of her *Inner Life of Syria*: Burton had finished his translation of Catullus, and Camoëns, the Portuguese poet for whom he had always held an especial veneration—but none of these were of great financial help. Burton reckoned that around twenty thousand pounds of his own money had been spent, over the years, subsidizing his various expeditions and scientific researches. Both of them were wildly extravagant in small ways. They took trains across Europe as other people took cabs across London. Burton had over a hundred pairs of boots, and large numbers of greatcoats, but always wore a shabby thin jacket to keep himself tough. Isabel, according to all contemporary accounts, was exquisitely dressed, and possessed some good jewelry. (Though it is not recorded if wifely pride overcame chic, and she wore the famous necklace of human bones which King Gelele presented to Burton during his expedition to Dahomey.) Their enormous quantities of luggage, the pets, servants, and possessions they collected (Isabel traveling about with a capricious Syrian maid, and several large dogs; and Burton with a favorite gamecock and a large part of his library—there were over eight thousand books at Trieste) represented a considerable outlay. From time to time there were some very odd schemes for money-making, such as the *Hadjilik,* or *Pilgrimage to Meccah Syndicate, Ltd.,* which had a capital of ten thousand pounds, a hundred shares at a hundred pounds each, and was designed as a sort of super-Cook's Tour, to enable the devout to reach Mecca with less hardships than were the general lot. Unhappily the scheme came to nothing, but for a time the Burtons took it very seriously. They were equally confident in a brew they tried to launch on the British public, called Captain Burton's Tonic Bitters; but this, too, failed, in spite of Isabel's insistence on pretty bottles. Burton's expedition to the alleged Gold Mines of Midian, undertaken at the request of the Khedive of Egypt in 1878, had also come to nothing. There seemed no way for the greatest Orientalist of his age to capitalize his talents.

All the splendor and surge of his life had passed, and he was sinking into obscurity, when, suddenly, at long last, he struck gold. It was there—beneath his hand—in the spartan workroom where he had spent so many hours of neglect working on the notes and translations of *The Thousand Nights and a Night* (*Alf Laylah iwa Laylah* in Arabic), commonly known as *The Arabian Nights*. He had begun it, in a desultory way, thirty years before, in his days of adventure, listening to the story-tellers in the bazaars. It had been a refuge from drab reality, over the years. In his foreword, he calls it a labor of love, an unfailing source of solace and satisfaction. "Impossible even to open the pages without a vision starting into view; without drawing a picture from the *pinacothek* of the brain; without reviving a host of dead memories and reminiscences. . . . From my dull and commonplace and "respectable" surroundings, the Djinn bore me at once to the land of my predilection, Arabia, *a region so familiar to my mind that, even at first sight, it seemed a reminiscence of some bygone metempsychic life in the distant Past.*" (The italics are mine.) Over this magic threshold, Isabel could never cross. Although she often copied and worked for him, in this book, this work, she sensed a barred door. This East—the glorious, scandalous, marvelous scene of cruelty, debauch and adventure was his —it could never be hers. But one day, and perhaps unconsciously, she was to have her revenge. It was the same East of *The Scented Garden;* if she could not share it with Burton, then no one else should. That may be one explanation of her burning of the manuscript.

At the beginning of his work Burton did not realize what a gold mine these Oriental stories—especially the *ars erotica*—would represent. He decided to bring out a privately printed edition, backed up by a group of Orientalists and enthusiasts. It would be obtainable by subscription only, for he would have no truck with an emasculated version. "I had knowledge of certain subjects such as no other man possessed. Why should it die with me? Facts are facts whether men are acquainted with them or not." Such were his views, and his reasons for both the notes and data accompanying his *Thousand Nights and a Night,* and later his translation of *The Scented Garden.* It is these notes which make Burton's *Thousand Nights and a Night* so outstanding, by comparison to other versions. *The Edinburgh Review,* traditionally carping at British bards, pronounced that of the most celebrated translations, Galland was for the nursery, Lane for the library, Payne for the study, and Burton for the sewers; and Carlyle denounced them all as "unwholesome tales." Burton was a man who had lived and adventured all over the East. He had no prurience, but rather an immense gusto, a roaring, Elizabethan quality of bawdry, which, oddly, found its counterpart in some aspects of Eastern sensuality. He had, too, the anthropologist's approach to every aspect of Oriental life. Its practices, natural and unnatural (by Western standards, that is), its beliefs and traditions were all set down meticulously, from astrological predictions to the use of jackal's gall as an aphrodisiac; female circumcision, the elliptical style of Oriental storytellers, or the preference of debauched matrons for blackamoors . . . the notes, as much as the "Terminal Essay," form what he describes as a Repertory of Eastern knowledge in its esoteric form. . . . "Having failed to free the Anthropological Society from the fetters of *mauvaise honte* and the mock-modesty which compels travelers and ethnographical students to keep silence concerning one side of human nature (and that side the most interesting to mankind) I propose to supply the want in these pages. . . ."

Mock modesty or no, Isabel said he made her promise not to read certain passages. Debarred from these virile delights, she was as usual wrestling with the business side of the venture, sending out thirty-four thousand circulars, attending to subscriptions, publishing, and proofreading under difficulties, since her sensibilities were not to be outraged, and Burton, she tells us, was constantly blotting out, or covering the juiciest bits.

But this statement was merely a public concession to Victorian *pudeur* as Isabel had her own copy upon which she fought a losing battle, when later she was preparing a blameless Household Edition. As Burton remarked, "*Les turpitudes* are a matter of time and place," and apropos the temple at Benares where twining figures assume every erotic posture imaginable, Keyserling has said "the erotic images in India never belonged to pornography, but to iconography." In Victorian London Isabel found whole passages quite beyond control. No, No! is scrawled across the margin in her handwriting, unsteady with exasperation as she battled with such stories as the "Tale of the Simpleton Husband," or "Queen Budur's Voluptés." INVENT OTHER WORDS! is another despairing note. *"Let us lie together,"* Burton's vigorous Chaucerian phrase, is Isabelized as "Let us enjoy life together," on the whole a fair rendering. She is less happy perhaps, though equally ingenious, in her transposition of *concubine* into "assistant wife." No doubt Burton enjoyed her version enormously, but when at last the Household Edition was presented to an eager public, titillated by the uproar over the original, it proved disappointing to all, and sales were poor.

Burton's unexpurgated translation appeared in 1883 and was an overwhelming triumph. The ten heavy volumes, bound in black and gold —the colors of the Abbaside Caliphate—were the sensation of London, both literary and otherwise. Under Burton's hand the legends glowed again, the medieval Orient took on new life: Haroun al Raschid, and the Queen of the Serpents; Afrits, eunuchs, reeking scimitars, bulbuls and Barmecides . . . Burton's notes gave the legends the added fascination of truth, and Swinburne's ode voiced the delight that many felt, on reading the fabulous tales.

> *Years on years*
> *Vanish, but he that hearkens eastwards hears*
> *Bright music from the world where shadows are.*
> *Where shadows are not shadows. Hand-in-hand*
> *A man's word bids them rise and smile and stand*
> *And triumph. All that glorious Orient glows*
> *Defiant of the dusk. Our twilight land*
> *Trembles; but all the heaven is all one rose,*
> *Whence laughing love dissolves her frosts and snows.*

And even Isabel, much as she deprecated Swinburne's unfortunate habit of egging Richard on towards risqué subjects, had to admit she found the poem beautiful, and *very* gratifying. The Burtons were basking in unexpected, unaccustomed sunshine. Money poured in: publishers fought for Burton's favors. All the same, he began compiling a Black Book of Biblical and Shakespearean indecencies. *Turpiloquium*, he called it, proposing to use it as his defense, were he prosecuted for indecency. *The Thousand Nights and a Night* was, he said, indecent but not depraved, which is exact. "Such throughout the East is the language of every man, woman and child, from prince to peasant, from matron to prostitute, and all are, as the naïve French travelers said of the Japanese, 'so coarse that they don't know what to call things except by their real names.'" Although Burton was not prosecuted, Isabel was very uneasy. She disapproved of his dragging in the Bible: she preferred his travel books. Those on archaeology were really safest, though with Burton you could never tell: sly references to hippic syphilis in Baroda, or happenings in the Sotadic zone might crop up anywhere. Burton said ironically, "I have struggled for forty-seven years, distinguished myself honorably in every way that I could. I never had a compliment, nor a 'thank you' nor a single farthing. I translate a doubtful book in my old age, and immediately make sixteen thousand guineas. Now that I know the tastes of England, we need never be without money."

Erotica or no, the financial success of *The Thousand Nights* was due in some measure to Isabel's unflagging energies. At the beginning, a publisher offered five hundred pounds to take it over entirely: but Isabel stood firm. All the work, but all the profits too. There were seventeen months of grueling toil for her; but they netted sixteen thousand pounds. "It came just in time to give my husband the comforts and luxuries and freedom which gilded the last five years of his life. When he died there were four florins left, which I put into the poor-box," says Isabel, touching in her selflessness.

Officially, Burton was still chained to the Consulate. The climate of Trieste, especially its raw winter *bora*, had never agreed with him, and Isabel had tried for some while to persuade the Foreign Office (if they would not give him another post) to retire him on full pay. When Matthew Arnold died she made a tactical blunder by telegraphing a demand that Burton should be given the lapsed pension. She was incorrigible, and Burton seems to have been either complacent, or fatalistic regarding her maneuvers. She now drew up another of her fulsome documents entitled "The Last Appeal," for which she canvassed fifty or more influential signatures; but without avail. Nor was her next round-up any more fortunate. For the last time, she was jockeying for the consulship of Morocco, at Tangier, which was just about to be vacated by Sir John Drummond-Hay. This post had been one of Burton's reasons for remaining in the Consular service; over the years it had become a sort of official mirage.

At Christmas 1886, the Burtons were at Gibraltar for their Silver Wedding, en route for Tangier, where Isabel, optimistic as ever, decided they should look over the place, preparatory to moving in. Though the post was never offered, there was a telegram announcing the Queen had conferred a knighthood on Burton. In a state of beatitude, Isabel wrote: "The Queen's recognition of Dick's forty-four years of service was sweetly done at last, sent for our Silver Wedding, and she told a friend of mine that she was pleased to confer something that would include both husband and wife." By which it seems that neither Burton's diabolic nor pornographic aspects blinded the Queen to his long and devoted years of service, nor, too, the devoted years of marriage which had been Isabel's earthly cross and crown. Isabel and the Queen both had worshiping wifehood in common. Indeed there are several parallels between Queen Victoria and Isabel Burton. Both of them were masterful women who struggled to gain, and keep an ascendancy over their empire.

Isabel's most bitter cross was the thought that if Richard died outside the Catholic Faith they would be parted forever. Then, too, there was the disquieting thought of all those houris Mohammed promised the Faithful after death. . . .) It was out of the question for her to abjure her faith, to join him in Mohammedanism, yet none of her proselytizing seemed to have borne fruit. Or was he, secretly, a convert? There had been that strange occasion when, during an attack, Burton had lost consciousness and Isabel, terrified by the doctor's pronouncements, seized some water, and kneeling and praying, baptized him. . . . "When I told him what I had done he looked up with an amused smile, and he said, 'Now that was very superfluous, if you only knew'; and after a pause, The world will be very much surprised when I come to die.'"

"'If I could only save Dick's soul!' she would cry, and I could not persuade her that his soul, if he had one, did not want her help. Women have such strange illusions as to what they believe to be their *charge d'âmes.'*" Thus Ouida, trenchant in her opinions, but a staunch friend to both of the Burtons. "To women," she wrote, "Burton had the unpardonable fault: he loved his wife. He would have been a happier and a greater man if he had had no wife—but his love for her was extreme: it was a source of weakness as most warm emotions are in the lives of strong men. Their marriage was romantic and clandestine; a love-marriage in the most absolute sense of the words, not wise on either side, but on each impassioned. . . . Throughout the chief part of their lives he was implicitly obeyed by her, but during the close of his, ill health made him more helpless, and compelled him to rely on her in all things, and then the religious ogre raised its head and claimed its prey."

Perhaps more than anyone else, Ouida pierced the mystery of Burton's personality, and saw, behind the mask, the face, and behind it all, again, the soul of this strange man. Had he known, when he married, that from then on he would be a prisoner of his own emotions as much as Isabel's? That love would demand the sacrifice of freedom—of even such a limitless freedom as his? And did he, in subconscious, or deliberate revenge, once trapped by his love, torment Isabel with his rejections and withdrawals within the domestic periphery? Did he take a sadistic pleasure in seeing her his slave, his puppet, his whipping-boy? Why not? For all his paladin aspects, every photograph betrays another side; that questing, wild-beast look can have boded no good to anyone who loved him, or worse, whom he loved. Such a man must have resented every tie; most of all, the ties of love; especially those which reminded him how Victorian England (an age and a climate so alien to him) in the person of Isabel, stood, like a barrier, between himself and the East. Perhaps, in certain aspects, his marriage had become identified with submission to the West, to domesticity—all he loathed, and longed to smash, to escape. But it is likely, too, that in spite of all his revolts, the actor, and this he indisputably was, submitted at last to the only wholly appreciative audience he had ever known. After all, if he remained so

profoundly attached to her in spite of everything, it was probably because he knew that in her eyes he had never failed in anything, that he
had never known defeat, and that for her, to her, his life had been a
succession of triumphant achievements; that he had, at least given her
the limitless horizons, the recognition and glory he had not obtained
himself.

When Isabel realized that Burton's strange attacks of paralysis, his
"fits" as she calls them, vaguely, agonies of gout and heart attacks, were
all part of his general decline, and that he must lead, now, at best, a semi-
invalid life, she decided they should have a resident doctor. Today, such
an adjunct to the household is unimaginable: it seems as remote as the
ages which employed jesters, astrologers or lady companions as part of a
wealthy entourage. But in the late Victorian age, when telephones were
still scarcely used, motor cars unknown and medicine primitive by our
present scientific standards, a resident doctor was the most practical solution to Isabel's problem of how to keep Burton alive, to look after him
without resorting to the presence of a trained nurse whom no doubt
both of them would have found exasperating; moreover, it enabled
Burton to live at his own tempo as no nursing-home could have done. It
also gave Isabel the support of professional help, always at hand, day or
night, if one of Burton's alarming attacks returned. Dr. Leslie arrived in
1887 and seems to have got on well with them both from the start.
Isabel spoke of his office, rather than person, as a disagreeable luxury.
Sometimes Burton lived an almost normal life, and was well enough to
work for weeks at a time, though when carried away by some Oriental
legend he would forget to eat, and have to be coaxed to take even a
cup of tea. Sometimes all three of them made journeys about Europe,
following something of the old pattern. Burton had mellowed considerably since his belated success. Both the money and the knighthood
had come too late, but at least they had come—particularly the money.
As Burton's horizons narrowed, little things were a distraction—watching the process of Swiss milk being condensed; reading *Little Lord
Fauntleroy* (we do not have Burton's opinion of it) or receiving the
news that Tussaud's wax works wished to include him in their Exhibi-
tion, in Arab outfit. "That will bring me in contact with the people,"

he said, beaming. Then there was that new and wonderful invention, the phonograph. Isabel says that Burton proposed to recite *Allah Akbar*, the Arab's call to prayer, into the magic wax cylinder; but somehow it was never done. "O! what a treasure it would be now!" she wrote later, and we imagine Isabel, the desolate widow, playing the fugitive strains threadbare.

These last years in Trieste were even more demanding on Isabel than the earlier ones. The Eastern horizons faded from sight and hope; their last afterglow was centered round the figure of Burton, stooping, hour after hour, over his Oriental manuscripts. In winter, the wind howled down from the mountains, rattling the palms incessantly; drafts gnawed, doors slammed; sudden gusts overturned the bazaar bric-a-brac, fluttered the Persian portières, making the little *prie-dieu* lamps smoke, in Isabel's Cross and Crescent salon. She had no hope or health left; she was too weak to go for even the shortest walk, now; although she still kept watch over Burton at night (an electric bell connected their beds, so that if he stirred, she woke, instantly vigilant). She came to rely more and more on the resident doctor. Stifled with love and care, Burton's restlessness assumed neurotic proportions. They were forever on the move. No sooner had they arrived at a new place—Berne, Algiers, Tunis, Rome—than he seemed, in Isabel's words, "to have sucked dry all his surroundings, whether place, scenery, people or facts before the rest of us had settled. . . ." He would anxiously say: "Do you think I shall live to get out of this and see another place?" And Isabel would calm him by offering to leave on the instant; feverishly, she would begin to pack up the trunks she had only just unpacked, making train and boat reservations, with all the added complications of transporting the invalid. Paying, packing . . . forever on the move; but now it was Burton who followed. He could no longer bear her out of his sight: she seemed his talisman for the life he no longer lived, but to which he clung. Dr. Leslie had been replaced by Dr. Baker; the trio traveled royally, a whole compartment to themselves, champagne picnics. Isabel pressed station masters and armies of porters or local officials into the battle for Richard's comfort. The desert eagle would look out of the carriage window apathetically: he was quiet, at last. But Isabel would have given everything to see him again in the independence of his youth, striding out of her life as he used to do so ruthlessly. "Alas! the birthdays' injury. . . ."

During their last visit to England they stayed at Folkestone with Burton's sister and her family. They must have presented a striking picture on the green lawns of the Leas. Both were painted; here, as once, in Damascus, their eyes were heavily rimmed with kohl, panda-like. Isabel wore a towering golden wig; Burton dyed his hair black—he still looked strongly Arab, said Walburga, Lady Paget; "an illusion which was strengthened by his staining his underlids with kohl. His wife still bore great traces of beauty, though she too shared the Eastern predilection for pigments." According to his niece, Georgina, family life at Folkestone was just what he needed. "Good English food, open fireplaces, the fresh winds from the Channel were preferable, we urged, to kickshaws, closed stoves and ill-smelling towns. 'True enough,' he answered, and forthwith took rooms at the Pavilion with his wife and doctor, lunching with us every day, and seeming for a while fairly happy and amused." But Isabel knew otherwise, and within hours the caravan moved on again.

Even such a noncomformist couple as the Burtons had the Victorian feeling for family life. Isabel kept up with Richard's relatives as meticulously as she kept up with her own. Still, there was no denying they both suffered from the grayness of England, both climatically and domestically. They thought of themselves as martyrs, living in Trieste—they spoke of themselves as exiles—eagerly awaiting the day of Burton's retirement, and would even plan a retreat in London, but the exile they really felt was from the sun—the East. Nothing could ever take its place, for either of them. Certainly not family luncheons at Folkestone, though Isabel recounts one aspect of the English scene which entertained Burton vastly. An August bank holiday found them by chance at Ramsgate, with Isabel wondering how he could be reconciled to the trippers. But Burton was fascinated by the whole scene; the crowds swarming over the beach, paddling, eating winkles with a pin or listening to the concerts, Pierrot troupes, with lovers, lost dogs and bawling babies everywhere. Anthropologically, it must have been absorbing. He could not be torn away.

There is a photograph of the Burtons taken about this time. Dr. Baker stands, deprecatingly, in the background. Burton has an air of bravado, puffing at a cigar, his white beaver hat set rakishly. He stares out—the eyes are still bold and raging. Isabel nestles at his side coyly—nothing left in the overweight, snugly corseted figure with the bang, of that ardent creature who had ensnared him in the Botanical Gardens. Nothing, either, of that sweetness, nobility and courage which her life must have stamped on her face. As Burton came to lean on her more and more, there were little exchanges of tenderness, shadowy love scenes, almost, which Isabel treasured. "What a horrible desert it would be if I had not got you to come back to," was wrung from him after some all-male celebration which Isabel had not attended. Another time, in London, speaking of their favorite lime tree in the garden at Trieste, Burton said, "Our tree must be in bloom, now; don't you wish you were there?" And Isabel replied, "My tree is wherever you are, darling." Burton seemed touched, and said it was rather a sweet thing to have said. . . . But he was not going to be caught making any really soft speeches. Isabel had to be content with that.

Looking back on her life of love, the love of her life, from her widowhood, Isabel had some pertinent things to say about men. "I always think that a man is one character to his wife, another to his family, another to *her* family, a fourth to a mistress or an *amourette* . . . if he have one—and so on, ad infinitum; but I think the wife, if they are happy and love each other, gets the pearl out of all the oyster shells. . . . My husband, whose character, naturally, expanded with me in the privacy of our domestic life, became quite another man the moment anyone else entered the room. I have often, in the early days of my married life, watched with great interest and astonishment things that in after life I became quite used to." This is the only veiled reference she ever makes to the years when she suffered, proudly, in silence, for the detached sarcastic manner Burton habitually adopted towards her in public, at any rate. As it was remarked earlier, his religion and his love for Isabel were the only two things about which he ever dissembled. After saying firmly that he was the best of husbands and the easiest man to live with, Isabel continues: "He was a man with whom it was possible to combine, to keep up all the little refinements of the honeymoon, which tends to preserve affection and respect. . . ." She is not very explicit, but if the "little refinements of the honeymoon" are a Victorian euphemism for the Eastern cult of *volupté,* and the prolongation of an infinite variety of delights (whether achieved, like the Frenchman Burton quotes in his notes to the *Arabian Nights, "en pensant à sa pauvre mère,"* or by those tours de force which form part of regular Oriental erotic education, and ever one of Burton's favorite themes, it will be recalled), then we see that however peculiar, or difficult this man she had undertaken, there had been compensations.

Yet we also have an eyewitness account of their chance meeting in Venice when each of them was traveling separately. "Hallo! what are you doing here?" asked Burton casually—indifference at all costs—no show of sentiment either to the public or Isabel. But by now Isabel was used to the performance, the pose. "Ditto, brother," she replied coolly, and they shook hands, to the astonishment of the onlooker. For a man to whom dramatic living was the breath of life, Isabel's buoyant calm must have been sadly frustrating, at times. Not to be able to ring up the curtain on daily domestic dramatics must have been exasperating. Isabel was his slave, his adoring doormat, his tireless publicity agent; but she would not play naïve spectator to his histrionic performances—it was the one thing she denied him, since this imputed a separate state, rather than the oneness she craved. If he chose to put on an act, then she would play it too: a husband-and-wife-team in all things. One soul in two bodies. . . .

\*       \*       \*

There were only another five months to go, they kept reassuring each other. In March Burton could retire, pensioned off. Freedom at last, they said; freedom to shake off the last shackles of official life, and Trieste. Isabel had come to love the beautiful house and garden, and even Trieste. Secretly, she feared their retirement and the enforced inactivity their reduced income would impose. Riches meant, it seemed, that Burton must be forever working at those licentious Arab translations. What a price to pay! But she hid her tremors, and they went on planning another Eastern jaunt. Constantinople, this time, with the pearly domes and minarets soaring up from the Bosphorus. Constantinople! The Sublime Porte! Eyoub! The fountain of Achmet! The cypress groves fringing the Sweet Waters of Asia! They saw themselves seated in the dappled shade of the great plane trees, in the cafes beside the Beyazit mosque, where the pigeons strut between the tables and the Turks rattle trictrac counters, or just sit, puffing at their *narghilyés* in the immemorial Eastern climate of contemplation.

Burton had finished his translation of the *Priapeia*, and followed it with another piece of erotology; this time a notorious Arab manuscript, *The Scented Garden Men's Heart to Gladden*, of the Shayk El Nafzawih, which he sometimes said (usually to bait the Grundys) was his *magnum opus*. When the lickerish cast of his labors was criticized he would reply that England, ruling the greatest Mussulman Empire, knew and understood nothing of Oriental psychology. (Though it is hardly to be supposed that he designed *The Scented Garden* as a manual for the Colonial Office.) Isabel regarded it in the nature of a distracting toy—a bright bauble for an ailing child—let him have it. She was overjoyed when he said, "Tomorrow I shall have finished this, and promise you I will never write another book on this subject, and I will take to our biography." Isabel was beginning to pack up their belongings, sorting the vast accumulation of years. There was a feeling of departure in the air.

"Let me recall the last happy day of my life," says Isabel, and goes on to describe in pathetic detail the routine of their lives, that Sunday, October 19, 1890. She went to Communion and morning Mass . . . came back, and kissed her husband as he sat writing. They both wrote letters home; there were visitors for tea; a robin was found drowning in a tank in the garden, and Burton held it inside his coat for hours, warming it back to life. . . . Three days before he died, he told Isabel a bird had been tapping at his window all the morning. . . . "That is a bad omen," he said, but Isabel stoutly contradicted him, reminding him he was in the habit of feeding the birds. "Ah, it was not that window," he said, looking out over the autumn hills. "These last few weeks Richard kept saying to me, 'When the swallows form a dado round the house,

when they are crowding on the window ledges in thousands, preparatory to flight, call me.' He would watch them long and sadly." They
were winging south. . . .

It was remarked that he lingered in his study that evening, putting
all his things in order with special care. At dinner, they discussed de-
voting their retirement to working for General Booth's Salvation Army,
Burton favoring a widespread Malthusian campaign as a partial solution
to the problem of the Submerged Tenth. As usual, he pained Isabel by
his cynical jests about religious observances. Still, they always said
prayers together, now. Round by round, Isabel was winning. At bedtime,
as she knelt beside him, praying, a dog began to howl dismally—that
dreadful howl which the superstitious say denotes death. Both Isabel and
Burton were excessively superstitious, and the uneasy Isabel sent a servant to look for the dog. Burton was settled for the night comfortably. He
asked for a novel "to cool his brain" as he said; *chou-chou,* he called it,
something light, as opposed to the scientific treatises or classics that were
his regular reading. Isabel gave him Robert Buchanan's *Martyrdom of
Madeleine.* At midnight he grew suddenly restive, complaining of gout
in his foot. Isabel sat beside him trying to soothe him. The doctor was
called, but found nothing alarming in Burton's condition. He dozed
uneasily and woke at intervals to speak of their future plans, and where
they would go when they were free. He slept on a truckle bed beneath
a large map of Africa, and an Arab inscription, *All Things Pass.* In the
small hours he said he was stifling; the doctor tried various remedies, but
Burton sank fast. Isabel roused the servants and sent them in all direc-
tions for a priest. At dawn, in the language of his *Arabian Nights,* came
Death, the Destroyer of Delights, the Sunderer of Companies. Clasped
in Isabel's arms and crying, "I am a dead man," Richard Burton died.

But Isabel would not have it so. He was unconscious—dying—but he
still lived! He *must* live until the priest came! His soul *must* be saved!
There would be time for grief later. When at last the priest arrived (he
was a Slav peasant from the mountain village nearby) he refused to administer Extreme Unction: it seemed too late; besides, Burton had never
declared himself a Catholic. "But I besought him not to lose a moment
. . . for the soul was passing away," says Isabel, recalling the anguish

of that moment. Over and over again, with frantic insistence, she maintained it was not too late: that her husband had long been a Catholic, in private, that the pulse still beat. At last the priest allowed himself to be persuaded, as much by Isabel's agony as by the doctor's noncommittal shrug. He gave the Sacraments, *Si vivis,* or *Si es capax.* Isabel, in transports of grief, was triumphant too. Richard was saved! He was absolved! He would enter Paradise—her Paradise (not that of Mohammed), and they would be together once more. She sat beside him all day, watching and praying, and expecting his return to her. "I thought the mouth and left eye moved, but the doctor told me it was imagination. But what was no imagination was that the brain lived after the heart and pulse were gone (Burton's journals, she says, show that he too believed this possible); that on lifting up the eyelids, the eyes were as bright and intelligent as in life, with the brilliancy of a man who saw something unexpected and wonderful and happy; and that light remained in them till next sunset, and I believe the soul went forth with the setting sun, though it had set for me forever."

> *The light of morn has grown to noon,*
> *has paled with eve, and now farewell!*
> *Go, vanish from my life as dies*
> *the tinkling of the camel's bell.*

It is one of Burton's most beautiful lines; it has all the sadness and longing of his exile from the East; for Isabel, it must have echoed all her grief, her longing, now exiled from him, forever.

The next twenty-four hours were a procession of priests, pious watchers, friends, officials and embalmers. The painter, Albert Letchford, made a sketch of Burton on his deathbed, a treasure which never after left Isabel's side. Burton had been greatly loved, greatly esteemed, in Trieste. The Austrian Government offered a *chapelle ardente* where the coffin might rest till Isabel could take it to England for burial. It was a faint, but definite comfort to Isabel when the Bishop of Trieste conceded "all the greatest ceremonies of the Church, and the authorities a gorgeous military funeral such as is only accorded to Royalty—an honor never before accorded to a foreigner." The coffin was covered by a Union Jack; Burton's sword, insignia, and medals, so few, for such a life, were carried on a cushion; there was a second hearse weighed down with floral tributes. "The entire Consular Corps," says Isabel with unction, "for the first time suspended their rule and in full uniform walked on each side of the hearse as pallbearers." She followed, too stunned to notice details, she says: "but they tell me no funeral has been equal to it in the memory of anyone living, not even that of Maria-Theresa, ex-Queen of Spain in 1873." In all there were three different funeral or memorial services. And Isabel was also sustained by knowing that a thousand Masses were sung for the repose of Burton's soul. But there is no mention of any Moslem rituals for "The Father of Mustachios," the Haji Abdullah of Mecca.

The drama of Burton's deathbed was the subject of violent attack from certain anti-Catholic quarters. Most notably, the Stisted family, whose temperate Anglican blood was roused to boiling point. They spoke of it as a sort of spiritual kidnaping. In her *Life of Sir Richard Burton*, Miss Stisted bursts into open hostility, not only against Isabel, so long the Stisteds' anathema, but against the Catholic Church too. This venomous passage rebounds on the family to which Burton belonged, by blood, but with whom he had, by choice, spent very little of his life, and who could not have known much of his true nature. "Rome took formal possession of Richard Burton's corpse," writes Miss Stisted, "and pretended moreover, with insufferable insolence, to take under her protection his soul. From that moment, an inquisitive mob never ceased to disturb the solemn chamber. Other priests went in and out at will, children from a neighboring orphanage sang hymns and giggled alternately." Miss Stisted, now positively intoxicated with the fumes of hatred, goes on to say (although relying entirely on hearsay) that "pious old women recited their rosaries, gloated over the dead, and splashed the bed with holy water; the widow who had regained her composure, directing the innumerable ceremonies."

And as a parting shot: "Burton's funeral . . . was made the excuse for an ecclesiastical triumph of a faith he had always loathed."

No one, not even Isabel, was ever able to say, positively, what Burton's true religion was: one friend described him as a mixture of Agnostic, Theist and Oriental mystic. Another friend, Madame Catherine de Ralli, writing to Cardinal Vaughan, said, "As regards those who claim to have known all about Sir Richard Burton . . . allow me to point out that the exoteric subtleties of his character were only exceeded by the esoteric." Burton himself used to say, "The only real religion in the world is that of Mohammed"; he had for many years made a comparative study of religion, but he always flatly declined to be drawn as to his own. One thing is sure. Isabel, his constant companion for so long, truly believed he had been for many years, in secret, a Catholic. She acted in good faith when she called the priest. She was a profoundly religious woman; would she, at this most terrible moment of her life, have tricked the priest on this most sacred of rites? Or was she, once again, unconsciously turning things to suit her ends? He had to be drawn into her fold, at last, so she convinced herself he had long been a secret convert to Rome. But knowing his curious withdrawn nature where either his love or his faith were concerned, she had never pressed him. Then, there was the paper he had signed, in 1877, which she had written out, a paper asking that if Burton should be on his death-bed, far from her, and unable, perhaps, to speak, but wish to recant his former errors and receive the Sacraments of Penance, he should make a cross on the paper to show his need. And there were those last years at Trieste: Isabel speaks of a mirror in their communicating rooms which used to reflect a corner of his room, where she used to see him praying. . . . But what prayers? To whom did he pray? Christ, or Allah? If his private journals told, they too have vanished in the widow's holocaust. Nothing was left which could part them, in death.

Isabel knew she was dying. It did not matter, now, returning to the overcast skies of England. It would not be long before she followed *him* into the sunrise, she said. But first there was much to do, and only she could do it. First, she must set all his affairs in order, negotiate with the Abbey, or St. Paul's, for his grave; above all, write his life story, something which would forever vindicate his memory and silence all those he had been too proud to answer himself. *The Labours and Wisdom of*

*Sir Richard Burton* was to be the last, loving gesture. She had fought for him throughout her married life; she would go on fighting in her widowhood.

*The woman without her husband is like a bird with one wing* is an Arab proverb. Its truth was borne home to Isabel, day by day, as she battled on. She returned from the splendors of the funeral to the silent shell of her home, the vast accumulation of years had to be packed; there were two hundred and forty crates, when she had reduced things to a minimum. Many possessions were given away; but Isabel could not bear to sell anything—it seemed a betrayal. For the last time, she set about the paying and packing. She would be following soon enough. On the day of Burton's death, she had locked his room from prying eyes. Now she steeled herself to sort and classify all his papers. For two weeks she locked herself in, among his life's work. She had been left sole literary executrix. Burton had always known her views on his erotology, yet he bequeathed her everything "to be overhauled and examined by her only, and to be dealt with entirely at her own discretion, and in the manner she thinks best, having been my sole helper for thirty years." It is curious that Burton did not bequeath *The Scented Garden,* or other such material to the Kama Shastra, or the Asiatic Society—especially in view of the incident related by Dr. Baker, who asked Burton if he realized such a work might easily be burned after his death. Burton turned a ravaged face to the doctor. "Do you really think so? Then I must write to Arbuthnot at once, and tell him that in the event of my death, the manuscript is to be his." He went on to reiterate this was his *magnum opus.* "I have put my whole life and all my life blood into that *Scented Garden;* it is my great hope that I shall live by it. It is the crown of my life." Though it must also be remembered that Isabel, in defending herself against the public outcry when she destroyed the manuscript, quotes an entry in Burton's journal for March 31, 1890. "Began, or rather resumed *Scented Garden,* don't care much about it, but it is a good potboiler."

Whether Isabel knew of the letter to Arbuthnot is not known, but since Burton left her no direct instructions, no one can dispute her right to act as she saw fit. Still, it is significant that Burton should lay such emphasis on this particular study, as the focus of his whole life—his whole life's blood. It was something Isabel never understood; something which came between her complete comprehension and possession of Burton, something she feared, of which she was jealous.

The burning of Burton's papers roused a violent outcry. It has been greatly misinterpreted. Isabel was condemned by large numbers of people who had never appreciated Burton during his lifetime, and were only now venting their annoyance at being balked of what they had hoped would prove salacious tidbits. Yet this act—Isabel's supreme act of battle—was also one of sacrifice, or abnegation in the Oriental tradition —a sort of Suttee, or widow's suicide, for with the flames she also destroyed all material security, the six thousand guineas it would have brought her to end her days in comfort. She had no pension, and Burton had told her this money was to be her jointure—the proceeds to be set aside for her annuity—he had worked on it to ensure she was provided for, in the event of his death. Now she was penniless.

There are two versions of the burning. She is commonly held to have shoveled the manuscripts on the fire in an excess of Victorian prudery. But legend has it that Burton's spirit appeared to her, ordering its destruction, and she herself recounted this to several friends. The apparition, she said, was stern, commanding. "Burn it!" said the revenant, pointing to the manuscript, and vanishing djinn-like, and true to type. After all, it was quite in keeping with Burton's character to issue orders, regardless of the cost to Isabel. Quite in keeping, too, with the tradition of mysterious spirit communications they had shared since the beginning, and she was as convinced of this as all the others. But when she wrote her bombshell letter to the *Morning Post* announcing her action, chiefly to silence the pressure of a greedy public awaiting posthumous Burton pornography, she wisely made no mention of the spirit orders. It was one of her usual outpourings; one marvels at an age when there was sufficient paper to print such letters, and enough leisure to read them, too.

All the same, she went straight to the point. "My husband had been collecting for fourteen years, information on a certain subject. . . . *The Scented Garden* . . . treated of a certain passion. Do not let anyone suppose for a moment that Richard Burton ever wrote a thing from the impure point of view. He dissected a passion as a doctor may dissect a body, showing its source, its origin, its evil and its good." She goes on to say that Burton had told her he anticipated *The Scented Garden* would cause a great outcry in England, and that by comparison, *The Arabian Nights* was a baby tale (Burton had written to a friend, his co-translator of Catullus, describing it in these terms: "It will be a marvelous repertory of Eastern wisdom; how Eunuchs are made, and are married; what they do in marriage; female circumcision, the Fellahs copulating with crocodiles, etc. Mrs. Grundy will howl till she almost bursts and will read every word with an intense enjoyment. . . ."). Not Isabel. "When I locked myself in his rooms," she continues, "I read this (manuscript). No promise had been extracted from me, because the end had been so unforeseen, and I remained for three days in a state of perfect torture as to what I ought to do about it."

It will be recalled that Ruskin faced a rather similar dilemma when he was appointed by the Trustees of the National Gallery to sort and classify the accumulation of work left by Turner. The painter had long been Ruskin's hero. Frank Harris writes that Ruskin, telling him of the incident, said, "It was one of the worst blows of my life. I had always believed that the good and the pure and the beautiful were one, various manifestations of the Divine. Again and again I had associated beauty of color in painting with holiness of life," he said, adding naïvely, "I knew of course that the rule was not invariable. Titian was supposed to have lived a loose life; they even talk about him in connection with his daughter, but it seemed to me like madness, a mere legend, not to be considered." He goes on to say that in 1857 he came upon a portfolio filled with painting after painting of the most shameful sort— inexcusable, inexplicable; ". . . I went to work to find out all about it, and I ascertained that my hero used to leave his house in Chelsea and go down to Wapping on the Friday afternoon, and live there until Monday morning with the sailors' women, painting them in every posture of abandonment. . . . What a life! and what a burden it cast upon me. What was I to do? For weeks I was in doubt, and miserable, though time and again I put myself in Tune with the Highest, till suddenly it flashed on me that perhaps I had been selected as the one man capable of coming, in this matter, to a great decision. I took the hundreds of scrofulous sketches and paintings and burnt them, where they were, burnt all of them. . . . Don't you think I did right? I am proud of it, *proud*," said the old man. Frank Harris thought it the most extraordinary confession he had ever heard—and he had heard some remarkable ones, in his day.

But Isabel, closeted alone with those hateful secrets of Burton's life and interests had no such clear-cut issue. Besides moral, there were financial angles to be considered too. "During that time I received an offer from a man whose name shall be always kept private, of six thousand guineas for it." This gentleman proposed to publish it for private subscribers, at four guineas for the two-volume set. But he had not reckoned with Isabel. "Out of fifteen hundred men, fifteen will probably read it in the spirit of science in which it was written; the other fourteen hundred and eighty-five will read it for filth's sake and pass it to their friends, and the harm done may be incalculable. . . . I sat down on the floor before the fire at dusk to consult my own heart, my own head. My head told me that sin is the only rolling stone that gathers moss; that what a gentleman, a scholar, a man of the world may write when living, he would see very differently to what the poor soul would see standing naked before its God, with its good or evil deeds alone to answer for, and their consequences visible to it for the first moment, rolling on to the end of time. Oh! for a friend on earth to stop and check them! What would he care for the applause of fifteen hundred men now—for the whole world's praise, and God offended? My heart said, 'You can have six thousand guineas; your husband worked for you, kept you in a happy home with honor and respect for thirty years. How are you going to reward him? That your wretched body may be fed and clothed and warmed for a few miserable months or years, will you let that soul *which is part of your soul* be left out in cold and darkness till the end of time, till all those sins which may have been committed on account of reading those writings have been expiated, or passed away, perhaps forever? Why, it would be just parallel with the original thirty pieces of silver!'" Thus Isabel, once again innocently having her cake and eating it— justifying her religious convictions with her violent determination to whitewash, or remove all traces of those aspects of Burton's nature which his detractors always fastened on, and which only her loyalty had at last stilled. "I fetched the manuscript and laid it on the ground before me, two large volumes. . . . Still my thoughts were, Was it sacrilege? It was his *magnum opus,* his last work that he was so proud of, that was to have been finished on that awful morrow— that never came. Will he rise up to curse or bless me? The thought will haunt me till death. . . . Sorrowfully, reverently, and in fear and trembling I burnt sheet after sheet, until the whole of the volumes were consumed."

What she did not say was that at the same time, and not commanded by the spirit Burton, she burned almost all of his journals, diaries and notes—an irreparable loss. The value of his *Scented Garden* was said to lie, like *The Thousand Nights and a Night,* more in the notes than in the text. The accumulated data were the fruits of a lifetime's ad-venture and study. "Burton's researches," writes Mr. W. H. Wilkins, "had this peculiarity, that whereas most of the writers . . . speak from hearsay, Burton's information was obtained at first hand. . . . Thus it came about he was misunderstood . . . a cloud of prejudices enveloped him." But Burton the Arab could not—indeed did not— hope to be understood by the West. He may have been indifferent or fatalistic—Isabel was not. It was these hidden, mysterious aspects of his life in the East of which she was always jealous. She had always stood beside him, her presence belying the insinuations—now in death, she saw her chance. His name should live on, untarnished. She would protect the legend from the man. And so the great and baffling char-acter of Richard Burton vanished forever.

It was probably with the destruction of his diaries, rather than his *Scented Garden* in mind, that Ouida wrote: "I never spoke or wrote to her after that irreparable act." Ouida, as all those who knew something of the nature of Burton's journals, spoke of "his genius, his force, his wonderful originality. His masterful powers," she said, "were tied up like great dogs in their kennels, and became savage as the dogs become." These journals—the key to his cryptic personality—were the record of his outer life and inner thoughts for forty-five years: they reached back to his earliest days in India, the fountainhead of all his Orientalism. There were two sets: a private journal, and another which recorded day-to-day events. The first has vanished. Most likely this told the complete truth, not only regarding his life in the East, but his marriage to the West, too. Perhaps he put in this journal all that remained for so long veiled, but perceptible, in those untamed eyes that stared out from the broken frame, following not only his enemies, but his wife, too. The journals were perhaps his final act of assertion, of escape to the freedom which he preserved mockingly, within. What the man no longer had the strength to accomplish, the writer achieved. It is not likely that he either wished, or envisaged the journals published. But it is possible that knowing Isabel, as literary executor, would go over every word he left, he deliberately, diabolically planned his revenge, a challenge, flung from the grave. The panther-cruelty flared up in one last terrible snarl. He meant her to know he had remained unconquered. But at the end, as in the beginning, he had not reckoned with Isabel. She saw her way to save his soul in heaven, his reputation, the repute of their marriage, on earth. The flames destroyed good and bad, legend and truth, West and East. He was safe. He was hers. She had reconquered her empire.

\*     \*     \*

She returned to London, where her sisters awaited her. Burton's coffin was sent by sea. She traveled up to Liverpool to meet the boat, although ill, and forgot herself, the spectators, everything, when she saw the coffin again, rushing to it, kissing it with heart-rending sobs. Meanwhile, Westminster Abbey had been unaccountably offhand. St. Paul's, too, had not proposed a place for "the greatest explorer England had ever neglected." Bridling, she dismissed a tomb in the Abbey as altogether unworthy, since Burton would have been listed along with Speke, Livingstone, etc.—"*his* name in a common list of theirs." She would do better. Burton had always lived apart—his tomb should be apart too. Long ago, they had chosen a plot of land together at Mortlake. Selecting cemetery plots was a favorite Victorian pastime; contemporary letters and memoirs are full of such melancholy outings, couples selecting and debating the respective merits of this tomb or that, in the romantic yet matter-of-fact manner associated today with the engaged couple's purchase of a double bed. Isabel decided that Burton's mausoleum—and later hers—should be built at the Mortlake Catholic Cemetery, where so many of her family were buried. Burton had always hated the dark, hated drawn curtains shutting out the light. He had once confided to her that he did not wish to be cremated—"I don't want to burn before my time" (levity, even at such moments, thought Isabel sadly) "but would like to lie in an Arab tent." She did not forget. At this time being without means (the one hundred and fifty pounds a year pension which was later granted her through the interests of friends had not yet materialized), she was obliged to canvass for public subscriptions to build the tomb. Fortunately loyal friends rallied round.

As a last exotic gesture she devised a setting worthy of his romantic personality. Alas! it also had that faint touch of the circus which sometimes marked Isabel's excursions into the Orient. Great blocks of Carrara marble were dumped and stone masons chiseled away feverishly. Presently an astonished public saw Islam rising from a suburban burial ground. Isabel had erected an Arab tent, fringed and gilded, surmounted by a golden nine-point star. Across the door was strung a rope of camel bells which sounded nostalgically in the little gusts of chilly wind which ruffled through the shrubberies of the "shabby sectarian cemetery" as the outraged Miss Stisted describes it. A space was left for Isabel, and she could not conceal her impatience to be at rest, with him, "in the most beautiful, the most undeathlike resting place in the wide world . . . an Eastern tent *above* ground . . . he has love, tears, prayers and companionship even in the grave," she adds, happy to think she had contrived it that Burton was not to be alone, even now.

The general sensation which the Arab mausoleum aroused delighted her. Richard was in the limelight once more. It was quite a distraction from all the abusive attacks, anonymous letters and general unpleasantness with which she had been surrounded since her statement on the burning of *The Scented Garden*. Miss Stisted was particularly savage. She spoke loudly of Isabel's vandalism. Her uncle's book, she said, could very well have been published with a few minor excisions. (Fellahs copulating with crocodiles . . . the Kama Shastras hundred variations of the kiss?) However, it was unlikely that Miss Stisted knew the precise nature of the book, in spite of a certain familiarity with Burton's tendencies. Its title was so pretty; . . . But Isabel had the last word. "It makes me sick to hear all this anxiety of the Press and the Literary world lest they should miss a word he ever wrote. When he came back in 1882 after being sent to look for Palmer he had a good deal of information to give, and he could not get a magazine or paper to take his most valuable article till it was quite stale. We used to boil over with rage when his books or articles were rejected. . . . and now, because a few chapters which were of no particular value to the world have been burnt, the whole country's literary minds are full of bitter plaint because anything has perished which came from the translator of the *Arabian Nights*."

She settled into lodgings in Baker Street, and once more Cross and Crescent strove for place in her drawing room. Burton's books and papers occupied the loft, where she liked to spend whole days, among his things. "Do not be so hard and prosaic as to suppose that our dead cannot, in rare instances, come back and tell us how it is with them," she said. Asked if she believed in communion with the dead she was positive: "I talk with my darling nearly every day," she said.

When the strain and labor of bringing out the Memorial Edition of Burton's works and her monumental *Life of Sir Richard Burton* were at last completed, she felt she could die in peace. Her earthly task was done. It had been a race against time; sometimes too weak, in too much pain to work for days on end. But gradually, the great formless mass of inaccuracies, biased and oddly selected material, was all gathered together. She claimed that Burton's spirit aided her. If so, it seems the spirits saw things differently from the man. With all his journals at her disposal, nothing vital emerges: there are pathetic little entries eloquent of Isabel's, not Richard's, sense of values. "Today my wife was sent for to the Austrian-Hungarian Embassy to receive from Count Lutzow a very beautiful portrait of the Empress of Austria in approval of her life and works. This has made me very proud, and her very happy. . . ." Is that all he had to note; all she could select? But in her passionate determination to present only the Burton *she* chose to remember, the secret Catholic, the perfect husband, she dismissed all other aspects, influences or recollections. Posterity should have nothing else to go upon. Alas! her zeal defeated its own ends. If we did not have Burton's own books, and the memoirs of his contemporaries, to recapture his essence, he would have faded away long ago, a man killed by kindness. Thus we see her loving greed, her destruction of the journals, and all her hopes of re-creating Burton of Arabia according to her own standards failed. To possess, she destroyed: but she could not re-create.

After her death, what few of his papers she had left were burned, together with many of her own, by her only surviving sister. The final siftings, the last few souvenirs found their way to the Public Library in Kensington High Street where, together with the bulk of Burton's library, they lie hidden away, forgotten, unknown to the scuttling throngs of shoppers outside. Isabel's books and some personal relics of their life found sanctuary in the Camberwell Public Library. His books, and her things—many miles of gritty London waste now separate all that remains of their life together, their homes and travels, the two hundred and forty crates, and the magpie trunk.

Although a dying woman, with a resident nurse in attendance, Isabel never became a crêpey widow. She still went about London, and stayed at various country houses. Much of her time was spent in a little cottage she rented at Mortlake, near the mausoleum. She had a tent put up in the garden, where she picnicked during the day. (Unkind tongues said she used to dispense tea in the tomb, but this was pure malice.) Her disease had crept slowly on; but now she began to suffer greatly; even so, she did not allow herself to give way. Lady Paget recalls her as being very coquettish in a pink dressing gown and frilled widow's cap. Conversation always turned, at once, on Richard. "He had a God, and a continuation, and said he would wait for me; he is only gone on a long journey, and presently I shall join him; we shall take up where we left off, and we shall be very much happier even than we have been here."

When she was asked to supervise the waxwork tableaux of Burton, at Madame Tussaud's waxworks, she was enchanted. The Abbey's slight was forgotten. She wrote to a friend: "They have now put Richard in the Meccan dress he wore in the desert. They have given him a large space with sand, water, palms and three camels and a domed skylight painted yellow, throws a lurid light on the scene. It is quite lifelike. I gave them the real clothes and the real weapons and dressed him myself." In another letter she said, "I am not quite content with the pose. The figure looks all right when it stands properly, but I have always had trouble with Tussaud about a certain stoop which he declares is artistic and which I say was not natural to him." She was hawk-eyed to the end. Neither a stoop nor a dubious line might be left to shadow Burton's memory. She was in great pain now, and very weak. "I think it will be so lovely when it is all over: I hope so" she wrote to Lady Paget. Her certain faith sustained her in death as in life. She closed her book on Burton with these words: "Reader! I have paid, I have packed and I have suffered. I am waiting to join his Caravan. I am waiting for a welcome sound—the tinkling of his camel-bell."

\* \* \*

Her passionate life ended, appropriately, on Passion Sunday, March 21, 1896. She was buried beside her "earthly God and King," Burton of Arabia, in the Arab tent at Mortlake. On a marble plaque is inscribed Justin Huntly McCarthy's sonnet to Burton. . . .

> *O last and noblest of the Errant Knights*
> *The English soldier and the Arab Sheik,*
> *O Singer of the East. . . .*

Beside it, the simple words "Isabel, his wife." No one goes to the tomb now. I found the dank little plot jumbled with weeds and graves. A depressing row of dun-brick cottages seemed to glare over the wall censoriously at the Arab tent, but there is now no trace left of that glowing and glorious East he had embodied and that Isabel had loved and striven to re-create round them at the end. English fogs have darkened the marble and rusted the gilded stars: the camel-bells are silent. The door caved in a year or two ago, I was told, and since no one could be found to replace it, it was thought best to wall up the opening against possible desecration. A tired-looking woman was cutting the rank grass nearby. I asked her if she remembered the tomb when it was open. A sudden warmth and interest was kindled: she smiled, and it was as if she was lit by a shaft of Eastern sun. "Yes, ever so well," she replied. "I often used to go in, it was so pretty inside. Very Oriental you know, all colored, with little lanterns, and jeweled golden coffins, and the lights went on when you opened the door, and then little bells rang . . . it was lovely." I looked across the lowering wastes at the gray sealed tomb. "He was a strange man," I said. "Was he?" she asked. "Yes, he must have been. It was so wonderful in there, so bright . . . sort of *different*." It was an epitaph they would both have liked I think.

It began to rain. The woman put on her plastic "mac" resignedly. I left by the little cinder path beside the track where the Southern Railway rattles past the windows of the hideous semi-detached cottage Isabel had taken to be near her "earthly God and King" until she could join him in his Arab tent. Neglected in life and death, they are still together . . . "never far apart, one soul in two bodies." Hagar's mysterious whispers echo down the years. It had all come true. Richard and the East . . . the lodestar East.

# ·II·

# THE HONORABLE
# JANE DIGBY
# EL MEZRAB

*Matrimonial Theme
and Variations*

THERE ARE TWO SORTS of romantics: those who love, and those who love the adventure of loving. The latter are less costive, more mobile, more able to blow where the wind lists. Jane Digby, my subject, who was successively Lady Ellenborough, Baroness Venningen, Countess Theotoky and the wife of the Sheik Abdul Medjuel El Mezrab, to name only her legal attachments, was of the latter kind. Romance alone was not enough, or not for long, at any rate. She craved adventure too; and was well equipped by nature to get life on her own terms.

She was a great romantic, but she was also an adventurer, in the precise sense of the word—one who has adventures, as opposed to an adventuress, since this word has come to have purely sexual implications—one who has lovers. Thus Harriette Wilson, the celebrated nineteenth-century courtesan, might be described as an adventuress, and most certainly not a romantic, while a contemporary, Lady Bessborough was the archetype of all romantics, loving young Granville Leveson-Gower to distraction, hanging on his words, drinking in the beauty of his complacent blue eyes. . . . ("Eyes where I have looked my life away" was found in her handwriting across his portrait, long after he had married her niece, and she had stood back, wilted, and died.) For her, loving Granville had been the supreme adventure.

In the case of Jane Digby it was less simple. Her love affairs were fabulous, and read, as she remarked in her last days (for it is impossible to use the term "old age" for such a woman), "like a naughty *Almanach de Gotha*"; an *Almanach* moreover which had covered a span of more than fifty pulsating years, and several unhappy endings. Yet she always contrived to start all over again with the same fervent yet naïve emotions. "Tomorrow to fresh Woods and Pastures new" might have been her motto.

Even such a charmer as she often came to grief and found herself deserted, weeping among the ruins. But she never spent long in that state: her ardent temperament, her perfect health, sought life—the adventure of loving, as much as love itself, and she was off again, plunging recklessly, deliciously, with the House of Lords thundering over her adultery; or her Bavarian husband dueling with her Greek suitor; or the two Queens who were her rivals sulking over the two kings, father and son, who were her lovers. . . . Wherever she was, in Almack's or an Albanian brigand's lair, it always added up to scandal. *"Torrents of scandal afloat"* wrote a contemporary, eyeing her first giddy spin. And on those torrents she whirled along until at last, with a positive tidal wave of scandal, she was swept into the black Bedouin tents of the Mezrabi, humbly washing the feet of her Arab lord and master. From here she was often to gallop out into the Syrian desert at the head of her husband's horsemen, leading them to one of those intertribal battles, all flourish and fantasia, which are the traditional pattern of Arab life. Adventurous loving was the pattern of her life, and this she found, in its fullest sense, among the Arabs.

She was an Amazon. Her whole life was spent riding at breakneck speed along the wilder shores of love. For her, each new affair was an encampment set up along the way; sometimes a palace, sometimes a tent, but always the supreme refuge. She was not a nymphomaniac, however, for at each camp she seems to have believed the journey over. As it happened, it took her thirty-five years to reach her true destination, a fact she sometimes deplored as much as her detractors. After each heartbreak there was a new dash, a new hope, and then, a new camp pitched hastily along the way. Too hastily, perhaps. But then, as some Mediterranean philosopher has said, life is three-quarters love, and Jane Digby loved life. Her error was probably that she believed she could force the hand of destiny, could find her fate by looking for it. So, in retrospect, we see this Amazonian creature galloping breathlessly from camp to camp, ever onwards towards a goal she *had* to reach, but which she could not reach alone.

The love story, so multiheroed, which is the life story of the Honorable Jane Digby El Mezrab begins in Norfolk, and ends in Damascus. She was born in 1807, and spent most of her childhood in a pastoral English landscape. It was the serene, golden sunset of eighteenth-century England, where Rowlandson's rosy yokels junketed on village greens, Moreland's equally rosy cattle drowsed in cozy styes, and distant thunders of faraway wars were drowned by the cawing of rooks in the elms. Only whispered tales of press-gang desperadoes, along with old Nanny's legends of Bogey Bonaparte, disturbed the sunset glow in which the country basked. The brisk yet dismal morning of the industrial revolution had not dawned. There were still the last rays of that splendid eighteenth-century sun which had seen St. Paul's rise from its ashes, Clive conquer India, Fielding write *Tom Jones*, and the great historic houses live their last days of splendor.

It was such a world that the little Jane Digby saw around her at Holkham Hall, the imposing home of her maternal grandfather, the first Earl of Leicester of Holkham. Prior to his ennoblement he had been known as Coke of Norfolk, and was the most powerful personality, and certainly the greatest landowner and agriculturalist of the county. Although sheep shearing, harvesting, Maypole frolics and other seasonal rustic delights were the background of Jane Digby's childhood, their homespun was interwoven with a scarlet thread of exoticism. Byronism was sweeping England, and Europe too. Don Juan's graceful verses were on every lip. The romantic East suddenly came into focus. Until then, to the English, it had been represented, for the most part, as remote and uncomfortable, smacking disagreeably of commerce and the East India Company's machinations. Now, a nearer East was sensed, the East of odalisques and scented fountains. There were Delacroix's sultry Algerian beauties, and *The Destruction of Sennacherib* . . .

> *The Assyrian came down like the wolf on the fold,*
> *And his cohorts were gleaming in purple and gold.*

Jane was a child of the Regency. Her taste was forming during this moment of such wildly stylized Oriental refulgency. In the great houses, romantic curiosities were the rage: Turkish slippers stolen from a seraglio, Genghis Khan's dagger. . . . The great English estates and gardens suddenly blossomed with a new crop of exotic little pavilions; *Chinoiserie* was elbowed aside by Moorish kiosks, and "temples in the Hindoo or Gentoo style." At Sezincote, in Gloucestershire, Sir Charles Cockerell imposed his Hindoo fancies on Cotswold stone, and the resultant grandeur plunged the landed gentry into frenzies of envy and emulation. The Prince Regent could not rest until he was installed in the Pavilion. Its fabulous onion-domes dominated the scene, shouting down the black pebble-fronted cottages which were typical of the little Sussex watering place. Later it was said it looked as if St. Pauls had gone down to Brighton and had pups.

But such an independent personality as Jane Digby could never be content with secondhand versions of the East, even when filtered through the architectural genius of Humphrey Repton. Nor was she ever one to sit sofa-bound, sighing over Moore's *Oriental Melodies,* or steel engravings of a desert sunrise. Adventurous travel was in the tradition of her family. Her father, Admiral Digby, was the typical buccaneering English seadog who struck terror into his enemies. When Jane was twenty, her cousin Henry Anson, together with John Fox-Strangways, set off for Mecca. They planned to pass from tourism in the Holy Land, to Arab disguise, and so, approach the Ka'abah. They do not seem to have been very well equipped for this desperate venture. How much Arabic they spoke is not known; but the first elementary precaution of removing their shoes in an Aleppo mosque was overlooked. They were discovered, and almost torn to pieces by an outraged mob. They languished in prison and awful tales reached London that they had been discovered in a harem, mutilated, poisoned, and so on: the embroideries were infinite. When at last they were released, Henry Anson was dying. He had caught the plague, and died a few days later, being buried in Aleppo, while his companion returned a pallid wreck.

In E. M. Oddie's delightful book on Lady Ellenborough, it is held that she was much influenced by a distant kinsman, Sir Kenelm Digby, the seventeenth-century poet and adventurer who sailed to Scanderoon, and whose associations with Syria had, perhaps unconsciously, or by a mysterious process of transference, or reinvestment of personality, come to inspire Jane with a similar hunger for the East. This reincarnationary theory is even held to show in the likeness between Jane, in the Steiler portrait, and one of Sir Kenelm Digby by Vandyke. This seems, to the present writer, a purely personal, and rather far-fetched supposition. As well say that she was influenced by the exotic aspects of the family arms. But perhaps she was. The crest of the Digby family is markedly Oriental by comparison to the general run of heraldic or mythological beasts, and must have intrigued any child. *An ostrich holding in the beak a horseshoe, all ppr. Supporters: two monkeys ppr. environed about the middle and lined or.* Monkeys and ostriches and emblems of good fortune, or travel, are rich material round which to weave stories of adventure in beckoning faraway lands. We imagine the little girl seated in her stiff-backed nursery chair, her round eyes tracing the crest engraved on her silver porringer. "Look Nanny! a monkey!" "Monkey! I'll give you monkeys! Eat up your supper this minute! . . ." The classic nursery exchange. An ostrich recurs again in her family heraldry; this time, curiously enough, in the arms of her first husband, Lord Ellenborough. But here, in keeping with the gentleman, it is a rather more pompous bird: *Gorged, with ducal coronets.* And there are no engaging apes, belted or otherwise, and no emblems of luck or travel either. Apart from ancestors or heraldry, however, her age, the Byronic age, must have colored her outlook and inclined her towards the exotic. This inclination being combined with her adventurous and vagrant temperament, brought her inevitably to the East. True it took her half her life to get there, and by the most circuitous routes. But once she reached it —the romantic revelation of her youth—she remained constant. The part of her story which belongs, properly, to this book begins in Greece, when she was over forty; it was from there, and because of her life there, that she took the first step into the desert. But first, her deviations en route.

Her childhood was uneventful, surrounded by easy wealth. It was the typical aristocratic upbringing of her age and station, embedded in layers of nurses, domestics and governesses, the most notable being "Steely," her lifelong friend Miss Margaret Steele, who tried with signal lack of success to fit her mercurial and melting charge into a more straight-laced mold. Her mother, Lady Andover, had been left a widow young, and married Admiral Digby *en seconde noces*; but she had clung with unabashed snobbery to her former title. She and her second husband seem to have been both ambitious and indifferent regarding their daughter's future. From birth she was a beauty, surrounded by admiration. Such a natural dowry must be capitalized, they decided. Before she was seventeen, they had married her off to Lord Ellenborough, a blasé, prematurely middle-aged and cynical man of the world. Harriette Wilson describes him in his youth, when already he seems to have earned the sharp side of her tongue. "Young Law, Lord Ellenborough's son, was a very smart, fine young gentleman; and his impatience of temper passed, I dare say, occasionally, for quickness. His wig was never on straight on his head. I rather fancy he liked to show his own good head of hair under it." She goes on to describe a scene in court, where "young Law" was cross-examining a flurried old country woman, and seems to have behaved with detestable bombast.

The marriage was a conspicuous failure, and conjures visions of the yawning boredom, the careless wealth and cynicism of Hogarth's "Marriage à la Mode."

Almost at once the husband went his own way, diverting himself with stronger meat, perhaps—or perhaps with none. He was said to have been a model husband to his first wife—he was also said to be profligate—to be impotent, to be anything, in fact, that gossip chose. Whatever he was, or was not, he cannot have been a wise choice for anyone of Jane's nature and youth. He was a most unpopular peer, exactly double her age, and a widower. But he was a brilliant catch, and so Jane was not consulted.

Before the honeymoon was over his young wife was left to her own devices. In Regency London, she was not long finding diversions.

There was a certain amount of tattle, naturally, but the general opinion was that if Lord Ellenborough chose to neglect his lovely young wife, who was then known as "Aurora," he had only himself to blame. It is possible that for a while Jane accepted the situation as normal, hoping, even, that her husband would return to her, and remembering Steely's teachings on self-restraint and decorum. But in 1827 she met Frederick Madden, a personable young man of twenty-seven who worked at the British Museum and was invited to Holkham Hall to catalogue the library. He kept a diary, which he bequeathed to the Bodleian, where it lay until 1920, and with it the secret of Jane's first love affair. In the spring of 1827, when Mr. Madden was deep in seas of calf-bound classics at Holkham library, young Lady Ellenborough arrived to visit her grandfather. Here is our first glimpse of her, through Frederick Madden's dazzled eyes. "She is not yet twenty, and one of the most lovely women I ever saw, quite fair, blue eyes that would move a saint and lips that would tempt one to forswear Heaven to touch them." Young Mr. Madden never set up to be a saint. Quite soon he was madly in love. There was a typical country-house timetable of walks and talks in the garden, card games, family prayers, the exchange of drawings for each other's albums, and music, Lady Ellenborough singing the most inflammatory songs. But one never-to-be-forgotten night "Lady E. lingered behind the rest of the party, and at midnight I escorted her to her room. . . . Fool that I was! I will not add what passed. . . . Gracious God! was there ever such fortune. . . ."

However, Steely's teachings still counted; Jane appeared to be overcome with remorse. She rounded on her lover, eluded him, and wasted several of their few remaining evenings together in moral scruples. Throughout her long life, her frailties and reckless passions were always weighing on her conscience. According to her journals, she was constantly reproving herself, setting herself a new and elevated standard, and then, falling from this state of grace, and finding the falling so agreeable, that it was all to do again. Self-censure, shame, and humble prayers for improvement, until the next emotional upheaval. In this instance, there was one last fond *rapprochement* in a damp grotto in the grounds, and the rest is silence. She returned to London, to the giddy world of Almack's and Mayfair. Madden tried to follow her, but Almack's and the British Museum are not contiguous. They never met again. Jane began to be seen everywhere with her cousin Colonel George Anson, and there was a lot of well-founded gossip. In February, 1828, she was delivered of the son and heir Lord Ellenborough desired, and accepted as his own. About this time he was appointed Lord Privy Seal in the Duke of Wellington's Ministry, and from now on he paid no further attention to his wife, whether in public or private, until the divorce proceedings which titillated all England.

Now for the first time since her marriage, Jane began to feel herself emancipated from the last echoes of Steely and Mama. She was a woman of the world—the adult world—at last. Now she felt equal to withstanding the chilly climate of her husband's house. The baby was christened Arthur, after the Iron Duke, and Jane seems to have been, with him, as with all her other children save one, an uninterested parent.

When she met the dashing Austrian Prince Felix Schwarzenberg, recently appointed to London as Secretary of Embassy, and now serving Prince Esterhazy, she was ripe for the *coup de foudre* which followed. Neither of them seems to have taken the least trouble to conceal their affair. There were the most imprudent afternoons behind scarcely drawn blinds at his house in Harley Street while Jane's green phaeton and bored groom waited below. There was a visit to the Norfolk Hotel at Brighton, where a Peeping Tom waiter witnessed the lovers' transports. Jane's relatives were beside themselves, though her husband remained resolutely blind. All kinds of press lampoons and scurrilous jests were circulated, for it was just the sort of situation the age enjoyed most. London society spoke of nothing else. The wife of the Lord Privy Seal and an Austrian Prince! Almack's and Boodle's buzzed. Busybody Creevy pursed his lips, and deplored the lovers' lack of *tenue*: in March, 1829, he writes: "Lady Ellenborough and the Pole, or Russian or Austrian,—whichever he is. . . . Anything so impudent as she, or so barefaced as the whole thing I never beheld."

Although he opined, earlier, that Lord Ellenborough was a damned fellow, he could not countenance quite such flagrant delights. No; it would not do.

Although the age was inured to the sort of scandals which rocked Carlton House, this seems to have taken precedence. Lord Ellenborough was said to be consoling himself with a pastry cook's daughter, or with the very lady whose house had been a *maison de rendezvous* for the guilty lovers. . . . He was challenging the Prince to a duel. He had blown out his brains. He was petitioning for a divorce. . . . Indirectly, the Prince passed into the English language as "Cad," which in view of his subsequent behavior seems appropriate. The nickname derived from a horse called Cadland which had just won the Derby, beating the favorite, named The Colonel. Then, said the Almack wits, let us call Schwarzenberg Cadland, since he beats the Colonel (Anson) to it for Lady E's favors!

Presently, and in his own time (a factor which was to tell against him in the legal proceedings), Lord Ellenborough did petition for divorce. But in the meantime the Prince had left England. Whether he had, as is probable, acted himself, or whether the Austrian Foreign Office had acted for him, he was suddenly posted to Paris. It was not far enough. Had they reckoned with Lady Ellenborough's inflammable nature, China would not have been too far.

Jane Digby was of that passionate and impulsive race of women who are found in all ages and countries. She was never a woman of causes; she did not canalize her emotions into politics or public works, but concentrated them entirely on romantic relationships; in a later age, and denied her beauty, or given a stronger sense of civic duty, she might have been a Communard, dying on the barricades, a suffragette, or one of those heroic and devoted women such as the Princess Marie Wolkonsky, who followed her husband, the Dekabrist, into his terrible exile in the Siberian mines.

As it was, the whole force of her nature was set on the Byronic lodestar, Love, at that moment embodied in the Prince Schwarzenberg. Useless to speak to her of duty, the conventions, her husband, or her baby son. Her parents appear to have been even more shortsighted than the Austrian Foreign Office. They descended on the Ellenborough home in outraged majesty and removed their erring daughter to the country. No matter that she was already several months gone with child by her paramour. They treated her like a naughty schoolgirl. She was banished to Ilfracombe, to be guarded by Steely, who though now duenna rather than governess, doubtless could not resist the temptation to moralize. It was unwise. And now this beautiful bored young thing, the toast and scandal of Almack's, but showing a most unmistakable *embonpoint*, was to be seen issuing forth from Steely's cottage for the daily walk. Each afternoon the incongruous pair set out briskly marching along the muddy high-hedged lanes of north Devon, where the sea mists steal inland, blanketing the lush pastures in a milky haze, and dripped softly from the overhanging boughs. "Where every prospect pleases, and only *man* is vile. . . ." No doubt Steely sought to turn her ex-pupil's thoughts to higher things. But it was a losing battle. The days stretched ahead, infinitely tedious. Embroidery in the mornings, walks in the afternoon, and at night, with the curtains drawn, the candles lit, and the silence closing in, no amount of elevating literature, bezique, or the pressing of ferns in albums could stifle memories of the Prince. Like a glittering harlequin figure of love and freedom, he seemed to flash across the low-ceilinged room in a trail of sparks. Steely was up against hopeless odds. Overnight, leaving behind her the tea cups, the albums, and poor Steely, Jane bolted. She went straight to Paris to find her love; and so the first step Eastward was made.

*       *       *

Her flight to Paris was not so much to avoid the scandals at home, for she had proved herself indifferent to them, but rather the gesture of a woman blindly in love. Alas! this was another fatal move. She found the Prince's ardor noticeably cooled. He was not of the same stuff as his mistress. He was neither naïve nor truly passionate. For him the world was not well lost for love. He did not reckon on a divorce. His Catholic family would never countenance such a thing. It was all very awkward. It reopened the scandal in a new setting and it was playing havoc with his career. It was most tactless of Jane. True, she was the greatest beauty of her day, and she had given up everything for him, fortune, good name, friends, all. . . . Most gratifying, still . . . He had recovered from the parting pangs, and now wanted no more. It was a painful situation for both of them. However, there were certain set standards, even in such situations, and these held them together for a while, proving more effective than Jane's overflowing love. "Poor Lady Ellenborough is just going to be confined," wrote Lady Greville from Paris. "Schwarzenberg going about flirting." The birth of a daughter did little to unite them. Nor, a year later, did the birth of a second daughter do any more. Their liaison wore itself out: and neither were, *au fond*, domesticated. Jane found herself alone just at the moment when her husband opened his petition for divorce before the House of Lords.

In passing, it should be recalled that at this time, in England, divorce was an exceedingly costly affair, demanding large outlays of both time and money. Few could permit themselves such a luxury. First, a Private Act of Parliament had to be obtained; then, a suit in the Ecclesiastical Courts, which was, in fact, no more than a judicial separation. Next, the petitioner must bring a case for damages from his wife's paramour. (Injured wives did not sue—they merely suffered their wrongs.) If the damages were granted by the Common Courts, the plaintiff could then proceed to the next stage. Now he must apply to the House of Lords for an Absolute Decree, with permission to remarry. If, after sifting all the evidence, the Lords were indulgent, they sent the case back to the Commons, to be reconsidered. If the Commons, too, concurred, the Decree finally required Royal Assent. After which, it is not surprising to learn that the number of divorces averaged two a year. Matters continued thus until 1856, when a Special Court for Divorce and Matrimonial Causes was established in the teeth of violent opposition from both the Church and Mr. Gladstone, who thundered his denunciations.

Jane made no defense, and does not seem to have been very much interested in the proceedings. Probably she was too stunned and disillusioned by the final break with Schwarzenberg. Her first child, Arthur Law, had died a few months earlier. There was now no heir to the Ellenborough estates. Even if she had wished for a reconciliation with her husband (and nothing is too wild for her unsophisticated mind), there was nothing to bring them together again. And Lord Ellenborough must have known it would be all to do again, soon, and late. In his cold legal way he probably assessed her shrewdly, and thought himself well out of it.

Meanwhile, the Ellenborough Divorce Petition was meeting with the most unexpected checks. In spite of the flagrant way he had been cuckolded (and by a foreigner too! said the masses. Still, it *was* a foreigner, said the classes, for they admired the influx of European aristocracy to the point of idolatry), the noble Lord obtained curiously little sympathy from either the classes or the masses. No one attempted to whitewash his wife's conduct; there were a series of salacious disclosures as ostlers, chambermaids and even her ex-governess were cross-examined. But, the Lords maintained, was there not something fishy . . . ? It smacked of collusion. Why did Lord Ellenborough demand a divorce from a wife whom he had not valued enough to treat as a wife? Did the noble Lord really attach so much value to his wife's chastity? Then why had he left her, a beautiful eighteen-year-old, to sleep night after night alone, and to go about London society with any escort but himself. Why was there no defense, too? Lord Radnor, waxing eloquent, attacked Lord Ellenborough's marital default by quoting St. Matthew. "He that putteth away his wife for any cause other than adultery causeth her to commit adultery."

No, the House of Lords was not satisfied. They spoke of the wife as victimized (showing a Regency width of vision which shrank considerably after the accession of Queen Victoria) and even said Lord Ellenborough had left her free "to prostitute herself in the most indecent manner by his *deliberate* neglect and indifference." The newspapers gloated. Prince Schwarzenberg had been seen lacing the Lady Ellenborough's stays! Miss Steele, the governess, admitted warning her ex-charge, who had, alas! laughed in her face. Quite forgetting her station, Miss Steele went so far as to accuse the whole aristocracy of being dissolute, a pernicious influence! The scandal had no equal until twenty years later the murder of the Duchesse de Praslin, probably by the Duke, menaced the French aristocracy of Louis Philippe's tottering court. Both the Lords and the Commons luxuriated in every detail of the evidence—again and again they re-examined pot-boys and housemaids, sifting the below-stairs evidence with gusto. The second reading of the Bill, on March 9, 1830 was sensational. We can imagine the scene—the solemn panoply of the law; the long-faced, whey-faced or empurpled countenances of the ranks of noblemen, bishops, and country M.P.'s, all sitting in judgment on "Aurora, the Light of Day."

Lady Ellenborough was described as "a lively woman who felt the enchantment of fashionable society." There were minute accounts of the fatal rendezvous at Brighton, where the porter at the Norfolk Hotel described the arrival of a foreign gentleman whose luggage consisted of a carpetbag and a cloak. "Why foreign?" asked counsel. "Because he wore moustachios," was the reply. The foreigner sent his card up to Lady Ellenborough, who invited him to a dish of tea, forthwith.

"And . . . ?" asked the Commons, anxious to be told, once again, how he was still there for breakfast. (Sensation.) Robert, the night porter, admitted that having the good name of his hotel at heart, he peeped through the keyhole. Unhappily the key was turned in the lock, and he could see nothing. But he heard something . . .

"What, pray?" asked counsel.

"Kissing," was the reply, producing a further excitement in court.

Still the Commons were not satisfied. They *must* know more; and were now furnished with details of how Jane and her Prince had left a rout at Wimbledon separately, but had both stopped on Putney Heath, where Jane had dismissed her equipage, and continued in that of the Prince. The Commons took the case as a battleground for discussing the license of a neglected wife. "Was she to sit at home, pining?" asked Mr. Hume, the Member of Parliament for Aberdeen, a most sententious bore. "Would anybody," he asked, "credit that a lady dressed to go to a dance could be guilty of anything improper?"

Here he was interrupted by an outburst of laughter—the loud, jolly laughter of Regency England, I fancy, overriding all the cant. But

Mr. Hume, as simple as sanctimonious, again tried to impede the passing of the Bill. Even at its third reading he was hinting collusion, and much enjoyed himself censuring the profligate aristocracy in the name of his granite electorate. Everyone agreed, however, that it seemed like deliberate intent on the part of Lord Ellenborough to remove on his own terms a wife who did not suit him. The two families, Digby and Ellenborough, wilted under the publicity as the case dragged on. This was the West, with all its solemn pomp, its prudery and hypocrisy.

At last, however, the divorce was granted, although a rumor persisted that Prince Schwarzenberg had been secretly bled of twenty-five thousand pounds by Lord Ellenborough, in order that he might avoid the cost of making his ex-wife an allowance out of his own pocket. If both Jane's husband and lover had behaved badly, Parliament was chivalrous towards such beauty, in such distress. Curiously, the same Legislators who could hang a child of eleven for sheep stealing now set aside the customary decree which then forbade the guilty party to marry the corespondent. Thus they left the way open for Jane to marry her Prince, and perhaps, one day, return to the Mayfair fold.

The ex-Lady Ellenborough now became a celebrated figure in Paris. She lived there with the Prince from 1829 to 1831, but as neither he nor his family even contemplated marriage, the sparkle of scandal invested her with an added fascination to Parisian society. She knew most of the outstanding personalities of the day in many different circles, literary, worldly and sporting. Balzac, with whom she had a brief liaison in spite of his unromantic appearance, cascade of chins and grubby splendors, is known to have drawn her, or caricatured her, rather, as the erotic Lady Arabella Dudley of *Le lys dans la vallée*. Yet Balzac, who missed nothing, saw in her, with strange prescience, those seeds of Orientalism, of Eastern fervor which were to develop so many years later, revealing the true nature of the woman. He saw in Lady Arabella, who is considered to be his portrait of Jane (although it has been said to be another English beauty then living in Paris, the Contessa Guidoboni Visconti), that vigorous and elemental creature who had everything to do with love, but nothing to do with drawing-room intrigues. He described her passions as *African:* a peculiar adjective. He likened her desires to tornadoes sweeping across the burning deserts. He sensed her true, and torrid, climate. He called her a swallow of the desert, belonging to the East. Did she, during their brief liaison, speak to Balzac of her childish, and possibly abiding, passion for the Orient? How else did he assess her so exactly, while she was still thirty years away from those black Bedouin tents, in the finicky Paris salons where they met? Throughout his book, Balzac stresses this tawny, *African* quality inherent in the blond English aristocrat whose careless elegance so dazzled him.

Contemporary correspondence proves that the Prince had become a tepid cavalier. Jane had slipped into the category of wives who are domestic appurtenances, if not encumbrances. Between one confinement and the next, she was left on the shelf—by him. According to his family, however, she consoled herself with the same ease she had done in London. Once again, she was searching for her destiny. She was surrounded by a large circle, many of whom were old friends, for Paris was the cross-roads of the world. And most people forgave her the dreadful sin of having been found out. After all, she had that charm, that childish simplicity which disarms. She kept it throughout her life. In spite of everything the most outraged moralists could say, she remained guileless, with nothing petty or false in her nature.

Paris at this time had reached one of its several apogees of brilliance. It surged with life and overflowed with astonishing personalities who were to leave their mark on the century. It was the cradle of the Romantics who had just discovered Shakespeare and were making a great to-do about it. Berlioz was transported to almost cataleptic frenzies by the sight of Harriet Smithson playing Juliet at the Odeon. She was a mousy English miss, but she inspired his *Symphonie Fantastique,* so much could be forgiven her. Liszt wrote, consoling Berlioz on her death many years after she had become his neglected wife, "She inspired you. You loved her. You put her into your music. Her task was done." Here speaks not only the supreme egotism of the artist, but that supremely egotistical creature, man—particularly nineteenth-century man, who for the most part regarded women from Olympian heights of superiority, for distraction, or breeding, or as unpaid slave labor, according to their class. It was an attitude which Jane Digby opposed all her life, although, curiously, this thoroughly Oriental point of view does not seem to have been held by the Arab she was to marry. With him she became as doting and submissive as any harem wife; not so much because he expected it, but rather because she, loving so greatly, wished it thus. So, we see her in contemporary memoirs, kneeling before him in joyous humility, washing his feet, like any other submissive Oriental wife and glorying in it, as one eyewitness records approvingly.

In Paris, at this time, since all things English were the rage, Jane must have enjoyed an even greater success on that score. Not only in literature, but in sport too, England led the fashion. The Jockey Club was founded by Lord Henry Seymour, whose profligate parent, Lord Hertford (the origin of Thackeray's wicked Marquis of Steyne) gave the most spectacular entertainments at his house on the site of the present Opéra. The Madeleine was only half built, and surrounded by wasteland. The Champs Élysées was a sinister cutthroat district; but much of the Left Bank, l'Ile de la Cité and the narrow streets running down to the Seine have changed little since that time. Paris was a carnival city given over to *bals masqués*. All along the boulevards they danced, winter and summer, exuberant scenes which Garvarni's drawings have immortalized. He found it ironic, to Eugéne Sue it was sinister; to Heine, tragic. To Jane it must have been at any rate a diverting place in which to steel herself to the Prince's indifference. The small world in which she lived, *le beau monde*, overlapped into the demimonde, and the world of the more successful Bohemians. Everyone knew everyone else. Extravagant poses were admired. Petrus Borel preferred to be known as the lycanthrope, or man-wolf. To keep pace with the English craze, all the dandies drove Tilburys. English pseudonyms were chic. Some, such as Philothée O'Neddy, were not really convincing. The Revolution of 1830 had blazed up, only to subside into steady bickering between Bourbon and Bonapartist factions.

Abroad, there was the Algerian war, and the name of Abd El Kadir became famous. (Thirty years later, Jane was to know this great figure well, when he was an honored exile in Damascus, and she the wife of a Syrian Sheik.) The distant wars revived an interest in Eastern exoticism.

Delacroix was obsessed by sultry harem interiors. A giraffe had lately arrived in Paris and was the rage and wonder of the city as its dusky retinue exercised it in the parks. Everything was *à la giraffe,* from towering bonnets to dappled gloves. Giraffes in palmy groves were painted on dinner services, or woven into chintzy motifs, on the *toiles de jouy.* George Sand was sketched by Alfred de Musset wearing Turkish trousers and the sort of Oriental dressing gown Balzac also favored. (With a positive autointoxication, they were all forever drawing or writing about themselves, or each other.) Merimée drew himself *à la Chinoise,* in a mandarin's robes and drooping mustaches. Liszt, always partial to fancy dress, favored blue Turkish trousers. Paris was peopled with such carnival figures, hardly less theatrical than the great Debureau who was then performing at the Funambules. Paganini was one of the most popular spectacles. He could be seen any afternoon, a diabolic figure, wrapped in an immensely long fur-lined overcoat, whatever the weather, sitting immobile in a music shop in the Passage de l'Opéra. And Rossini, struggling and hungry, was at that time delighted to play all the evening, at anyone's party, for thirty francs.

As Prince Schwarzenberg's mistress, and nobody's wife, there were a number of his official social engagements from which the ex-Lady Ellenborough was debarred. This must have thrown her back on her own resources, bringing her into a less exacting circle of writers, musicians and such. For all that the pale romantics earned their reputations, they were a robust lot. Hugo, Dumas, Balzac, de Musset, Gautier —they all knew how to live well. Such a society must have done much to mold the impressionable young creature Jane still was. Soon, she emerged from the schoolgirl chrysalis of her early married days in London, where even at Almack's, a society not distinguished for its intellect, her vapidity was as remarked as her beauty. Now, she gradually assumed, or developed, an unexpected brilliance. She became an outstanding conversationalist, witty, widely read, and full of those unexpected quirks of personality which, linked with her peculiarly airy, English humor, made her such good company.

Sometime during the year 1831 Schwarzenberg had finally taken himself off, and suddenly Jane decided to move on too. She seems to have deposited her two children with the Prince, who was obliging enough to take them over for good. Now entirely unencumbered, the *ci-devant* Lady Ellenborough left Paris in a cloud of rumors. Imperceptibly, the black Bedouin tents were one step nearer: she had moved eastward again, over another frontier, towards other loves. "Tomorrow to fresh Woods and Pastures new."

\*　　　\*　　　\*

In the early nineteenth century, travel was for the most part still interpreted in terms of the eighteenth-century Grand Tour. It was a polite circuit, a well-beaten track where the great houses of England were linked by a series of inns and posting houses, with the châteaux of France and the castles of Italy. Vienna, the Rhine, and the Alps were part of the tour. Hungary, Greece and Russia were not. A sunrise or a sunset on Mont Blanc were considered a "must." In dust and rain, by ravines and through forests, the cumbersome family coaches rocked their way along, overloaded with luxuries which were almost necessities considering the state of most hostelries. Traveling light was unknown. Gold or silver fitted dressing cases, great calfskin portmanteaus, *batteries de cuisine* and bed linen, these too were "musts." When Lord and Lady Blessington and the ubiquitous Count D'Orsay set off from Paris in 1821, the city turned out to see them start. "The Blessington Circus," as it was dubbed, included a specially designed satin-padded carriage for Milady, with a folding bed and a small but choice library. Lord Byron took along seven domestics and five carriages, furniture, horses, and livestock by way of portable larder, too.

We do not have any record of how Lady Ellenborough traveled, but she seems to have been considerably more mobile, except for certain lesser whims, like her own bed and table linen, and plate. And then, her travels, or *déplacements*, rather, were so often in the form of elopements; sudden whirlwind dashes, galloping off to join a new lover, mounted on the spirited thoroughbreds she liked to ride. She was a splendid horsewoman, and outwardly the embodiment of the heroine of every extravagant novelette. Inwardly, however, hers was at once a simpler, and more subtle, nature. She was without pose, transparently honest, eager, and touchingly trusting. Each new love was to be the love of her life. She never acquired the faintest trace of cynicism, even after forty years of adventures. The freedom of her ways never coarsened either her nature or her beauty. Her conduct was deplored, particularly by most of her English family, who turned her picture to the wall, and grew with the century's smothering growth of prudery to acquire a horror of the least domestic irregularity. And it must be admitted that Jane's were on a monumental scale. Yet however much she outraged public opinion by the cold statistics of her affairs, she retained the love and respect of all who knew her well, wherever she went. In this, as in her indestructible qualities of youth and beauty, ...d desirability (which, like Ninon de Lenclos, she kept until past seventy), she was without parallel in her time. But then, what was her time? She was a child of the Regency, and all that it implied in raffishness. Yet she lived out her life through the Victorian age, when the Queen refused even to countenance the remarriage of widows.

At the moment of her leaving Paris Jane was still limelighted by the Schwarzenberg scandal, so that on her sudden departure following on so many alleged affairs of short duration, such as that with Balzac, the gossip-mongers of London, Paris and Vienna all had their own versions of her disappearance. She was in romantic hiding with Bernadotte of Sweden. . . . She had run off with an innkeeper's son, the Schwarzenbergs said. . . . She had taken refuge in a convent, said others. Thus they speculated, buzzing happily. Quite soon, she was discovered to be in Munich. How, or with whom, or why she arrived there is not known: but before long gossip was fattening on new, delicious tidbits. Lady Ellenborough had taken another lover—a king, this time. Tongues wagged, but heads nodded in approbation, too. Kingly lovers were very much in the Regency tradition.

King Ludwig of Bavaria was a Wittelsbach, a godchild of Marie Antoinette, and Napoleon's protégé; an amiable eccentric, though he never carried the family eccentricity to the lengths achieved by his grandson Ludwig II or even his niece the Empress Elizabeth. He was content to plunge into an unbridled Philhellenism. He lavished enormous sums of money on rebuilding Munich in the Greek style, rushing between Athens and Rome, importing unwieldy archaeological trophies, laying foundation stones of triumphal arches, at once a romantic and faintly comic figure, with the haunted eyes of a visionary, the baggy umbrella and crumpled coat of a professor. His Philhellenic indulgences cost money, but in all else rigid economy was the order. At the *Residenz*, the royal children ate black bread. On their housekeeping budget, the royal cooks could not possibly serve onions, they said, when the king asked for these humble delicacies. But Ludwig was easygoing over such details, only waxing exigent over beauty in various forms. Such enthusiasm carried all before it. His new Bavarian *Griechenland* was becoming the art center of the world, after Paris. Its citizens groaned under the expenditure and taxation, but also glowed with civic pride, as blueprints multiplied, and architects and builders, goaded on by the king's enthusiasm, worked day and night. The exquisite rococo of the Asam brothers was forgotten. Cuvillié's perfections went out of fashion. The new Munich was a grandiose jumble: Romanesque, Renaissance and Athenian architecture was firmly superimposed. The Alte Pinakothek was built to house the king's splendid collection of family art treasures which he now presented to the nation. Then there was the new Pinakothek, the Hof-Theater, the Glyptothek, and dozens of classic obelisks, arches and such. The apotheosis of such Philhellenism was achieved by the Walhalla, or Teuton Hall of Fame, an almost exact replica of the Parthenon, which sprang up at Regensburg, and was a bizarre gesture of Pan-Germanic fervor in the classical idiom. This, then, was the new and splendid camp into which our Amazon now rode.

Sometimes, however, the king showed a less abstract love of beauty. He was besotted on beautiful women, and was, indeed, to lose his throne on account of his infatuation for Lola Montez. But that was nearly thirty years ahead. Now he was a cultivated, charming, if eccentric man in his prime. When the celebrated Lady Ellenborough arrived she caused an instant stir. She seems to have lived in some style. She was invited to Court, and at once the king was her slave, and she his mistress. He commissioned Carl Stieler to paint her portrait for his celebrated Schönheits Gallery, a collection of beauties which he liked to contemplate daily, in a sort of inspirational communion, as he explained. This collection of charmers contained not only those ladies with whom he was personally, or romantically involved (as the series of beauties of the bedchamber which Charles II commanded Lely to paint, and which hangs at Hampton Court Palace, a zenana full of sly sideways-glancing houris) but also his own daughter and the daughter of the butcher who delivered meat to the *Residenz*. Stieler was not much of a painter: his beauties have the glossy quality of oleographs— they are sleek and succulent, distinguished less by their looks than by their national backgrounds or costumes, their local color, romantically introduced, as in the case of the Greek girl in her tasselled cap, beside an Ionic isle. The over-all impression is merely an amalgamate of beauty, pre-Winterhalter, post-Gainsborough.

It does not seem that Stieler has done justice to Lady Ellenborough. We cannot judge her beauty from the few portraits left, certainly not from his. She must have been all that was radiant, animated and fascinating, apart from her perfect coloring and features, with reddish-gold hair (Balzac calls it a soft tan), violet-blue eyes and a delicate aquiline nose. But what do we see? A placid if not stolid matron with a pseudospiritual expression in the vacant eyes which are certainly not those Balzac had in mind when he described Lady Arabella Dudley's: "the desert, whose burning vastness is to be seen in her eyes, the desert, all azure and love. . . ."

The air of complacency, the padded shoulders, as much as the rich draperies, all give the picture an air of being more a mechanical exercise in the style of beauty and painting then in vogue than a portrait of the sitter as she really was. From all accounts, Lady Ellenborough had that delicate, careless type of English beauty at its best in muslins and the morning light, and which Gainsborough has immortalized. At all events, we must accept that she was one of the great beauties of her century; with some added charm, a sensuality which was vital rather than languorous, perhaps, which made her irresistible to men of all ages and races, throughout her life.

In Munich Jane lived in tranquil happiness. Her royal lover fostered her interest in the arts and first fired her with that love of Greece which was to have so much meaning for her later. She took lessons in sculpture and painting and studied classical Greek. The king consulted her on all his Periclean projects. They exchanged blueprints with the same fervor as billets-doux. She enraptured the king by addressing him as "Basilli"—the Greek version of his name. He turned "Jane" into "Ianthe." It was a serene idyl. Perhaps she even believed she had reached her destination. But it was only another interlude: her life was made up of such; she was forever darting from one campfire to the next, warming herself at the flames, and forever wondering why they flickered out. She and the king were always to remain close friends: however, Ianthe was to find another royal lover in Ludwig's son, Otho, when he became King of Greece. She had been foretold three Kings by Madame Lenormand, the celebrated fortuneteller who had made such tactlessly accurate predictions to the Emperor Napoleon. According to Edmond About, the French writer who was in Athens in 1852, and found Ianthe, as he always calls her, the most interesting personality in the whole city, she had also had some romantic entanglement with the future Emperor Napoleon III when he was an impoverished exile at Baden. If so, this would justify Mme. Lenormand's prophecy.

Presently Jane's English relatives learned with relief that she was married to the Baron Carl-Theodore von Venningen, a Bavarian nobleman. It was said that the king had arranged the marriage to ensure that his favorite should have a place at Court, or even that his child should be born in wedlock. But these stories seem to have been untrue. The Baron was young, handsome, rich and proud. It is improbable that he would have married to cover up the king's liaison. As to the child—it was the image of the Baron, and silenced all gossip as to its royal parentage.

How the Baron, as a staunch Catholic, succeeded in obtaining the permission of his Church to marry a divorcée is not known, though it was held that King Ludwig had personally interceded with the Vatican. At any rate, the marriage was celebrated in Italy, on November 10, 1832. The king was in Sicily that winter, and in December Jane gave birth to a son, Heribert, at Palermo. For two years the Venningens lived in Sicily in sunshine and content. No doubt the Baron felt he had domesticated Jane, who showed no signs of straying. But when they returned to Munich to settle on the family estates, Jane, although pregnant again, was becoming very restless. The honeymoon was over; she did not take well to the more humdrum pattern of matrimony. She was brought to bed of a daughter, Bertha, and began to look about for what she thought of as diversions, but which were in reality the adventures, the dangers and changing scenes which her vagrant nature always craved.

At this time there was a constant exchange of visitors between Munich and Athens. King Ludwig welcomed the excuse of advising his newly crowned son Otho of Greece on how to revive the classic glories of his kingdom. Each nation was fashionable in the other country. Athenian dandies were careful to wear their national dress, and wrought havoc among sentimental German *Mädchen*. They strode about, splendid and exotic figures in the *fustanella,* stiff pleated white skirts, heavily encrusted gold boleros, tasseled caps set rakishly, cummerbunds stuffed with daggers, and their liquid black eyes darting passion right and left.

And now, a swaggering Byronic figure, the Count Spyridon Theotoky enters the scene. He was of a noble Corfiote family, poor, proud, and as irresistible to women as Jane was to men. They met at a Court ball, and plunged headlong into deep waters. In him, Jane saw all the glorious color and adventure of life which her marriage to the Baron had denied her. She loved Carl, she admired his upright and generous nature: but even her naïve hopes for domestic bliss with the love of her life—since each fresh venture was always seen as such— she cannot have imagined herself settling down, at twenty-seven, to a Munich matron's life.

When the Venningens left for their estates in Baden, the Greek Count followed hot-foot, staying nearby at Heidelberg. There were long romantic rides in the twilight green forests, where the now impassioned lover importuned the Baroness Venningen to fly with him. He offered much, to one of Jane's temperament; not only love and adventure but the burning isles of Greece . . . Byronism . . . the climate of love. She could not resist. There were more and more indiscreet rendezvous, when she galloped through the night towards Spyridon's embraces, while her unsuspecting husband made the rounds of his estates. But at last things came to a head. The Baron was becoming suspicious: he was not the sort to accept cuckoldom meekly. It is said the lovers slipped away during a court ball for the King of Prussia, and that as soon as their absence was noticed by the Baron he rushed off in pursuit, raging. He must have ridden fast, or perhaps they dallied; at any rate, he caught up with them, and brandishing his pistols called the Count out. Jane watched, horror-struck, from the post chaise. The postilions acted as seconds, and at the first shot Theotoky fell, bleeding terribly from a wound in the chest. So far there had been romance, and drama, all that Jane could have wished: it was succeeded by tragicomedy. Theotoky lay on the grass livid and apparently doomed. But with what everyone took to be his last breath he swore their love had been innocent: that up to now there had been nothing dishonorable between them. The Baron appears to have been as credulous as noble. It was decided that as the Count was such a long time expiring (in Jane's arms) he had better be moved off the roadside to breathe his last in comfort at the Schloss Venningen. But it was not so simple. After floods of tears and devoted nursing on Jane's part, remorse and doubts on the Baron's, and a series of harrowing eternal farewells, the Count began to recover. It was a ludicrous situation, but no doubt lost on the trio.

There was no going back: for Theotoky to return to Greece, for Jane to return to her stern but forgiving husband, was, for her, the closing of all doors. It meant a life of sober matronhood behind the drawn blinds of respectability. No horizons, no loopholes. It could not be. Her children, Heribert and the infant Bertha, did not anchor her any more than her other three children had done. More tears, more self-recrimination and agonies of indecision. Theotoky, pallid but increasingly passionate on one side, Venningen austere but less patient on the other, awaited her decision. As it has been remarked before, Jane was never one to be coerced. At last it was done. Once again she fled matrimony for the honeymoon. Once again, home, husband, children, if no longer her good name—for that had been lost some time—were exchanged for the chimera of love. The infatuated pair left for Paris (it seemed wiser not to flaunt their affair under the nose of Greek patriarchal society), where they were to live for the next few years. Contrary to all moral dictates, they were very happy. Only a faint regret for the sorrow she had caused the Baron remained to shadow Jane's second life in Paris. She was to remain in affectionate correspondence with him, and her children by him, for the rest of their lives. But she was not the maternal type; she was always more feminine than womanly, more mistress than wife. Balzac, watching her ride, said, ostensibly of Lady Arabella: *"J'ai remarqué depuis, que la plupart des femmes qui montent bien à cheval ont peu de tendresse. . . ."* Yet like so many daughters of Albion, she always showed an overwhelming love and tenderness towards animals, a contradiction which never fails to bewilder and exasperate other nationalities.

After some carefree years in Paris, swimming in an aura of high romance, the storm center of international scandal, the lovers seem to have arranged the delicate matter of Jane's new divorce satisfactorily. She is said to have been baptized into the Orthodox faith, and they were able to marry. In 1841 they left Paris for Dukades, the Theotoky home on Corfu. The family, who accepted her as the former Lady Ellenborough, and voluntarily or by reason of their remoteness appear to have skipped both the Schwarzenberg and Venningen episodes, were enchanted with Jane and she with them. In an atmosphere of domestic felicity, Jane laid out new gardens, planted a cypress which, a few years back still towered darkly over the landscape, imported silver and china from England, entertained all the notable travelers, and bore a son, Leonidas. She loved this child as she had never loved any of her others. She appeared to have settled down. At last! her English relatives said, triumphantly, complacently.

When Count Spyridon was appointed King Otho's aide-de-camp (and was this, perhaps, a move on the part of both kings, father and son, to bring the beautiful Countess back into their orbit?), the Theotokys moved to Athens, leaving behind them forever the pastoral happiness of their island home. It had been the peak of Jane's romantic life. She was at the zenith of her beauty, and she had discovered newer, deeper delights in the little Leonidas. In Athens she was soon surrounded by admirers and temptations. But so, too, was the Count. The young King Otho was as enslaved by her as his father had been: scandal flared up again, and most disquieting rumors of the royal affair reached London, silencing the premature complacency of Holkham. Jane's relatives seem to have made no further attempts to keep in touch: they gave her up as lost, all but her younger brother Kenelm, who remained staunch, although in Holy Orders.

In Athens Queen Amalie began to make difficulties. She was jealous of Jane's conquest of both King Otho and the capital. Whenever the Countess Theotoky rode abroad on her fine white horse, the crowds followed cheering the Queen of Love and Beauty, as she was called. Spyridon seems to have been indifferent to the scandals. He retaliated in kind; they drifted apart, united only by their son, Leonidas.

But Leonidas was not to be left to them. One summer when he was about six, the idolized little creature accompanied his mother to Lucca, where she was taking the waters. He was on the top-floor nursery of the tall old house where they stayed. Looking down through the balustrade he saw her far below in the hall. He started to slide down the banister, overbalanced, and crashed to his death at her feet. She never recovered from this, her first profound tragedy. With her child's death she broke camp once more.

\*       \*       \*

For a long while she remained hidden away. When she returned to Athens she and Theotoky had separated. There was no divorce, but each went his own way. To still her grief, she plunged into more adventures and travels. Now the scandal which had coupled her name with King Otho's redoubled. There was talk of Italian husbands, Turkish lovers; she had eloped with her groom, with the king himself. . . . People were never so tolerant or generous towards Jane as she always showed herself to others. *Judge not that ye be not judged* was inscribed on the flyleaf of her Bible; she held to its generous principle throughout her life.

Athens had an Oriental passion for scandal. It ran through the salons and cafés as through a bazaar. It was in keeping with the city's many other Oriental traits. If it was not, truly, the East, neither was it the West—it was a wild scene, part Turk, part Slav, and part Levantine. There were the seething Turkish bazaars, the cafés where the population spent most of the long hot nights smoking their *narghilyés* and drinking innumerable cups of coffee. The ill-lit, noisome streets were crowded with exotic costumes from the various islands and provinces. There were wafts of incense from the dark icon-studded churches where the chanting of the monks mingled with the piercing sweet mournful songs the peasants sang. Along the waterfront the Levantine sailors lolled by their gaudily painted boats, dozed, drank raki and gambled, up to no good. In the center of the town where the Bavarian architects had spasmodically re-created a few Philhellenic façades, Greek society lived as much *à l'Européenne* as their surroundings permitted.

Athens was a come-by-chance capital, having been chosen for archaeological rather than political or economic reasons. The young King Otho had selected the site, probably in deference to the classical interests of his father. Before he had been installed as monarch, Athens had been a fishing village, scarcely remembering the legends of its glorious past. The new capital would have been better placed strategically at the Isthmus of Corinth. But health and commerce had to take second place; so the village mushroomed up, overnight, into an agglomeration of booths and palaces. In 1852 it was said to have twenty thousand inhabitants, but only two thousand houses. A great number of the population lived and slept in the streets. Ministries and tribunals were situated oddly, over shops, or behind noisy *gargottes*, and high government officials were lodged in inns. There were few diversions: Karaguez, the puppet whose lewd antics are known all over the Levant; gossip, which always attained the malevolent stature of scandal; and cards—cards morning, noon, and night. When About asked the Countess Theotoky if she was interested in cards, she replied, "We are in Greece—don't ask me to speak ill of its religion."

Still, the tiny capital was the world, the flesh and the devil to the Balkans. Rich Moldavian nobles traveled great distances to spend their patrimony there in riotous living. All around were the wild hills and mountains. It was described as being Arcadia, infested by brigands. But Athenian society did not venture far afield, unless joining a religious pilgrimage to some inaccessible rockbound monastery. Few people paid any attention to "The Ruins," as they were called. Archaeology, though favored by a few cultivated foreigners, left the modern Greeks comparatively unmoved.

Of all the many races who crowded into the little city it was the Pallikars who were the most striking. They were a legendary lot, mercenaries—and cutthroats, some people said—from the Albanian mountains. They had fought magnificently in the War of Independence, and it was to keep them amiably disposed that King Otho nominated their chief, the General Xristodolous Hadji-Petros as his new aide-de-camp in succession to Count Theotoky.

Albania was all the rage. Jane recalled *Childe Harold's Pilgrimage.*

> *Land of Albania! where Iskander rose,*
> *Theme of the young and beacon of the wise . . .*
> *. . . Land of Albania! let me bend mine eyes*
> *On thee! thou rugged nurse of savage men!*
> *The cross descends, thy minarets arise,*
> *And the pale crescent sparkles in the glen*
> *Through many a cypress grove within each other's ken. . . .*

Wicked, romantic Lord Byron! He was a little out of fashion, now, but he had been the music of her youth . . . and really, no one could conjure the beauty and nobility of Greece as he. No one else ever captured the voluptuous and mysterious East with such a mixture of poetry and truth either. Byron's ornate overlay does not blind us to his almost photographic sensitivity, when we know the places of which he writes. The notes form a curious counterpoint to his poetic flights; historic, personal, geographic: they are as informed and accurate as the rest is romantic.

When the Albanian General swooped down on Athens from his mountain lair, he was soon the most talked-of person at Court. He was much feted by the women, for he was a handsome and romantic figure.

And since he was the Chief of the Pallikars, the King found it expedient to appoint him Governor of the province of Lamia, too. He must have been a splendid man, towering over the tallest, ferocious-looking, and as handsome and seductive at sixty as many men half his age. He ruled in a princely fashion, as he dressed. He wore Albanian costume, all crimson and gold embroideries, and he bristled with pistols and yataghans, which he did not hesitate to use. His horses were trapped out in gold and silver. His men swaggered about, wildly mustachioed and reeking of garlic. They wore great shaggy cloaks, and looked like bears, some said. Like wasps, said others, remarking their incredibly small waists, induced, or maintained, surprisingly, by the habit of tight lacing. Edmond About calls them the wasps of Aristophanes. This ruthless and theatrical band put the Athenian ladies in a flutter. The Queen was said to have particularly tender regard for their Chief, Hadji-Petros.

But it was the old, old story. In a short while Jane had fallen in love again, tempestuously, sincerely. No matter that he was over sixty, a widower with children somewhere in the background. He was a Pallikar, a man from the mountains who breathed fire and adventure, and who stood for all the wildness which Jane had always craved. They lived together in the mountains, galloping over the savage wastes by day, sleeping in camp, surrounded by the brigands, at night. She lived among them, as their Chieftain's wife, sharing their reckless adventures and hardships. It must not be forgotten that Jane was by upbringing athletic. She was proud of being able to shoot a pheasant from her saddle at full gallop. Now, at last her vagrant cravings were satisfied. The cushioned comforts of her former life seemed stifling. She decided to divorce Theotoky and marry Hadji-Petros. This prospect appeared both romantic and practical to her lover, who was penniless and eyed her fortune longingly. Not that it was such a large one, still . . . and not that he did not love her passionately, and had fallen a willing victim to such charms, especially as he was in his late sixties, when to carry off such a prize was especially flattering. But the Queen was not to be trifled with. She had been jealous of Jane before. First on account of her husband; then, she had resented Jane's popularity with the people. And now the irresistible Hadji-Petros was snatched from under her nose.

When Jane began negotiations for her divorce and remarriage the Queen struck. Hadji-Petros was relieved of his command of the Pallikars as well as the Governorship. The lovers returned to Athens in disgrace. Alas! the brigand proved to be a sycophant. He wrote to the Queen, pleading for reinstatement. *If I am this woman's lover it is not for love's sake, but purely for self-interest. She is wealthy, I am poor. . . . I have a position to maintain and children to educate.* But the Queen did not relent. She retaliated by publicizing the letter. Even then, Jane remained infatuated—more perhaps with the brigand than the man, or with what he represented in terms of adventure and escape. It was escape, too, from middle-aged inactivity, the settled pattern which was her anathema, and which she tolerated no more at forty-six, in Athens, than at twenty-seven, in Munich. It was not so much that she wished to remain young—who does not? But rather that she did not age, inwardly or outwardly. Along with the freshness of her beauty, "the morning hue," she retained the irresponsible optimism and greediness of youth.

Since not only the Queen but all Athens now showed hostility towards Jane's latest affair, the lovers, with surprising restraint, decided against aggravating public opinion by setting up house together. That could come later, with the marriage. Jane, who as usual was paying, rented two small houses side by side on the outskirts of the city, where she and her domestics lived in one and the brigand chief and a few of his Pallikars in the other. It deceived no one.

She set about building a magnificent mansion, something to dazzle all Athens, which was to be the fortress of their love. If the world wanted none of them, the world would be well lost. For the present, however, they lived rather shabbily at the wrong end of town. Very few people called. Still, if it lacked style it was not humdrum. Jane now preferred the garlic-eating *tchibouk*-smoking Pallikars to all the scented, internationalized Phanariotes and courtiers. Flinging herself as wholeheartedly as ever into her latest entanglement, she saw herself the ever-loving wife of Hadji-Petros, a second mother to his children and the inspiration of his men. She was ready to submerge her personality and acquire the submission required of Pallikar women. She would live sequestered, prostrated before her lord and master. . . . It was a lovely pipe dream, engendered by the wreathing smoke of the *tchibouks*, perhaps, as the Pallikars sat immobile, belching genially, round the campfires they insisted on lighting in her newly planned garden.

It was at this time, in 1852, that Edmond About first met her. He found her a fascinating study, the outstanding personality of Athens, and still a great beauty, looking nowhere near her true age. He rhapsodized over her perfect figure, her aristocratic hands and feet, her chestnut-golden hair, her large deep blue eyes. "As to her teeth, she belongs to that section of the *élite anglaise* who have pearls in their mouths, beside which other women's teeth look like piano keys." He went on to say her skin had the milky whiteness, the transparent clarity so essentially English. She colored, he said, at the slightest emotion: ". . . her passions," he said, warming to his theme, "could be seen agitating in their imprisonment." She made a profound impression on the inquisitive Frenchman who was as impressed by her reputation as her beauty.

Yet not all her beauty, nor what was by now her considerable experience could save Jane from another disaster. A less romantic or childish woman might have been warned of Hadji-Petros' true nature by the manner in which he had tried to reinstate himself in the Queen's favor. But Jane was always the giver, emotionally as well as materially. She continued loving Hadji-Petros, and sharing out her fortune between the absent, forgotten Spyridon, who seems to have applied for some Consulate post, and been delighted to continue in the state of pensioned-off husband, and the brigand lover, who was as impecunious as picturesque, and quite unable to contribute to a ménage which ran on Jane's extravagant plane. Financial questions never bothered her greatly, and she was fortunate in that so much of her life was spent in times and countries where her English income, set at around three thousand pounds per annum, represented great wealth. Besides, there were sometimes rich lovers, and *gages d'amour*, too, splendid jewels—her emeralds were famous; and no doubt there was always credit, the comfortable habit of the age.

So she went on reigning over the Pallikars, ignoring the slights of Athenian society, supervising the building of the fortress of love and enslaving Hadji-Petros even more by her care for his youngest child, the little Eirini, whom she loved tenderly, and in whom she found something of her lost Leonidas. She saw herself atoning for her past ways by being a second mother to the brigand's baby . . . a better, wiser, more stable parent than she had been for even Leonidas. She spent whole days playing with Eirini, reading to him French *contes* and English nursery rhymes. Perhaps she sang him the traditional lullaby of the Pallikars. Behind its innocence there is a surprising note of violence and possession . . . in it sounds all the plundering adventure of the people. It is the lullaby of a warrior race used to a life of constant warfare, pillage and conquest; in it sound the envy and fury and devotion which are the texture of Balkan life. It runs something like this:

> *Dozey, Pozy, Pallikare*
> *My little sleeping boy.*
> *I will give you a golden toy*
> *My little sleeping joy.*
> *Alexandria for your sweet*
> *Great Cairo for your bread*
> *Constantinople as your kingdom*
> *You shall be its head.*
> *And three big villages,*
> *And three big monasteries*
> *My little sleeping boy.*
> *The villages to stay in*
> *The monasteries to pray in*
> *My pretty sleeping joy.*

The brigand idyl drifted on, domestically enough, until Jane discovered Hadji-Petros was in reality more enamored of her maid Eugénie. It was a severe disillusion, a blow to both her heart and her pride. Eugénie had been her discreet and faithful companion for many years, and through so many, many adventures. She is an enigmatic figure. It is not known when, precisely, she entered Jane's employ, nor from where she came. Probably she was French; perhaps she had begun her years of service during the Schwarzenberg liaison in Paris. We imagine her, rather bilious-looking, dark-browed and taciturn; a Frenchwoman from some remote province; from Auvergne, perhaps; her brilliant, small black eyes ever watchful, alert for the least rumpling of a collar. A faint down emphasizing her thin, unsmiling lips, her face softening rarely, but her whole life's force of loyalty and devotion centered round Madame; round Madame's comfort— Madame's toilettes, Madame's position in *le beau monde*. Defending Madame from all-comers and occasionally defending Madame from herself. Yet it was she who told her mistress of the General's conduct. I cannot help feeling she acted less in the interests of her mistress for once (if the story was true, which is not proven) than in a desperate bid for self-preservation. Jane must have been an exigent mistress, and the numbers of moves, sudden flights, new homes and countries must have been tiring to Eugénie. No doubt she saw it all in terms of her work. Packing; unpacking; finding soap or curling tongs in outlandish places. Walking Jane's adored dogs. Making-do in temporary quarters, making all those foreigners understand . . . And now, the Pallikars. What self-respecting lady's maid could have faced with composure the prospect of life in a brigand's lair? No doubt she acted for their good. The good of herself and her mistress, that is, in making the disclosure she reckoned would bring an end to the affair. Poor Eugénie! how could she foresee it would have the effect of launching Jane into yet another precipitous flight, this time to undreamed-of deprivations, to scenes wilder and stranger than any Pallikar encampment, and finally, the arms of an Arab Sheik?

Jane was both loving and forgiving. She had ignored Hadji-Petros' manner of explaining away their liaison to the Queen. She knew he enjoyed her money—that was nothing—but to enjoy her maid, too, that was insupportable. He had humiliated her in public; now he humiliated her in private: it was the end. She told Eugénie to pack.

Overnight, she decided to break camp once more. Without disclosing her plans to anyone, least of all to her lover, she left Athens with the subdued but still devoted Eugénie. They sailed for Syria, where she had for some time past thought of going to buy an Arab horse worthy of her Pallikar. Now it was an escape, a distraction, the first place that presented itself, and above all, fresh ground, a new world, far from any painful echoes of her past. And so the black Bedouin tents came into view, at last.

*       *       *

Jane Digby, or Countess Theotoky, as she was still, landed in Syria thinking herself heartbroken: it was the first time she had admitted to herself that at forty-six, life, as she interpreted it, was probably over. It can have been of no comfort to know she had enjoyed more of it than most women. "A hundred summers when they're done, will appear as short as one." But travel had always helped her before: the fabled Orient would be a distraction. She would fling herself into archaeology. Those interests first fostered by King Ludwig twenty years ago had never left her—sometimes they had been elbowed aside by more ardent matters of the flesh, but she had remained one of the few Athenians who had followed the sporadic excavations knowledgeably. "Schliemann of Troy," the extraordinary little German grocer's boy who was to teach himself Greek and astonish the world fifty years later by his excavations and the discovery of the buried golden jewelry of Troy, only came to Greece after she had left, or they would no doubt have met; and perhaps it would have been she, rather than the beautiful Greek girl who became Schliemann's second wife, who would have worn the diadem once worn by Helen.

Arrived in Syria, Jane planned to visit Baalbeck, Jerusalem and Palmyra. She would track down Zenobia's legendary kingdom. Perhaps she was fired by *Eothen*. She must have read Kinglake's account of his travels in the Near East, for she was always an energetic reader, keeping abreast of new literature by means of large packets of books sent regularly from London and Paris, many on the recommendation of her younger brother Kenelm, with whom she remained on devoted terms. They exchanged intimate accounts of each other's doings, although they had not met since she left England in 1829 at the peak of the Schwarzenberg scandal. She had become a deeply cultivated woman. The manner of her living had not affected the quality of her thinking. She was musical; she painted; and her sculpture was said to be remarkable; she followed the intellectual developments in Europe closely, and she spoke and read eight languages: later, she was to add Arabic to the list.

She may have felt that only archaeology remained, and no doubt Eugénie fostered this attitude which promised a more reposeful way of life for both of them. But it was not to be. Less than a month after she left Athens she was involved with an Arab of surpassing attractions. Not much is known about Sâlih. He was young, handsome, lusty, and as conscious of her charms as she of his. There is no suggestion that he was the sort of opportunist dragoman who could be hired out by any lonely lady. He appears to have been a splendid creature, very possessive, who swept her off her feet and into the black Bedouin tents of his encampment out in the desert. Jane was enraptured. The Pallikars paled. When Sâlih's tribe entertained her with the traditional and picturesque Arab hospitality, she was lost. . . . All at once she discovered the living East, and it went to her head. No use for Eugénie to purse her lips, waiting with the heavy luggage at the inn. Her mistress was away savoring the desert life along the Jordan, discovering its climate, at once languorous and fierce, primitive and subtle. Another *coup de foudre!* This time her love for the Arab people and their ways was to last all the rest of her life. Once again she had found the perfect love: she would be united forever, suspended in Time in a state of perpetual bliss. They would marry! His people should be her people, his ways her ways. . . . Suddenly it was imperative to proceed with the divorce from Theotoky, which up to now had hung fire. The building of Hadji-Petros' love-nest must be stopped. Sâlih was all. By which it will be seen that Jane's heart had remained as young as her person. For so experienced a woman, she was really astonishingly naïve.

But before returning to Athens to obtain her liberty, she decided to visit Palmyra. Archaeology elbowed even emotion aside. Sâlih was piqued. He had not reckoned on an inanimate rival. Besides, he could not accompany her. Probably there was some question of intertribal warfare. The desert Arabs were in a permanent state of battle, plundering and skirmishing. Safe-conducts, an ironic term, were often given to travelers, but were for the most part not worth the paper they were written on. Even if it was convened that the tribes of the Shammar, the Fedáan, Gomassa or any other, should respect the traveler, once out of their zone, the trail would lead to fresh dangers from another tribe or nomad band, all of whom had their system for raids, and apparent rescues (with a division of the reward) worked out among themselves. One band of brigands would swoop on the caravan of unsuspecting travelers, with a terrifying display of horsemanship, much firing of flintlocks and brandishing of spears. They would take all they could lay their hands on, and at a given moment, there would be a dramatic swoop by yet another band of horsemen, who would drive off the first, appear to vanquish them, and return to claim the reward for saving the lives of the travelers. This way, double profits could be made to the benefit of all concerned—all the Arabs, that is. It was, in fact, a racket.

No one was safe; and although this particularly transparent technique was not practiced between the Arabs themselves, still it was often a matter of life or death for one tribe to venture across alien territory. The two great rival factions were the Shammar and the Anazeh. The Euphrates lay between them, and centuries of blood feud too. Such an atmosphere of drama was, as always, the breath of life to Jane. Nothing Sâlih could say dissuaded her. She would go alone. She set about negotiations for the journey. Damascus had all the provincial town's curiosity,—added to which there were the bazaars where rumors began but never ended. Jane was a conspicuous figure and getting herself talked about, as always. Her fatal mixture of beauty, careless wealth and complete disregard for the conventions interested both the Arab and European population. Directly her project was known, there were half a dozen rival bands planning their raid-and-rescue maneuver. Arabs are, by nature, a predatory people.

Jane was fair game. Whispers of her adventure with Sâlih had reached the European colony, too, who were scandalized but perhaps not surprised. The English Consul deplored her arrival in Damascus. Perhaps he was thinking of the many inconveniences suffered by a former consul, on behalf of another eccentric English noblewoman, Lady Hester Stanhope. The Countess Theotoky was so very beautiful too. It might lead to all sorts of unpleasantnesses; from the official, Foreign Office viewpoint, affairs with Arabs came under that heading.

Edmond About cites a highly colored incident of Jane's early days in Syria, which he attributes to Medjuel El Mezrab, the Arab Sheik she was later to marry. But in reality, if it occurred, and it is very likely, it must have concerned Sâlih, for About learned of it on his second visit to Athens, in 1853–1854, soon after Jane had herself returned there to wind up her affairs; to strike camp, in fact. As she was always a great talker, and given to disclosing with disarming frankness, the most personal details of her life, it is probable that the incident in question was one she herself enjoyed telling to her gaping Athenian audiences. If so, it must have concerned Sâlih, and not Medjuel El Mezrab, with whom there was no question of marriage until some time later, on her final return to Syria.

Here is About, inquisitive as ever, on the fascinating Ianthe.

"For a year I asked for news of her in vain. But I heard something of her, this week." He describes how Ianthe had been building the love-nest for Hadji-Petros, and had rushed off to Syria to purchase an Arab mare worthy of her stables, and her brigand lover. He remarks that her departure was sudden, and surprised her friends. Evidently he does not know of the real reason behind her flight, which was not general knowledge, and which she had only confided to her journal, at that time. He goes on. "Ianthe found an Arab mare of the pure blood she sought. It belonged to a Sheik. The Sheik was young and personable. He said to Ianthe 'The horse, alas! is untamable; even were it tamed I could not name a price, for I love it more than anything in all the world, more, even, than my three wives.' Ianthe replied, 'A beautiful horse is a treasure, but three wives are not to be scorned, if they are beautiful. Send me your horse, and I will see if

I can tame it.' [This has the authentic ring of the Amazonian Ianthe.] Two Arabs brought the horse to Ianthe, who subdued him. While she was galloping, as the Sheik was escorting her to a fantasia, he found her more lovely than all his three wives together. He said: 'Woman succeeds where man fails, for woman knows when to yield. The animal is beyond any price, now that you have tamed it, but if you still wish to buy it, it will not be with money that you must pay.' " According to About this pronouncement made Ianthe fall silent for some moments: we imagine her eyeing the cavalier with sidelong glances, at once speculative and provocative. But she was accustomed to getting her own way. She replied that since she had not come all this way to haggle over terms, she would pay his price. But—she, too, had her price. He must get rid of his harem.

The young Sheik demurred: it would be contrary to custom: by tradition a Moslem had as many wives as he could afford: did she want him to look like some pauper, with only one? He even invoked his religion, and the Turkish law then prevailing in Syria. In short, he found Ianthe's terms too high.

And here we have the astonishing spectacle of the Countess Theotoky, the former Baroness Venningen, the onetime Lady Ellenborough, Balzac's "African" mistress, the beauty who subjugated kings, bargaining with a young Arab Sheik for the terms of her surrender. About goes on to say that they made a covenant; and a very odd one, at that. Ianthe should become the sole wife for a period of three years, and that if at the end of that time the Sheik should wish to reinstate his harem he should be free to do so; otherwise, the contract should be renewed, on the same terms. If About's details are correct, then it would seem that Ianthe had indeed preserved her naïve optimism, and to the point of madness. Even so great a beauty as she can hardly have hoped to keep an Arab, fifteen to twenty years younger, on strictly monogamous terms.

At any rate, it was a sustaining piece of tattle, and Athenian society was nourished on it for months. When About's book *La Grèce contemporaine* was translated into English, this incident was removed, perhaps in deference to, or at the request of Ianthe's sensitive English relatives. The Greek historian and statesman Spyridon Trikoupis, who lived in Corfu and was three times Greek Ambassador in London must have known her well; probably he acted as a filter through which only the more reassuring aspects of Ianthe's life in Athens sometimes reached England.

But back to Damascus where Sâlih sulked, while Jane continued planning her journey to Palmyra without him. Once again we see the irresistible attraction which adventure held for Jane. Not even a new love could hold her long, when she sensed the desert and the excitement of new scenes awaiting her. All her roving blood rose.

It was while negotiating for a camel caravan to take her across the desert, a nine days' journey at that time, that she encountered the man who was to become her fourth and last husband, her great love, the Sheik Abdul Medjuel El Mezrab. His tribe were a branch of the Anazeh. They controlled the desert round Palmyra and were, for the tribal habits of their day, a particularly honorable and cultivated lot. They were neither rich nor numerous, but their blood was blue. The Sheik Medjuel was the second of nine sons. His father, the ruler of the tribe, had been a remarkable man, who had insisted that all his children obtain a wide education. That Medjuel could read and write was a distinction among the Bedouins. He spoke several languages, and was well-read; he had studied the histories of ancient Syria, and knew the desert and its legends as few others. Sometimes he acted as escort to distinguished travelers. It augmented the tribe's finances, and it brought him interesting contacts with the outside world. It was suggested that he should act as Jane's guide. And so they met.

Medjuel El Mezrab was only a few years younger than Jane. He was not at all the novelette version of the blazing-eyed desert Adonis, though it must be remarked that nearly all Arab men possess those glittering and impenetrable black eyes so irresistible to European women. When Richard Burton was appointed Consul in Damascus, in 1869, Mrs. Burton came to know Medjuel and his wife well. Isabel Burton was a snob, and she reverenced Lady Ellenborough, as she always preferred to call her, though she deplored Medjuel's particularly dark cast of countenance. She condoned the Schwarzenberg lapse, while ignoring all the others, but, as she confided to her journal, "The contact with that black skin I could *not* understand. His skin was dark—darker than a Persian—much darker than an Arab generally is. All the same, he was a very intelligent charming man in any light but that of a husband. That made me shudder."

Medjuel El Mezrab followed the pastoral and nomadic tradition of his people. (It was only after fifteen years of marriage that Jane persuaded him to a knife and fork.) He was both scholarly and virile, with character and humor. He was of the desert. He had none of what Doughty calls "the glozing politic speech of the town Arab." He impressed all the distinguished travelers who were later to visit him when he and Jane were man and wife. Byron's granddaughter, Lady Anne Blunt, and her husband the poet Wilfred Scawen Blunt, encountered him during their wanderings in Syria, where they were buying the Arab horses they afterwards introduced into England, and wildly planning an Arabian Caliphate to be headed by Abd El Kadir. They did not see him as *le mari de Madame*, but a personality in his own right; and there were no invidious references to his complexion.

But at the moment of their first meeting, Jane was still under Sâlih's spell. Medjuel was merely a courteous Arab with whom she was negotiating terms. Medjuel, however, was at once intrigued by his odd and beautiful client. "*Engleysi*"—a madwoman, shrugged the Arabs, lounging in doorways, eyeing the heavy baggage being loaded. Eugénie, so efficient, so long-suffering, always had to unpack silver, damask and fine bed linen for every wayside halt. She had done it right across Europe, from Paris to Greece and all over the Balkans; now, it was the desert. If, up to the present Jane had not traveled with an excessive attention to luxury, neither had she yet learned to live *à la Bedouine*. That was to come. Only a very rich maniac could travel about like that, the Arabs decided, and among themselves they discussed plans for raiding her caravan.

The expedition started out in style. Medjuel had brought a large retinue: there were outriders, baggage camels, horses, and of course the foster-camels which were used as traveling dairies, or mobile milk supplies for the highly bred Arab horses who could obtain no pasturage in the arid desert wastes. The slow plodding sway of the camel train was a base from which Jane and the by now enslaved Medjuel galloped off into the tawny distance to visit the ruins, lonely encampments or oases that lay off their route. Jane was as tireless a horsewoman in her forties as in her twenties, when she had astonished Balzac. Perhaps she began to realize that, for women, travel, in its real sense, only begins where love leaves off. You cannot serve two masters. Most women find their views of countries have been filtered through the personality of their companion. An emotional life presupposes a concentration of time and energy lavished on one person: there is little left over for places. Now Jane and Medjuel hunted antelope and wolves, and shot partridges, and Jane did some sketching in the true Victorian tourist's manner. Romantic ruins, and those poor dear camels, as she often called them. She was still "doing the East," the sights, as an outsider, in polite perspectives, reminiscent of the drawing-room albums then in vogue.

For Medjuel, it was probably love at first sight. Love tinged with bewilderment and a sense of daring. It was unheard of that he, a Moslem, a Sheik, should consider *marrying* a Christian. Yet, very early, he sensed that if he wished to have her for himself, he must take such a drastic step. By now he had heard of Sâlih. There would be others. He did not wish to be one of a string of experimental Arab amours. She was, he knew, a great lady, but he had no feeling of aspiring to her hand. He was an Arab noble—his blood quite as blue as hers. If anything, he considered whether he himself was not risking too great a *mésalliance*. But he said nothing for the time, and the expedition went on its way. At night they all sat round the campfire, and flames lit up the swarthy faces as they laughed and talked among themselves in the guttural Arabic Jane could not follow. (She and Medjuel spoke a mixture of the French and Turkish he knew passably well.) It was all a series of exotic picnics, to Jane, as she sat among the Bedouins eating roasted lamb basted with sheep's yoghourt and wild honey. Outside the circle the camels groaned and barked in their melancholy fashion, and the horses whinnied in the darkness, or far away a jackal howled. Jane, sleeping unmolested in her black Bedouin tent, still dreamed of Sâlih; but Medjuel dreamed of Jane.

Once again, as in the duel between Venningen and Theotoky, there was a dramatic episode of drama verging on farce. This time the duel was a tribal rather than personal matter, but it was still fought over Jane. The caravan was on its way, about six days out from Damascus, when they were suddenly surrounded by a ferocious-looking band of horsemen, brandishing spears, and demanding their money or their lives. Damascus had rung with ghastly stories of the fate met by desert travelers. Some never returned: there was talk of whitened bones, carrion crows, ransoms, tortured hostages, death by thirst . . . two Englishmen had lately crawled back stripped of all but a copy of *The Times*. Jane turned trustfully to Medjuel.

Now it is possible that since this was one of the customary pre-arranged holdups, and was in fact conducted by some of Medjuel's own tribe, he was aware of the plan and allowed it to proceed in order to appear as Jane's defender, a chivalresque figure, *sans peur et sans reproche*. It is equally possible he knew nothing of it, was taken by surprise, but being by now emotionally involved, decided to defend the object of his love. At any rate, he behaved with what the tribesmen found a bewildering loyalty to his client, rather than themselves. He rushed into battle, rallied his own men round him, and at the point of his lance routed the marauders, who fled nonplussed. The whole thing had taken place in a few moments of violent action and counteraction. Jane, who always throve on drama, found the incident most stimulating; Medjuel was brave as a lion, a hero, her savior! There were some tender passages which led Medjuel to hope. It was said in Damascus, later, that he had pressed his suit then and there and that out of gratitude she ceded. But this does not seem to have been the truth, for when a little while later she returned to Athens to settle her affairs before returning to live permanently in Syria, she was still planning to marry Sâlih. There is no doubt, however, that the incident raised Medjuel enormously in her esteem. She always had a weakness for dashing men.

Back in Damascus, Jane tore herself away from the desert and Sâlih with reluctance; but it was imperative to wind up things in Athens. She was back there in 1853 for just long enough to cold-shoulder Hadji-Petros' renewed advances, and to titillate her friends with accounts of her latest adventure. The reaction of cramped Athenian salons must have decided her finally. No more salons, no more Europe. She returned to Syria before the year was out. But the Bedouin Lovelace had not waited. Jane found a rival installed; not merely the harem she had dismissed in her contract, but a young person called Sabla, very young, and very impudent. Jane retreated before Sabla's invincible youth.

Once more there were tears and regrets and wild longings for the past and the golden heyday of her own youth. Evidently only travel and archaeology remained. She might have known as much. In a somber mood she set out for Baghdad, trusting once more in the restorative effects of travel, but this time without much faith. She saw before her the awful abyss of remorse and a solitary old age. Still, there could be no turning back. England was closed to her; so was Bavaria. Paris—? No; she had done with big cities. To return to Greece would have been unthinkable. She had burned her boats. The East, which had lured her and punished her could still comfort her. She loved the land and the life. She set about learning Arabic, and decided that she would retire to a little house hidden away in the Arab quarter of Damascus. Eugénie was still to be counted on. They would grow old together, surrounded by the cats and dogs she loved. Now there would be more time for them. There are natures which need love, a lover's presence, to enjoy a landscape, a symphony, or even their food. Love seems to be a part of their basic metabolism; age does not change such natures; their craving only perishes with life itself. Jane was such a one. Therefore, it was in a mood of black depression she set about making the best of the dust and ashes that remained to her.

She began to explore the country. Edward Lear, returning from Petra on one of his sketching tours which produced the meticulous and lovely water colors now forgotten beside his *Nonsense Rhymes*, mentions meeting her about this time. "Lady Ellenborough in a crimson velvet pelisse and green satin riding habit, going up to complicate the absurdities of Jerusalem," he writes, tantalizingly. We long to know more. Did they meet at some verminous wayside inn? Did they exchange travelers' platitudes, insecticides and sketching notes? It is unlikely they were much together—they could have had little in common, this painfully shy, neurotic, "pixilated" man, always building barriers of illness, nonsense and inhibitions between himself and reality, and Lady Ellenborough, entirely uninhibited, very healthy, living life to the full, all barriers down.

At this time Syria appeared to most Europeans as far more remote and ill-regulated than India. For centuries it had been under Turkish rule. The Porte appointed local Sheiks to administer the different provinces, but often with the intent to set them at each other's throat. Once a year the great religious pilgrimages to Mecca roused the country to a ferment. There were various routes, according to the place of departure: from North Africa; from Arabia; from Cairo. The Western Hadj or caravan of pilgrims used to leave from Damascus, where it was swelled by more pilgrims from Constantinople. Side by side with this immemorial scene, there were now prospectors, working on the proposed Euphrates Valley Railway, which was to be a short cut to India, but which was finally abandoned in 1872. Greek boats called at the ports bringing mail about twice a month. For trans-desert communication there were dromedary couriers: the Damascus-Hit route was known as the Road of Death, for it was infested by bandits, and the wells were two hundred and fifty miles apart. As early as 1160 the Fatimid Caliphs of Cairo had established a special courier pigeon service which had been in use for generations. The birds flew in relays: Cairo, Basra, Beyrout, Constantinople: on the Little Desert route they winged from Damascus to Palmyra and Meshed Rahba. There were bird towers every fifty miles.

Out of these savage wastes, rockbound and arid, rose the ruins of Zenobia's empire, and the veined pink cliff-face of Petra, "the rose-red city half as old as time." To the west, Damascus bloomed among its gardens. Damascus, "Shaum Sheref," the Holy or Blessed, it was called. Mohammed is said to have gazed on it and called it Paradise.

He declined to dally, however, holding there must be only one Paradise—Allah's own. "Minarets peered out from the midst of shade, into the glowing sky and, kindling, touched the sun," says Kinglake. It was a landscape of milk and honey. But it was not insipid. In the winter the snows came down, wolves howled in the foothills, and the tribes moved south on their annual migratory trek, always searching pasturage for their sheep and camels. These tribes were accounted by their numbers of flocks, or in the case of warrior tribes, by the spears they mustered.

Syria was as violently picturesque as its history, which still echoed with the name of Rustem and his elephants, and great Tamburlaine. Within living memory Mahommed Ali, who butchered the Mamelukes, had coveted Syria, but his sieges and schemes came to nothing, and he had been seen languishing in a Neapolitan hotel, playing whist with a young American tourist, said those who returned to Damascus to tell of the old tyrant. His son, Ibrahim Pasha of Acre, too, had come to no good, and was last heard of in London at the Reform Club. Syria settled back again with relief. Not that anyone could call it a really peaceful place, or one recommended to tourists. Very few travelers passed through, in the forties and fifties. The spate of books which were to come in the sixties and seventies, *A Summer Ramble in Syria, Cradle Lands, My Friends the Bedouins,* or *Damascus Day,* had yet to be written, as so much of the land had yet to be explored. After Lady Hester Stanhope, Jane Digby was one of the first European women to venture there alone.

In the early spring of 1854 she set out for Baghdad. She was still brooding over Sâlih, still recoiling from the specter of old age. But presently there was a revivifying interlude with another Arab, the Sheik El Barrak, who found her as seductive, in her grief, and late forties, as other, earlier lovers had done in her heyday. Perhaps the crimson velvet pelisse had something to do with it. To the Arab eye it must have seemed a queenly outfit for the rocky ravines. The Sheik was insistent, the lady was lonely. We have no record of what Eugénie thought about it all, huddled up beside the campfire, regretting, no doubt, the comparative civilization and restraint of the Pallikars.

There were a few voluptuous days and nights together in the desert, most agreeably distracting to one in Jane's melancholy mood. But the affair proved as worthless as the man. They quarreled: first over his unkindness to "those poor dear camels," and later his unsympathetic attitude toward her sketching. The final break came when El Barrak made free with her tent and invited several strangers inside. There was a violent scene; Jane was angry with herself, that she could have accepted such a man as her lover; El Barrak was furious when he saw her slipping from his grasp—the lady, and perhaps, her money.

When they reached Aleppo they were on very bad terms, but they continued their journey together. It is not easy to shed a caravan en route. There were no regrets on Jane's side, for there was no love, no disillusion, here. It had all been a great mistake, and it was far, far better to live without love, in solitude and dignity. But her mind still harked back, painfully, to Sâlih, and sometimes she thought affectionately of Medjuel, who had been such a different type from El Barrak; so *simpatico*, such a gentleman. . . .

Jane was now well known by repute to most of the Syrian Arabs, and her latest amorous adventures had been discussed throughout the camps and bazaars; news of her return from Baghdad soon reached Medjuel in the desert. When he heard she was riding towards Damascus, in company with the Sheik El Barrak, he acted quickly. Suddenly, he rode up out of the horizon to meet her, bringing a beautiful Arab mare as a present; their meeting was decisive. The Sheik El Barrak disappeared, with tact, or prudence perhaps; together Jane and Medjuel returned to the city. During the next few days, Jane discovered in Medjuel all the qualities and attractions she had so often imagined were centered in other men. This time she was not deceived. Medjuel had character, brains, and breeding; and he loved her for herself. (This was to be proved, over and over again. During the thirty years of their life together, he was always profoundly disinterested in her fortune.) Medjuel was a man of honor and kindness; a man of romantic passion, too, she discovered. A man of purpose. During her absence he had set about divorcing his wife, who had borne him sons and was, by Arab standards, an old woman. No one seems to have found it cruel that she was sent back to her people. She was given the dowry she had originally brought, and was in fact honorably pensioned off.

Now Medjuel was free to marry Jane on her own European terms. He proposed to her, as they rode towards Palmyra once more; and Jane, still full of girlish excitement and rapture, recorded in her journal their first kiss. He was accepted unreservedly. Suddenly there was no more loneliness and disillusion. She had found the perfect man and the perfect life. She was reborn. *"Si je n'avais ni miroir, ni mémoire, je me croirais quinze ans,"* she wrote in her journal. Mirror or no, all contemporary accounts agree that she did not look anywhere near her age. Even when sixty-eight, she was thought to be forty. "Those Englishwomen have the devil's own trick for keeping young," said one French traveler, rather grudgingly.

There was a stormy interview with the English Consul, who was outraged at the idea of the marriage, questioned her sanity, and tried to prevent it, or at any rate delay matters until he had consulted the authorities in England. But Jane was adamant. Official barriers were swept aside, and the marriage took place at Homs, where Medjuel owned a house, although he always preferred living under tents in the desert. Jane was at once loved and accepted by the Mezrab tribes. She was known as Jane Digby El Mezrab—the Arabs called her the Sitt, or Lady; more picturesquely, Umn-el-Laban, Mother of Milk, in reference to her fair skin. She was supremely happy among them. She felt she had come home, as indeed she had.

At first Jane and Medjuel divided their time between Homs and the desert tents, those black hair tents of Kedar which had remained unchanged through the centuries. Later Jane was to build a fine house on the outskirts of Damascus where they lived six months of the year *à l'Européenne*, the other six being spent *à la Bédouine*. Each of them adapted to the other's way of life, though Medjuel, like all Bedouins, found cities and houses stifling and made frequent dashes into the desert, which not only his nature but his interests, the flocks and horses, demanded. Jane was quick to adopt Arab ways. She smoked the *narghilyé* and liked to go barefooted, wearing the traditional blue robe and yashmak. She learned to outline her huge blue eyes with the smudge lines of kohl that are an essential part of an Arab woman's *maquillage,* and flung herself into the life and habits of the tribe. Both outwardly and inwardly, she was one with them.

Her splendid horsemanship, her knowledge of horses, and her methods of caring for them, keeping them in condition and doctoring them, all legacies from the Holkham stables, were greatly valued by the Arabs. They hunted; there were falcons, and Persian hounds; and soon Jane had mastered the art of dromedary-riding, and was often to be seen racing at the head of a group of Bedouins. The dromedary is not an easy mount. It can go very fast but it pitches and tosses uneasily. To such an Amazon, however, it was no problem. "Dear useful animals," she called them. Like another expert on horseflesh, Lady Anne Blunt, she loved and appreciated the dromedaries and found them patient, intelligent and affectionate. Sheep breeding, horse breeding, crops: this pastoral life awoke many echoes of Holkham. Jane had never been, at heart, a drawing-room or city woman. She had loved the primitive life at Dukades, and in the Albanian mountains too. This was a thousand times better. She glowed with content, but was torn with a mixture of emotions—pride, astonishment, and sadness, when Medjuel went off alone into the desert for a two months' sheep-herding expedition, in order to earn money for his tribe. She remarked the independence of his attitude towards her money: it had not occurred to him to avail himself of her fortune, as Schwarzenberg, Theotoky, Hadji-Petros and many others had done.

Perhaps, during such times, suspended between more vibrant phases, she was able to assess and savor the desert stillness, that immemorial Arab climate of nothingness, of being, simply, as a state of well-being. Perhaps, she too began to share their special *optique* on life. It has been said that the Arab object in life is to Be—free, brave, wise—or just to Be, contrary to so many other peoples, whose aim is to Have—wealth, knowledge, a name. Perhaps, too she was aware of that mighty whirring of wings, that pulse of nineteenth-century endeavor sounding tensely beyond the desert's rim, heralding a new way of life, where it was enough to Do. Movement and action for their own sakes; a sort of nervous tic. How gloriously rich the life of a Bedouin shepherd seemed, compared to that of a city scuttler. Perhaps she remembered, ironically, that bombastic Ellenborough, her husband so many lives and loves past, had also reached the East—but another East to hers. He had become Governor-General of India. If she had stayed to reach the Orient as his consort, how stifling, how frustrating she would have found those pearl-fringed pavilions. A thousand times better, the black Bedouin tents of her Mezrabi.

She began to speak Arabic fluently, though those who knew her later, such as the great Orientalist, Sir Richard Burton, record that she spoke with a strong regional accent, a sort of country burr, acquired from her tribe, and of which she was sensitive. But Medjuel, according to Abd El Kadir, spoke the most classical Arabic in all Syria.

It was a busy life: there were intertribal affairs, and family affairs too. She had eight brothers-in-law now, and all their wives and children, and two stepsons, Schebibb and Japhet and their wives, too. She was on excellent terms with all of them. Gradually they began to turn to their Umn-El-Laban for advice on more and more questions: farming, medicine, law, domestic affairs, education and such. Medjuel's elder brother, the Sheik, was childless: Medjuel was virtually head of the Mezrabi, first by reason of his linguistic abilities, and then, by virtue of his two sons, who were the Sheik's heirs.

It must not be imagined that Medjuel and Jane always lived a serene October idyl. "So calm we are, when passions are no more." For them, there were still many years of overboiling emotional stress, lovers' quarrels, reconciliations, jealousies, a torrid climate of love. Sometimes there were romantic snatched honeymoon journeys alone together in the desert. Sometimes there were misunderstandings and partings. When they married there had been a most peculiar pact instigated by Jane. If at any time Medjuel felt constrained by European monogamy, he was free to take another wife—but she must be kept at a distance, and Jane must never know. To Jane, in the first fiery transports of her love, as certain of its everlasting glow as she always was, this had seemed reasonable. And indeed it was so—but when did reason ever live with love? In time, Medjuel's occasional absences and casual bazaar gossip was to torment Jane bitterly. There were scenes. Nor was Medjuel always easy on her account. She continued fatally attractive, though now so deeply, so long, in love, that there were probably no more than sidelong glances. . . . Still, mystery and hints surround the name of the Sheik Farés El Meziad, and there are certain incidents which remain dark and clouded with passions. Medjuel was as possessive as all his race. It is inconceivable that he would have tolerated any freedom on his wife's part.

It was never dull. Besides personal dramas there were intertribal feuds and raids where enemy tribes swooped, snatching the best cattle; and once Jane's favorite mare. The Government dallied, no action was taken. Jane boiled with indignation and scorn. At the head of the troops she and Medjuel galloped off to battle. There were three weeks of desert warfare: Holo Pasha attacked their camp with a force of ninety, at dead of night, but Medjuel and Jane rallied their men and he was routed. She gained even more stature in the Arab world by her adventurous spirit. She was a law unto herself; the Arabs, like the Europeans, came to realize that Jane upset all preconceived notions, and fitted into no category—woman, Amazon, wife, mistress . . . she was Jane Digby El Mezrab, and as unique in the East as the West. Sometimes her money was helpful in buying the newer sorts of arms for the tribe's defense. (For the most part the Bedouin tribes were armed with spears or crazy old horse pistols.) In this instance Medjuel occasionally accepted her contribution, and she was even more respected by his people. Here is a bellicose entry in her diary: "Cannon and musketry was heard in the morning, and about twelve dozen Arab horsemen rushed into the town with the too true news that Hassaim Bey had indeed attacked our camp with Ebn Merschid, and after pouring a volley of balls into our tents, had carried off all our camels, but, thank God, had killed none of our men." Then there was more buckling on of armor, more priming of flintlocks, more reprisals. No; it was never dull.

Some of these desert skirmishes continued for weeks at a time, with savagery. Others were more formal and conducted on the lines of medieval tourneys—that is, with more ceremony and tradition than bloodshed. Some of the Syrian tribes, and notably the Rowála and the Ibn Haddal, still maintained the immemorial custom of the *Uttfa,* a huge camel-howdah which on the occasion of a pitched battle was in the center of the fight. It was an immense bamboo structure, a sort of cane pavilion, lavishly decorated with ostrich feathers. Inside sat a girl whose business was to sing the slow, nasal Arab chants which can express both love and fury with so slight a change. Her object was to whip up the fighting spirit of the Rowála, to keep them on the attack. Her defense or capture decided the battle. It cannot have been an enviable position, amid whistling spears and savage tribesmen. But as a legendary spectacle it was probably one of the many historic and now vanished Arab customs which Jane Digby El Mezrab was able to see first hand.

She often speaks of the *djerid,* or fantasia, the wild, plunging charge of the Bedouin horsemen, a traditional Arab flourish, practiced from Morocco to Arabia. She does not go into any details, however; she accepts it all in a very matter-of-fact manner. But her compatriot, Isabel Burton, new to Syria and as englamored by the East, describes it in detail. "When I say the men are riding *djerid,* I mean that they are galloping about violently, firing from horseback at full speed, yelling, hanging over in their stirrups with their bridles in their mouth, playing with and quivering their long feathered lances in the air, throwing them and catching them again at full gallop, picking things from the ground, firing pistols, throwing themselves under the horses' bellies and firing under them at full gallop, yelling and shouting their war cry. . . . The wildness of the scene is very refreshing," she adds; "but you have to be a good rider yourself, as the horses simply go wild."

In 1857 Jane decided to visit England. She wished to see her family, her lawyers, the trustees of her income, and to settle her will in Medjuel's favor. But the visit had to be of a surreptitious nature for an aura of vice surrounded the mere mention of her name in England, where if ever she was alluded to it was in terms of opprobrium, as the scarlet woman. It was very trying to her family, who still smarted when they read references to *"undesirable persons . . .* [such as] *the notorious and polyandrous Jane Digby El Mezrab. This lady had been the wife first of Lord Ellenborough, who divorced her; secondly of Prince Schwarzenberg, and afterwards of about six other gentlemen. Finally, having used up Europe, she made her way to Syria where she married a dirty little black Bedouin shaykh."* And except for the adjectives "dirty," "little," "black," which the Digbys were not in a position to refute, there was really nothing they could say.

Jane had not been back to England since the Schwarzenberg scandal of 1830. She had left a society of Regency gaiety and latitude. Now she was to find it smothered in the clinging creepers of Victorian prudery. All her contemporaries had become stout, or withered matrons. Home life was the altar at which everyone worshiped. There were long engagements, sentiments, but not passions. Divorce was never mentioned. Widows who remarried were not received at Court. Missionaries were much in vogue. All races who were not of the European strain were dismissed as black or yellow, poor heathens, to be converted, or patronized—but emphatically not to be married. The mere idea was indecent. Especially when you looked like Jane, who returned to the family fold with an unrepentant air of youth and romance. At fifty she seemed in her early thirties. She had kept her figure; her hair was still the chestnut tan Balzac had admired; the few silver strands merely seemed becoming. It was noted that she had that horrid Eastern habit of blacking her eyes. Painted! All her elegance and charm and loving gaiety were as nothing: the over-all aura of disapproval could not countenance a happy sinner. If only she had come back wasted, bathed in tears of repentance! How stimulating, how gratifying that would have been. . . . They would have shown her how charitable they could be towards a fallen woman. Instead of which she positively gloried in her Arab marriage (on top of all those others too . . .). The visit was not really a success, although some of her relatives rallied round with a show of warmth. Jane's temperament and perennial youth were a fatal barrier to all except Kenelm, who was as loving as ever. Even Steely, her old and faithful governess, was not to be won by graphic accounts of Syrian delights. Jane had married a black—Steely did not care to discuss it. To the whole family, Medjuel was unmentionable, which hurt Jane's pride. The damp and chilly English spring depressed her; there were no letters from darling Medjuel. She fretted: she did not belong in England any more now than in her youth. Soon after her fiftieth birthday, it seemed better to hurry back to Syria, the sun— and Medjuel. She stopped in Paris just long enough to buy a piano, a lot of elegant clothes, and a stock of poultry. She pressed on, Marseilles, the Mediterranean; she was fuming as the boat lingered in the little ports of call. At last the low apricot-colored coastline of Syria came into view. The East! Beyrout, and the mountains of the Lebanon, at last! She rushed ashore. Baggage, the piano, the poultry, the Parisian toilettes—all were forgotten. She rode on through the night. "With beating heart, I arrived in Damascus. . . . He arrived, Medjuel, the dear, the adored one, and in that moment of happiness I forgot all else." The wanderer had come home, at last.

*       *       *

Medjuel was a profoundly religious man. He never missed the sunrise and sunset ritual prayers of his Mohammedan faith. Jane had not been noticeably pious, but she became, by way of thankfulness rather than repentance, a devout churchgoer. She knew there was no question of converting Medjuel to Christianity; she respected his religion as he respected hers, but she seems to have regretted that she could never win him over from the crescent to the cross. Perhaps the devotion, the matter-of-fact mysticism of the Moslems around her affected her—perhaps their deep inbred piety awoke her own dormant religious principles. At any rate, she came to redouble her now active participation in church affairs. As time went on missionaries were welcomed at her house, and their schemes for schooling the infidel young were encouraged.

There was never any suggestion of the reformed rake about Jane. She was not trying for redemption. She simply realized her good fortune and happiness with Medjuel, thanked God humbly, and tried to share some of her happiness with others—with the missionaries, who were trying to help the dear Bedouins—her people; with the Bedouins, who might (who knows?) profit by the Bible classes and kindergarten schools. There is an account of a Sunday school class in Damascus where she slipped in, unobserved, and squatted on her heels among the other Arab women. She was dressed as they, and veiled—besides which her long chestnut hair was now dyed black, in accordance with the Arab superstition that fair hair is unlucky. It is not surprising that the missionaries did not recognize the former Lady Ellenborough. She lingered to chat politely and congratulated them on their work. And here I seem to see a flicker of the other Jane, the mischievous creature who described her long list of lovers as a naughty *Almanach de Gotha*; the Jane whose ironic banter delighted Balzac and all who knew her.

But even at sixty she was by no means given over to religion. In Damascus, among both East and West, she had become a celebrated and much-loved figure. The Burtons had lately arrived at the Consulate where he, as an unequaled Orientalist, could profit by and savor her remarkable knowledge of Arab life. Abd El Kadir too had settled in the city with his retinue of faithful Algerians. The Burtons, the Mezrabs, and Abd El Kadir spent many of the breathless summer nights stretched on the rooftop of the Burtons' house at Salahíyyeh, where, with their *narghilyés* beside them they spent the time smoking and exchanging Oriental lore. Burton was still collecting notes for his *Arabian Nights,* and particularly the "Terminal Essay" which says all there is to say on Arab sexual life and customs.

Now when Burton, as a young and daring traveler disguised himself as a Persian peddler, he succeeded long before his journey to Mecca, in penetrating that other sacred Moslem fastness, the harem. All he wrote has the ring of truth; but Jane Digby El Mezrab had become a Moslem wife. She knew their ways, their harems, as not even Burton could do. There is no doubt he consulted her on many things. Mrs. Burton, who was always a little left out, on these occasions (one senses her eager, reverent, but spectator's attitude), speaks of those evenings on the rooftops, when the other visitors, the twenty-odd Europeans then resident in Damascus, the members of the Consular and Government services and passing visitors, had left, since few people cared to be out after dark in the lonely mountainside where the Burtons lived. "How I look back to those romantic days . . . when the mattresses and cushions of the divans were spread on the housetop . . . then the supper was prepared on the roof, and there remained with us the two most interesting and remarkable characters of Damascus, the two who never knew what fear meant—the famous Abd El Kadir and Lady Ellenborough. . . . She was a most beautiful woman, though at the time I write she was sixty-one, tall, commanding and queenlike. She was *grande dame au bout des doigts*, as much as if she had just left the salons of London and Paris, refined in manner and voice, nor did she ever utter a word you could wish unsaid. My husband thought she was out and out the cleverest woman he ever met; there was nothing she could not do. She spoke nine languages perfectly, and could read and write in them. Her letters were splendid; if on business there was never a word too much, nor a word too little [unlike Mrs. Burton, who rambled and gushed]. She had had a most romantic adventurous life, and she was now, one might say, Lady Hester Stanhope's successor." Mrs. Burton goes on to describe how Jane divided her time between the house in Damascus and the Bedouin tents. "When I first saw her in Damascus," she writes, ". . . she led a semi-European life. She blackened her eyes with kohl, and lived in a curiously untidy manner. But otherwise she was not in the least extraordinary," she says firmly. "She was honored and respected as queen of her tribe, wearing one blue garment, her beautiful hair in two long plaits down to the ground, milking the camels, serving her husband, preparing his food, giving him water to wash his hands and face, sitting on the floor and washing his feet, giving him his coffee, his sherbet, his *narghilyé*, and while he ate he stood and waited on him, and glorying in it. [Mrs. Burton heartily approved of this attitude, for she too was a submissive and enraptured wife.] She looked splendid in Oriental dress, and if you saw her in the bazaar you would have said she was not more than thirty-four years of age."

Though when living *à la Bedouine*, Jane seems to have for the most part worn the simple draperies which were general, she evidently blazed forth at times. In her will there are references to some sumptuous Oriental trappings. "My Arab ornaments, belt and jewelery in gold and silver and my silver gilt headpiece, breast ornament and bridle studded with coral . . . my colored diamond sprig for the head." Was this a European piece, legacy of her more fashionable days, or was it one of those elaborate, loose-wired trembling sprays of brilliants which are found in the Tunisian jewel *souks* and which were made by Italian craftsmen for the Eastern market? It is of no consequence, but I like to imagine her loaded in the trophies of her beauty, discreet European *gages d'amour* mingled with the more barbaric splendors of her adopted race, presiding, perhaps, over one of the traditional Arab fantasies, with cavorting horses, thundering hooves and volleys of shots scorching the spectators; presiding with that same grace that had once adorned Almack's or the salons of Paris, Munich and Athens . . . the camps along the way.

The Honorable Jane Digby El Mezrab, as she was now called (her brothers and sisters had had the rank of Baron's children conferred on them in 1859) saw everyone of note who visited Damascus, although there is no record that she ever met two of the most interesting Englishmen, Doughty and Holman Hunt. The pre-Raphaelite painter arrived in 1854 resolved, in his own words, to find out for himself what Christ looked like. For two years he wandered about painting Biblical types and scenes. Doughty, the scholarly traveler, his head full of fossils and Chaucerian English, lived hidden away in the Arab quarter of Damascus, in 1875. He was studying Arabic in preparation for his travels across Arabia. To such people, Jane Digby El Mezrab and her husband were always hospitable and warm. But those who regarded her as one of the sights (a onetime beauty, with four husbands still living, and now married to a black, was their attitude) were icily repelled. Anyone with letters of introduction from friends was sure of being received in the lovely house she built on the outskirts of the city by the Bab Menzel Khassab, one of Damascus' many gates. It was as beautiful and personal as all her homes had been. The garden was filled with lily ponds and rare plants, as well as English fruit trees. There were English flowers, too: the chintzy cottage borders that must have recalled the Norfolk of her youth—pinks and candytuft, sweet williams and Canterbury bells. Medjuel eyed them longingly. As a nomad he was not interested in horticulture; but what pasturage for his camels! The stables and outbuildings centered round a courtyard where a fountain played, and where Jane's ever-growing menagerie was fed by the still faithful Eugénie. At one moment, besides horses, donkeys, dromedaries, a pelican, Persian hounds and parrots, there were around a hundred cats. Each one was required to have its own plate. No wonder only Eugénie was entrusted with this task: it would have seemed both unseemly and incomprehensible to the Bedouins. The house was furnished, for the most part, in the European manner, with ormolu, and mirrors, *grospoint,* knickknacks, and family photographs too. There was a splendid octagonal drawing room of great size and elegance, where Jane received her guests amid the lovely things she had amassed during her wanderings. Her clothes, if a little outmoded, were still unmistakably Parisian; round her neck she wore magnificent pearls. The Emperor of Brazil called one morning at the odd hour of 6 A.M. but was received graciously. He was immediately under her spell. She said that he was the pleasantest royal person of all the pleasant royalty she had known.

*       *       *

Jane's acceptance of her husband's people and their ways was unquestioning. Isabel Burton says she was "more Bedouin than the Bedawi," and not only accepted, but was party to their habits of raiding, and levying large sums of safe-conduct money from desert travelers crossing their territory. This is Mrs. Burton's account of how they got the better of a suspicious character recommended to them by Jane, as guide-protector, or *Ghafir* on their expedition to Tadmor. "This journey was an awfully difficult thing in those days. . . . First of all, six thousand francs used to be charged by the El Mezrab who were the tribe who escorted for that journey. . . . There was no water, that is, only two wells the whole way, and only known to them. The difficulties and dangers were great; they traveled by night and hid by day. You may say that camels were about ten days on the road and horses about eight days. . . . Lady Ellenborough" [to Mrs. Burton she was always a peeress, rather than a Mezrab) . . . "aided the tribe in concealing the wells and levying blackmail on Europeans who wished to visit Palmyra, which brought in considerable sums to the tribe." The Burtons were determined to go, but had no money to spare for such tourist indulgences. Richard Burton had no need of interpreters; to the man who had penetrated Mecca as a Moslem, such an expedition was in the nature of a stroll. When he asked his wife if she were prepared to risk the trip, her answer was characteristic. "Whither thou goest, I will go." Isabel says that on hearing their decision Lady Ellenborough was in a great state. "She knew it was the deathblow to a great source of revenue to the tribe. She was very intimate with us, and distantly connected by marriage with my family, and she would have favored us if she could have done so without abolishing the whole system. She did all she could to dissuade us; she wept over our loss and she told us that we should never come back—indeed everyone advised us to make our wills; finally, she offered us the escort of one of her Mezrabi, that we might steer clear of the Bedawi raids, and be conducted quicker to water *if it existed*." This is Mrs. Burton's view; it may be a rather high-handed interpretation of a perfectly innocent offer on Jane's part. Or it may not; in any case, Burton was a match for any Bedouin. He often spoke of the rapid decline in Arab chivalry: in the increasing treachery and decay of traditional honor. When once the sacred ceremony of breaking salt together rendered travelers safe among the tribes, now hunger and want had changed all. "Useless to plead *Nahnu malihin!* (We are salt-fellows!)" wrote Burton. "They rejoin, 'Thy salt is not in my belly.' The great majority of these sons of Antar who had ceased to be gentlemen, ignore or rather deride the rococo practice of their forefathers. And there are scoundrels who will offer you a bowl in one hand and stab you with the other."

Nevertheless, the Burtons decided to go: they accepted Jane's offer of a Mezrab *Ghafir*, but to make quite sure, took seventeen camels laden with water. Both were dressed in Arab clothes, and armed to the teeth: there were several grooms, *kavass*, outriders, and Mohammed Agha, Burton's faithful Afghan guard. This considerable cavalcade set out in style: even so, every precaution was taken. They slept in their clothes, revolvers at their sides; the men watched by turns, and the camel bells were removed, so that absolute silence reigned in camp at night. A day or so out from Damascus Mrs. Burton records that she thought the Mezrab wore "an uncanny, *amused* look." She discussed it with her husband; they were sure he would presently lead them into a trap. Burton called to the faithful Mohammed Agha, giving him some orders in Persian. The Afghan darted off. Mrs. Burton says that whenever Burton told him to fetch someone he would go off saying, "Yes, by Allah! Excellency, if he were in hell I would have him out— . . . "The Bedouin had his mare and his arms taken from him, and he was mounted on a baggage mule. *Every* kindness was shown to him, and he enjoyed *every* comfort that we had, but two mounted guard over him day and night, and he was thus powerless. We knew quite well that the Bedouin, on his thoroughbred mare, would have curveted off in circles, pretending to look for wells, when in reality he would have fetched the tribe down upon us and we should have been captured; orders would have been given to respect and treat us well, and then we should have to be ransomed, and this would have *proved* the impossibility of visiting Palmyra without a Bedawi escort at six thousand francs a head, and the Foreign Office would have smartly reproved, and perhaps recalled their Consul for running such a risk. We stuck our Mezrab up for a show, to prove that we had a Bedawi escort, whenever Bedawi raids were near, but he was not allowed to move or make a sign." Jane must have raged at this insult to her beloved Mezrabi: or did she perhaps secretly rejoice that the tribe had been taught a salutary, bloodless lesson? We have no record that she ever made any attempts to change the Bedouin pattern of violence, any more than she ever attempted to convert them to Christianity. She lived with, and among them, keeping a few of her own tenets inviolate, but never proselytizing. Then, too, if Medjuel the adored, the noble, lion-hearted, independent lover had never availed himself of her fortune, he must not be criticized for acquiring funds in ways traditional to his people. No, in all probability Jane's sympathies were more with the Bedouins than the Burtons. But she maintained a discreet silence, and having wept over their departure into unknown dangers, welcomed them back with every appearance of relief. It was Fate! Inch'allah! God had willed it so.

\*     \*     \*

The year 1872 brought a lot of adventure, and some high comedy too. Intertribal warfare flared up dangerously. The Mezrabi supported the Saba against their traditional rivals the Rowála over the vital question of pasturage, and trading concessions. After a series of underhand dealings and intrigues with the Turkish administration (who delighted in such), the Rowála provoked the Saba to battle; the Mezrabi joined in, but things went badly for them, and they suffered great losses of men and cattle. Their camps were sacked. Jane rushed off to be in the fray beside Medjuel. The Saba were licking their wounds. Presently they re-formed to attack. There was fierce fighting, and this time the Rowála were beaten at Jabul, in a battle of such ferocity that all Syria heard of it. The losses suffered by the Mezrabi led to the rumor that the Chief's wife, the Umn-El-Laban had been killed. There was no news of either Jane or Medjuel. The rumors multiplied: Jane was now as celebrated a figure in the Levant as she had been in Europe. In both life and death she made headline news. Now the papers vied with each other in raking over old mud. The obituary notices made racy reading —all of them told the same tale, in varying degrees of accuracy. One of them opened on a very impertinent tone. "There had just died a noble lady who greatly used, or abused marriage." . . . The writer credited her with six husbands in Italy alone. "She was at her seventh husband when she married, in Athens, a Greek Colonel, Count Theotoky, who could hold her no longer than the rest." . . . and so on. This obituary stated her ninth husband had been a camel-driver who had preceded her to the grave, showing little more accuracy than *Burke's Peerage* which, in one edition, described her first and second marriages correctly, and then lost all control: ". . . was married thirdly, to General Sheik Medjuel of the Greek Army, and fourthly, to Medjouel, an Eastern gentleman." Such variations on the matrimonial theme were altogether outside Burke's experience. The obituary notices continued to flood the English, French and German press—vying with each other in highly colored embellishments. Jane's surviving relatives were mortified. Even from her grave, it seemed, sex reared its ugly head once more.

But such calumnies were not to go unchallenged. Mrs. Burton, no longer at Damascus, since the sinister business of her husband's recall, had not forgotten her veneration for Lady Ellenborough. She still remembered the magic of those rooftop evenings at Salahíyyeh. With her customary energy she rushed to defend her dear friend's memory. Pages of denial and defense were dispatched to *The Times* and other European newspapers. Her motives were loyal, but she was almost as inaccurate as the rest. With a sweep of the pen she dismissed any aspersions of an irregular life. After listing Lady Ellenborough's many virtues she dwelt on her regular attendance at the Protestant church, "often twice on Sundays." . . . After announcing that she always fulfilled the duties of a good Christian lady and an Englishwoman, she continues with mounting zeal, "She had but one fault, and who knows if it was hers? [she adds generously] washed out by fifteen years of goodness and repentance." Thus Mrs. Burton, who admitted the Prince Schwarzenberg as Lady Ellenborough's *one fault* but ignored all the other slips from grace. She went on to say that she possessed autobiographical notes and material dictated to her by Lady Ellenborough, who had wished her to write the biography.

But Jane was not dead. When at last she rode back to Damascus by Medjuel's side in triumph she had the doubtful pleasure of reading her own obituary notices. Mrs. Burton's statements seemed to have annoyed her more than all the rest, and she wrote categorical denials all round. She was not dead—she had not had nine husbands—nor sanctioned *any* biography. There was a sharp exchange between the two ladies— and then it is likely that since Jane was without rancor, she forgot the whole business of her death in the more agreeable business of her life. But poor snubbed Mrs. Burton felt it all bitterly; she had meant so well.

Now Jane was a grandmother. But she had never been a really rapt mother, except in the case of Leonidas, whom she still mourned. The

Schwarzenberg children left her unmoved. The two Venningens, Bertha and Heribert, whom she had abandoned for Theotoky, had never caused her any particular maternal longings either. So a grandmother's state, too, did not seem to touch her as she could be touched, now, by the affairs of the tribe. Although she never saw the Venningen children, they corresponded. Bertha was a problem: her mind was slightly clouded, and she was finally consigned to an asylum. Poor Bertha! writes her mother, genuinely distressed, reproaching herself for her defaulting parenthood. Could she have saved Bertha's mind by staying? No, that would be a sentimentalist's view (Jane was always romantic, seldom sentimental); Bertha was a baby when she left; and Bertha had never known her—she was brought up in love and riches by the Baron, but she remained clouded. Heribert was another story. He was no problem, and although they never met, mother and son were on affectionate terms. He sent her his photograph, which she treasured: she was delighted when he sent his friend Count Louis Arco-Valley to visit her. We can imagine Heribert urging his fellow-student to visit his exotic parent. "Do go and look up Mama, she lives there, you know." But did the Count know? We see him, a student from Heidelberg, perhaps, touring the Holy Land, arriving in Syria, struck dumb by the wild welcome of a cohort of yelling Mezrabi tribesmen escorting him across the plains to Damascus, to their Chieftain's wife—Heribert's mother.

The whole tribe were proudly devoted to their Sitt. They appeared at all times of the day and night for advice and help. Sometimes, in moments of great intertribal stress, they would descend on the Damascus house in large numbers, and spread themselves all over the place, watering their camels at the fountain, camping in Jane's beautiful gardens, and even swarming over the house and sleeping on the stairs. But they were Medjuel's men—Jane did not mind at all. She sat unmoved in her octagonal drawing room, at her needlework, or discussing archaeological projects with would-be excavators. She was considered one of the foremost authorities on Syrian ruins, at that time. When Carl Haag, the fashionable Bavarian painter, visited Syria in 1859, they went sketching together, and Medjuel and his men escorted them to the more remote and picturesque panoramas. We can imagine the scene: Haag, the successful artist, whose satiny engravings adorned so many London homes, grown perhaps a little pompous, secure in the royal patronage of Queen Victoria and the Prince Consort. But always the professional artist, with his green-lined umbrella lashed to his light traveling easel, his camp stool, and his array of paints— water colors of course. Beside him, Jane, with rather less paraphernalia, and now quite inured to the sun, dabbing happily and skillfully, too, the pleasingly factual landscapes of her time. There is something touching in the scene: the dashing adventures, the Arab chieftain's wife, the Honorable Jane Digby El Mezrab, sitting quietly in the desert, painting a delicate water color in the manner Steely had taught her, so long ago, in the schoolroom at Holkham. These are the sort of paintings which few families value now, except historically. They are not to be taken seriously, as art. But they have the nostalgic power to evoke a place, an hour, an episode, as more intellectual approaches fail to do. They are still to be found, these delicate little water colors, stacked away in attics or junk shops. A pale gleam of gold proclaims the frame. The quarry is brought to light. Evening over the Bay of Naples; Swiss Lakes; The Cedars of Lebanon; a little carriage drawn up before some ornate villa. . . . They are pathetic yet abiding personal tributes to beauty, and another age.

So Jane sketched the romantic East around her, and chattered on about mutual friends in London and Munich. And in the shade of some stunted olive trees, or a crumbling mosque, Medjuel and his Mezrabi sat wrapped in their burnouses, immobile, silent, staring with that curiously inward-turning gaze of the Arab, as if they saw, absorbed the subject, and then contemplated it at length, from within. When Jane learned that Haag had painted the Prince Consort, she instantly commissioned him to paint Medjuel's portrait. Not that she saw Medjuel in the light of a consort: rather, he was her adored Lord and Master, for whom nothing—not even Queen Victoria's court portrait painter—was quite good enough.

"Sixty-two years of age, and an impetuous romantic girl of seventeen cannot exceed me in ardent passionate feelings," she wrote on her birthday. This romantic tenor continued throughout her sixties. She was evidently of that rare band of women to whom perennial youth and desirability are granted. Impossible to dismiss the legends, to say that she was importunate, all-devouring, or that her money and birth gave her the means to acquire lovers long after other women were on the shelf. Just as it had never occurred to Jane that she could lose her English birthright or individuality by becoming an Arab wife, so it never seemed to occur to her to become old.

In his memoirs, Lord Redesdale records how she spoke of the friends of her youth, of Regency London, as if time had stood still for them, too. She asked after an old friend, Lord Clanwilliam. Mr. Mitford, as Lord Redesdale was then, replied that he was wonderful, "cutting us all out at skating at Highclere two or three months ago."

She looked puzzled at that. "But why should he not?" she asked.

"Well," he answered, "you must remember that he is past seventy years of age."

"Dear me!" she exclaimed, "is it possible? That handsome young man!"

But Jane still felt young; she looked young, and she remained young too. Admiration and love are the best beauty treatments. Her life had never led towards the armchair, being divided, it might be said, between the saddle and the alcove. Until within a very few years of her death the pace never slackened and the pattern did not change. Lord Redesdale also speaks of her describing some of her many battle sorties to avenge some tribal affront. "In fact," she added, "we have one foot in the stirrup now, for we must start for the desert tomorrow morning." That was in 1871, when she was in her middle sixties.

She remained passionately, romantically in love with Medjuel, and except for that one mysterious episode of which nothing is certain, the episode concerning the tempestuous attentions of the rival Sheik Farés, she was always faithful to Medjuel. But was he faithful too? Certainly he loved her deeply, and there were never any Sablas, any flaunted mistresses, nor did he ever admit to another wife, such as their original marriage pact had convened. In the main he must have been a most satisfactorily ardent husband, as her diaries showed. But there were persistent rumors of his attachments to a stepdaughter-in-law, Ouadjid, Schebibb's widow, who, it was said, became far more than a daughter-in-law to Medjuel; Jane suffered torments of jealousy.

And then, to go back, there had been the estrangement caused by Jane's attitude in defending the Christians during the massacre of 1859. This hideous chapter of Syrian history was opened by an unprecedentedly snowy winter, devastated crops, famine and growing unrest among the heterogeneous population. Presently, Moslem and Christian fell on each other. In Beyrout, in May, the Druzes almost wiped out the Maronites, a Christian sect, in a massacre which spread in waves of terror across the country. In July, it reached Damascus, where the horrors of the Indian Mutiny were equaled. Kurds and Druzes set fire to the city, smoking out the Christians, who were put to the sword, raped or dismembered. The piled-up corpses rotted in the gutters and the pariah dogs savaged them. It was an appalling scene. All who could, fled. But Abd El Kadir and Jane Digby El Mezrab remained, to do what they might. Abd El Kadir plunged into the center of the bloodshed, trying to reason with the mob. When he found he could do nothing, he opened his house as sanctuary to any Christians who could reach it. From her house near the Moslem quarter Jane heard the battle raging round. As the Christian wife of a Moslem, and a conspicuous personality, her position was dangerous. Medjuel and his men had turned the house into a fort. The fires raged on. The foreign consulates were burned. Some of the Consuls and their staffs escaped—some were wounded, or killed outright. Few of them seem to have had the sense to act together. United they might have made a stand. But one, the Greek Consul, showed some fight. He retreated to the top of his house, with a gun and a bottle of *raki*. From this vantage point he picked off every Moslem who approached. Presently quite a litter of corpses were strewn outside his door, and seeing this the mob turned back. But even such resourcefulness was powerless against the spreading flames.

The heat of the Syrian July combined with the fires. It was a furnace. The reeking corpses and the shouts and groans of the tortured filled the air. Damascus, the golden city, the second Paradise, was an inferno such as Hieronymus Bosch imagined.

Yet Jane Digby El Mezrab left the protection of the Mezrab household, and quite alone went into the city, trying, like Abd El Kadir, to do what she could to turn the tide of carnage. She was less qualified to succeed, but she went on, unflinching. Neither her person nor her house was touched—a remarkable tribute to her position among the Arabs. But she had made a public and very positive admittance of her own Christian faith, which she continued to underline. There was never anything circuitous or compromising in her character. Even her love for Medjuel and the Arabs had to give place, here. In her middle age Jane had developed so strong a faith that she would have no more denied it than, many years ago, she would have denied her love for Schwarzenberg.

Such directness lacked tact, now as then; but there it was. It never occurred to her to love, or pray, in secret. And here it seems that Medjuel took an equally firm stand. There was an estrangement, and he went back to the desert, leaving Jane desolate.

Though not alone. Even after the massacre, when she was branded as a defaulting Moslem wife—an infidel—there were a series of highly colored improbably *opéra bouffe* scenes, where the Sheik Farés pressed his suit with a renewed cunning very disagreeable for Jane, deserted in Damascus, without the support of either the Mezrabi or such assistance as the English officials could have given were she still English. By her marriage and residence in Syria, she had now become a Turkish citizen —a fact she could no more accept than her age. Farés was a puissant prince, who owned enormous territories: but that he lusted after and coveted Medjuel's legendary wife for herself is undisputed. Her fortune may have been, as Burton once cynically averred, her passport in the desert, but it did not affect either the attitude of Medjuel, who though impoverished was totally lacking in worldly sense, or Farés, who was rich enough to be unmoved by her money. Even in middle age, and in another, Eastern world, Jane's charms were all-conquering. Which seems to confound the general theory that Arabs (unlike the Chinese) are only susceptible to extreme youth. Though perhaps in this, too, Jane was a law unto herself.

*       *       *

The trajectory of her emotional, or sexual, life must have risen from the innocent coquetry of the young girl to the hungry flirtations of the young wife, which in turn developed into the first burning love affair. After this there was no turning back. There are suffragettes, women who fight for their equality with man: there are women who spend their lives complaining that they are "the second sex," trying to revolt, to protest, to stand up to man in all the various fields of human activity. But Jane was not one of these. She never had to fight for equality: it came to her naturally. The problem of inequality between the sexes never arose in her mind, because, being born an Amazon, she was born equal. In today's jargon, she was uninhibited. She was entirely feminine; beautiful, fragile in appearance, but she rode through life jumping all her fences, social and moral. And if there was any way in which she was not equal to man, it was only because men loved less, tired quicker. Even in her early twenties she seems to have impressed Balzac by her ardors. The distorted portrait of her in *Le Lys dans la vallée* (which was all the more overdrawn, since Balzac deliberately used Lady Arabella's passions to heighten the lily-purity of poor, pinched Madame de Mortsauf) is all we have firsthand of the woman who was to rouse so many kinds of men. Here is Balzac, on his mistress: "*Lady Arabella prit plaisir, comme le démon sur le faîte du Temple, a me montrer les plus riches pays de son ardent royaume . . . Elle etait la maîtresse du corps.*" Madame de Mortsauf was of course *la femme de l'âme* . . . not perhaps an altogether satisfactory role.

It could be argued that as she met Medjuel in her late forties her appetites had diminished; her attractions too. But she adored Medjuel as she had never loved another man. She seemed more completely fulfilled, in this union, than in any other. Perhaps the legendary prowess of the Arab lover had something to do with it. It is probable that by her wayward life she had acquired a hunger the more pallid Western men could no longer assuage. But for twenty-five years her marriage to Medjuel continued on an ardent plane, with no slackening into Darby-and-Joan coziness. When we remember that she did not marry him until she was nearing fifty, we must admit she was in every way an exceptional creature. Her beauty, for so long celebrated in Europe, must still have seemed dazzling to the Arabs, used to the monochrome brown tones of their own women. Jane's brilliant coloring, white and gold and blue, like her soft voice, apparent youth, vitality and independence, were fascinatingly different. Everyone who knew her in Syria, from the local missionaries to Dom Pedro, Emperor of Brazil, was enchanted with the timeless charm and simplicity of the real woman—it was a charm which had survived all the storms and scandals to bloom on to the end, in a long golden afterglow. True to the East, there was no twilight.

\*     \*     \*

But at last the years "like great black oxen" were moving nearer implacably. From all over Europe the posts brought news of death. Few of Jane Digby's contemporaries were left, now. At seventy-four she began to find life in the Bedouin tents too rough, as she found the long desert rides too exhausting. For a few months before her death she had to remain in Damascus, while her horses grew restive in the stables. Medjuel went to and from the desert without her, and she felt it bitterly.

Sometime earlier, become realist at last, she had bought her grave in the Protestant cemetery. Probably she knew that to the Mezrabi, like all other Arabs, the body, after death, is an object of no concern, a package, to be disposed of quickly, and forgotten. Perhaps she thought of the shallow graves in the desert, the shroud that suffices for a coffin, and the jackals prowling. In death, she chose to lie among the Christians.

During the summer of 1881 cholera swept through the city. Most of the Europeans left for the hills. Jane and Medjuel stayed on in the beautiful house, with its fountains, its gardens, and the menagerie . . . but Eugénie was no longer there to dispense the pets' hundred dinners on the hundred plates. Whether she had died, or at last, exasperated by the demands of such a household, had returned to France, is not known. At any rate, another old and loyal friend was gone. The end came quickly, with an attack of dysentery, on August 11. Medjuel was with his wife when she died: Medjuel who had been for nearly thirty years the embodiment of all the adventure and romance and beauty of the East which was the revelation of her life. With Medjuel, in Sir Richard Burton's splendid phrase, "life's poetry never sank to prose."

In her death, as in her life, Medjuel brought her the drama she loved. As the funeral cortege wound its decorous way, black-beetle slow, towards the Protestant cemetery, the wild desert Bedouin he was at heart rebelled. The awful funereal gloom and ritual of his wife's faith appalled him. He electrified the few mourners by hurling himself out of the first carriage and taking to his heels like a madman. The cortege went on its way, considerably shaken. The service was conducted to its close: the last majestic words of the burial service were being read by the parson, when there was the sound of horses' hooves thundering nearer. Medjuel had returned. On Jane's favorite black mare he galloped up to the open grave. *Dust to dust, ashes to ashes* . . . Her Bedouin husband and her Arab horse were there beside her, at the last. For Jane Digby, life's poetry had never sunk to prose.

# ·III·

# AIMÉE DUBUCQ de RIVERY

## *Message from a Ghost*

WHEN THE CORSAIRS led Aimée Dubucq de Rivery through the teeming lanes of Constantinople towards the Seraglio, a path was cleared for her by the slashing hippopotamus-hide whips of the Sultan's Eunuchs. She was a present from the Dey of Algiers to his master, the Padishah, or Sultan of Turkey, Allah's Shadow upon Earth. She had been on her way home to Martinique from her convent schoolroom in Nantes, where she was a special favorite with the Sisters. She was a beautiful, intelligent, pious and charming young creature. There had been tears and prayers when she set sail, and even the Mother Superior had been on the jetty, to wave farewell. How many more tears, how many more prayers, if they could have forseen her fate!

But Aimée, now swaddled in sumptuous brocades and bundled in veils, must have remembered the prophecies of the old Negress Euphemia David, in Martinique, when Aimée and her cousin, a dark, skinny little girl, Joséphine Tascher de la Pagerie, whom the world was to know as Joséphine Bonaparte, crept through the sugar canes at dusk to cross the old sibyl's palm with silver. At the time, her mumblings had seemed a wild farrago of crowns, thrones and pirate ships. The children had listened breathlessly—they did not believe her, but they remembered. . . . Now, with a thud of terror in her heart, Aimée saw an enormous figure waddling towards her, his ermine-lined pelisse sweeping behind him, his towering turban nodding with flamingo plumes. It was the Chief Black Eunuch, the Kizlar Agha, a princely Nubian, *Son Altesse Noir,* come to the Gate of Felicity to inspect the Dey's offering to his Sublime master. Beside him Aimée saw a great pyramid of heads, some so newly severed that they reeked and steamed with blood. The future seemed to close round her. It was not a nightmare! It was her destiny, and she could not escape! Her large blue eyes stared out wildly over the yashmak, and then closed. Aimée had fainted.

*           *           *

Very little has ever been known or written about Aimée Dubucq de Rivery, "the French Sultana," mother of the Sultan Mahmoud II, The Reformer, whose sweeping changes laid the first foundations of the new Turkey. But once we know of her existence, her influence can be traced in many ways, from vast sweeps of international policy to salon revolutions such as the introduction of a French dancing master to the Harem, or the Sultan Mahmoud's predilection for champagne. By nature the Turks are secretive and withdrawn, especially concerning their homes and their women. Significant Turkish intrigues, particularly those centered round, or originating in the Seraglio, as so many of them did, have remained veiled through the centuries. Since Aimée Dubucq de Rivery lived in the Seraglio as an infidel, a *Giaour,* she was a thousand times stranger, more suspect than all the other odalisques, the Georgians and Circassians. As a Frenchwoman, she had every need to remain a shadowy figure; not only was her own life threatened, but that of her son, who, if he was to inherit the throne she coveted for him (and which had been predicted for him, too) must never appear to be tainted by dangerous European influences.

Thus she has remained a romantic cipher, a ghost, sensed rather than seen, flitting through the kiosks and pavilions of the Seraglio, a baffling phantom. Her beauty was acknowledged by the whole Seraglio; but to a small inner group of statesmen and courtiers she became a symbol of horizons breathlessly new to the ingrown world of Ottoman administration; a symbol of justice and liberty and gentleness far removed from the passions and corruption of the decaying oligarchy that ruled the Turkish Empire from the inner fastnesses of the Seraglio.

In Aimée Dubucq de Rivery we see a remarkable illustration of the saying "character plus opportunity equals fortune." The only known portrait of the French Sultana, made when she was about sixteen, shows a face full of spirit. It has nothing placid, or resigned. It is likely that once she accepted the impossibility of struggling against her lot, she made the best of it, extracting the maximum from its fabulous resources. The nose is witty, delicately upturned; the brows strongly arched; the mouth small and pouting, the perfect cupid's bow so much admired at that time. The eyes are large, a clear blue, we are told, and seem to have at once a languishing and quizzical regard. It is a determined, self-contained face; softened, no doubt, by her fair Norman complexion. In the Harem she was known as *Naksh*, The Beautiful One, which must be taken as high tribute from a world where the odalisques and slaves were of unparalleled beauty.

She was born in Martinique, at Pointe Royale, in 1763. Her family was of noble Norman stock. An ancestor, the Sieur Pierre Dubucq, had been a young officer in Cardinal Richelieu's own regiment, exiled for dueling and killing his adversary. At that time dueling was rigorously proscribed, punishable by death. The boy had fled the country, joined a ship sailing for the West Indies and took service under the Governor of Saint Kitts. He did well, and presently was sent as aide-de-camp to the new Governor of Martinique, where he settled, subdued the natives, built a sugar mill, the first on the island, and ran a large, flourishing plantation at La Trinité. Settling down is a comparative term, however; he continued to see much active service, thrusting and parrying his way from one swashbuckling engagement to the next, several times wounded, but always emerging victoriously. In 1701 he was granted letters of nobility, in recognition of his services to France and her Colonial expansion. His sons remained on Martinique, continuing to cultivate the family estates, and to marry among the daughters of the other settlers. One of Pierre Dubucq's descendants, François Henri Dubucq de Rivery, was to become the father of the French Sultana. He died the same year she was born, and when his widow, Marie-Victoire Menant, died six years later, their daughter, the little Marie-Marthe Aimée, was adopted by her guardian, a relative, Monsieur Dubucq de Sainte Preuve.

There were a lot of relatives, uncles and aunts, greataunts and cousins of first, second and third degree. The child was loved and petted by them all, and adored by her *da*, the fiercely loving mulatto nurse who reared her. Among her favorite playmates was her cousin Maria-Joseph (or Joséphine) Rose Tascher de la Pagerie. There seems to have been something in the air of Martinique which bred a race of queens. Joséphine, who was to become Empress of the French, her daughter Hortense, who became Queen of Holland, Madame de Maintenon, morganatic wife of Louis XIV, and Aimée, the Sultan Valideh, or Queen Mother, of Turkey—all these seductive women were Creoles from Martinique.

It was an agreeable way of life for the big French families. The days slid by, the months merged together, year after year, without any perceptible break. Only the hurricanes, and, rarely, the muttered threats of Mount Pelée, the volcano, ever threatened the calm. Everywhere, tropic vegetation coiled overwhelmingly, the scarlet flamboyant tree, purple bougainvillea, palms, breadfruit, calabash and papaya. The plunging gorges and mountain slopes seemed choked in luxuriance. Over all, the trade winds wafted their spicy breezes from one bay to the next. The island was dotted with the spacious but simple white houses of the plantation owners, such as that belonging to Aimée's guardian, at La Trinité. The slaves were, on the whole, well treated; they were gay and childlike, passionately devoted to the fripperies of dress peculiar to Martinique, the madras muslins, the checked and striped foulard handkerchiefs they wore like shawls, and the countless variations of starched turbans, *tête calendée*, set so coquettishly on their blue-black heads. Beneath all this, however, ran a deep strain of superstition; there were tales of prophecies, and black magic, of hauntings, incantations and zombis; a dark breath of poison behind the frangipani.

The strange story of the prophecy told to the young Joséphine is too well authenticated to be dismissed as a mere legend. There is a detailed account left by Mlle Lenormand, herself the most famous of all French fortunetellers, who was to become an intimate friend of the Empress Joséphine. It is from Joséphine herself that Mlle Lenormand claims to have obtained the details. Mlle Lenormand, who had been consulted by such as Talleyrand, Napoleon, Marat and Alexander of Russia, published her *Mémoires historiques et secrètes de l'Impératrice Joséphine* in 1820, six years after Joséphine's death, and it is easy to dismiss the prophecies she records as opportunist fabrication. But they are attested by many; indeed, the Empress herself sometimes spoke, in her heyday, of the tragic end predicted for her by Euphemia David. Sir Walter Scott, too, claimed that the prophecies were related to a friend during Napoleon's Italian campaign, long before either Joséphine's rise or fall.

About fifteen miles from the Dubucq estates at Pointe Royale, was Trois Islets, belonging to the Tascher de la Pagerie family. Aimée and Joséphine were often together and one day the two children, then about twelve, decided to visit a celebrated old fortuneteller, who lived near Trois Islets. The seer lived in a tumble-down shack, the path bordered by huge lilies, *amaryllis gigantea*, to which Joséphine, always of a horticultural bent, took a great fancy. In later years she cultivated them at Malmaison, and it is said she would often sigh over them, recalling the Pythoness of Martinique.

When Joséphine and Aimée entered the shack, they found her crouched on a mat, muttering. Mumbo jumbo and abracadabra, all of it; sharpened, no doubt, by Mlle. Lenormand, who, herself, lived by such abracadabras. The two girls crossed the plum-pink paw with silver and watched her as she peered intently at their hands. Together, the future Empress of France at the apogee of its glory, and the future French Sultana, mother of the Grand Turk, Allah's Shadow upon Earth, stood gaping at history.

After outlining, in detail, the chequered opening to Joséphine's life of adventure, touching on her loves, the disastrous marriage with Beauharnais, the Revolution, her widowhood and her two children, Euphemia predicted that Joséphine's second husband would be a dark, apparently insignificant man; nevertheless, he would fill the world with his glory. Many nations would bow before him as a mighty conqueror. Joséphine would become a great lady, a queen—but having been the wonder of the world, she would die unhappy, repudiated, and often regretting the free, peaceful life of Martinique. One statement has never been disputed, for many witnessed the phenomenon. She told of a strange meteor, or light, which would appear out of the heavens, on the moment of Joséphine's departure from Martinique. And, as is well known, on the day Joséphine sailed, a glowing light appeared overhead; it was the phosphoric flame, known as St. Elmo's fire, and, in Mlle Lenormand's words, "seemed to attach itself to the ship, forming a sort of wreath around it." The young Joséphine, sailing to unknown worlds and an unknown husband, was hardly consoled by this strange augury of fortune. She preferred the dolls with which she still played.

Aimée approached the old witch with some coffee grounds, one of the methods of divination she used, and again the prophecies appear to have been equally exact. *"You will be sent to Europe to complete your schooling,"* she told Aimée. *"Your ship will be seized by Corsairs. You will be taken captive and placed in a Seraglio. There you will give birth to a son. This son will reign gloriously, but the steps of his throne will be dyed with the blood of his predecessor. As to you, you will never taste the outward honors of the Court, but you will live in a great and splendid palace where you will reign supreme. At the very hour when you know your happiness is won, that happiness will fade like a dream, and a lingering illness will carry you to the tomb."*

It can be imagined how the cousins hung on her words. Such a future was to be both dreaded and desired. It was nothing if not romantic. Were they to believe it or not? In any case, it seemed best kept away from family mockery, at present. However, such a pronouncement was not likely to be forgotten, and when, a few years later, it was decided Aimée should complete her education in France, she must have recalled the warning note on Algerian Corsairs, and trembled. Or was it, rather, a tremor of excitement? For a thirteen-year-old beauty, life at Sainte Rose would soon pall. If she had any doubts about the voyage she said nothing, and so, in 1776 she sailed for Nantes, accompanied by her devoted *da*. At Fort de France—then Fort Royale—the brightly clad crowds of slaves gathered at the harbor to wave farewell. *Adieu madras, adieu foulards,* the traditional song of the Martinique girls to their sailor lovers, sounded faintly across the gathering distance. The ship set its course—eastward.

*       *       *

The convent of the Dames de la Visitation, at Nantes, where Aimée was bound, was then regarded in the light of an elegant finishing school for the daughters of the nobility. While living a cloistered life, its inmates were not subjected to the rigors of a nunnery. Not that they enjoyed the license associated with some eighteenth-century convents, such as that in Venice, which, if we are to believe Casanova, was little more than a *maison de rendezvous;* nor that of the convent at Beja, from which the immortal Portuguese nun wrote those burning evocations of her lover's visits. At the convent of the Dames de la Visitation, the pensionnaires spent their time in light studies, needlework and polite accomplishments. This sojourn, it was thought, would fit Aimée for her future life. And perhaps it did: perhaps it succeeded better than anyone could know. It is likely that after such an austere regime, the voluptuous tenor of life in the Seraglio may have seemed particularly agreeable. Seated in the refectory, eating wholesome fare, her eyes cast meekly down, at her devotions, or lying stiffly in her narrow bed, did she ever recall the prophecy? At her embroidery, or helping Soeur Angélique with the conserves, she must have remembered the episode, as fantastic as a fairy tale, as remote as *La Belle aux bois dormant.* But perhaps, being a Creole, and accepting the superstitions of Martinique, she accepted the prophecy too, and secretly cherished her fearful and wonderful destiny. It is recorded that she was a pupil of exceptional abilities, with a wide range of interests. As children, she and Joséphine had both playing the guitar; now she studied singing, the harpsichord, choosing, perhaps, with a little secret smile, the quasi-Orientalisms of Couperin's *Sultane.* Perhaps she showed an extra animation, an added application for geography, "the uses of the globe," with a leaning towards the Eastern hemisphere. And Racine, having had a century or more in which to become a classic, was probably allowed as light reading in the Convent. If so, she must have pored over the noble sorrows of *Bajazet.*

Aimée spent nearly eight years at the Convent; far longer than had been anticipated, for the war between France and England, over the American Colonies, had broken out in 1778, and it was thought unsafe for her to risk the return voyage at a time when the high seas raged with battles. Aimée said nothing: what would be, would be. She would return home safely, God willing, marry, and follow the placid, cradle-full pattern of her kind. In 1784, when she was twenty-one, the war being over, Aimée set sail from Nantes for Martinique; she took with her the prayers of the whole Convent, where she was much loved, a number of books to relieve the tedium of a two months' voyage, and the company of her dragon, the old *da*.

A few days out, in the Bay of Biscay, a fearful storm broke. The vessel was small and leaky—it could not stand up to the violence of the waves. Soon its seams were gaping. At nightfall, all hope was abandoned as the ship listed and began to sink. But miraculously, a sail was sighted. It was a large Spanish trader, speeding to the rescue. In inky darkness, with waves breaking over them, the sodden passengers and crew were transferred to the Spanish ship, which was heading for the Balearic Isles. Next day, the sun blazed down. Nature had been vanquished. The rescued passengers preened themselves dry, and were in a mood to savor the smooth roll of the ship as it sailed towards land. But not for long. After nature, man. As they were congratulating each other, in full sight of their destination, the pink spires of Palma de Majorca, they perceived that they were pursued by Algerian Corsairs. No sooner sighted than overhauled; there was no escape, no defense. Pirates! Even the bellying sails seemed to sag. Soon the pirate galley was alongside, and Aimée, now doubtless resigned to her fate, and perhaps buoyed by the ultimate splendors forseen by Euphemia, caught her first glimpse of the dreaded Corsairs. Swarthy, red-capped, and grinning derisively, they scarcely bothered to draw their cutlasses. It was child's play to overcome the Spanish trader's resistance, and the ship, with all on board, was taken to Algiers in triumph.

During the eighteenth century, piracy was on the decline, but Tunis and Algiers were still the Corsairs' lair. Algiers, in particular, by its natural formation, had become a towering fortress, dominating the snug harbor, offering a hideout for both men and ships. It was under Turkish domination, but all along the Barbary Coast, pirates of every race knew they would be protected and encouraged by the Turkish Governor. The dazzling white cubes of the Kasbah piled up the hillside, under the shelter of Turkish cannons menacing any unwelcome newcomers. In the labyrinthine climb, where overhanging eaves left only a slit of sky to pierce the sinister depths, all races were congregated, Spanish, Italian,

Berber, Nubian, Greek and Arab, eating, sleeping, loving, thieving and brawling together. The uneven cobbled alleys were slimy with filth; rats fattened on the refuse; entrails glowed red on the butchers' stalls, beside the bouquets of carnations or jasmine with which the Arabs love to surround themselves. Sometimes, behind a tattered calico curtain, a blue tiled courtyard could be glimpsed, with a fig tree, or a fountain, and a group of Negro slaves fanning a charcoal brazier. The old bawds squatted in their doorways shouting their wares, and sometimes the sound of a flute, or a sudden scream, echoed across the flat roofs where the women gathered at sunset. The sinister reputation of the Kasbah had grown with the centuries. Even the pirates trod warily, there.

We have no record of Aimée's emotions, as she was led, a captive, through these mazes, up and up, to the palace of the Dey, an inner fortress, set deep in the Kasbah, more protected there than the original Governor's palace, the Djanina, in the lower part of the town. At this moment, Algiers was commanded by Baba Mohammed Ben Osman, a foxy septuagenarian, and worthy successor to Barbarossa the Terrible, who first captured Algiers for the Turks, and now dead two hundred years or more, lying in a splendid tomb beside the Bosphorus. Baba Mohammed, too, was the terror of the Mediterranean. As master of the Barbary pirates, he defended his men and ships against all comers—his raiding expeditions went unrevenged, and although all Europe set a price on his head, he continued to taunt the world from his Algerian stronghold. Only that year, he had defeated a force of three hundred Spanish men-o'-war with his handful of ships. The old tiger was adored by his men, and their finest plunder was always brought first to him.

Thus it happened that when the Corsairs boarded the Spanish ship where Aimée and her *da* were standing on deck, their captain, realizing her beauty, set her apart as prize booty, to be reserved for Baba Mohammed. Slave trading flourished all along the African coast, there was a constant stream of ebony flesh being shipped to Turkey alone. Those unfortunate boys designed to supply the demand for Eunuch guards were a trade in themselves. So few survived the operation, from which they were left to recover, or die, plunged up to their waists in the burning sands. White Eunuchs, mostly recruited from eastern Europe, were also in steady demand, white female slaves, especially the beautiful Circassian or Spanish women, fetched high prices. If the pirates could come by the comparative rarity of a blond young European, they earned their chief's particular approval. Aimée was a splendid haul. Useless for her distracted *da* to plead and curse. The captain merely locked Aimée in his cabin and ordered that she be treated with respect. What happened to the rest of the ladies on board, we do not know. Nor do we know the fate of the *da*. Was she allowed to accompany her young mistress, was she sent packing (in view of the tale she could tell, it is unlikely she was returned to Europe), or did she simply vanish into the shadows of the Kasbah? We have no records, but it seems that when Baba Mohammed Ben Osman saw Aimée, he at once realized she would be a rare and worthy offering to the Sultan himself; a really sumptuous present, reflecting a lasting luster on the giver. He ordered that she be kept apart, inviolate, and heavily guarded. Aimée was not consulted, of course, but by now she can have had no doubts as to the workings of Destiny. The pirates fitted out a splendid ship, a vessel of state, worthy of a future favorite of the Sultan, and presently, adorned in the most lavish Oriental style, and heavily veiled, Aimée set sail for Constantinople.

She was now committed irrevocably to her fate. Another voyage began, and she sailed away from all she had ever known, from last echoes of France, or Martinique. Now there were no handkerchiefs waving fond farewell; no pious prayers, no soft voices singing . . . *Adieu madras, adieu foulards* . . . henceforth she was to be quite alone . . . as she remained, ghostly and apart. But sometimes it seems as if the ghost beckons, or signals to us from the obscurity of history. The signs take many strange forms: the fantastic balloons of Montgolfier floating over the minarets of Santa Sophia; Prince Selim's letter of friendship to King Louis XVI; the introduction of a system of quarantine; even an expression in the eyes of her son the Sultan Mahmoud, The Reformer, when he greeted a Western European . . . an expression which was to culminate, one day, in the massacre of twenty-six thousand Janissaries, the arch enemies of all that progress along Western lines which she craved, and for which she worked; as well as being the embodiment of the cruel and tyrannous system of which she, the captured, enslaved French girl was a victim. Of all the signals so long ignored by the outside world, the most unmistakable is the sudden, inexplicable manner in which the Sultan Mahmoud II was to turn against Napoleon, turning the tide of history, to bring about his downfall. This can perhaps be attributed to a purely personal motive, one of family revenge: the loyalty of one little French girl from Martinique defending another —her cousin Joséphine—whom Napoleon by his divorce was to repudiate so ruthlessly.

\*      \*      \*

The Corsairs' ship skirted the last of Africa. The ruins of Carthage and the little white huddle of Sidi Bou Säid were visible in a line of red earth that was Tunis. Far away, inland, rose the lovely blue silhouette of the Bou Kornëin, and behind it, faintly, the phantom of another peak, Djebel Ressas. . . . Africa faded.

The voyage was long; it seemed an eternal moment, becalmed between past and future. Sicily, Greece, the Aegean islands, the Syrian coast, and then, one day, the forlorn wastes of the Dardanelles, widening at last to the milky blueness of the Marmora, dotted with frisking dolphins and little islands. As they drew near to Constantinople, there were busy lanes of shipping, galleys and *mahouns*, and gilded caïques, all converging on the Porte. The ship rounded the point, and Stamboul rose before them, its thousand domes and minarets lit by the westering sun. It was the capital of the Ottoman Empire, home of the Caliph of the Faithful, Padishar of the Barbary States, Shadow of the Prophet upon Earth, the Sultan Abd ül Hamid I—Aimée's fate.

As they anchored, and all the tumult of the harbor rose from below, Aimée could see the great mass of the Seraglio, the Royal Palace, set on its promontory between Asia and Europe, lapped by the waters of the Bosphorus and the Golden Horn. This fabulous conglomeration of palaces and kiosks, stables, kitchens, barracks, prisons, torture chambers, pleasure gardens and mosques was capable of housing twenty thousand souls. The cypresses rose black and chill beside its battlemented walls— it was at once menacing and fabulous—like nothing else. And so Aimée came at last to the Gate of Felicity, and being received by the Chief Eunuch, fainted away.

*      *      *

When Aimée Dubucq de Rivery came to herself she was in the heart of the Harem, one of the hundreds of odalisques who entered it like convent novices to acquire a new name, a new personality, and to live there, according to rule, immured, for the rest of their lives. To Aimée, it must have seemed almost as if her school days at Nantes were all to do again. The same strict surveillance, the same crowds of girls, giggling, childish and silly, with their petty feuds, secrets and gushing friendships. Their ages ranged from twelve upwards; none of them spoke French, and Aimée could not understand a word they said to her. They might have been mocking her, tormenting her, proffering friendship or criticism. There was only the tone of the voice to go by: but jealousy is unmistakable. Such a striking newcomer must inevitably find it a hard school.

If the girls seemed much the same as those at Nantes, everything else was wildly different. The food was neither plain nor wholesome. As to the hours spent lolling in Turkish baths, naked and sleek, ladling perfumed water over each other, twisting pearls and peacock feathers in their long hair, nibbling sugary comfits, gossiping, idling away the hours, becalmed in the dreamy, steamy limbo-land, nothing could have been a more violent contrast. Aimée recalled the convent's views on baths; dangerous reminders of the flesh, and only to be permitted if the body was shrouded in a voluminous calico robe. Yes; it was very different in the Seraglio. Slowly, she began to accustom herself to her new life and its strange mixture of luxury and restraint, etiquette, ritual and abandon.

The Seraglio has always represented mystery in its most absolute form, and remained, through the centuries, an impenetrable legend. Few outsiders ever crossed its threshold, or were privileged to penetrate further than the Second Courtyard. On rare occasions an Envoy Extraordinary would be granted audience, and has left accounts of as much as he was able to see around him; but for the most part, until the fall of the Osmanli dynasty in 1909, the inner life of the Seraglio was almost unknown. Few who had entered ever escaped, or lived to tell of their experiences. The Turkish passion for concealment amounted to a fetish—their homes, their women, and their monarch, all were shrouded, not only from the foreigner, but from each other, too. When the Sultan rode abroad in his capital he was surrounded by guards who carried large banners, pearl-fringed umbrellas, and even wore helmets topped by forests of waving ostrich plumes, the better to screen their master from curious eyes. Those persons granted an audience found it quite an ordeal (though in no degree approaching the severity imposed by one Byzantine Emperor who used to put out the eyes of visiting emissaries, as a precaution against prying). The foreign visitors were first submitted to a ritual bath, and then, being clothed in magnificent robes, they were lifted bodily into the presence of Allah's Vice Regent, supported on each side by high court dignitaries, lest, it was supposed, the overwhelming honor should paralyze them. After which introductory flourish, they were seldom vouchsafed more than one jeweled finger, extended for salutation through the drawn curtains of the throne. This was like a gigantic four-poster bed, its framework silver-gilt, and encrusted with a blinding array of precious stones, slabs of emerald, rubies the size of farmhouse eggs, its brocaded hangings stiff with pearls and bullion.

The Seraglio is variously referred to as the Sarail, Le Grand Serai, the Serayi or the Harem, though this latter is incorrect, to describe the whole palace, since it applies only to the women's quarters, the core, within the whole. The word "Harem" derives from the Arabic *haram*, forbidden, unlawful. A certain area of land centered round the Holy Cities of Mecca and Medina were considered as set apart, inviolate, and so described as *haram*. The word came to be applied, in its secular sense, to the women's quarters of a Moslem household—it was their *haram*, or sanctuary, territory apart, inviolate to all but the master of the household. The Selamlik, or men's quarters, derived from the word *selam*, a greeting, the Selamlik being the one part of the house where it is permitted to receive visitors.

Although the Seraglio has always remained shrouded in an aura of mystery, there have been, through the centuries, a few eyewitness accounts. In the fifteenth and sixteenth century those foreigners admitted were mostly physicians or craftsmen. The Italian doctor, Domenico Hierosolimitano, has left a detailed account of his visit during the reign of Murad III; and an Englishman, Thomas Dallam, went there in 1599 to install an organ specially commanded by the Sultan. He did not see very much: "At everie gate of the surralia there always sittethe a stoute Turke . . . the gathes ar faste shut, for thare pasethe none in or oute at their owne pleasures. . . ." He speaks of the pavilion where he was ordered to set up the organ as being "no dwellinge house, but a house of pleasure, and lykewyse a house of slaughter; for in that house . . . the emperor that rained when I was there had nynteene brothers put to deathe in it and it was bulte for no other use but for the stranglings of everie emperors bretherin." Perhaps he had seen enough.

In the early eighteenth century, a daring French traveler, Aubry de La Motraye, succeeded in persuading a Swiss clockmaker of Galata to take him as assistant when he went to repair some pendulums in the Seraglio. La Motraye prudently donned Turkish clothing, and tried to note all that he saw, as a black Eunuch hurried them from one timepiece to the next, through perspectives of overwhelming grandeur. They visited part of the Harem, though the women were absent, and La Motraye closes his observations on a censorious note. *"In comparing the Chambers of the Grand Seigniors Women to the Cells of Nuns, we must except the Richness of the Furniture, as well as the Use they are put to; the Difference of which is easy enough to be imagin'd without Explication."*

In the heart of the Seraglio was the Harem and the Selamlik. Between the two, dominating both, and focal point of all, were the apartments of the Sultan Valideh: the Veiled Crown, or mother of the Sultan, who, next the Sultan, occupied a supreme position. The layers of walls and courtyards encircling the center were a warren of subterranean passages leading to prisons or treasure vaults; or stairways giving on to unexpected terraces and pavilions set in tulip gardens, with distant vistas of the Bosphorus and the mosques of Scutari, on the far Asiatic shore. There was the Corridor of the Bath, or Hamam, the pivot-point of daily life; the Golden Path, down which the chosen odalisque was led to the Sultan's bed; the aviaries and libraries, laundries and hospitals; the kitchens occupied almost the whole of the southeastern side of the enclosure. There were great ice pits, too, where snow, wrapped in flannel, was brought on muleback some seventy miles from Mount Olympus, was stored for the making of sherbets and other cooling delicacies.

There was the Confectioner's Mosque, the Black Eunuchs' quarters and those of the White Eunuchs, too. The slaves' lodgings, the guardhouses of the six hundred Janissaries, with their line of "kettle drums" ever muttering threats. There was the Divan, or Council Chamber, the Pavilion of the Holy Mantle, dormitories of the dwarfs, mutes and buffoons, as well as the place of execution and the Chief Eunuch's suite. There were, too, such necessary adjuncts to Moslem life as the Hall of Circumcision, the Place of Consultation of the Djinns, and the Kefess, or Cage (which was described by Thomas Dallam), where the heir to the throne was immured until his accession or slaughter by rival claimants. Added to all this there were such personages as the Keeper of the Pedigree of the Prophets' Descendants; the Chief Turban-Winder, Nightingale Keeper, and Tent-Pitcher, and myriads of gardeners, pages, waiting-women, grooms, scribes, apothecaries, astronomers and messengers, besides.

Over all, ranking with the Grand Vizier, ruled the Chief Black Eunuch, the Kizlar Agha. His power was absolute. Aimée soon realized that he was the most important person in this new world around her. He alone had the right to speak directly to the Sultan. He was at once Comptroller of the Household, Master of Ceremonies and the Sultan's confidant. He was in supreme control of the Harem and the odalisques, and in consequence ranked higher than the Chief White Eunuch, the Kapi Agha, who controlled the Selamlik. Between the two Chiefs lay centuries of rivalry: the corruption of the White Eunuchs had gradually led to a decline in their authority and the concentration of power being invested in the Black Eunuchs. Like most of the Seraglio's personnel, both black and white Eunuchs were imported from afar. It was held that coming to the palace as children, knowing no country, no master other than the Grand Turk, they would be more likely to be loyal, less swayed by internal politics and the intrigues which exercised so galvanic an effect on the otherwise supine Turks.

At the time of Aimée's arrival, the Kizlar Agha represented a moderate and humane influence within the Seraglio. He was not to be bought, and the Sultan was known to like and respect him. Therefore, when she remembered that he had been waiting at the Gate of Felicity to receive her, she knew it was proof of the prestige she enjoyed, as an offering from the Dey of Algiers. Perhaps the attitude of the other odalisques, or the deference of the Eunuchs who guarded them, had already made her sense she was set apart. It was then, in all probability, that she first began to regain her courage, and try to calculate, with shrewd French common sense, just how much she could rely on the Kizlar Agha's support, steering her solitary way. She may have hoped, wildly, innocently, that he would take pity on her awful fate. We imagine her, the calm, reserved French girl, flung down among the cushions, her long golden hair falling in confusion around her tear-stained face, sobbing tears of rage and misery . . . and then, raising those large blue eyes which were to prove so compelling, to fix them, thoughtfully, on the majestic figure of the Kizlar Agha, who had come to pay his daily visit to his protégée, the Dey's offering. Perhaps she thought that through him she might be able to send a letter to her uncle at Nantes; and then he would hasten to Versailles, to the all-powerful King Louis, who would personally appeal to the Sultan for her release. . . . But perhaps there were also a few appraising glances at the opulent setting in which she found herself. To her thrifty French mind, especially after those eight convent years, the Seraglio must have been dazzling, calling Euphemia David's mumbling prophecies to mind again, sharply. *You will live in a great and splendid palace where you will reign supreme. . . .*

There is no doubt that the Kizlar Agha, too, was eyeing her speculatively. Like Baba Mohammed Ben Osman, he was aware of her exceptional quality; here was a young woman who had grown to maturity in the outside world, who could offer perspectives of which they were ignorant; who breathed the air of liberty which was in itself a new and heady perfume not only in the Seraglio but to all Turkey, too. By which it will be seen that the Chief Eunuch was of a progressive nature.

In the inner factions which revolved around the throne with the slow, ritualistic cunning of a chessboard, moves and countermoves of life, death, the Kizlar Agha was allied to a small group of liberally minded statesmen and courtiers headed by the Mufti Vely-Zadé, and a beautiful Circassian Kadine, once the favorite of the late Sultan Mustapha III, the father of her son Selim, now heir apparent. Turkish succession did not go direct from father to son, but went by age, the eldest surviving Osmanli always succeeding. This explains the holocausts by which ambitious mothers of younger sons would murder any elder claimants standing between their sons and the throne. Selim's life was in constant danger from the jealousy of other Kadine, the reigning Sultan Abd ül Hamid's favorite. She was a cruel and treacherous woman in the scheming manner of the Seraglio, where violence as much as *volupté* was the tradition. It was her son Mustapha, Abd ül Hamid's sole surviving child, who would succeed, were Selim removed. Not only did Mustapha's mother covet the throne for her son, but even more she coveted the position which would then be hers, one of supreme power, as Sultan Valideh, the Sultan's mother, or crown of the Veiled Heads, or all Moslem women, throughout the Empire.

The history of the Ottoman Empire is a long testimony to the power wielded by women—by the Harem. This Oriental state, where women are generally believed to have no place or status and to be submissive playthings, to be petted or abandoned at will, was, in fact, governed for centuries at a time by the secret influence of the Harem, and the intrigues which originated in the kiosks and alcoves of the Seraglio. Capricious, cruel and cunning, ruthless and ambitious . . . such were many of the Kadines who enslaved their Lord and Master, and virtually ruled the country. Women such as Roxelana, the unscrupulous Russian, who in Turkey was known as Khurrem, the Joyous, and whose influence was such that she persuaded Suleiman the Magnificent to murder his eldest son, thus clearing the way for her own child. For the most part these scheming voluptuaries contented themselves with internal policies, material acquisitions and the advancement of their protégés: above all, the accession of their sons. Foreign policy was of less consequence to them.

But now, since the middle of the eighteenth century, there had been a more progressive group within the Seraglio who were beginning to be conscious of a world outside its walls and of horizons of thought and progress which must come from the West, and which it was folly to ignore. Such were the views of this inner, liberal group headed by the Kizlar Agha and the Circassian Kadine; and as such they were opposed violently by the Janissary Corps who feared their own powers might be wrested from them. This Corps centered round the heir apparent, Mustapha, who could be their puppet were he to reign in Selim's place. Together, the Janissaries and Mustapha's mother were of a mind. Nothing must be allowed to stand in the way of Mustapha's accession.

The Janissaries were an age-old institution: this dread body, a sort of Praetorian guard, had come to represent all that was most reactionary and corrupt. They were recruited from the numbers of Christian children levied from the provinces, who were forcibly removed, and converted to the Moslem faith. They underwent a rigorous military training, but always enjoyed certain privileges. Some of them became the Sultan's picked troops, but for the most part they were mercenaries, and moved from one battle zone to the next. They were expected to live austere lives, the better to harden them. Celibacy was the rule. They were also forbidden to wear the beards that were almost universally worn by the Turks. Instead, they cultivated long mustachios, hanging to their waists, which, it was held, increased the ferocity of their appearance.

Their dress was curious; the color of their boots, red, yellow or black, proclaimed their rank, as did certain enormous paradise plumes, falling from their turbans in an arc, nearly to their knees. Their titles all derived from the kitchen—the Chief was called the Chorbaji-Bashi, or Head Soup-Distributor; next came the Head Cook, and so on. Their standard displayed a vast caldron, or kettle. In time, these kettles came to have a special significance, and were used by the corps as a symbol of revolt. When the Janissaries were in camp, their kettles were piled before the tent doors in the manner of regimental drums. And in the same manner, beating upon them furiously was a call to battle or revolt. Each week, their rations were fetched from the Seraglio kitchens in these kettles. If they were dissatisfied, they would reverse the kettles and begin drumming on them ominously with the long ladlelike spoons each man wore fixed into his cap. So terrible were their uprisings that the whole Seraglio, the Sultan, too, would listen for the dreaded sound. Some Sultans stayed to argue, others acted swiftly. Ringleaders were seized and executed on the spot, the decapitated heads piled up in a huge silver dish, for all to take warning. But as time went on, the Janissaries became more puissant, the Sultans less decisive: at least six Sultans were dethroned or slaughtered by their orders. This decay in loyalty is supposed to have originated with the decline in successive Sultans' military prowess. When they were a picked guard, campaigning with their Padishah, a fine military morale prevailed—but as the Sultans waxed fat, never venturing beyond their harem, so the Janissaries began to abuse their power, grew lax in turn, and thrived on corruption and intrigue. They looted the city, terrorized its citizens, extorted money, sold preferment to their favorites and opposed all progressive measures on principle. In the beginning of the nineteenth century there were around one hundred thousand of them. They were often to be seen issuing forth on plundering forays in the bazaars. They thought nothing of trying out a new scimitar blade on a passing infidel, and brooked no discipline, or remonstrances on the part of either the Grand Vizier or the Sultan himself.

While the Janissaries muttered, their kettle drums sounding ominously, it was obvious to the Chief Eunuch that they were only biding their time, before rising, to dethrone Abd ül Hamid and install Mustapha. On that day his head would no longer be safe: a reign of terror and reaction would set in. But he was not altogether without hope: he thought he saw a new way to outmaneuver his enemies; and so, hurried off to the apartments of his friend the Circassian Kadine, to recount his impressions of the new French slave, and to air his theories as to how best she could be used to their advantages. This Circassian woman was the daughter of a Christian priest in Georgia. She had been abducted into the Seraglio as a child, and was a woman of brilliant intellect, and kindness, too. All her force was directed towards saving her son Selim from his enemies, and, while avoiding the terroristic methods adopted by so many other Seraglio mothers, yet see him placed upon the Osmanli throne. She listened to the Kizlar Agha attentively. Yes, she agreed: this new French odalisque, *Giaour* or no, might be used to their advantage. Gaining the Sultan's favor, she might well become the decisive factor in their game. Was she really so lovely? Yes . . . ? It might work out very well, then. . . . We can imagine them, the Chief Eunuch, *Son Altesse Noir,* his gigantic sugarloaf turban nodding, as both of them puffed contentedly at their jeweled *techibouks,* while the hanging lamps cast a swaying shadow on the cushioned alcove where they sat, two old friends, planning the next move in the eternal game of life and death.

*       *       *

At the moment when Aimée was first pitched into this sinister game, a pawn who was to become a Queen, there was no Sultan Valideh, for the Sultan Abd ül Hamid's mother was long dead. Mustapha's mother, the favorite Kadine, retained her rank and influence, not so much by her charms as by the lassitude of the Sultan. All these things Aimée was only learning by degrees; from someone who had a smattering of French to answer her questions, perhaps, or as she began to pick up some Turkish, herself. The Sultan's four wives, or Kadines, were always known by their distinct titles, taking precedence accordingly. The Bach-kadine, or first wife, the Skindji-kadine, or second wife, the Artanie-kadine, or middle-kadine, and the Kutchuk-kadine, or little Kadine. It was this latter title which Aimée was to assume, on the birth of her son. But at first, although singled out for the Royal alcove, she merely ranked as one of the novices. First, she must be put through the school for odalisques, to perfect her in every seductive art her Royal Master's jaded palate might demand. There was so much to learn; to accept; and as she began to look about her with that shrewd French eye, intensely practical for all its languorous blue depths, it must have been clear to her that the heir apparent, the young prince Selim, was worth cultivating.

The Sultan Abd ül Hamid was her master—the present. But Selim was the future. He was said to be gentle, and good; perhaps he could be persuaded to help her smuggle out a letter? The thought must have given her renewed courage, fresh hope in her solitary battle.

*     *     *

The first months which Aimée spent in the Harem must have been a shattering experience: her whole way of life, even her name was changed. The women were known by descriptive titles—the Lily, Moon-Face, Nightingale, and such, and it is a tribute to Aimée's loveliness that in this paradise of houris she became *Naksh*—The Beautiful One.

The Seraglio has been described as a kind of huge monastery whose religion was pleasure and whose God the Sultan: but although this might apply to the Seraglio as a whole, it is by no means applicable to the Harem, where a disciplinary tone prevailed. There are those who imagine it to have been a temple of unbridled license, one long riot of indulgence conducted on the lines of Scheherazade's revels as presented by the *Ballets Russes,* where unleashed slaves bound from one inviting bosom to the next. But however licentious or indulgent the principle, in practice the Harem was maintained on lines of the strictest formality. It was a hierarchy, with its own protocol and etiquette. Some of the inmates never saw the Sultan, and spent their whole lives inventing ways of passing the time . . . consoling themselves with useful works, bookkeeping, jam making, overeating, other people's babies, or distractions of a Lesbian nature. Once incorporated, they could never leave; those few who were discovered to have been unfaithful were executed, or dumped in the Bosphorus in weighted sacks. The Sultan Ibrahim, being of a particularly self-indulgent nature, once dispatched his whole harem, three hundred strong, for the pleasure of being able to restock it with refreshing newcomers. A diver off Seraglio Point came up with tales of dead bodies all standing upright, weighted by their feet, swaying and bowing in the underwater swell with a sort of ghastly *politesse.*

The odalisques were bored, and disillusioned, too, perhaps, by the rigidity of life beside the legends that had lured them there. All of them lived for the moment when, perhaps, they would attract the Padishah's eye, and then . . . Some of them contrived to establish a sort of relationship with the Eunuchs, for it was well known that not all the mutilations were effective, although the Seraglio doctors were ever-watchful on this score. For the most part, the Eunuchs were, as may be imagined, a resentful lot, full of malice and envy, lashing out with their hippopotamus-hide whips. The women took a delight in tormenting them. They were known ironically as "Keeper of the Rose," or "Guardian of Delights." Occasionally it happened that a Eunuch loved and was loved by an odalisque. The Harem is reported to have admitted, on occasion, the "marriage" of Eunuchs; in which case the Eunuch was generally appointed to another palace, further down the Bosphorus, or at Broussa, or Adrianople.

All this regiment of ungratified creatures existed for the sole pleasure of the Grand Turk. He had absolute power over them, in life, in death. Sometimes it happened that a Sultan preferred boys; many of the White Eunuchs, when young, were beautiful creatures, we are told, slim and smooth, their faces lavishly painted, their rich costumes smothered in attar of roses. Sometimes the Sultan would pass on one of his odalisques to a minister he wished to favor, or perhaps liquidate. No man could refuse, even if he suspected it to be his death warrant. This was one of the accepted techniques by which the Seraglio disposed of their enemies. The favorite would install herself in her husband's house and proceed to spy on the outside world, reporting back to the Seraglio. Or else, she would proceed to remove her husband, in her own way. Her task accomplished, she was reintegrated into the Royal household and rewarded for her services. In the argot of the Seraglio, this was known as "earning a passport."

The hierarchy of the Harem was founded on the law that there could be no liaison between a Sultan and his subjects. The Harem was therefore always recruited from outside—from Circassia, Georgia, Syria, Roumania, with an occasional Italian or Spaniard to vary the menu. Thus the succeeding Sultans were always the sons of slave-mothers, and only half Turkish, themselves. Agents from the Porte scoured eastern

Europe and the Levant for recruits—Circassians ranked first, on account of their beauty. Dramatic stories of the kidnaping of young children are not to be altogether believed, for large numbers of girls grew up with the fixed intention of entering a Turkish harem—if not the Seraglio itself—much as, fifty years ago, country girls decided on domestic service in the big cities. (And, strangely, there were also numbers of voluntary Eunuchs, both black and white). The odalisques were usually well treated, as one of the family; and if they were chosen for the Seraglio, there was always the glittering possibility of Royal favors. Even without, it promised a life of luxury, which many girls preferred to the hard toil of a peasant's lot. There was never any question of dishonor—a moral Mason-Dixon Line might be said to have divided Europe over the question of white slavery. The Sultan's concubines, so shocking, so pitiable to the West, were congratulated and envied by the East. Aimée, being groomed and schooled for the Sultan's favors, found that she had to change her viewpoint considerably. Useless, now, to cast backward glances to Martinique, or Nantes, or to view the intricacies of Seraglio living through European, let alone convent, eyes. Useless to cling to the notion that she was a sacrificial lamb, being decked for the slaughter, when it was obvious that everyone around her, from the Wardrobe Mistress to the Chief Eunuch, felt she was singled out for glory.

Like all the other slaves, Aimeé must pass through the *Academie de l'Amour,* or school for odalisques, where they were instructed in the finer shades of pleasing. The young candidates for the Imperial alcove had to pass an examining board, usually presided over by the Sultan Valideh (who, as mothers, were nothing if not thorough). Nothing was left to chance. It was really a very sensible arrangement, and saved the Sultan many a disappointment. When the newcomer was pronounced perfect, she passed into the ranks of ladies-in-waiting. . . . Around her would be at least two or three hundred more, all lovely, all voluptuous, jealous, bored; all specialists in those arts they could so seldom practice; all waiting for their chance to prove themselves.

In general, this came when the Sultan paid a state visit to his Harem. It was announced by the Eunuchs, who rang a big golden bell. Then followed a feverish rush for the grandest toilettes, the most brilliant *ma-*

*quillage*. The Chief Treasurer of the Harem, together with the Sultan Valideh, received the Sultan in state, at the entrance to the Harem, and conducted him, with the Chief Eunuch, to the reception, held either in the apartments of the Sultan Valideh or those of the reigning favorite. A Eunuch walked before, magnificently dressed, chanting in a nasal voice: "Behold our Sovereign, Emperor of the True Believers, Shadow of Allah upon Earth, The Prophet's Successor, The Master of Masters, Chosen among the Chosen, our Padishah, our Sultan! Long live our Sultan! Let us admire Him who is the glory of the house of Osman! "

The Sultan would then pass between the breathless ranks of beauty, each slave holding herself in the prescribed Court pose, head thrown back, hands crossed on the breast. The reception room would be crowded with the more favored members of the hierarchy, past favorites, the family, daughters, or Sultanas, the Kadines, or wives by whom the Sultan had children, the Ikbals, those who had already enjoyed the Royal attentions, and the Guzdehs, "those who had caught the eye," odalisques who had already been remarked, but not yet been tried. The Sultan then knelt before his mother, who raised him, and signified that the long ceremony of obeisance might begin. When all the rituals were at last over, the Sultan took his place on the divan, flanked by the Chief Eunuch and the Treasurer. The Sultan Valideh sat on an opposite divan. To this rigid setting, the young odalisques were now admitted. The Sultan would eye them speculatively. Such ceremony, such protocol, especially when under maternal supervision, must have been dampening to spontaneous desires. But perhaps it was an artificial barrier, cunningly contrived, to stimulate a jaded palate. While the youngest slaves, little newcomers of eight or ten years old, skipped about with silver trays of coffee, or sweetmeats, the older ones gathered round the Sultan; perhaps not quite "the rosebud garden of girls" which Tennyson had in mind, but still, a flowerbed of lovely faces, all turned towards him as to the sun. Hundreds of charmers, each yearning for a chance to charm! All of them twittering round in fevered efforts to catch the Royal eye. O! happiest of men! No competition! No rebuffs! All of them hanging on his word, applauding his every quip . . . while in the background, the professional laughers tinkled with discreet but festive gaiety, the caged nightingales outvied each other, the perfumed breezes (reinforced by incense burners) wafted through the pavilions, and over all, unseen, but powerful, brooded the reassuring presence of the Court Abortionist.

Sometimes a Sultan would take a malicious pleasure in ending the revels abruptly by stalking out in dudgeon. In which case there were reproaches and nerve-storms, tears, dramas, and extra doses of opium all round. (Opium, it must be remembered, was the aspirin of the East.) But if the Grand Turk singled out a charmer, he would ask the Valideh Sultan her name, and the odalisque would be then authorized to approach the dais, and kiss the cushion of his Majesty's divan. This was an official consecration—now she became a Guzdeh, and from that moment set apart from the rest, installed in a special apartment, where, pampered, polished and perfected, she waited the summons to the Imperial alcove, while all around, her rivals strove to spoil her chances by any mischief they could devise.

Nor must it be supposed that formality and protocol ceased at the doors of the Royal alcove. When the Sultan received a favorite, the date and duration of the nuptials were meticulously entered in a special register. If, nine months later, a child was born, it was attributed to the Sultan, and the fortunate Ikbal passed into the ranks of the Kadines, with all the privileges attached: a larger establishment, more slaves, jewels and money. Those Kadines who had sons were at once placed in the highest rank of the hierarchy; all of them lived in the hope of seeing their son as Sultan, themselves as Sultan Valideh. Those who had daughters were also ranked as Kadines, but without any special privileges. Throughout the Moslem world, daughters were always at a discount.

That the Seraglio was not overflowing with children was due not only to violent methods of liquidating any possible claimants to the throne, but also to the strict surveillance of the calfas, old slaves who watched over the girls minutely, and at the first signs of pregnancy informed the Court Abortionist, who was empowered to exercise her calling at once. For a slave to become a mother, it was necessary that the

Sultan be so enraptured with her charms that he prove his fondness by thus permitting her to acquire Kadine's rank. Occasionally, a determined Ikbal, aided by her companions, succeeded in disguising her condition until the accouchement, in which case the child became the adored and petted plaything of all the other thwarted odalisques, or was strangled, drowned or otherwise removed.

Sometimes the Sultans themselves, surfeited by plenty, and the tedium of etiquette attendant on selecting a new favorite, preferred to live austerely; or, fearing for their lives, would not risk an unknown newcomer who might be the instrument of vengeance; whose very kiss might be poisoned. Sultan Selim III (who was a gentle young prince at the time of Aimée's arrival) was so horror-struck by the fate awaiting so many infant and possible claimants to the throne, that, we are told by Lady Craven (who was then visiting the capital), "as soon as he knew the horrid custom of strangling every infant which is born in the Seraglio not the child of the reigning Sultan, he declared he would never be the cause of a human creature's death, and has constantly avoided any opportunities of becoming a father." This attitude must have seemed to undermine the very foundations of the Harem.

*       *       *

Like all the visitors to Constantinople, Lady Craven was eager for every scrap of information regarding the Seraglio. She was staying with the French Ambassador, in 1785, and from his windows at Galata, used to follow the ceremonial comings and goings on Seraglio Point, across the Golden Horn, by means of the Ambassador's telescope. *"Yesterday I saw the Sultan (Abd ül Hamid) sitting on a silver sofa, while his boats and many of the people who were to accompany him were lining the banks of the garden. We had a large telescope and saw the Ottoman splendors very distinctly. The Sultan dyes his beard black to give himself a young look; he is known at a considerable distance by that, which contrasts singularly with his face, that is extremely livid and pale."*

Lady Craven was an insatiable traveler and gossip. She had driven the length of Europe to Moscow, and from there to Turkey by way of the Crimea, staying, en route, with the governors or princes of each province. She noted everything with lively interest, in a series of letters to the Margrave of Brandenburg and Anspach, whom later she was to marry. The letters were published in book form in 1787. From them we have a vivid picture of Constantinople at its last truly magnificent moment. She describes a rambling city, an extraordinary jumble of marble and wood; of luxury and waste lands where gypsies and beggars camped in the shadow of the glorious Suleimanyé Mosque, much as they do today. She conveys something of its sinistry too: for it must not be imagined that Constantinople basked in the refulgent gaiety of sun and song; there was nothing Mediterranean about this city, at once fierce, voluptuous and squalid; a dramatic atmosphere peculiarly its own; like nothing else.

It has been said that the history of Constantinople is a costume drama, and it is certain that with the decline of the ceremonial and specialized clothing which was reserved for each rank and each occasion, much of the city's splendor and unique interest vanished. Alas! It was Aimée's westernizing influence upon her son that may be said to have brought about many of these lesser, sartorial reforms. Today's cloth cap is a poor substitute for yesterday's fez, which, in its turn, is a miserable object, beside the towering turban (in Turkish *dulbend,* from which "tulip" derives, the flower being fancifully likened to a turban). Its various forms, height and color, like the width of a fur edging, or the length of a train, were all Imperial edicts—law. Admirals wore scarlet and gold; the Tressed Halberdiers were so named because of two locks of false hair falling from their helmets, on each side of their face (its purpose being, originally, to prevent the wearer's casting glances at the odalisques whom they might encounter during their duties of stacking firewood in the Harem). Furs, too, had a hieratical significance. While the Janissaries wore splendid robes trimmed with lynx, sable was reserved for the Master of the Stirrup. Many costumes were copied *in toto* from the conquered Byzantine Court. Splendor was the prevailing note throughout the Seraglio. Even as late as the last days of the Sultanate, in 1909, we are told of solid silver dustpans, and real diamond buttons sewed onto the modern kid boots imported from Paris to assuage the Harem's craving for Western chic.

When Aimée Dubucq de Rivery entered the Seraglio, its splendors were still unshadowed by restraint; indeed many of the subsequent reforms probably originated in her thrifty French brain, as we shall see. But in 1784, we read of umbrellas with gold ribs studded in sapphires, pattens for the bath inlaid with pearls, and hand towels stiff with gold embroidery. No favorite ever appeared before the Sultan in the same dress twice. The first visit was an occasion of unparalleled grandeur, and Aimée must have felt herself very far from the convent, as they robed her in the innumerable gauze chemises, velvet and fur caftans, the vast pantaloons, or *chalvari*, and the three-trained overdress tradition demanded. There are no portraits of her, thus adorned, but there is one eyewitness description which has been preserved: she was remarked above the other three black-haired Kadines for the beauty of her coloring, her fair skin, and pale golden hair. It seems she was always dressed resplendently, *à la Turque*. On her head, and tilted to one side, she wore a tiny, flat pillbox cap, blazing with jewels. Her flowing hair fell to her waist, and was powdered with diamonds which trembled among the gold and seemed scattered carelessly, but were, in fact, cunningly attached by fine golden chains. Her hands and feet were hennaed, though she had little need of the paint so much a part of the other women's toilette, and an essential part of Turkish tradition.

But before Aimée had arrived at this point of acceptance, of total integration, there were some scenes unparalleled in the history of the Seraglio, where no woman ever questioned her lot, much less repulsed the Sultan's favor. When the Kizlar Agha announced to Aimée that she was singled out for the Royal alcove, and that he would conduct her, personally, along the Golden Road, she resisted with violence. Shrewd and ambitious as she was, and carefully as she had planned her line of conduct, it is likely that she had not envisaged this decisive moment with all its implications. She must have realized that there was no other way for her to obtain power; but it was the spontaneous reaction of a young convent-bred girl, terrified of her fate. Through her birth and privilege in Martinique, she was proud, still unbroken in spirit. A Dubucq was not to be intimidated by the Turks. But this was a terrible moment: a point of no return. Her outbreak was perhaps the reflex of a slaveowner's daughter, now being led, herself, to the couch of a man she must have regarded in the light of a savage. For all her strategies, the outburst was uncontrollable: it was the last of all that remained of that girlish, perhaps childish creature who could still recall so clearly, her home, her family, and her old *da*.

The Kizlar Agha had never seen such a display of resistance. At all costs he must avoid an uproar in the Harem; his Royal Master's appetite was whetted by descriptions of Baba Mohammed's French catch; it would never do to disappoint him. Aimée's fury and independence were such that the Kizlar Agha feared she might be not only unco-operative but downright dangerous. The more she stormed, the more the other odalisques regarded her with astonishment . . . a crazy creature . . . if only *they* could be in her place, summoned by the Sultan! . . . The Chief Eunuch recalled some old story of a *tzigane* who had bitten a Sultan to the bone. . . . Well might he shudder, imagining the sort of tortures, culminating in the silken bowstring, that would be his lot, were he to sponsor another such wildcat. He left Aimée storming and padded off to be soothed and advised by his old friend, the Circassian Kadine. She listened sympathetically, and then, being a woman of great tact, her wits sharpened even more by the atmosphere of danger which was now concentrated round her son, she thought she saw a way to aid the Chief Eunuch, calm Aimée, and further her own plans too. She sent for Aimée, and had the sense to speak frankly. Again, we wonder, in what language these two women talked together? Aimée cannot, at this stage, have acquired much Turkish; it seems unlikely that the Circassian Kadine, who had entered the Harem at the age of eight, had learned to speak French, or Italian, but perhaps she had. Some of the women obtained all sorts of cultivated graces, studying astronomy, languages or even medicine; though it must be admitted that they were usually the less successful members of the Seraglio, those who had never succeeded in catching the Royal eye, and who thus fell back on learning, in the long interval between their integration and retirement to the Old Seraglio, a sort of almshouse, or old ladies' home, down by the water on the Seraglio Point.

The Circassian woman played on the French girl's good sense, her emotion, and her vanity. She impressed on her that all thoughts of escape were hopeless. It was for life: then why not accept the honors offered to her? She could be the first—the favorite, and, perhaps, mother of a son who would one day rule. (There was a striking precedent in Saladin's mother, Berengeria, though it is unlikely that this was known to either of them.) Then, reassuring Aimée as to the character of the Sultan, she spoke of the part Aimée could play influencing him towards the reforms Turkey needed so urgently. Lastly, she painted a fearful picture of the dangers to which she, her son, Selim, and all her adherents, the liberally minded, progressive group, were exposed by the enmity of the present favorite, Mustapha's reactionary mother. They looked to Aimée to protect them: the way led down the Golden Road.

Aimée was before else of a practical nature. Her innate common sense told her that the Circassian Kadine spoke the truth. There were no more rebellious outbreaks. Resigned to her fate, Aimée was to become, in time, its master. In triumph, the Chief Eunuch, *Son Altesse Noir*, conducted Mlle. Dubucq de Rivery to the Sultan Abd ül Hamid I.

The Sultan was no Terrible Turk, but a cultivated voluptuary, a patriarchal figure to whom the intrigues and violence of the Harem were abhorrent. Aimée seemed a creature apart; her blond beauty, her Western intellect, her Frankish background. . . . He was delighted with her. Very soon, as the Circassian Kadine had forseen, she had supplanted Mustapha's mother in his affections. *Naksh*, The Beautiful One, was formally installed as the new favorite.

One year later, on July 20, 1785, her son Mahmoud, was born. Thus Aimée Dubucq de Rivery found herself a key figure in the succession to the Ottoman throne, and the words of the old Euphemia David must have echoed in her ears again. . . . *You will be taken captive and placed in a Seraglio. There you will give birth to a son. This son will reign gloriously.* . . .

The whole Seraglio was illuminated to celebrate the birth of the Sultan's son. The aging Abd ül Hamid felt himself reborn. None of the other favorites were so enchanting; and none, except the shrewish woman who was Mustapha's mother, had given him a son. It is said that Mustapha and Mahmoud were the only fruits of all his five hundred wives. There seems to have been no question that the Sultan was as delighted with Aimée's child as with Aimée herself. There was no talk of strangling this newborn infant (except by Mustapha's mother, in secret longing). The Sultan ordered a magnificent fête. There were fireworks and wrestling matches, and a pavilion made entirely of spun sugar, decorated with palms, to symbolize the fertility of the union. Cages of nightingales (the bulbul of Oriental literature) were hung in the boxwood thickets. To crown the celebration there was a tulip festival, where decorative arrangements of the flowers were illuminated by colored lights, set between glass globes of colored water which reflected the lanterns and fountains. The Turks were particularly fond of such displays; they liked to set off the beauty of tulips or roses in illuminated booths, a sort of floral theater, where bird-song and the soft notes of a rebeck were a background to the aesthetic spectacle.

While the nightingales sang and the fountains plashed and the great showers of fireworks sparked across the night sky, Mustapha's mother probably skulked in her apartments. The new baby was next in succession to Selim, after her son Mustapha. She must see to it that both Selim and the baby were disposed of; it would simplify things. But Aimée, hanging over the ruby-studded cradle, must have felt complete confidence in her child's future. Euphemia David had predicted his glory—and so far, all she had foretold had come true.

At the time of Aimée's entrance into the Harem of the Sultan Abd ül Hamid, Selim, his nephew, was about the same age as Aimée. He had been brought up almost as a son by the Sultan, who, after spending forty-five years in the Prince's Cage himself, did not wish to impose this cruel incarceration upon his heir. Abd ül Hamid showed the greatest indulgence towards Selim, who had grown into a scholarly, sweet-tempered youth, passionately devoted to the ideals of his mother's liberal faction. He was in hourly danger from the assaults of Mustapha's mother, who had already succeeded in having him poisoned once, and awaited a second chance. Selim's life was only saved by the resourcefulness of his mother, who, anticipating such attacks, kept a skilled toxologist at hand, day and night. Although she had saved Selim by this promptitude, he was considerably enfeebled.

He was of that pallid delicacy seen in the Persian miniatures; one of those sighing Princes, whose vellum-toned features have a feminine cast, at odd variance with their blue-black beards, thick and trim as a yew hedge. Their long, almond eyes gaze sidelong in liquid pathos, and are emphasized by a thick sweep of painted brows, often meeting across. The Oriental manuscripts depict them, poetic and languid, riding their steeds across a barren landscape, locked in heroic but unconvincing combat with leopards or Asiatic hordes; or surrounded by courtiers, playing the lute, in fountain courts or tulip gardens. Lamartine tells us Selim's face was beautiful, his character gentle, his enthusiasm ardent; his mother had insisted that his education should befit him for his duties as Sultan. If he was to rule, it would be his strength; if he was doomed to remain vegetating in the eternal captivity of the Seraglio, then it would be his consolation. Turkish poets and philosophers surrounded his youth: as he grew older, greatly daring, he sometimes talked with an Italian doctor, Lorenzo, accredited to the Seraglio, and would interrogate him minutely on that strange faraway Western life outside the frontiers of Turkey. He was sensitive, shy and abstracted, seeming more suited to the mosque than the palace. We are told that he was faintly pitted with smallpox, very tall, and stooped slightly, from long years of study. Gossip substantiated Lady Craven's claims that he neglected his Harem and even declined to assume the responsibilities of parenthood, being so revolted by the Seraglio's general practice of strangling newborn infants. This, then, was the lonely, dreamy young prince who was to fall under Aimée Dubucq de Rivery's spell when she first appeared in the Seraglio so dazzlingly fair, so extraordinarily different to all the rest.

Aimée was now in the bloom of her northern beauty, which had nothing of the Creole exoticism so marked in her cousin Joséphine Bonaparte. Hers was the fresh silvery beauty of her Norman ancestry, so remarkable among the sultry inmates of the Seraglio. (And it must not be forgotten that she had also been through that celebrated school for odalisques where all the Oriental arts of seduction were taught.) It is therefore not surprising that as she gained in ascendancy over the Sultan Abd ül Hamid, so Mustapha's mother dropped from power, until she became a dispossessed malefic force, biding her time—that moment when her weakling son would succeed to the throne, and she would become Sultan Valideh. The Janissaries, confident of her future support, continued to center round her, a reactionary clot. But it was Aimée and her immediate circle who now had the Sultan's ear. Aimée was of the Seraglio—and yet, she always retained something of the West, quite unchanged by the ritual, costume and language she had adopted. However meltingly pink and white and gold she appeared, a steely streak remained. It was probably about this time that she first began to work at something which can be regarded as her most striking, most powerful message to the outside world of which she was born—the education of her son. The little Prince Mahmoud was a robust child, strangely independent, yet disciplined, compared to the fretful princelings who only struggled to maturity in spite of overpetting and indulgence or abortive attempts upon their lives. Aimée succeeded in imposing Western nursery restraints along with certain hygienic and dietetic measures unknown to the Seraglio. Beneath the great cypress trees that fringed the gardens, she could be seen, all summer long, playing with the child. . . . The loved, lost echoes of France sounded round her once more.

*Sur le Pont d'Avignon on y danse, on y danse . . .*
*Les beaux monsieurs font comme ça. . . .*

The little boy must have listened delightedly, watching his mother as she went through the pantomime of curtsies and courtly bows, hand on heart, toe pointed with a classic flourish. She could never return to France, but she was slowly contriving, within the Ottoman Empire, a breach through which the Western air would one day pour.

She spoke French with Mahmoud in secret. As he grew older, she steeped him in the legends of France: in the high deeds of Charlemagne and le Vert Galant, no doubt, though she probably respected the Turkish tradition which forbade any mention of defeat at the hands of the Crusaders, so that Richard Coeur de Lion was not likely to have been a nursery hero. With his mother, the little Prince lisped the fables of La Fontaine, and entered into the enchanted kingdom of Perrault; but with the rest of the Seraglio, he enjoyed the antics of Nas-reddin, the Moslem Tyl Eulenspiegel, and all the bare-faced audacities of Karageuz, the Turkish *polichinelle*. His profound love of all things French or Western, an atavistic force, was to remain with him all his life. The formation of his character was Western: its restraints and purpose, its energy, overlaid the Orient. Behind all his most decisive actions we sense the French girl from Martinique. Her influence in the Seraglio, too, was extreme. It is even said that she succeeded in converting the Sultan Abd ül Hamid to Catholicism, though this does not seem probable to the present writer. On this point, as on so many others regarding Aimée Dubucq de Rivery, all is conjecture and reconstruction. But it is certain she was loved and respected, even by her rivals in the Harem (all save Mustapha's mother) and among the high dignitaries of the Porte, those few privileged ones who were familiar with the Seraglio, she was a respected, if veiled, figure.

Behind the outward semblance of a pampered Kadine we see that Aimée was, in fact, the inspiration and guiding force behind various significant political intrigues stretching far beyond the Seraglio's walls, or even Turkish frontiers. Behind the unprecedented letter which Selim, as heir apparent, wrote to Louis XVI, in 1786, we sense Aimée Dubucq de Rivery. It was the first of a long series of pro-French gestures she was to engender. To understand the whole significance of this letter, it must be remembered that until that time there had been no regular diplomatic exchange between Turkey and the West: a French ambassador was suffered, rather than encouraged, to reside in Constantinople, but no Turkish ambassador had been appointed to Paris. Any negotiations that were made were circuitous affairs, conducted by temporary agents, recalled to the Porte as soon as their mission was completed. The Sultan and his Grand Vizier remained legendary and remote. Therefore, when the French Foreign Minister received a letter addressed to Louis XVI, proffering friendship and admiration, signed by Selim, the heir apparent to the Turkish Empire, he was nonplused. It was a departure from both protocol and procedure; highly unorthodox, very suspect.

The Foreign Minister could not be expected to see, behind the inept overtures, a convent miss. Up to that time, no one in France knew of Aimée's fate. Her family had given her up for dead. No one, not even her cousin Joséphine, who must have recalled the prophecy, could imagine she was now not only the reigning favorite of the Seraglio, but a potential influence in international affairs. Then, too, a letter from the Turkish heir apparent was in itself curious, since the Princes were by tradition always immured in the Kefess, from the age of seven onwards. And even though Selim had not been so immured, he still lived sequestered, playing no part in the policies of the Porte. By custom, the Princes saw no one from the outside world. The majority of mothers preferred to act as filters; it kept their sons more dependent and gave them greater power, themselves. Only their immediate family and their tutors ever visited them; though at fourteen they had the right to claim their own slaves and odalisques to share their confinement. Such distractions apart, these unfortunate Princes lived in absolute stagnation, awaiting their summons to rule, or die.

Why, then, did Selim, if not a prisoner, still of no acknowledged power, suddenly decide to write such a letter? What was his motive? Who was the motivating force behind such an extraordinary step? But the answer is obvious. This clumsy, naïve overture was not really addressed to Louis XVI—to France, but, rather, to the beautiful French odalisque, Aimée Dubucq de Rivery. It proves how ably Aimée had played her part; not only that assigned her by the Kizlar Agha and his faction around the throne, but also that which she had chosen to play for herself. It shows unmistakably the power that this twenty-three-year-old French girl now exercised over the young heir apparent. However strong Aimée's influence over the Sultan Abd ül Hamid I may have been, she can hardly have hoped to persuade this tired, conservative old ruler to take so drastic a step. But Selim was young and idealistic. He had fallen completely under Aimée's spell, and believed in her judgment. They were of an age; to him, she appeared the incarnation of all that liberty and civilization he sought in vain around him. There were a few happy hours when Aimée visited his mother's apartments, and they could be together. In secret, no doubt, for Aimée, as the Sultan's favorite, the youngest Kadine, was not permitted, officially, to meet even the heir apparent. But the complicity of the Kizlar Agha must have smoothed the way to many such stolen meetings. After all, if the young creatures enjoyed it, so much the better; it was to the advantage of the Kizlar Agha, and all the liberal faction, too, that Aimée should enslave the heir apparent. Selim must have seized his chance to talk to Aimée of the West, and of her ideas and hopes, so similar to his own; and eager to please her, he needed no persuasion to write the French monarch. No doubt Aimée dictated the simple phrases—too artless to seem other than madness or extreme Oriental cunning, to the stilted circle of diplomats who received it.

\*       \*       \*

This message from a ghost reached Versailles in October, 1786. But nothing came of it. The King did not trouble to reply until the following May, and then only by empty phrases. Aimée was not discredited by the failure, however. Her supporters accepted the rebuff fatalistically, and went on with their efforts to reorganize an army which should be modeled on the French system, disciplined, loyal, and uncorrupted by the Janissaries.

Even though Aimée's influence on Turkish foreign policy has never been established, and must always remain a matter of conjecture, there is strong evidence that she was behind Selim's letter, for the same messenger to whom the letter was entrusted also carried one from Aimée to her uncle, Monsieur Dubucq of Havre. At last she had achieved the dreamed-of letter. But now it was too late to think of escape. Everything was changed. There was the little Mahmoud, who could never leave. He must stay there, to meet his destiny, and she must stay beside him, to help him meet it well. The letter was her first communication with her family since leaving the convent. They had probably given her up for dead. Her news must have been at once reassuring and disquieting. We have no record of how the Dubucqs viewed their lost Aimée: whether they were disinterested, proud or horrified by her exotic fate.

Did they hush up the whole matter, speaking of it in whispers, and never before the servants or children? *A fate worse than death* . . . but that is probably a Victorian attitude: theirs would have been robustly eighteenth century; and since they were French, tinged by a worldly approbation. Viewed that way, Aimée had done rather well for herself, ensnaring no less a person than the Grand Turk. Though, on the other hand, the Osmanli were not perhaps quite the family the Dubucqs would have chosen for an alliance. We do not know if they replied to Aimée, but we can imagine with what longing the ghost waited for an answer from that living world to which she had once belonged.

\*     \*     \*

In April, 1789, the Sultan Abd ül Hamid died, and was succeeded by his nephew, Selim, who became the Sultan Selim III, Allah's Vice Regent upon Earth. He was twenty-seven years old, and the nation rallied round him, confident that his youthful eagerness could overcome the abuses of government and taxation under which they now labored. But for all his enthusiasm, his bold resolves, and Aimée's support behind the scenes, Selim was not strong enough for such a monumental task. At every turn he was harassed: at home by the Janissaries; abroad by his enemies, the Russians. Everything depended on achieving a new army, disciplined along French lines, and loyal to the Sultan, alone. He set about creating such a body, called the Nizam-Djedid, or new troops. This was a blow aimed directly at the Janissaries: and following it up by another, he decreed that the pick of the youngest Janissaries should now be incorporated into his Nizam-Djedid. The Janissaries were thunderstruck. Evidently this weakling meant business. The Agha sent for his captains and they began to plot their countermoves. But it was not so easy. Selim was proving himself firmer than they had thought; and the people were on his side, too. It was a stalemate. Once more, both factions drew back, waiting. . . .

When the Revolution swept France in 1793 Aimée followed events as well as she could, from behind the Seraglio's high crenelated walls. It was discouraging to have to admit that such a great country as hers was now gripped by a violent mob displaying a positively Oriental savagery. But Selim was not shaken: he agreed with her; it was the terrible outbreak of a misguided minority. France as a whole was sound. It is likely that from time to time she had news of her family; of her cousin Joséphine, too, now the mother of two children, now Beauharnais' widow, and now wife of a dynamic little Corsican general. News traveled slowly, then. Perhaps the gossip of the Paris salons reached the French Embassy at Pera. But no further. That last mile, across the caïques that bridged the Golden Horn, past the spices and serpent skins and perfumed roots piled along the Egyptian Bazaar, news from Europe faded, and was lost. It was said that ten thousand people crossed the bridge daily—but not one idea. This was the East, enclosed, remote. Time, like Western thought, flowed past the bubble-domed roofs of the Great Bazaar, past the minarets of the Suleimanyé, on past the gates of the Seraglio. The East had its own rumors, its own dramas. No echoes of Paris reached so far. Within the courtyards of the Seraglio, where a strange, oppressive silence was always remarked, no such small talk reached Aimée. Only the barest outlines of her cousin's story were known to her, over the years; the more spirited episodes in Joséphine's life during the Terror; but after, Joséphine, *la femme galante,* Barras, the mirrored bedroom in the Rue Chantereine—all this was certainly unknown to her, until—marvelous justification of all Euphemia David's most extravagant claims—Joséphine was crowned Empress of the French.

There was no record that the cousins ever corresponded; although it is known that much later, during Selim's reign, when Aimée enjoyed almost as much authority as the Sultan Valideh, she was able to dispatch magnificent presents to the Emperor and his family; diamond aigrettes, pearls, and a hundred of the delicate *cachemires* that Joséphine wore so incomparably. But beyond this formal gesture there is no record of any personal exchange. They were very different characters. One, a frivolous, cynical, calculating, extravagant charmer. The other, serious, idealistic, practical and sentimental. Only ambition and a sense of adventure seem to have been common to both these beautiful Creoles.

But Aimée cherished a special affection for the memory of her

cousin. She had been cut off from France for so long; all that she remembered of her childhood and home in Martinique was now embodied in Joséphine. It was a lonely life within the Seraglio; there can
have been so few outsiders that she could ever meet. It was only some
thirty or forty years after her death that the stream of distinguished
French visitors began to arrive. We can imagine with what delight
Aimée would have welcomed the state visit of the Empress Eugénie, on
her way to the Suez Canal, and for whom Aimée's grandson, Abd ül
Medjuel, decorated the sugary little palace on the Bosphorus.

Even such an austerely dedicated woman as Florence Nightingale
would have been welcomed: indeed, she would have probably found
the practical and energetic temperament of the French Sultana a great
help in her struggles to establish the hospital at Scutari, just across the
water from Aimée's kiosk. Gérard de Nerval, too, wandering giddily
about the Levant, collecting material for his *Voyage en Orient,* how
welcome a guest he would have been! And how much he would have
enjoyed her story: his book is full of such vignettes, blazing with color.
But of all of them it is really Pierre Loti who should have been there in
Aimée's day, instead of sixty years later. Would he have written *Aziyadé,* if he could have feasted on the drama and mystery and pathos
of the French Sultana's story? How Loti would have luxuriated in the
delicious melancholy of it all . . . and set within the fastness of the
Seraglio, too! *Pauvre petit fantôme . . . chère petite Sultane. . . .*
We imagine them, sitting together in some shadowy pavilion; Aimée, the
ghost, trying, through him, to return to the West; and Loti, the writer,
the Turcophil, trying, through her, to become one with the East; each
aching with voluptuous nostalgia . . . talking at cross purposes, but
still, talking in French, the language of Aimée's heart.

\*          \*          \*

Selim had a positively childish enthusiasm for all that was French. He
must have had unlimited confidence, revolution or no, in a land from
which the incomparable Aimée sprang. During the early years of his
reign, after the peace of Jassy in 1792, by which Russia was ceded
the Crimea, Turkey withdrew to lick its wounds, and Selim con-

centrated a new and powerful army on completely French lines. French and Swedish engineers were employed. The cannon foundry at Top Hané was under French command. French artillery officers were employed to effect a series of drastic changes in army administration. Next there were translations of French manuals on mathematics and military tactics. French naval officers trained the navy; French shipbuilders organized the shipyards. In 1795 Selim sanctioned a French weekly, *Le Moniteur de l'Orient*, to be published in Constantinople. We have no doubt why it was sanctioned, or for whom. Selim himself had only the barest smattering of French, but no doubt he enjoyed the extracts Aimée read him. Most significant of all, the first permanent ambassador was appointed to France in 1797. He became the sensation of Directoire Paris, where everything was *à la Turque* for a few weeks. Napoleon received him warmly. He had long had his eye on Constantinople as the greatest strategic prize Europe could offer. Perhaps he remembered how, in 1793, when the Porte had first sent for French military experts, he had been one of the officers who had volunteered; but his application had been turned down, and he had stayed behind, to become First Consul, to conquer Europe, and aspire to becoming Emperor of the world, Turkey as part of the spoils.

When news reached the Seraglio that General Bonaparte, the First Consul, had married none other than Aimée's cousin, the Vicomtesse de Beauharnais, Selim must have felt confident of French interest and support in his progressive dreams. But Napoleon was less interested in dreams than schemes. It was a severe shock to the Sultan to learn, in July, 1798, and after all Napoleon's professions of amity, that a French army thirty thousand strong had landed in Egypt intending to wrest it from Turkish rule. However, Napoleon's mirage of Oriental conquest (of which this was the first step) faded. In 1801 there were a flurry of treaties and a general, though brief, era of peace was established. Napoleon acknowledged the sovereignty of the Porte in Egypt and the Sultan, in return, favored French interests in Turkey. No doubt Aimée rejoiced that this painful breach had been healed. She must have had to employ all her arts, persuading Selim, the proud, the just, to overlook so many unprovoked acts of aggression at Napoleon's hands. And so, one by one, sharper, more distinct each time, signs were coming from the fastness of the Seraglio, signaling to the world, of the mysterious presence of a *French* mind behind the close-latticed window of the Divan, where, by custom, the Sultan could watch, unobserved, from a secret gallery, the workings of his Divan, or ministerial conferences.

During these years, there was one man who went between Paris and the Porte, and was becoming a revered figure among the Turks. The name of Pierre Ruffin recurs over a wide span of time. He was born at Salonika in 1742, the son of a dragoman who represented French interests in the Levant. He grew up to become an Orientalist of high attainments. He was six times Chargé d'Affaires in Constantinople, and had become so influential with the Turks, so much loved by the successive Sultans, who addressed him as *Père*, that on his retirement, his mere presence in the city enfeebled the authority of the succeeding Ambassador, who asked for him to be removed elsewhere. Ruffin must have come to know Aimée well; he probably helped her to form the Francophile tendencies of both Selim and Mahmoud. With his scholarly interests, his knowledge of European and Oriental literature, it was probably he who guided Aimée in the daring innovation of a new library containing enormous numbers of French books, the classics, the Encyclopaedists, many of them translated into Turkish. When we consider that the first Turkish press was only established permanently in 1784, the year of Aimée's arrival, it seems likely that her influence was already at work here, for it needed the direct encouragement and protection of the Sultan, the *ulemas*, or priests, being opposed to any diffusion of knowledge. The Koran was only authorized to be printed and sold publicly as late as 1850. Between them, Selim, Ruffin and Aimée were beginning to open windows onto the world.

At this time Selim's reforms had not yet aggravated the people. Whatever the Janissaries felt, it was wiser to wait. The Sultan's faction was both purposeful and powerful. Behind Selim stood the puissant Pasha of Rustchuk, governor of a province in the north of Bulgaria, a loyal and devoted servant; there was the Kizlar Agha, the Sultan Valideh, the Mufti Vely-Zadé, and, it now seemed, French support. No; it was not yet time to strike. Across the courts, the two factions watched each

other implacably. Sometimes, in the dusk, the scuttling figure of
a dwarf, or one of the mutes could be glimpsed, carrying a message between the pavilion of Mustapha's mother and the Court of the Janissaries. There were eyes and ears everywhere. Nothing passed unobserved. As the atmosphere became increasingly tense, the Janissaries
would break out with some fresh piece of insolence or cruelty, which
Selim was not powerful enough to quell. When their kettle drums
sounded, even the bravest quailed, and Aimée, knowing the price she
and her son might one day have to pay for her years of hostility to the
Corps, and her influence over the Sultan, must have closed the shutters
and stopped her ears against the sinister beat. And in the morning there
would be fresh tales of violence and anarchy, and some loyal member of
the Sultan's party would be discovered hanging from the great plane tree
outside their quarters; or another head would be added to the pyramid
beside the Gate of Felicity. During those years Aimée's hatred was
forming into that implacable force which one day was to overthrow the
whole Corps and all the violence they represented.

But that day was still far away; now, there were golden interludes,
when Aimée and her son enjoyed an almost serene family life beside
Selim and his mother. Selim loved his young cousin Mahmoud devotedly. It was Aimée's child; he loved him like his own; or, perhaps, as
a younger brother. The Circassian Kadine and "the French Sultana"
had violated all the traditions of the Seraglio when they joined forces
to foster loyalty and affection between their children, the rival claimants. From the beginning Selim had shown a devoted interest in the
child. As the baby grew into the boy, and the boy into the young man,
the gap in their ages seemed to dwindle, until, by the time Mahmoud
was twenty, to Selim's forty and Aimée's forty-one years, there
were times when they all seemed of an age. Serene and golden days,
when they picnicked in the hyacinth gardens overlooking the Golden
Horn; or made expeditions to one of the Royal *yalis*, or summer palaces
reflected in the blue waters of the Bosphorus, lapping below its windows. Sometimes the Sultan Selim would hold an archery tournament,
beyond the city's walls, and a splendid tented-pavilion would be
pitched; wherever it had stood remaining, ever afterwards, as free land—

a gift to the people. Often, Selim sat beside Aimée in her kiosk as she worked at her embroidery frame. The needle flashed in and out of the petit point garlands, hung poised, and then plunged; her long hair fell over her face like a burnished golden veil; the diamonds glittered and trembled on their invisible chains. Selim thought her the most beautiful creature in the world: he would have done anything for her—anything. He drank in her words; and all the while she was talking about France . . . the West; the world outside the Seraglio . . . the world she had known before she became a ghost.

Sometimes she showed a naïve, and rather touching nostalgia for odd aspects of her French past. Within the Seraglio, anything she commanded was hers. Selim gratified her every whim: yet she harked back to her youthful memories. The Montgolfier brothers and their marvelous balloon had been the rage when Aimée was at Nantes. All France talked of their extraordinary invention; there were pictures and prints, and even wallpapers of "Montgolfiers," as the striped and decorated balloons were called. First the balloons had been tested with goats sent aloft as victim-passengers, rather in the manner they are now used for atomic experiments. Later, it became fashionable to make an ascent, several hundred feet up, in a beribboned basket: Aimée must have recounted it all to Selim and Mahmoud many times over. So one day, and probably to gratify the wish of *Naksh*, The Beautiful One, a Montgolfier rose from the fields of Dolma Bagtché. Not only that, the Sultan himself proved to the French Kadine that he was as fearless as her Western men, by making an ascent himself, and there was the astonishing spectacle of the Padishah of the Faithful, Allah's Shadow upon Earth, soaring over the five thousand domes and minarets of his capital, while far below, pandemonium reigned among the caïques that crammed the Sweet Waters of Asia, as their occupants craned skywards in delicious apprehension, cheering wildly. And at sunset, the mosques filled with the Faithful, all gathered together to hear the *ulemas* rendering thanks to Allah for the safe return of their Sultan. These gaily striped balloons were like so many airy bubbles of frivolity and elegance, gigantic *articles de Paris,* soaring in the blue skies of Turkey. Yes; it was evident in many ways that there was a French woman behind the throne, and her power was perhaps even more striking than that exercised by her cousin Joséphine, in France.

Under Selim's protection, Aimée found much to enjoy. She was of a sanguine nature and did not anticipate disaster. There were many agreeable aspects of life now. Her son; Selim's love and admiration; considerable liberty; increasing power and the most seducing luxury. There were her gardens, her study of Oriental culture, her French books, her music, and her warm friendship with the Sultan Valideh, who had helped to make her path easier. But on October 16, 1805, the Circassian woman died, and with her Aimée's carefree days. She was buried in one of the sumptuous Imperial Turbehs, as befitted her state, and Selim and Aimée and Mahmoud, the Kizlar Agha and all her friends mourned her loss. But the Janissaries knew that one of their keenest adversaries had gone: they began to take stock. Now Aimée stood alone between them and the two Princes, Mahmoud, her son, and Selim, the gentle Sultan, so unfitted to oppose them, and for whom she felt, perhaps, more than a protective love.

The sixteen years of Selim's reign had not given him the authority he required, surrounded by such enemies. His wars had weakened the country, as his reforms had weakened his popularity. Napoleon's invasion of Egypt had proved a weapon in the hands of the anti-French faction. Mahmoud was barely twenty, without any claims to the throne while Mustapha lived, but he had grown into a self-reliant, withdrawn character, bound up in the secret world of all things French, which he shared with his mother. He had studied military tactics with the French officers, learned to ride his horse with a European saddle, and to read everything of the West he could come by; but he had no place in official life. He could do no more than encourage Selim.

It was a Turkish tradition that every Prince of the blood must have a profession. Mahmoud chose to be a scribe, and spent long hours perfecting the graceful arabesques. The beauty of his calligraphy was such that he was often asked to inscribe the prayers or verses on public monuments about the city; many of them are still to be seen, great sweeps of black and gold, decorative and splendid, an ironic monument for a Sultan who had the force to break away from the bondage of his ancestors, and who was to pass into history as The Reformer.

Between 1805 and 1806, Selim, actuated by Aimée, had made two more overtures to the French. Friendship at all costs. Their need for a powerful ally was desperate, now. Not only was anarchy spreading within the country, reaching outward from the very Seraglio itself, but Russia was waiting to pounce on the weakened country. Selim's cry for help sounded a desperate note. Ruffin's reports enlightened Napoleon as to the urgency. For Mustapha's supporters were closing in. They, too, had been making outside overtures—to Russia, Turkey's traditional enemy, and to the English, too. The Tzar's troops were marching south. The British fleet was sailing east. Selim sent another, more agonized appeal for support, and now Napoleon acted quickly. He appointed one of his young staff officers, General, later Marshal, Sebastiani, as his special envoy to the Porte. Sebastiani, like Napoleon, was a Corsican. He was a brilliant soldier, capable of conceiving and executing the boldest schemes. He traveled fast, driving on, through the plains of central and southern Europe, blinding white in the dust of midsummer. He reached Constantinople on August 10, 1806, to the fury of Mustapha's faction. They were outmaneuvered.

The British Ambassador was in a great taking too. Under his very nose, General Sebastiani was being received in private audience by the Sultan, an honor not accorded their Ambassador, even under great stress. There was no stopping the General. French officers commanded Turkish ships—Good God! even the sailors' turban badge was a tricolor beside the Crescent! Colonel Sebastiani was in daily conference with the Seraglio; he was arming them, advising them, organizing them, *running* them in a most irregular fashion. It was not diplomacy . . . it was unheard of—it amounted to an act of war! Thus the outraged British Ambassador to his Government.

The British fleet sailed up the Dardanelles, their object being to demand Sebastiani's recall. Under threat of their guns, Selim weakened. But Aimée stood firm. There must be no negotiation, unless the fleet withdrew beyond the Dardanelles. Meanwhile, Sebastiani must be invested with absolute power. The Turkish people, now roused to the danger, flung themselves into preparations for defense, dragging their few cannons into the positions Sebastiani chose. They closed their ranks for battle. Selim pitched his tent next to that of Sebastiani and ordered his ministers to establish themselves beside the various batteries along the walls. For many of the Seraglio sycophants this was a most disagreeable order, but they knew better than to question it, then. Sebastiani's presence was both galvanic and reassuring. Under his orders the city was turned into an arsenal and fortress. The people were now ranged solidly behind him: neither the Janissaries nor Mustapha's party could turn them in favor of the English. While the foundries were contriving clumsy grapeshot and cannon balls made of rough stone, the British men o' war lay becalmed off Prinkipo Island, in sight of the city. The wind had turned against them, and for several days they were helpless. Those few days were crucial. They gave Sebastiani the time he needed to consolidate his defense. He achieved miracles, was everywhere at once; in the foundries, at the Seraglio, in conference with the Divan, about the city, at the Arsenal, on the Galata Tower, scanning the city's outer defenses. Even the Corps Diplomatique were fired—young attachés helped drag the guns; the Dutch Chargé d'Affaires flung gold coins right and left, to encourage the mob. The secretaries from the French Embassy, in lace-edged shirts, toiled beside ragged brigades of Armenians or Greeks. When at last the wind changed, Constantinople had been transformed into a fortress, commanded by a daring General, supported by the entire population. Admiral Duckworth decided discretion was the wisest course, and sailed for home. Aimée had won the first round.

*       *       *

The pro-French element around the throne could breathe easier, now. They foresaw a period of security and more progress along French lines. But progress, like beauty, is apt to lie in the eye of the beholder. "Orthodoxy is my doxy—heterodoxy is the other man's doxy." The mere word "reform" sounded ominous to many. The Janissaries smoldered with resentment. But while Sebastiani, representing Napoleonic force, was in control, there was no chance of gaining power. Their puppet, Mustapha, and his mother waited, too. . . .

In Aimée's apartments, safe from prying ears, there were many conferences. The atmosphere must have seemed dazzlingly European to Selim. Some years earlier Aimée had refurnished a suite of rooms in the French style, delicate Louis XVI chairs, satinwood commodes and curtains of *toile de Jouy*. The bold silhouette of Directoire or Empire furniture was unknown to her. She had recreated the salons of her youth, of the few visits she had made to her friends outside the convent. There were mirrors with swagged and gilded frames. Porcelain bowls full of potpourri stood on spindle-legged little satinwood tables. The love seats and *bergères* were plump with pale striped satin cushions; but they were unmistakably strict in form; they were for sitting, in the formal, European style; no lolling, as on the Turkish *minder,* or couch. A harp stood in one corner, though Aimée preferred to play the guitar. Sometimes Selim persuaded her to sing, and Lully or Couperin sounded across the courtyards of the Seraglio, tinkling, ghostly music, sung by a ghost, scarcely heard, above the clanking of the Janissary guard, patroling below the latticed windows.

In this frivolous setting, Selim loved to savor the West (not a *tchibouk* or divan in sight!) He liked to listen to Aimée's clear voice.

> *Nous n'irons plus au bois*
> *Les lauriers sont coupés . . .*

Even her saddest songs seemed gay, beside the minor *mélopées* of the East. Sometimes the Sebastianis came to join them and then there was champagne, a taste Aimée was much criticized for fostering in the young Mahmoud, who, like all Moslems, defied the Koran with every sip. Selim would sit silent, listening to the many plans which, in the light of Sebastiani's experience and Aimée's enthusiasm, seemed feasible. Sometimes there were more frivolous exchanges; Sebastiani would recount life at the Tuileries, and his wife, the charming Fanny de Coigny, would give Aimée accounts of the day-to-day doings of cousin Joséphine, and elegant Paris. Before that there had only been Monsieur

Ruffin, who had represented a rather arid aspect of France, and was, besides, so much of an Orientalist that he preferred to speak Turkish. Aimée herself, although long established in the Turkish way of life and dress, was still undeniably French; while Mahmoud's upbringing and ancestry left no doubt as to his sympathies. He had a strong conviction of his duty towards his people. They *must* be westernized. Then, once more, the pashas would be shaken out of their habits of graft and inertia; flail-like, the reforms struck right and left, and across the inner courtyards of the Seraglio, Mustapha's mother noted everything, the Sultan's visits to *Naksh,* The Beautiful One, the infidel; Sebastiani's comings and goings—nothing escaped her: everything was noted and reported to her masters, the Janissaries. But when their kettle drums sounded, not all Selim's devotion, not all the brocaded *bergères* and harps could give Aimée a feeling of ease. To her, the drums were the pulse of that hateful Orient which had enslaved her; to her they symbolized all the savagery of the East; the very cannons of the pirates who had dragged her, a captive, through the alleys of the Kasbah.

Not only in the Sultan's immediate entourage, but throughout the city, among the people, Sebastiani's popularity was enormous. He was the savior of Constantinople, the hero of the hour. But then he usually was. He had formed the pattern of success early. Throughout his long and vivid life he went from glory to glory. He was, besides, fitted by nature to be at once a compelling and alluring figure. He charmed everyone by his magnificent physique and romantic good looks: "a creature who caused drawing-room riots." The Abbé de Pradt described him as *le Cupidon de l'Empire.* He must have been the perfect type of Napoleonic Marshal. Today, all that is left to us of this dashing band is the line of stone figures in their grimy niches along the façade of the Louvre beside the Rue de Rivoli. They stand there, the stone Marshals of France, while the buses grind past and the pigeons perch on cocked hat and flourished saber.

Sebastiani is a particularly highly colored figure. We imagine him galloping across Europe, looking like one of Gros' equestrian portraits, his charger rearing, a leopard-skin saddlecloth flung over the dappled rump, his plumed shako set rakishly, his uniform smothered in soutache, his hussar's jacket falling from one shoulder, his drawn saber gleaming as he spurs forward into the smoke of battle. Onward! Eastward! To Vienna! To Belgrade! To the walls of Constantinople! To glory!

He was born in Corsica in 1772. His father was a shoemaker, comfortably well off, and said to be related to the Bonaparte family. The young Horace François Bastien Sebastiani was destined for the church, but having other ideas, he left Corsica for France, where he joined the army. His rise was spectacular. He saw much fighting, played a conspicuous part in the Coup d'Etat of 18 Brumaire, after which Bonaparte marked him out for success and appointed him to his staff. After fighting at Marengo and Austerlitz, he was created a Colonel, then Count of the Empire; presently Bonaparte entrusted him with a delicate mission in the East. He was to go to Egypt and discover the relations between Turkey and the Mamelukes: he was to sound the Arab chiefs, reassure the Christian Syrians as to French support, and return by way of Constantinople, where he was to flatter and reassure the Padishah on Bonaparte's behalf. All this Sebastiani executed with his customary adroitness; so that when Selim's second desperate cry for help reached Bonaparte, Sebastiani was the obvious choice of envoy extraordinary, a diplomat and soldier, already familiar with the Levant, and fit to meet whatever emergency he might find at the Porte.

That he succeeded brilliantly, we know; had it not been for his wife's sudden death, he would have probably stayed beside Selim indefinitely, and Aimée's cherished dreams of progress might have been achieved in full. But when Fanny died giving birth to a daughter Sebastiani asked to be recalled, and returned to Paris, heartbroken, to bury himself in military life once more. He fought through the Russian campaigns, was with the Emperor during the Hundred Days, and retired to live in England after the battle of Waterloo. In 1816 he returned to France to enter politics, becoming successively *Ministre de la Marine, Ministre des Affaires Etrangères,* Ambassador to Naples, and London, where he was succeeded by Guizot. His old age was embittered by the terrible death of his daughter, Fanny, Duchesse de Praslin, who was found hacked to pieces in her canopied bed in the Praslin house, in the Rue St. Honoré. She was said to be a passionate and nagging creature, and there is little doubt that her husband, the Duke, was responsible for her death. He had fallen under the sway of an apparently mousy young English governess, whom the Duchess accused of alienating not only her husband's love, but that of her children, too. The drama rocked France and almost ruined the already tottering government of Louis Philippe. Sebastiani had rushed to Paris to press the charges against his son-in-law. But the Duke refused to speak, and escaped trial by taking poison.

As a fiery septuagenarian, Sebastiani was still to be seen pacing up and down the olive yards of his Corsican estate. An American diplomat recalled seeing him, a dynamic figure, even then, sheltering from the heat under a yellow umbrella, muttering as he walked . . . alone with the huge sweep of his memories. *La Grande Armée,* the Mamelukes, Joséphine's dinner parties in the Rue Chantereine, to which, as *le Cupidon de l'Empire,* he was no doubt welcomed. Austerlitz, Waterloo, Constantinople, the secret life of the Seraglio he was one of the few to have penetrated. . . . And Aimée, the veiled figure he and Fanny came to know so well, so long ago. . . . An attack of apoplexy carried him off suddenly, one golden spring day. He had been seated at the luncheon table, and, suddenly, was no more. It was a perfect death. He had wished to be buried in the Invalides, among his peers, the other Marshals of France: the following August, with all the pomp and honors he commanded, his coffin was carried there. At that moment, a mysterious fire burst out; the banners and standards taken in battle from his defeated enemies went up in tongues of flame, thus conspiring, to the end, to surround him with an atmosphere of heroic drama.

\*     \*     \*

At the moment when Sebastiani's path crossed that of the French Sultana, at the very moment of their joint triumph (though, it must be remarked, for different ends, his for his Emperor, hers for her son) all was turned to ashes. Just as, once before, Fate had stepped in, turning the wind against the British fleet, so, now, it stepped in again. Death struck, and all was changed. Fanny Sebastiani suddenly sickened and died. Her husband was broken. He blamed himself for bringing her to this Asiatic waste of dirt and disease, of burning suns and icy winds.

Aimée, too, was desolate. She had welcomed Fanny like a sister. Fanny had brought back her girlhood in France, and had seemed to represent everything of *la douceur de France*. She had been the first, and only, French woman, besides Aimée, whom Selim and Mahmoud had known. Her charm, and Sebastiani's strength, had confirmed all that Aimée had told them of her people. And now Fanny was dead. To Sebastiani, Constantinople was haunted, accursed. He fled.

Now, at last the Janissaries' hour had come, and they unleashed their long-pent fury in a rule of terror. In the name of nationalism, a wave of reaction set in. Playing on the dangerous French influence dominating the Sultan, they suppressed his Nizam-Djedid, seized the throne, deposed Selim, and proclaimed Mustapha as Sultan, his mother as Sultan Valideh. All this less than a month after Sebastiani's departure. Aimée, Mahmoud and Selim huddled together in captivity, went in hourly terror for their lives. Many of their entourage were killed outright, others disappeared or were imprisoned. Their officers of state, generals and governors of provinces were recalled, to be met with the bowstring. The Janissaries gave no quarter. Cruelty and reaction reigned once more.

When the news reached Paris, in spite of Sebastiani's advice, Bonaparte made his first open move towards annexing Turkey. He had always been perfectly cynical as to the protection he had extended, and he had never believed in the staying power of the pro-French faction. It had suited him to send Sebastiani; he could not have the English established there. Now, with reports of anarchy and terror coming in by every messenger and a sinister silence from Selim, he decided the time had come to disclose his plans. He was deaf to Sebastiani's pleas; deaf, we must suppose, to anything Joséphine may have said concerning the fate of her cousin. (Bonaparte was always able to be ruthless where family considerations did not coincide with his own policies.) In June he thundered off to Tilsit to meet the Tzar Alexander, where, embracing flamboyantly on an ornamental raft moored in midstream of the Niemen, the two demigods swore eternal friendship and concluded an agreement that the Ottoman Empire should belong to Russia. Such was their private understanding. Publicly, however, the treaty read otherwise; it provided for Russia's evacuation of the Danubian provinces. As Bonaparte saw it, this would clear the way for his ultimate conquest of Turkey, besides allaying the suspicions of the Porte as to his intentions. As Alexander saw it, the gesture would earn him French co-operation in his dreams of occupying all Turkey, from the Danube to Salonika. The two Emperors were delighted with themselves; each thought the other his dupe. Their standards floated over the pavilion on the raft; their aides-de-camps clanked their spurs and swords up and down the landing stage; at night, beside the long lines of horses pick-eted on the banks, the Cossacks broke into their wild dances. There were fireworks and military bands, and the junketings went on into the pale summer dawn.

*     *     *

While Mustapha and the Janissaries were liquidating their enemies, they had overlooked the one man who was to bring about their ruin. Baraiktar, Pasha of Rustchuk, a Bulgarian province on the Danube, was himself of Bulgarian origin, but a devoted servant of the Turkish Em-pire, and in sympathy with the French reforms. He was a Three-Tailed Bashaw by rank, a loyal supporter of the Sultan Selim by in-clination. As soon as word reached him of Selim's deposition, he rallied his troops, and set out for Constantinople, leading an army of scowling Albanians. From the flat dun-colored banks of the Danube across Bul-garia to Turkey was a formidable march, especially in the torrid climate of midsummer, but Baraiktar pushed on, through the wild defiles of the Balkan mountains, beside the looped windings of the Yantra River, where it races yellow beneath Tirnovo, the ancient Bulgarian capital. On, by Kazanluk, where the Valley of the Roses melts into the moun-tains, always south, through those strange, secretive Slav villages, where Turkish domination rankled and Bulgarian patriotism smoldered for nearly five centuries. The avenging army marched on, till, come at last to the Turkish border country, the great mosques of Adrianople rose suddenly into sight. Turkish soil at last! Baraiktar found the konaks, or inns, full of rumors. The Sultan was dead! His French faction were im-paled on the gates of the Seraglio; the Janissaries were in possession of the Divan. . . . Baraiktar pressed on, and reaching the outer walls of the Seraglio, surprised the guard, stormed the first courtyard, and was at the Gate of Felicity before Mustapha and his ministers were roused. But once the alarm was given, Mustapha's mother struck, serpent-quick. Her son's life was safe only if he represented the last of the Osmanlis. An old superstition held that both dynasty and empire stood, or fell, together. No one would touch Mustapha, were he the sole survivor of the Royal house. Selim and Mahmoud must die. She dispatched the guard to kill them where they languished in the Princes' Cage.

Selim, the gentle, the scholar, died like a lion. As the soldiers broke into his room, only one man stood beside him, Taiher Effendi, who flung himself between the Sultan and his assailants. But Selim knew his hour had come, and that it was Mahmoud who must be saved, to carry on the reforms he, Selim, had failed to achieve. Selim loved Mahmoud not only as a brother, but as the child of Aimée, *Naksh*, The Beautiful One, his Beautiful One. . . . Ordering Taiher to find Mahmoud and warn him, Selim drew his dagger and rushed on the guard, to fight a delaying action, and die of a hundred thrusts. But Mahmoud had been saved. Taiher reached him in time to help him escape onto the roof, by way of a chimney. Legend has it that Aimée succeeded in hiding her son in the disused stove of a bathhouse: in any case, his enemies found him gone. As they rushed after him, their way was blocked by one of Aimée's devoted slaves, a Georgian woman of formidable physique, known in the Harem as The Strong. She, too, would defend Aimée's child with her life. She hurled a brazier of red-hot coals at the guard, who fell back for another few, vital moments. By now Baraiktar had battered down the Gate of Felicity and was raging through the Seraglio calling for Sultan Selim, his master. But silence met him everywhere. The courtyards were deserted, the kiosks empty, the Harem silent; the Eunuchs, the cooks, the gardeners and the ministers—all had fled. At that moment, Mustapha's voice was heard. "Hand over Sultan Selim to the Pasha of Rustchuk, if he wants the pig's carcass," and he kicked his cousin's body across the threshold, where it lay, terribly disfigured, under the blazing noonday sun.

Baraiktar flung himself down beside it, weeping bitterly, and vowing vengeance: "Is it for the Pasha of Rustchuk to cry like a girl?" said his captains. "Let us avenge our Sultan!" "Let us save Sultan Mahmoud!" replied Baraiktar, and at that same moment Mahmoud himself appeared, blackened by soot, but in no way shaken by his ordeal. With that majestic force which characterized him, even so young, he took command. He told Baraiktar that he would avenge Selim himself, in his own time, in his own way. And there sounds the first note of implacable determination, of unhurried, calculated revenge which Mahmoud was to nurture within him, unknown to all, save his mother, for so many years, until at last it was unleashed in all its fury, crushing, forever, the Janissaries and their way of government. In this aspect of Mahmoud's nature we see Oriental cunning restrained by Western discipline; the luxury of revenge was sublimated to long-term strategy. Not for nothing had he studied French military tactics; not for nothing had he hung on Sebastiani's words; absorbing from Ruffin, from his mother, from the French artillery officers, all that he could, of the West.

He gave his orders coldly. There must be no more bloodshed; no more dramatic gestures, by Baraiktar or anyone else, until he, Mahmoud, commanded. His dynamic personality dominated the scene; his powerful voice rang through the courtyards. It was apparent that this was no vitiated princeling, but a strong man. He led the way to the Hall of the Sacred Mantle, where the Prophet's Standard, the Sanjak Sherif, and other holy relics were kept. It was here that the new Sultans always prayed; here that Mahmoud now prayed alone, for some hours. When he emerged, his mere presence silenced the throngs who had crept out from their hiding places and now prostrated themselves in terror and obedience. Mahmoud gave his orders, and Mustapha and his mother were led away to their imprisonment. Baraiktar was created Grand Vizier. That night the cannons of Top Kapou roared out a Sultan's salute. Mahmoud was proclaimed Padishah of the Faithful, Allah's Vice Regent upon Earth.

In the shadow-filled mosques the people prayed, rocking backwards and forwards, prostrating themselves towards the East; in the *tekkées* of Scutari the Dervishes spun and howled in mystical frenzies. A new Sultan and a new time had come. It was Allah's will! They prayed for Mahmoud. Alone in the splendors of her Royal kiosk, Aimée prayed, too. She had never relinquished her Catholic faith; it had sustained her through so many trials. Now she was the Sultan Valideh; her son the Sultan; her enemies confounded; the future all before her. Thus we see the French convent girl, the trembling slave, who, so many years ago was carried from the Corsairs' *barque* to the Gate of Felicity, now mistress of those who believed they could enslave her. Once again, the words of Euphemia David must have rung in her ears. . . . *This son will reign gloriously, but the steps of his throne will be dyed with the blood of his predecessor.* . . . Surely it was God's will that she had been sent to Turkey, that Mahmoud had been preserved, to rule, and to reform. Perhaps, that night, she was the only one who prayed for Selim's soul.

*       *       *

At this point let us examine the impression which the young Sultan made on those around him. His energy and commanding air have been already noted; he is described as having a curious fixed stare, which he turned, like an unspoken question, upon any foreigners. Even the sight of a *Giaour*, among the crowds that cheered him as he passed, would produce this haunting gaze. It was as if he searched for civilization, for this magical, long-desired Western myth. He had what was described as a *severité mélancolique*. He was rather above middle height, powerfully built, with his father's livid pallor and jetty black beard. Prior to his accession he had remained unknown, unseen, living protected, rather than a prisoner, in the Princes' Cage, or his mother's apartments, known only to Selim's closest followers, or the French faction. Now it was seen with misgiving that he had many marks of the *Giaour* about him. He preferred a chair to cushions or a divan. He scorned to eat with his fingers, and used an elegant gold knife and fork. Worse still, he drank champagne at every occasion. (Indeed, after his death, which was wrongly attributed to drinking, by his enemies, his widow flung the whole contents of his cellar into the Bosphorus, in a gesture of grief and Moslem repudiation. The spectacle of thousands of bottles of fine French wines sinking off Seraglio Point, where once the unfaithful odalisques had perished, must have been edifying for those of the old school who had opposed such manifestations of infidel leanings.) When he rode, it was with a European saddle and in the style of the French cavalry officers. Later, even more audacious, he wore a costume where an odd blend of tradition and innovation was apparent. The sable-lined brocades and glittering turbans of his youth gave way to a pair of pleated trousers, a topcoat cut like a uniform tunic, topped by a fez. The turban was condemned. His only mark of distinction was a heron's plume, or aigrette, attached to his fez by a gigantic diamond crescent. But he wore a sweeping green cloak, and his horses' trappings were still ablaze with jewels, and the Seraglio was still maintained in a style, which, even if it began to feel a slight pinch from Aimée's more thrifty French management, was, all the same, sumptuous. During his reign the numbers of odalisques declined, and while being in no way an ascetic, he showed a less Oriental approach to his pleasures and was positively domestic in his attitude towards his Armenian favorite, Besma, a simple creature, once a bathhouse attendant, by whom he had six children, and to whom he remained greatly devoted, over the years.

Like Selim before him, all things French found favor in his eyes; his reforms were spectacular, and disquieting, too. Once again, the people muttered. No more conservative nation than the Turks ever existed, and Mahmoud, in a gush of youthful enthusiasm, tried to sweep away all the old ills along with many time-honored customs. All must be shining new and Western, from knives and forks and fezzes to a system of taxation, or administrative changes. His enemies multiplied. In vain did Signor Donizetti, the new court musician, and brother of the celebrated composer, laud the Sultan's musical abilities, compose the *Sultan's March* and give Mahmoud lessons in counterpoint, dwelling on the special grace and melancholy of his songs. The Turks preferred their own cadences, those lovely minor airs, which unfold like an intricate arabesque, and seem suspended, languorous, on the air. Gérard de Nerval heard such a song in Egypt: "something pastoral, something of the dreaminess of a lover poured from these words so rich in vowels and cadenced like the song of birds. Perhaps, I thought, it is some shepherd's song from Trebizond or the Marmora. I seemed to hear doves cooing upon the tips of the yews: it was a song to be sung in blue valleys . . ."

Mahmoud concentrated largely on reforms of internal policy, aiming to set his house in order and complete the work Selim had left unfinished. Over the years he was responsible for such startling innovations as a system of quarantine which saved the city from a terrible outbreak of the plague in 1838. (That the plague had long been considered as endemic, rather than sporadic, in Constantinople, may have been due to the habit of barely covering the bodies, in their shallow graves.) He founded a school of medicine, and even sanctioned a treatise on anatomy, something which the conservative regarded as a piece of flagrant disobedience to the Koran, which is categoric on this point. *Even if the dead man had swallowed the most precious pearl, and that pearl not his,* the opening of the body was forbidden. Nor was Mahmoud any more approved when he ameliorated the lot of his Christian subjects, Syrian Christians, Orthodox Greek or Bulgarian minorities; and when he moved, though unsuccessfully, towards the suppression of the trade in Eunuchs, it was felt he had really gone too far. Next, he would be suppressing their Harems. He also constructed a theater at Pera, where he was often to be seen in the Imperial box. All things Western were welcome. When the nuns of a convent in France wrote asking if he would replace the carpets looted from their chapel by the Revolutionary mob, in exchange for their prayers, he and Aimée were very gratified. Christians turning to a Moslem Prince! It seems curious that French nuns should have conceived the idea of addressing the Sultan of Turkey, but it is not perhaps too wild a conjecture to think it was Aimée's old convent at Nantes (which had been a center of Terrorist manifestations), who received news of their former pupil's high estate and now appealed, circuitously, for her help. The ghost must have been overjoyed, and a pair of sumptuous carpets were dispatched, forthwith, in the Sultan's name.

Much later, Mahmoud was to proclaim the right of free worship in Turkey, and to establish the first Turkish gazette, but that was the work of the older monarch. Now he had to content himself with small-scale, though significant, moves. Once, overreaching himself in a touching gesture of imitation, he issued invitations for a ball at the Seraglio. But very few of the Turkish nobility would countenance their wives leaving the Harem to meet and mingle—let alone *dance*—with the Sultan's other guests. They preferred to brave the Imperial displeasure; so Signor Donizetti's fiddlers played, and the French dancing master Selim had originally appointed (no doubt at Aimée's suggestion) went round the waxed floor bowing and scraping before the ladies of the Seraglio. But it did not turn out the sort of ball they held at the Tuileries, such as Sebastiani and Fanny had so often described. . . . It was not a really successful evening. The conservative Turks could forgive the fez, could overlook such dubious experiments as schools or hospitals, but a ball . . . ! Dancing partners! The valse! They locked their harem doors, set the Eunuchs on guard and went to join the Janissaries, who were plotting in undertones.

If Aimée and her son imagined their enemies were vanquished, they were mistaken. Very soon, Mahmoud's policies were proved too indigestible for the country as a whole, and he was forced to be even more discreet. But the first signs of moderation were taken for weakness. Once more the Janissaries' kettle-drums were heard; once more their enemies were strung up under the great plane tree which was their rallying point, and Aimée shuddered. Mustapha and his mother were the focal point for all their plans. Mahmoud could no longer afford to be merciful. He had seen Selim butchered; he had grown up in the shadow of the Princes' Cage. Violence was a tradition of his race. Only force could quell force, only terror could terrorize. He ordered the death of Mustapha and his mother, while all those women who were pregnant by Mustapha were to be thrown into the Bosphorus. It was in the accepted pattern; but it was Mahmoud's first act of violence. Alas! it was not to be the last. It came to be said of him and his sons, *"Mahmoud, lover of blood, Abd ül Aziz, lover of money, Abd ül Medjid, lover of women."*

Yet when we consider the antecedents and surroundings of the young Mahmoud, such action is seen to be more in the nature of self-defense. It was kill, or be killed, in the Seraglio. His ancestors, on both sides, had been a hot-blooded lot. In the great days of medieval Turkey, his forbears lived hard. The young princes who survived were often governing whole provinces at the age of fourteen; "victorious in battle, they were rewarded with voluptuous young slaves. They were fathers at the age of sixteen, and again, at sixty. The princes were gentle in the harem, ferocious in the camp, humble in the mosque and superb on the throne." How, then, expect Mahmoud to show clemency towards an unscrupulous enemy? Moreover, Aimée had brought him up to believe in his sacred mission, that ultimate goal of Westernizing the country. No doubt they both held that the ends justify the means.

Although despotic by nature, as Selim never was, Mahmoud was benevolent by intent. Yet to attain even a moderate degree of civilizing humanity, such as his attempted reform of the trade in slaves and Eunuchs, he was compelled to adopt the most autocratic, if not tyrannous, methods. On occasion, however, he could show remarkable patience. When one of his admirals had sentenced a malefactor to five hundred blows on the stomach, and killed him, by the hundredth, Mahmoud flew into a terrible rage, but, inviting the admiral to the Seraglio, merely ordered him to eat as many rich cakes. When, after seventy, the swooning admiral begged for mercy, Mahmoud replied that if a mere seventy *cakes* were unendurable, how could anyone be expected to endure five hundred *blows?*

It is probable that Aimée Dubucq de Rivery was often beside her son in his most ruthless actions. She had not lived twenty years in the Seraglio for nothing. The Koran could be interpreted comfortably as sanctioning the removal of rivals, saying, "If there be two Califs, kill one." She had perhaps grown, if not blunted, at least in agreement that he who struck first lived longest. Just as her Creole blood and those languorous charms with which so many of the island race were endowed may have helped her to adapt to the requirements of the Harem, so, too, the sultry background of Martinique, with an underlying menace beneath its tropic brilliance, may have given her an adaptability towards the sinistry of Turkish intrigues. It was not, perhaps, as alien to her as it would have been to an ordinary, convent-bred French girl, or one from an English schoolroom. Martinique was in her blood, with its centuries of dark spells, volcanic storms, and serpents darting from the surrounding luxuriance to strike down an unsuspecting victim. The parallel is there: Aimée, advancing through the savage luxuriance of the Seraglio; her cousin Joséphine showing an equal, though different, address in making her way through the jungle of revolutionary, court, and Bonaparte family life in France. Both were pliant and resourceful women.

Creoles are by nature given to display. Joséphine's extravagance bears this out. At the Seraglio Aimée was able to gratify such tastes to their full. Contemporary accounts speak of her elegance, the splendor of her jewels, and how the passion for precious stones was a salient feature of the whole nation. Many noblewomen, so festooned, and unable to attach so much as one more ornament to their person, used to adorn their slaves with their surplus jewels, thus admiring their possessions objectively. Sometimes, as a refinement of luxury, they would wear comparatively few jewels themselves, at great functions, weddings or such, but would be followed by a slave carrying a treasury of precious stones on a golden tray. Sharp-eyed Lady Craven speaks of a moment during the reign of Abd ül Hamid (about the time of Aimée's arrival in Turkey) when the nation's defenses were crumbling, "while the Porte delays building batteries upon the most important posts, under pretense of needing money . . . yet the jewelers cannot find diamonds enough to supply the demands of the Harem, for which they are paid in ready money." This was something which even Mahmoud could not hope to reform.

Lady Mary Wortley Montagu, describing her visit to a harem in 1717, wrote that her hostess wore "a girdle as broad as the broadest English ribbon, entirely covered with diamonds. Round her neck she wore three chains which reached to her knees; one of large pearls, at the bottom of which hung a fine colored emerald as big as a turkey egg; another consisting of two hundred emeralds closely joined . . . every one as large as a half-crown piece. . . . But her earrings eclipsed all the rest. They were two diamonds, shaped exactly like pears, as large as a big hazel nut. . . . She had four strings of pearls, the whitest and most perfect in the world, at least enough to make four necklaces, every one as large as the Duchess of Marlborough's." She goes on to speak of a gigantic ruby surrounded by twenty drops of clear diamonds, a headdress covered with "bodkins of emeralds and diamonds," large diamond bracelets, "and had five rings on her fingers, except Mr. Pitts, the largest

I ever saw in my life. It is for jewelers to compute the value of these things . . . but I am sure that no European Queen has half the quantity."

There were all sorts of lesser splendors, too. The Sultan's opium pills were gilded, in one, two, or three layers of gilt, thus spacing or timing the speed of their effect; which is possibly the origin of the phrase "gilding the pill." Luxury, as such, was considered all-desirable. When the painted and gilded caïques were rowed up and down the Bosphorus, dallying between the Sweet Waters of Asia and the ornate summer houses, or *yalis*, along the shores, they were followed by a sparkling shoal of jeweled fish attached by chains, so that they seemed to be escorting the caïque, bobbing in its wake. These caïques were sumptuous affairs, less secretive than the hooded sleek gondolas of Venice, and seemed to be made not so much for the assignation as the state visit. They were piled with brocaded cushions, and over the stern, Persian rugs, or a richly embroidered velvet carpet, in crimson, or purple, the *hirame* trailed from the stern, out over the surface of the water in a fan of splendor.

Some Sultans allowed their Harem considerable freedom; the ladies were permitted to picnic at the Sweet Waters of Asia, heavily guarded by the Eunuchs, or drive through the town, to the bazaars, though this was a concession which was only granted during the middle and latter part of the nineteenth century. In Aimée's day, the Seraglio remained sequestered. However, Selim, when Sultan, was, as we know, very indulgent to Aimée's innovations, and by the time she became Sultan Validé, she had probably enjoyed more liberty than all the other Seraglio women. She was deeply interested in every aspect of her son's empire, not only in the political intrigues which were the passion of other Seraglio mothers, but in its cultural and historic heritage, too. It is known that Mahmoud went about his capital disguised, like Haroun al Raschid, and like him, had for close friend his barber, who kept him informed of the everyday life and opinions of his people. It is probable that Aimée, too, made secret sorties about the city. Even after twenty years she must have still seen it with something of a traveler's sense of wonder, and marveled at its dreamlike quality, the crumbling Byzantine splendors, the great subterranean cisterns, dank and still, lying beneath the city's surging surface, and all the history and legends of this place, where Crescent rose on Cross, where the Bazaar had once stabled Justinian's two thousand horses, and where there were any number of such strange-sounding, forgotten churches as St. Mary of the Mongols, built by a Paleologue Princess to celebrate her safe return after being sent as bride of an aged Mongol Khan, who died before the marriage was consummated.

Both mother and son had the adventurous strain of their ancestor Pierre Dubucq. It would not have suited either of them to be bound by the conventions of their rank. What interest, for either of them, to be escorted in state through the streets surrounded by Three-Tailed Bashaws and other Satraps? It is probable that Aimée, bundled in the heavy black *feridjie* worn by all Turkish women who ventured abroad, sometimes accompanied her son on these outings, mingling with the crowds along the slippery quays of the Fish Market, or crossed the bridge to Galata, among the throng where the peaked black lambskin caps of the Persians, the white skull caps of the Albanians, and the Turkomans' turbans were jostled together, all the hordes of the East, "with that dark dignity of bearing common to the men of the East," as one enraptured lady traveler puts it.

Everywhere, the Janissaries were apparent, slicing off heads, leaving the body to sprawl across the streets, head placed ignobly between the legs, nailing malefactors to their door by one ear, or setting off, down the Bosphorus, with a boatload of prisoners, to be executed as soon as they came to a suitable spot. (The Turks were prone to choose agreeable spots for their executions, as others might select harmonious surroundings for a picnic. With Arab fatalism the victims would embark, discussing the scenery their executioners chose for the fatal act.) At this time, the Janissaries' evil had reached a peak; and Mahmoud went about, in the streets and coffeehouses, noting it all, storing a horde of secret hatred, against the time when he could crush them forever.

The fearful risks which they ran, mother and son, on such incognito expeditions, must have brought them even closer. It was unthinkable for any Moslem woman of Court rank to go about unescorted, or in such dubious quarters. Mahmoud must have realized, even more, the remarkable nature of this enlightened, independent French woman who was his mother. We can imagine them, a humble-looking pair, mother and son, shambling past the impressive façade of the French Embassy, or Palace, as it was called, with its scarlet-coated kavass on guard (Janissaries, these, as most other officials about the city); past little booths full of honied confections, up and up, mounting the disreputable alleys leading to the heights, "that primrose path of Galata, winding upwards to depths of depravity," as an American social worker was to describe it, rather wildly, half a century later, when embroiled in the organization of homes of rescue for fallen women, or those misguided girls who arrived at Constantinople lured there by legends of Harem grandeurs. The missionary even went so far as to have all the trains and boats met by social workers wearing caps embroidered with their calling, and chosen for their linguistic abilities . . . but alas! the response was not encouraging. So many of the girls spoke another, more universal language, and did not seem to care about being saved.

*     *     *

Within the Seraglio Aimée, as Sultan Valideh, now reigned supreme. She had her own palace, entourage and revenues. Her son consulted her, and her alone, on every move. Besides affairs of state there was the organization of the Harem, with its etiquette and protocol; visits from the ladies of her Court; the supervision of the hospital, the library; the planning of new gardens, such as that which Melling, the French landscape painter had come to Turkey to design all along the Bosphorus. Now, the floral conceits of the Bostanji Bachi, or Head Gardener, were tempered by the introduction of a brother of the Head Gardener at Schönbrunn. Aimée's kiosk overlooked the Bosphorus, and was beside a little, hidden garden, shaded by cypress trees and planted with hyacinths, where she loved to walk in the cool of the evening, watching the golden sparks that flittered among the tombs in the dark groves of Scutari, across the water. Superstition held that they were departed souls, but they were more prosaically explained as being a phosphorescent glow induced by the agglomeration of bones. Another superstition held that the wheeling and dipping black birds that haunt the Bosphorus, neither sea gulls nor starlings, and which are never seen to rest, are damned souls condemned to wander, like Paolo and Francesca, "forever together on the unresting air. . . ."

Aimée cannot have had much time for such somber thoughts, however. The Sultan Valideh's hand was apparent throughout the Seraglio, from foreign policies to household accounts. There were many curious traditions which must be observed, too. At Ramadhan, when the month-long fasting drew to an end, and the beat of drums throbbed through the city, announcing the Night of Power, one of the Seven Holy Nights of the Moslem year, when the Sultan went in high state to pray in a mosque outside his palace, it was the Sultan Valideh who, custom decreed, must select and present him with a new bride, one of the latest recruits, a little creature fresh from the mountain valleys of Georgia perhaps, some luscious child who, it was expected, would not fail to produce a male heir.

Sometimes there were distractions of a more European nature: packets of the latest books from Paris; or the visit of a passing musician, recommended by Signor Donizetti's clever brother, Gaetano, whose operas were beginning to be remarked in the West. Or accounts (secondhand, and garbled, but entertaining, for all that) of Lord Byron's behavior, over at Pera, where he was, as usual, getting himself talked about while staying with the British Chargé d'Affaires. Once, a stately giraffe, or camel-leopard, arrived from Cairo, as a conciliatory gesture from Mohammed Pasha. This marvelous creature delighted the Sultan, and his Grand Vizier held levées, to which the whole Diplomatic Corps were invited, to watch the giraffe being put through his paces by Nubian grooms. But for the most part, Aimée's diversions were of a more homely character; a new Circassian dancing girl, or, perhaps, the compelling spectacle of Babaluk frenzies, where, in a sort of cataleptic trance, the harem Negresses divined the future, a proceeding which must have recalled to her the voodoo practices of the West Indies.

Most popular of all, among the Turks, was Karageuz, a puppet shadow-show full of robustly lewd antics, handed down from one generation to another. As Gérard de Nerval says, "The East does not share our ideas either of education or morality. It seeks to develop the senses: we endeavor to extinguish them." Whatever Aimée may have thought about such episodes as *Karageuz, the Martyr to Chastity*, she must not appear censorious, or even unappreciative.

One day there was the visit of some strolling players, which was to link Aimée's Oriental court with the Paris boulevards. All unsuspecting, she saw the great Debureau, many years before he became the idol of Paris, and his theater on the Boulevard du Temple was the rendezvous of such as Balzac, George Sand, and the Romantics. Debureau's luster has remained undimmed since his death in 1846. He has remained a symbol of all that was most brilliant in the tradition of pantomime. He was of Bohemian origin, born at Neu Kolin in 1796. He came of a straggling mountebank family who wandered about the world, thirsty in summer, shivering in winter, and always hungry. They dragged themselves from one little town to the next, across mountains and plains, wherever a few coppers could be earned, tumbling, wire-walking and juggling, competing with gypsies' tambourines and dancing bears. It was an inauspicious beginning for the greatest of all tragic clowns.

Around the year 1810 the Debureau family arrived in Constantinople and were, of course, commanded to appear before the Sultan. O! brilliant fortune! Their molting spangles were resewn, their tights washed, their act rehearsed to the point of exhaustion. But for an empty triumph. They were ushered through the sumptuous halls into a mirrored pavilion. Absolute silence reigned: it was completely deserted. It was, in Janin's words, "like the silence and desolation of the Théâtre Français when they play a piece by Monsieur Bonjour." The troupe were mystified. How could they divine that from behind slits in a brocaded curtain the Harem's élite were watching? As they hesitated, a turbaned Negro motioned them to begin their act. In silence, they spread out their threadbare strip of druggeting, pitiable against the Seraglio's Persian carpets. In silence they went through their act. In silence they proceeded to its climax, a human pyramid. Father stood on uncle, brother supported cousin. Greatly daring, the young Debureau topped the whole swaying edifice, balanced on a ladder. . . . *"Et voila!"* says Janin. *"Voila! au sommet de son Art. O surprise! O recompense de l'Artiste. . . ."*

From the summit, Debureau could look down over the curtain, into the forbidden paradise below. Here the Sultan's ladies were gathered, "the voluptuous odalisques of the Seraglio, sacred Sultans of His Highness, those redoubtable Houris, whose very regard could lead to death." His eyes met those of an unveiled odalisque. Overcome, he crashed to the ground, bringing the whole performance to an ignoble finish.

\*       \*       \*

It must not be imagined that Mahmoud, for all his devotion to his mother, was tied to her apron strings. Everything about him indicates that she had brought him up to be a man of action, who spent a minimum of time in the ennervating confines of the Harem. The British Ambassador may have opined that Mahmoud was an Oriental potentate at his most despotic, but seen in perspective, with the knowledge of his French blood, or rather, the manner in which his mother had deliberately fostered the Western strain, we see that it was this, rather than Oriental despotism which gave such force to his character. Nor must we overlook the influence of the British Ambassador, himself, Stratford Canning, afterwards Lord Stratford de Redcliffe, the Great Elchi, or Ambassador, as he was to become to the Turks. In the early years of Mahmoud's reign, he was only a fledgling Minister of twenty-four (to Mahmoud's twenty-five), yet between them, they might be said to have given the final blow which brought Napoleon to a halt.

From the beginning, Mahmoud had followed Selim's precedent, and made overtures to France: but these had gone unanswered; Napoleon saw Turkey as a vassal rather than an ally, and was confident of obtaining it, in his own time. Meanwhile, he had other problems; his divorce from Joséphine, and his plans for the Russian campaign. On December 16, 1809, Napoleon repudiated Joséphine to marry Marie-Louise. When the news reached Constantinople, Aimée and Mahmoud were thunderstruck. They took it as a personal, family insult. Although Aimée had never seen her cousin since they parted, as girls, in Martinique, she had taught Mahmoud to revere the legend of brilliance and charm which surrounded the Empress—his second cousin. Now Mahmoud felt a chivalresque urge to defend her; moreover, it was conclusive proof of Napoleon's perfidious nature. It was no longer possible to over-look many past treacheries, notably the Egyptian campaign and the se-cret understandings behind the Treaty of Tilsit, which Mahmoud had been unwilling to admit, for some time. From that moment, Mahmoud turned against Napoleon and his government implacably.

Overnight, the French Minister Latour-Maubourg found the Turkish Foreign Minister's attitude one of marked hostility. The Minister was acting on the Sultan's instructions, which, though categoric, were not explanatory, for Mahmoud showed a headstrong inclination to act on his own, without consulting his ministers, as the British Ambassador ob-served with misgiving. Overnight, as the French found nothing but hostility, so the British found gracious favor, the Ambassador (then Can-ning's predecessor, Robert Adair) being suddenly granted an audience and received with bewildering marks of esteem. Mahmoud, ever self-contained, gave no hint of the reasons behind his *volte-face*, but smiled, inscrutably, as news reached him of the French Minister's agitated dis-patches sent off in feverish speed, one after the other, to advise Napo-leon of the Sultan's change of heart. "The Porte has become *plus an-glaise que les Anglais*"—"more English than the English"; he, the French Chargé d'Affaires, might as well leave, for all he could do to change matters, he wrote bitterly.

In a dispatch to the Foreign Office dated November, 1811, there are the following succinct headings: *Violent language held by the French Chargé d'Affaires in a note to the Sultan. . . . Mons. Maubourg fails in an attempt to open direct intercourse with His Highness.* And in July, heavily underlined, *The* CREDIT *of the French at Constantinople absolutely* GONE.

For the next two years Mahmoud continued to show marked cold-ness to France: once again he was looking westward for an ally—always the old atavistic longing for the West—but this time, it was towards Eng-land, Napoleon's arch-enemy, that he turned. Perhaps the English could provide as civilizing an influence, and prove more trustworthy allies. Thus Mahmoud; and Aimée, with Joséphine's divorce rankling, did not oppose the anti-French move. Besides, Stratford Canning was a man for whom Mahmoud felt an instinctive respect. Over the years their mutual respect was to grow into something akin to affection: though the period of Canning's greatest influence in Turkish affairs was only to come much later, when, as the Great Elchi, he ruled the Porte beside the Sultan Abd ül Mejid, Mahmoud's son.

While Napoleon dismissed Mahmoud's attitude as being of little importance, Stratford Canning saw a way to turn it to his country's advantage, and, to that end, he succeeded in persuading the Sultan to make peace with the Russians, with whom Turkey had been engaged in a long and costly war over the territories of Bessarabia, Moldavia, and the control of the Danube's Black Sea ports. The war had dragged on with considerable loss of life and prestige to Turkey. But now Mahmoud had decided he would come to terms with his enemies. That he chose such a moment, when Russia had the French knife at her throat, seemed madness. It was obvious that by flinging all his weight against Russia he could obtain victory, at last. But Mahmoud never acted on impulse. He had his reasons. His country was not strong enough to win, not humble enough to lose. The treaty could save lives—and face, too, even with its humiliating terms (many of which were not incorporated, or even demanded, at first). But behind all this reasoning we may conclude Mahmoud was also swayed by a long-cherished, private vengeance. He was settling an old score, on his own behalf, and on behalf of his mother. If we read between the lines of history we can interpret his action as being due, not only to Stratford Canning's persuasive powers, but also to an Oriental sense of revenge, of cunning, to arrive, however circuitously, at the downfall of one who had betrayed him, snubbed all his advances and those of Selim, and humiliated his mother's cousin Joséphine. At last, he, Mahmoud, the neglected Oriental, could meet the great Frenchman on his own ground, and prove the decisive factor in his fall. Revenge is sweet. Mahmoud was thoroughly Oriental in this respect: he savored it to the full.

Dispatches to the Foreign Office about this time, speak of the Treaty's ratification being prepared.

*Suspicion entertained by the Porte of Mr. Canning entirely done away with.*

In a glow of mutual esteem and united aims, Sultan and Minister were as one. On May 28, 1812, a month after Napoleon invaded Russia, he signed the Treaty of Bucharest. This freed the Russian Army of the Danube to march north, against Napoleon, now standing before Moscow. It was a vital blow, and it came from a ghost: another message, but this time a deadly one, from the ghost of a Creole girl from Martinique. The old Euphemia David had foreseen many strange things; but life was to take an even more fantastic turn than anything she had foretold the two children who came to visit her, their white muslin dresses glimmering through the canebrakes in the summer dusk. What even Talleyrand did not foresee was that when the Grand Turk turned so inexplicably, so implacably, against Napoleon, it was really only one little French girl avenging another.

Meanwhile, the Russian campaign had not been going according to plan; there were the usual series of victories, yet Victory, that total victory to which Napoleon was accustomed, still eluded him. Too late he realized how decisive the Sultan's support could be in the south, and, to that end, sent a series of ingratiating overtures which remained unanswered. The prolonged silence was disquieting. He began ordering his ministers to dispatch couriers "once or twice a week, to Constantinople to carry the bulletins, and all possible news." And again: "Mere couriers do not have the same effect as officers. Send, therefore, some Polish officers. Have the Polish Confederation send an embassy of three members to Turkey, to act on behalf of the Confederation, to demand the guarantee of Turkey. You will realize the importance of this step." Now, at last, he saw the vital necessity of Turkish co-operation; of Turkish ships blocking the Crimea, and Turkish troops occupying Moldavia and Wallachia; in short, of keeping a large Russian force busy in the south. All this was in July, two months after Mahmoud had signed the Treaty of Bucharest with such secrecy. During all the rest of this fateful summer Mahmoud waited, for once displaying a truly Arab fatalism. He had done all he could. The rest was with Allah.

In August, the Russians were defeated at Smolensk; in September, at Borodino; the French still seemed invincible. In October, the humiliating terms of the Bucharest Treaty leaked out at the Porte, and when the people learned Bessarabia had been ceded to Russia, they turned against the Sultan. The Janissaries set fire to the city and it seemed that Mahmoud must be overthrown. In Moscow, Napoleon, too, had now heard of the Treaty, and realized its terrible implications for himself. Now his own words, *"le sabre est toujours battu par l'esprit"*—'the sword is always beaten by the mind'—were coming home to roost. It was Mahmoud, with the incisive French side of his nature, who had seen the way to deal the fatal blow, and by a stroke of the pen, turn the army of the Danube against the Grand Armée. In December, the French met disaster at Beresina. Napoleon fled to Paris: his men and horses perished in the retreat. It was all over. Aimée, looking out across the Golden Horn, must have wondered if Joséphine understood the message.

When news of the debacle reached London, where Stratford Canning was enjoying a prolonged holiday, he must have smiled, in his glacial way. It was the first of a long series of diplomatic triumphs. It may be recalled that while Canning's biographers claim it as his master-maneuver, the Duke of Wellington, in his memorandum on Napoleon's Russian campaign, claims the *coup de grâce* as being the work of his brother, the Marquis of Wellesley, then head of the Foreign Office (though a rather inert one, from whom Canning never received any instructions of worth). The Iron Duke described the Treaty of Bucharest as being a piece of strategy which gave his brother "the opportunity of rendering the world the most important service that ever fell to the lot of any individual to perform." Against this, David Morier, who was one of Canning's staff at the Porte, writes of the Foreign Office, "then asleep under the Marquis of Wellesley" and how Stratford Canning "without one word of instruction . . . or encouragement took it upon himself to undertake the task . . . of effecting the peace between the Porte and the Russian Government just in time to release Chichagov's army. . . . *Quod ego attestor."*

But while the great statesmen and diplomats each claimed the master stroke for themselves, they all overlooked the part played by a French woman who remained faithful to the memories of her childhood.

\*  \*  \*

Piece by piece, in fragments and snatches, the history of that faraway moment is reconstructed, much of it, indeed almost all that centers round Aimée Dubucq de Rivery, a matter of shadowy conjecture. The walls of the Seraglio were high, dispatches were terse and did not dwell on the more personal aspects or shades of influence round the Sultan's throne. Even so, a thread is traced, through the great calfbound reports, stuffed away in the Foreign Office Archives or among the cliffs of parchment in the Records Office. This was before the printed reports, or Blue Books, gave a spurious air of simplicity to the minutia collected on each question where H.B.M. Foreign representatives were concerned. Page after page of elegant flourishes, faded longhand by some forgotten Embassy clerk . . . each dispatch opening dramatic perspectives, however laconic the entry. Mahmoud's terrible struggle with the Janissaries is summarized thus:

*Feb. 19, 1815. An attempt to reform the Janissaries. Disturbance in consequence.*

*Feb. 25. Conflict in consequence of the perseverance of the Sultan to reform the Janissaries.*

On March 10 a more sinister note sounds. *Atonement of the Janissaries for the late Acts of Violence against the Sultan.*

Mahmoud also seems to have made a good many gestures of purely domestic *politesse* which are also scrupulously recorded in the files. We read: *The Sultan's answer on the accouchement of the Duchess of Cumberland,* or again, *The Sultan's answer to the Royal Letter on the death of the Princess Charlotte.* Sometimes there are entries which rouse wildest speculations and set one off on a further paper chase, burrowing through the parchment cliffs.

*Arrival of a Confidential Person from Vienna, with disclosures relating to Bonaparte's marriage.* Or this, sandwiched between passages dealing with the Elgin marbles (referred to as Lord Elgin's Antiquities).

*Relative to a Dagger Intended for Constantinople, Messrs. Rundell and Co., London.* But for what purpose, we wonder? Are we to suppose no worthy blade could be obtained in Turkey? Was violence afoot, and could no member of the British Embassy risk purchasing a weapon openly in the bazaars? Or was it intended as a present, best Sheffield steel, a token of esteem to some Three-Tailed Bashaw?

*       *       *

For so much of the year 1812-1813, not only the French, but the British, too, were kept wholly in the dark as to the Sultan's real intentions, their only means of information being through their dragomans, or Embassy interpreters, who were Turks, and when their Sultan chose, singularly ill-informed. Mahmoud must have found a certain cynical satisfaction in appearing to comply with Canning's designs, while in reality following his own. If he had no counselors, neither did he seek confidence. Save for his mother, he always walked alone. One thing is clear: behind his acquiescence to the terms of the Treaty, behind his risk of internal anarchy, there seems to lie some purely personal motive. Why not? History is made by man, and man is made up of such impulses.

All through his life, a curiously malign fate seemed to stalk Mahmoud. His internal reforms were often balked by exterior causes; his armies decimated by overwhelming odds; and his country cynically used as a pawn in the game of international power politics. No sooner was the Russian threat removed, no sooner had Napoleon fallen, than the great pashas of his distant provinces banded together in defiance of his authority. In Egypt, Mohammed Ali, after butchering the Mamelukes, settled himself more firmly in his palace, and ruled there in defiance of the Sultan's orders. In Albania, Ali Pasha of Janina held the southeastern provinces in thrall, and it was not until 1820 that Mahmoud was strong enough to crush him. None of his most cherished reforms could be achieved, he knew, unless he had, behind him, a strong and loyal army. It took him twenty years to build up such troops, for, at every step, there were the Janissaries to be reckoned with. But Mahmoud's invincible will, his growing sagacity, and above all, his quiet patience, held firm. He felt himself utterly alone, for although, when Canning was reappointed to the Porte in 1826, he proffered friendship, it was primarily a means of furthering British interests. The Great Elchi's real love for the Turkish people was only to grow, slowly, with the half-century he spent among them, culminating in the Crimean War of 1853. In the middle years of Mahmoud's reign there was still some mistrust, and many misunderstandings, which faded slowly, but did at last vanish in the glow of mutual respect and friendship.

Unhappy Mahmoud! He was born before his time; he chafed against the ignorance and prejudice of traditionalism; his enemies were quick to capitalize on his failures; even his progressive measures were regarded as the work of an iconoclast—an infidel. Alone together, mother and son went over the problems which beset them: it always came back to the same point: no reforms could be lasting, so long as the Janissaries remained to block the way: and as long as Mahmoud's army was inefficiently equipped, or harbored any Janissaries in its ranks, all hope of real progress was out of the question. All then, hinged on the formation of a new army, and like Selim before him, Mahmoud set about it, laboriously. Step by step, mother and son continued to plan, in secret, those various reforms which gained Mahmoud his title, and, at long last, overcame the taunts of *Sultan Giaour* or *Infidel Padishah*. Between them they had opened the windows. A bracing northern wind swept in from Europe, stirring the falling leaves of the Seraglio courtyards, rattling at the casements, imperatively. Before it, the phantoms faded; at last even tradition was overcome.

But long before that day, Mahmoud had lost the guiding inspiration of his life. In 1817 the little French girl from Martinique, *Naksh*, The Beautiful One, The Powerful One, she who was to change the face of Turkey, died in the Seraglio, where she had lived, since entering it thirty-three years before. Just as the old fortuneteller had foreseen, great triumphs and glories had been hers, and at the very moment Mahmoud's innovations seemed triumphant, when her happiness seemed won, it was to fade, with her life.

\*     \*     \*

On a winter night in 1817, five years after that snowy evening when mother and son had learned of Napoleon's defeat, a boat crossed the Golden Horn, and two men hurried to the Convent of Saint Antoine, at Pera. It was a time of tempest; the winds howled round the creaking

wooden houses, rattling the shutters. No one was abroad: only the five
watchmen continued their rounds, striking their iron staves on the stones
as they walked, forever on guard for the outbreaks which perpetually
ravaged the city. The Superior of the Convent, Father Chrysostome,
was kneeling at prayer in his cell, when he was disturbed by a violent
knocking on the doors. Two guards stood before him, and bowing ceremoniously, presented a letter bearing the Imperial *tughra*, or cypher.
Escorted by the guards, Father Chrysostome went down the steep descent to Galata, where a splendid caïque, with twelve pairs of oars, was
waiting. The caïque shot away from the shore, and was lost in the
blackness of the night. Arrived at the farther shore, the priest was led
through deserted gardens, and ushered into a room, decorated with
silken hangings, fine carpets and candelabra. It was, for all its luxury, a
lugubrious room. On the bed lay a dying woman, attended by a Greek
doctor. Beside the door two black slaves were ranged. A few paces away
stood a man whose bearing showed great distinction, but who seemed
overwhelmed with grief. "This man appeared to be about forty years
of age; his height was above the ordinary; his brow high, and noble;
his expression commanding. His beard was black, and gave his face an
impressive, grave beauty. His costume was simple, but of a singular elegance. The sobs and lamentations, which he was unable to control, told
of his anguish." When Father Chrysostome entered the room, this man,
whom all in the place obeyed, signaled the slaves to withdraw, the doctor, too. Approaching the bed, he bent over the dying woman. "My
mother," he said, "you wished to die in the religion of your fathers. Let
your wish be fulfilled." He motioned the priest forward, and stepped
back into the shadows.

The priest listened to the woman's confession, her prayers and repent-
ances; for more than an hour he prayed with her. Then, as she sank, he
gave her Absolution. As the words of Extreme Unction sounded, the
bearded man, sole witness of the scene, approached the bed, flung himself down beside it. The Padishah of the Faithful, "the Sultan *Giaour*"
was calling upon Allah, in his loss.

*       *       *

Father Chrysostome was escorted back to the Convent by the same guards who had fetched him. Not a word was spoken. When he reached the Convent he found the Brothers waiting for him anxiously. In silence he went past them to spend the rest of the night before the altar, praying for the soul of Aimée Dubucq de Rivery, Sultan Valideh of Turkey.

Aimée died, as she had lived, in the Catholic faith. But she lies in one of the most splendid of all the Imperial Turbehs not far from Santa Sophia, in the high state befitting a Sultan's mother. The sunlight pierces the grilled windows, falling across the velvet catafalque; the trees in the little garden outside cast dappled shadows on the shimmering walls. Her epitaph is full of flowery phrases, and there is one oblique reference to her French blood. She is "Naksh, The Beautiful One, the Queen Mother, of noble foreign blood."

*Of her, Mahmoud, the Sultan of the World, was begotten,*
*Of her, the Majestic Emperor of Shining Soul, was born . . .*
*He, who opened the Gate of the Orient to a new light.*

She, who may truly be said to have opened the Gate of the Orient to a new light, remains veiled, all her work attributed to her son; but then, perhaps, to achieve such a Prince had been life's work enough. Mahmoud, the son, had surrounded his mother's tomb with all the grandeur an Ottoman Sultan could devise. But Mahmoud the Reformer had one more tribute to pay.

At the first opportune moment, in 1826, nine years after Aimée's death, that Sultan whom she had taught French nursery rhymes, and so many other things, besides, crushed forever the Janissaries, so long her enemies, the butchers of Selim, the enemies of all that progress she had so ardently desired.

Mother and son had worked all their lives for this moment, and when at last it came, the mother was dead; but the son was ready. For years they had been compiling a list of the Janissaries' ringleaders. His new troops had been trained in secret, on the lines of a Western army. Thousands of muskets had been purchased in secrecy, too. So, when on that June morning, columns of smoke rising from Stamboul told the citizens of Pera that once again the Janissaries had mutinied, and were burning and looting the city, Mahmoud rode out to meet their challenge.

He went first to the Sultan Achmet mosque, where he raised Mohammed's sacred green banner, the Sandjuk Sherif, and standing beneath its fluttering silk, he denounced the Janissaries, and called on his people to destroy them. With pistols and daggers stuck in his belt he led his troops to the attack. The Janissaries knew their hour had struck, and fought desperately. The slaughter went on all day. Their barracks were fired. They were shot down and hunted out, their leaders hanged from the great plane tree outside their quarters in the Seraglio, where for so long they had strung up their own victims. From his house at Pera, Stratford Canning, newly returned to the Porte, watched the smoke rising ominously, and reflected on the monstrous abuses of power practiced by the Prætorian Guard, the Streltzi, and now the Janissaries, all of whom were to perish by their own corruption. His diary goes on to say that the sea of Marmora was mottled with dead bodies. *"The entrance to the Seraglio, the shore under the Sultan's window . . . are crowded with dead—many of them torn and in part devoured by the dogs."* No quarter was given. By nightfall five thousand had been killed. Next day, the formal abolition of the Corps was proclaimed in the Mosques. On June 22, Canning notes, *"All is as quiet here as the bowstring and saber can make it. . . . Executions and transportations go on incessantly. . . . Everything seems changed, or changing. . . ."* Canning was amazed to see how the Sultan's authority grew daily more assured. There was no murmur of counterrevolution. Mahmoud had proved himself master. His people were ready to follow him in his new policies. It had been a terrible tribute which Mahmoud the Reformer paid to Aimée Dubucq de Rivery, his mother; and it was a last triumphant message of victory sent by the ghost, to that Western world to which she had once belonged.

# ·IV·

# ISABELLE
# EBERHARDT

*Portrait of a Legend*

Everything about her was extraordinary. She was a woman, dressed as a man. A European turned Arab. A Russian who transposed "nitchevo" into "mektoub," whose untidy mystical torments, *l'âme slave*, found peace in Islam's faith—and flesh. She was born on the prim, pale lakeside of Geneva. She died in the burning desert. She was an expatriate wanderer whose nomadic Slav background led her to range the desert insatiably: yet she dreamed of a *petit-bourgeoise* haven, a grocer's shop in some obscure little Algerian town where she and her Arab husband and all his hordes of relatives could conduct a modest business. She adored her insignificant husband, but her sensual adventures were without number. Her behavior was outrageous; she drank, she smoked hashish, but *déclassée*, she remained *racée*. She was the outcast, despised and rejected by French Administration and the colony in general. But she was General Lyautey's trusted friend. She was a writer who was almost unrecognized, and quite penniless till after her death, when, ironically, posthumous editions of her books earned a small fortune—for others. Her death was strangest of all, for she was drowned in the desert.

In her brief lifetime she aroused violent interest. She was loathed or loved, respected or despised. No one was indifferent to her. Her echoes have never died. No one who knew her ever forgot her. Those who had never known her felt the strange, compelling force of her character. She was a legend during her lifetime. After her death the legend grew monstrous and distorted. *La Bonne Nomade, L'Amazone du Sable, L'Androgyne du Desert,* or *Le Cosaque du Desert* . . . these were romantic, but reasonable epithets. But she was also vulgarized as *l'Esclave Errante* in a cheap farrago of nonsense played at the Théâtre de Paris in 1924. In 1939 she was *Isabella d'Afrique*, in another lamentable piece which would have revolted her fastidious nature. For fastidious she was, and naïve and dignified, and pious too. All these, in spite of excesses and brutalities of living which would have made a Légionnaire recoil.

Her writings have not been translated, and even in the original most of them suffered a posthumous process of "editing" which amounts to rewriting by the late Victor Barrucand, who took it on himself to distort her by mazes of overwriting. Since little of Isabelle Eberhardt the writer is known to the English reader, it may be better, here, to speak more of her life than her work, and the woman, or man, Si Mahmoud, as she was known, than the writer. There are few people, now, who knew her. She died in 1904, at the age of twenty-seven. But when, in 1951, I talked of her to General Catroux, he told me that although he had never known her himself, being in Indo-China while she was with the French troops in the Sud-Oranais, she was a legendary figure in Southern Algeria, when he arrived there later. It was the General's elder brother, then a young officer serving under Lyautey, who had known her well.

She was one of the very rare women whom Lyautey had liked: she had, in fact, charmed him by her bizarre character, her knowledge of the desert and her profound understanding of the Arab people. Lyautey was at once poetic and practical: with her, he "talked Sahara," as General Catroux put it, for hours on end. Her close contacts with the powerful Arab religious leaders were often used by the French. Her experiences, and the unexpected range of her conversation, delighted Lyautey as much as her knowledge impressed him. "No one knows Africa as she does," he said. General Catroux's handsome, haggard face softened, lightened to enthusiasm as he told me of the pilgrimages he had made to her grave in the Moslem cemetery of Aïn-Sefra. He had talked with many of the Arabs, the venerated marabouts, or priests, the Spahis and the nomads. To all of them she had remained a legend.

\*　　\*　　\*

Isabelle Eberhardt's background was Russian, the mixture of races which Russian-Jewish stock implies, which may account for the force of her nomadic cravings, just as her youth in the insipid Geneva country-side may account for her appreciation of the Oriental landscape. But although her background was Russian, it was not Russia: it was that changeless emotional, intellectual and fatalistic life of all Slav exiles, gathered round the samovar, the air blurred with cigarette smoke, husky centrifugal Slav voices discussing Nietzsche or Bakunin, universal brotherhood, anarchism, chemistry, music . . . disordered, timeless discussions, till the stove grew cold and shawls were huddled round shabby shoulders and someone coughed, and someone snored, and someone played the violin, and the gray morning seeped through the shutters. Often, such discussions left no time to eat, but there was always tea, the inevitable glasses of tea. This was the exiles' climate. They lived in it everywhere, in Paris, or Rome, or London. The pattern is familiar to anyone who has known them.

Isabelle Eberhardt spent her first eighteen years in this setting, in the smug suburban ambiance of Meyrin, outside Geneva. Her mother, Madame Nathalie de Moërder, née Korff-Eberhardt, was the wife of a Russian general. She was beautiful, gentle, and pampered. Outwardly, she had seemed a conventional wealthy St. Petersburg matron; but was she? Little is known of her life in Russia. Abruptly, around 1870, she left the country forever, with her three children, and settled in Switzerland. Nothing unusual here. There were Russian expatriates everywhere. Turgeniev becalmed in Paris, beside Pauline Viardot. Herzen raging in Turin. Bakunin in London, and the palmy Riviera promenades thick with noble Slav families basking in the warmth and liberty of France.

But the presence of Alexander Trophimowsky, her children's tutor, immediately changes our estimate of her character. We observe her more closely, and we find she is not so true to pattern. She was the illegitimate daughter of a Fräulein Eberhardt and a rich Russian Jew named Korff, which in itself must have been a scandalous secret to be hidden from the rigid society of St. Petersburg. Moreover, she had run off with the tutor, though here, she is perhaps more in the convention of misunderstood wives. With a singular sense of timing the General died a year or so later, leaving her all his money, which is far less in the convention of deserted husbands.

Alexander Trophimowsky was Armenian, splendidly handsome, an ex-priest, or pope, of the Orthodox faith, born in Khison in 1826. He was an intellectual, atheist and utopist; tall and bearded, the disciple of Tolstoy and the friend of Bakunin. Whether he left Russia expressly to join Mme de Moërder or also for more abstract reasons of faith or politics is not known. At any rate, he abandoned a wife and children, and he and Mme de Moërder settled down together in the Villa Tropicale, renamed the Villa Neuve. With them were the de Moërder children, Nicholas, Nathalie, Vladimir, and Augustin, born in 1872, in Switzerland, but recognized by the still devoted General who had followed his wife to attempt a reconciliation. However, Madame de Moërder preferred the tutor. Five years later, on February 17, 1877, a natural daughter was born. She was registered as Isabelle-Wilhelmina Marie Eberhardt.

It was not a really harmonious atmosphere. The tangled green maze of subtropical vegetation, for which the villa had been named, occupied Trophimowsky, who cultivated his plants in a scientific rather than a horticultural spirit. He also cultivated the children's education, which was wide and tangled too. He forbade them any schooling except that which was filtered through his own violently personal prejudices. Isabelle learned six languages, including Greek and Latin and Arabic. Philosophy, metaphysics, and chemistry were thrown in as makeweights.

The elder de Moërder children deeply resented the presence of "Vava," their mother's lover. There were feuds and jealousies, and none of them seems to have appreciated the ironic ex-pope's many admirable qualities. Though perhaps, domestically, such an iconoclast was difficult.

"Jésus-Christ canaille!" was one of his favorite remarks. He was thought to be connected with some of the Nihilist Societies which skulked in Switzerland. At any rate, he was vilified by his neighbors, who pitied and dramatized the lot of the de Moërder children in his grip. A Swiss governess who had known them as well, perhaps, as any outsider ever could, left a series of rather censorious recollections, which call to mind another governess, Malwida von Meysenburg, in another equally chaotic Slav household, that of Alexander Herzen. (Though Fräulein von Meysenburg, with Germanic thoroughness, did not stop at criticism, and succeeded in wresting Herzen's younger daughter from him forever.) It needed no outside influences, however, to turn the de Moërder children against Trophimowsky. Nathalie the eldest daughter was openly at war. Suddenly, she escaped by marrying into a very humble Swiss family, tradespeople whose son was a lawyer's clerk. This rocked the Villa Neuve to its foundations. Trophimowsky raged. Her mother wept. They could have forgiven almost anything but a flight into small-fry respectability. But Nathalie held firm. In 1888 she walked out of the house forever to become Madame Jules Perez-Moreyra. It was the end. She was cut off. Her name was never mentioned again. Her departure had a profound effect on the little Isabelle. She had stood for some stability and the more accepted hygienes. Now dirt and disorder reigned. No sheets, no tablecloths, no more regular meals. . . . When, years later, Isabelle Eberhardt made occasional references to the affair, she always said her sister had returned to Russia and married an officer of the Imperial Guard. Even *La Bonne Nomade* had her snob weaknesses.

One by one, one way or another, the de Moërder children escaped from Trophimowsky's influence. After Nathalie, Nicholas, who returned to Russia. He seems to have been a reactionary type and may have had something to do with Tzarist agents said to have driven Vladimir to his death. Vladimir, "le cactophile," bristled with complexes. It is probable he was connected with the underground Revolutionary and drug-peddling organizations to which Augustin had belonged. At any rate, he killed himself in 1898. Later, Augustin, too, killed himself, and later still, Augustin's daughter. They were a doomed family. It was Augustin, the youngest, who most nearly approached Isabelle in years and was her childhood companion. They loved each other with a morbid tenderness, and as they grew up, they began to romanticize their affections. On Isabelle's side it was perhaps the love of her life. Some of her later letters show how her childish emotions grew into an adult, or perhaps adolescent passion which may or may not have been returned. When, in his twenties, Augustin was married, miserably, to a common-place girl, "Jenny *l'ouvrière*," as Isabelle dismisses her, she made no secret of her resentment. Augustin, committing suicide in 1914, was perhaps not only ending the failures and miseries of his life in a culminating *cafard*, but also stilling the longings for his dead sister. These are problems no one will ever know, but the emotional overtones they conjure were the dominant influence of Isabelle Eberhardt's unstable nature. In a curious letter of nostalgia, written on Christmas Eve, 1895, when Augustin had left the alternate stagnations and uproars of the Villa Neuve to fling himself into the Foreign Legion at Sidi Bel Abbes (a typical gesture of his period), Isabelle writes of her longings: "of the kisses we gave each other at 10 o/c that night of Saturday Oct. 12 . . ." She quotes Loti, for of course she is steeped in *Aziyadé;* its beautiful pseudo-Oriental melancholy has already reached her inner ear. She has already begun to read and write Arabic easily, but she is enmeshed in the more superficial, sensuous mysticisms of Islam. She luxuriates in her abandon of grief. "Separated, separated, my beloved, perhaps for all eternity. No hope, no faith; absolute solitude . . . No one will ever know the depths of our suffering. . . ." She is in a bad way: she continues in Arabic characters, quotes some Greek, and recalls again their love. She speaks of a Turk with whom she has been in love, but he is dismissed. "*Toi, toi,*" she writes passionately, "*ô! avec toi, toujours—toujours avec toi, de près ou de loin, toujours.*"

If these spontaneous affections for her half-brother—or possibly her full brother—were dammed up, or diverted by convention, this is, I believe, an explanation of much in her subsequent melancholy, her neurotic cravings for stronger meat, deeper draughts. I do not mean to imply that had she been able to marry Augustin she would have settled into a contented matron. That could never be, with Augustine, or anyone else: but something occurred between them, I believe, which affected her emotional balance profoundly, and which accounts for those restless cravings for oblivion, which were more powerful than her Slav heritage alone.

But all that belongs to the tragic nomad of later, of the desert. Now she is still at Meyrin. She is surrounded by all the *va et vient* of exiles, and friends of many races. Gradually, Moslems predominate. The villa vibrates with Pan-Islamic fervors. About this time she and her mother were toying with the idea of becoming converted to the Moslem faith. Certainly the atheist Trophimowsky would have raised no objections. And anyhow, was there so great a change? A comforting fatalism prevailed in both religions, both races.

Isabelle Eberhardt's later-day habit of wearing only men's clothes, of dressing as an Arab cavalier, and calling herself Si Mahmoud was often criticized as being a pose, a love of attracting attention. But it had its beginnings in her childhood, and was fostered by Trophimowsky, who encouraged all nonconformism on principle. Later, as General Catroux observed, it was practical. Her nomadic life, her comings and goings, passed less observed, and by then she was very poor, too. She had no wardrobe. Not for her the background of another ardent, though less highly colored Arab authority, Gertrude Bell. Not for her the resources, the worldly trappings such as those which Miss Bell commanded, when she wrote home asking for crepe de Chine blouses, purple chiffon evening dresses, or parasols.

Alas! Si Mahmoud's coquetries were limited to a rather fine pair of red boots. Her hands, long pale aristocratic hands, were often remarked: they were as handsome as her face was plain.

But to return to Geneva in the eighteen nineties. Perhaps since she was growing into a plain girl she felt herself more suited to men's clothes, and her lifelong love of travesty, of dressing up, was in part a defense, or calculated effect, as well as an inherent craving to escape from herself—her sex. Even in her own mind she does not seem decided as to which sex she is—or wishes to be. This indecision or ambiguity is emphasized in her journal, where, for the first part, she always refers to herself in the masculine gender, and only later adopts the feminine. By today's standards I do not think she would have been thought plain: indeed she might be found fascinating: but she had nothing of the rosy-posy prettiness of her epoch. She was tall and slim, with high Kalmuck cheekbones and black eyes, set Chinese-slanted, in a sallow face. Her build, and her dragging gait, so different to the admired young ladies' tripping steps, made it easy for her to pass as a boy. She loved the adventure of it all, and was photographed as a French sailor, her hair cropped. She fancied herself in Syrian costume, and in Arab robes, a synthetic, photographer's outfit, dagger and all. She was moving unmistakably, even in this superficial sartorial way, towards Islam.

It is curious to reflect that she, who was to know the desert and the Arabs as perhaps no other European woman has done, living among them, with them, without reserve, in dirt and disease and dust (no haughty Lady Hester Stanhope approach, here), where long spells of debauch alternated with meditative withdrawal, was to leave us a fancy-dress image, the photograph of a round-faced girl, posed in a fake Bedouin dress; a soaped, brushed Isabelle, who would reluctantly remove the burnous, lay aside the dagger, and take the horse-omnibus home to tea.

About this time she began a correspondence with a young officer stationed in the Sahara, who, bored, advertized for a pen-friend, and found himself launched into a flood tide of political and metaphysical outpourings, bewildering, though rewarding and far removed from his original cosy notions. Eugène Letord remained her friend for life. Whether they were ever more to each other is not known.

\*     \*     \*

Writing of Eugène Letord, I remember a strange meeting I had, the night before I left Tunis, when I was told of an old French woman, once a friend of Isabelle Eberhardt's, now living in an almshouse outside the city. Someone who had known her well, who could recapture, perhaps, the essence of this enigmatic figure. I rushed off, bumping over the mud tracks and refuse heaps of the waste lands behind the Arab town. I went from almshouses to asylums and hospitals. I could not find her. . . . But she was run to earth at last, an hour or so before my plane took off. She was a wild, wrecked, yet romantic figure, still with traces of great beauty. She, too, had turned Moslem. Her skeletal blue-veined hands were tattooed with the symbols of Islam. She had lost her sight but not her memory.

It was evident she had known Si Mahmoud well. There was no condemnation in her attitude. "She was an alcoholic," she said, briefly. "That was the only thing out of key with her profound religious acceptance of Moslem faith. Yes, she was deeply religious—the stuff of mystics and martyrs. . . . She lived like a man—or a boy, because she was far more like one, physically. She had a hermaphrodite quality—she was passionate, sensual, but not in a woman's way. And she was completely flat-chested," she added. "I know—we often used to bathe together in the mountain streams. She had her vanities, but they were more those of an Arab dandy. Her beautiful hands were tinted with henna, her burnous was always immaculate, and she was, when she could afford it, drenched in the overpowering perfumes all Arabs love. . . .

"At one time she used to spend whole days in the *souks*; when she saw a man she wanted, she took him. She'd beckon him over and off they'd go. She never made any pretenses; she never hid her adventures. Why should she? They were only one side of her character. She had her deep religious ecstasies, I believe, and those she did hide. She was very strict in her observance of ritual. Five prayers a day, in the mosque, the street, or the desert. Wherever she was, she prayed. And whatever she did, she remained well-bred. That sounds absurd, perhaps, but it's true. . . . She was very poor. There was a man called Eugène . . . I don't know who he was. She often spoke of him. She used to say Eugène sent her money when things were desperate. . . . Eugène or Allah! It is all God's will. . . ." She shut her eyes. "Why do you want to know all this? I'm tired. Go and read lies about her in the Bibliothèque," she said sharply, and I could get nothing more from her.

"She's very weak, she'll sleep now," said the nurse, and I left, reflecting that probably such a lonely end would have been Isabelle Eberhardt's, had she not been drowned. Neither Eugène nor anyone else could have saved her from old age.

\*       \*       \*

If a life could be said to be predestined, Isabelle Eberhardt's was such a one. All the threads drew her to Islam. There were more and more Oriental ties. Presently Mme de Moërder and her daughter were persuaded it would be agreeable to move to North Africa. Augustin had left the Foreign Legion and was roaming about Algeria looking vaguely for work. They had many Arab friends. There was Eugène, eager to welcome them. All the more reason for the move. Mother and daughter arrived at Bône in May, 1897, and Isabelle's fluent Arabic was the wonder of all her new friends. She had the astonishing facility of her race. When, later, she was asked how she had begun, she replied it had been no trouble at all—she was too lazy to take trouble, "To speak Arabic—well, I just began to speak."

The Moërders were completely happy. It was a new life opening before them. Isabelle began to write stories, notes, her remarkable journal, and the first draft of her novel *Le Trimardeur;* a local paper published her charming little story "Yasmina." There were expeditions into the *bled,* the burning countryside, and Isabelle began to sniff the faraway desert. Now she, and perhaps her mother, were converted to Moslem faith. They knew no Europeans, and the better to become absorbed into their new life, they lived in the Arab town: on the fringes, rather, and there is something symbolic, here. They still had one foot in the West, a window which looked down towards the broad streets of the French town. The future seemed full of exotic promise. The damp lakeside vistas of Geneva evaporated under the blazing African sun.

Soon this happy life at Bône was ended forever. Mme de Moërder died of a heart attack. Her daughter was distracted. Trophimowsky, arriving late for the funeral, found her raging that she must die with her mother. He coldly offered her his revolver. When she talked of suicide, he showed her the stone-flagged terrace far below their windows. But his ironic detachment gave way before the loss of his mistress and he returned to Geneva broken. Isabelle erected a marble *stèle* over her mother's grave in the Moslem cemetery, in the name of Fatma Manoubia, and was often to return there, luxuriating in her loss of "The White Spirit" as she called her dead mother, always writing this name in Russian. All her life she was to savor morbid griefs. Her preoccupation with death, her mother's, her own, with the mystery of death, was of neurotic intensity.

Now began a period of wanderings, the foretaste of her real nomadic life. Dressed as an Arab she bought a horse and left Bône at a gallop heading for the Sahara. This brief fling crystallized forever her cravings for the nomad life, above all, for the desert. She had found her country, her people, her tempo of living. But her journeys cost money: she had not yet learned to live like the Arabs, on a handful of grain, sleeping anywhere, anyhow. She came to the end of her money, and had to return to Geneva. There, in the shadow-haunted Villa Neuve, she was followed by Rehid Bey, a Turkish suitor she had known some years before. He was now aflame for the eccentric creature. He proposed, and was accepted. He was a diplomat at The Hague, and expected to be nominated to an Oriental post. Isabelle was enraptured. Love and the mysterious East went hand in hand.

But suddenly all was changed. The diplomat was nominated to Stockholm. The Oriental mirage faded. . . . Isabelle recoiled from the bleak prospect of northern lights and protocol. The engagement was broken off. Augustin, who had returned to the villa to rot, spent his days with her beside the failing Trophimowsky, haunted, all of them, by memories. The green depths of the garden offered no repose. There were ghosts at every turn. Nathalie vanished, Vladimir, the suicide, in his grave, Mme de Moërder among the *stèles* of Bône, Trophimowsky dying. It was a tomb. On the night of May 14, 1899, Trophimowsky called for chloral, he had cancer of the throat, and was in great pain. Isabelle and Augustin who had both made fitful studies in medicine prepared the draught. It was fatal. No one will ever know whether this was accidental or deliberate, their typical family inefficiency or a bold decision, but in the morning the lonely, strange old man was dead. The brother and sister buried him beside Vladimir, and with him all their youth. They went their separate ways.

Augustin, in the Midi, soon married an insipid girl, "Jenny *l'ouvrière*." From Paris, Isabelle joined them in Caligari. But all was changed. It was a trio, now. The two women faced each other antagonistically. Augustin stood between. Isabelle decided to return to North Africa for good. She would like to live at El-Oued, the thousand-domed little town which was to have such a profound significance for her. Why El-Oued? There was the whole Sahara from which to choose. But she was probably fulfilling that destiny in which, as a good Moslem, she believed so blindly.

"If only we could foretell, at each hour, the vital importance of certain actions, even words, which appear of no consequence at the time. . . . There are *no* moments of our life that are without consequence or significance for the future. . . . Mektoub! it is written. . . ." She was Islam's ready pupil.

Before shaking the dust of Europe from her feet, however, she must return to Paris: there were practical questions to be settled. Perhaps she could find some work, some geographic reportage to do in Africa. Her friend Madame Lydia Paschkoff, the Russian explorer and traveler, could be invaluable to her. This fascinating woman is only glimpsed, in her relation to Si Mahmoud. She flits through the journals like an exotic bird. She made voyages of discovery in the regions of the Upper Nile, was correspondent for *le Figaro* in St. Petersburg, lectured to the Geographic Society, and wrote several long-forgotten novels and travel sketches. She was at once eccentric and worldly, an ardent feminist and warm-hearted. She gave Isabelle Eberhardt much excellent advice which, it is not necessary to remark, was ignored. "To live the life you and I prefer one needs fifty thousand francs' income." She also gave her many useful introductions. *"Tout Paris"* came to her *salon,* and she calculated astutely just how far Si Mahmoud's exotic appearance and adventurous aura could be exploited to the nomad's material advantage. Her advice was sound. Isabelle must always appear in Arab costume, as Si Mahmoud. It would *"épater"* the so-useful *bourgeoisie.* She must not offend the Jews, who were powerful. She must get in touch with such explorers as the Prince of Monaco, or Prince Henri d'Orléans. She must beware of French appetites, which often demanded payment in kind for good offices rendered to lonely young ladies, especially those of an unconventional nature. She presented her to a world of interesting people, but Isabelle was too *gauche,* perhaps too direct to play their game. There was a meeting with the Marquise de Morés, widow of the explorer who had been assassinated, mysteriously, in 1896, on the confines of Tripoli and Tunisia. The widow is said to have commissioned Si Mahmoud to return to the south and try to find traces of the Marquis, or his assassins. This would have been after Si Mahmoud's heart. Probably the deal was concluded. Probably the Marquise provided the funds. In any case, it was a pretext for Si Mahmoud's departure, although nothing more was ever heard of the project, or the funds, her detractors said.

Yet the legend of this venture still lingers on, in the little lost villages of southern Tunisia, on the Sahara's edge, where the sand drifts up to the window ledges of the solitary *bordjs*, reclaiming, grain by grain, the puny, man-made outposts. It was in such a one that I listened to an old Arab servant recounting the tale. He had been a Spahi, and spoke some French: I asked him about a track, a few footprints, a straggle of stones and alfa grass which led away, into the dunes.

"Where does it go?" I asked, idly.

He peered out into the dark, beyond the circle of lantern light. The palm trees rattled, scaly and sinister, in a cold wind that blew suddenly in gusts.

"It goes south," he said; "that is the way the mad woman went to find Monsieur le Marquis de Morés. . . . but she never found him." He spat, ruminatively, and it was a long time before we could get him to tell us the little he knew, the legend of Si Mahmoud passing that way with a servant, and a gun.

\*       \*       \*

But in Paris she made no lasting impression. After a few weeks of appearing, shy and insecure, among that most arrogant and enclosed circle, *"tout Paris,"* and one which is generally particularly receptive to highly colored personalities, she left France, abruptly. It is a sad reflection that this odd girl, with all her character, her aristocratic background, her wide culture and originality, did not find sooner that milieu, which could have truly appreciated her, of a certain French *élite*, men of real style and brilliance such as Lapperine, Motylinski, le père de Foucauld, or Lyautey and his officers, Catroux and Berriau, whom she only came to know, and by whom she was so justly valued, in the last year of her life. Had she found them earlier, perhaps her fate would have been otherwise. Certainly she would have found a focal point, a pattern for her life, and a use for her extraordinary knowledge and intuition in Arab affairs. Perhaps she might have found, at last, the long-sought Truth, and even come to peace, in the shadow of Père de Foucauld's hermitage at Tamanrasset.

\* \* \*

In July, 1900, she was back once more in Algeria, where she now began the most intense phase of her nomad life. It is impossible to realize the range of such a restless creature without studying the map where, even so, vast, overwhelming distances are telescoped between one pinpoint and the next, and a finger-nail's span covers a trail which takes the camel caravans she so often followed as much as two months' march. She is everywhere, up and down the country: in the desert, in the oasis, across the High Plateaux. She is indulging her *"goût d'espace,"* as she describes her ruling passion. She spends days and night in Arab villages, sleeping on the filthy mud floors of a *fondouk,* or caravanserai. She follows the marauding tribes in the south till she is half-dead in the saddle. She is with the Spahis; spends days immobile, in contemplation of the Great Desert: is in the squalid brothels with the troops. She tries to convert the Berbers to hygiene, but is too lazy to look after her own health. Now she is integrated into one of the religious societies, the Kadryas, and dreams of becoming initiated into Sufism, of becoming, perhaps, a woman priestess, a *maraboute,* like Lallah Zeyneb. Her integration has practical benefits too: she is protected, and closer to the people of her choice.

She blazes with happiness—with triumph. On her horse Souf, followed by her dog Loupiote, she is off again. Her journals record the intoxication of these days, drawn always further and further into the limitless distances. It was an elective affinity: "I wanted to possess this country," she wrote, "and this country has possessed me." She loves it all with passion: the people, their legends, their life. She is young, poetic, free. E. M. Forster has said that "only in youth, only in the joyous light of morning can the lines of the Oriental landscape be seen and the salutation accomplished." I do not altogether agree, but that is neither here nor there. In Isabelle Eberhardt's case it was true. It was her morning, and she was greedy. Like Marvel, she could not make her sun stand still, yet she could make him run. No one ever tore their pleasures "through the iron gates of life" more voluptuously than she. All, all was wonderful. She plunged. To appease her yearning for spiritual development there were long, reverent discussions with the religious leaders. Wisdom from the graybeards. Lovers, ardent Arab lovers without number. She knew how to enjoy the senses blindly, brutally. There was hashish and anisette for forgetfulness, and always her wild dashes into the desert. Violent delights. Although, writing of her wanderings in the Sud-Oranais, where she lived alone, or with the nomads, she speaks of the quality of nothingness, "the long hours with neither sadness nor boredom—nothingness—where one is nourished by silence. . . . I have never regretted one of those lost hours. . . . I felt myself immortal, and so rich, in my poverty." And of the desert, again: "In this country without vegetation, this country of stones, one thing exists—the hours. Here, sunrise and sunset are each a drama in themselves."

But for Si Mahmoud there were always many other kinds of drama too. At El-Oued she encountered a Spahi, Slimène Ehnni, an Arab quartermaster of the garrison, who spoke French well, and was even naturalized French. He was a handsome, rather ordinary young Arab, it seems, with consumptive tendencies. But they fell in love, madly. He is Adam to her Eve, and they are in Paradise. They exchange burning letters and keep delicious secret rendezvous—secret from whom, one wonders? For who was there, now, in all the world, to care whom Isabelle loved, or how? Unless perhaps the shadow of Augustin fell across the palms that formed their alcove.

Soon there were no more secrets of the alcove. They talked of marriage: their ecstasies would endure: nourished on such a love, they would need little else. Still, a grocer's store or a *café maure* would be a good idea: something to assure their lodging, and a few sous over for cigarettes. Slimène's brother could run it for them when they felt the urge for the desert. But even this modest utopia needed cash. Slimène's pay was negligible. Madame de Morés was dissatisfied with Isabelle's elusiveness, her dilatory ways, and now withdraw her subsidy. Isabelle had rashly entrusted the settlement of her mother's inheritance to Augustin, who in turn abandoned it to a shady lawyer. There was nothing left to pawn when Isabelle's iron cot and inkwell had gone. Even a pipe of *kif* cost money. *Nitchevo! . . . Mektoub!* The lovers abandoned themselves to wilder transports, and were consoled.

Isabelle, or Si Mahmoud, was for Slimène at once man and woman, the young boy, or *bel idéal* of so much Oriental literature. She had become completely accepted by the Arabs, most of whom knew her to be a woman, but respected both her and her disguise. Her affiliation to the Kadryas, and her friendship with Si Lachmi, their Sheik, had assured her position among them, and at this time she saw no Europeans. In January, 1901, as an initiate to the order, she went into religious retreat, studying their mystical tenets. One cannot help wondering if Slimène felt neglected by these sudden withdrawals, but perhaps he was sufficiently enthralled to accept his cavalier mistress as she was.

It is likely that even now, still enthralled by Slimène the lover, Isabelle was becoming aware of his rather mere personality, especially in contrast to that of the masterful Si Lachmi, by whom she was dazzled. This handsome and unscrupulous figure possessed a personal magnetism, an authority which enabled him to live in almost piratical manner, while yet retaining the self-appointed position as Grand Master of the Kadryas. He had seized this office over the heads of his brothers and against the wishes of his father, who had not appointed him his successor, and large numbers of the Kadryas, who did not consider him even a *marabout*, let alone their spiritual leader. But Si Lachmi always rode on, roughshod, getting the best of both worlds: wearing the green robes of piety, and heading a religious pilgrimage one day; the next, flinging himself into the saddle to lead a wild charge of horsemen in the fantasia, that dash of maddened men and animals, all gunshot and flourish which is the ritual Arab festival.

Here is Isabelle's description of such a scene: "They charged on us, discharging their arms all at once, into the smoking sand, close to our terrified horses . . . the acrid, intoxicating stench of burnt powder maddening the men and horses more than the savage music of the war cries."

Naturally, Isabelle's nature was fired by such surroundings. Geneva seemed another life, a flat echo. Had it ever been, that tepid existence beside the chilly lake? Now she lived; now she had come into her birthright; *Dar El Islam,* the house of Islam—home.

So far, her life had been a picturesque curtain-raiser to the Orientalism of her choice. On January 29 the drama proper began. She was with a religious pilgrimage of Kadryas headed by Si Lachmi at the village of Béhima, near El-Oued. But a rival religious sect, the Tidjanis, had marked her down. An infidel, a woman, a Kadrya—an enemy spy. She must perish. While she was in the act of translating a letter for an illiterate Arab, she was struck by a fanatic wielding a sword which glanced off her head, but nearly severed her wrist. It was a Tidjani, who said Allah had commanded him to destroy Si Mahmoud.

Uproar! Isabelle was bleeding to death while murmuring she forgave her attacker. The fanatic prayed and feigned madness; the Kadryas were in a ferment. The French intervened, and Isabelle was taken to the military hospital, to recover slowly. The Tidjani was arrested, pending trial. Rumors, accusations, and uneasiness simmered. The atmosphere grew hostile. Slimène was posted to Batna. The trial, which was to be held in the Military Courts, was fixed for June 18. It was a unique occasion for the French colony. The fabled Amazon of the desert, the *déclassé* ex-European journalist, the ambiguous cavalier, the scandalous creature. . . . The press of Algiers descended in a body to pack the tiny fly-blown courtroom.

What odd motive decided them to report Isabelle's age as thirty-five is not clear. Did they fear that, given her true twenty-four, she might appear too intriguing a figure, who might sway public opinion dangerously? Had they decided this, in a sort of left-handed gallantry, a sop, directed towards their outraged women-folk, or was it suggested to them, through some official channels, that this drama, set in the tinderbox of southern Algeria, would be soonest forgotten were the principal figure to appear a *vieille fille,* without allure, and thus, unlikely to fire the public's imagination?

In any case, *l'affaire* Eberhardt hid much that it was not politic to disclose. Too many aspects of the matter were better left unexplored: it was a moment when the French position in North Africa was extremely delicate: when to alienate a religious body might lead to untold difficulties: when, besides, each faction delighted in playing each other off against the French, displaying a most practical and militant address. It is held that Si Lachmi instigated the attempted assassination, partly because he wished to liquidate a mistress who had become a complication, and partly because he hoped, by using one of his own Kadryas, who passed as a Tidjani, to compromise the rival sect. So much was known, so little was said, and nothing was proved. Through it all, Isabelle moved with dignity, a solitary figure, disarming in her simplicity. *"J'ai toujours eté simple, et dans cette simplicité j'ai trouvé des jouissances fortes . . ."* "I have been happy in my simplicity." Such childish innocence was incomprehensible to sophisticated French natures who envisaged women as mothers, or mistresses, but not as adventurous mystics who looked for love, in man or God, with the same ardent innocence.

The verdict was bewildering. While the fanatic was sentenced to twenty years' hard labor, the victim was expelled from North Africa. Even those who most disliked Si Mahmoud found it unjust. But she could be used by the Kadryas to ferment trouble against the Tidjanis. The pacification of the Sahara was not yet complete. The French feared any excuses for local disturbances. She must go.

Was it only the work of a religious fanatic? Or were there other motives? Was it planned by a personal enemy, or by political *agents provocateurs?* Or even, as some say, inspired by the French? It is possible. The puzzle has never fitted into place. The attitude of certain French officials is unexplained. Did Si Lachmi, probably her lover, think it convenient to liquidate her as an awkward encumbrance likely to meddle dangerously in Arab affairs, and those of his confraternity, the Kadryas, in particular? Nothing is impossible for the time, place and people concerned. From her journals, it seems that Si Mahmoud herself never had any suspicions of other, sinister undercurrents. To her, it must have seemed a continuation of the violent traditions she had first encountered with *l'affaire* Morés.

In despair, Isabelle Eberhardt left for Marseilles, where, cut off from her lover and the country of her choice, she speaks in her journal of an attempted suicide. She was not an efficient person in affairs of everyday life, and she did not achieve her attempted suicides either. Such attempts run like a dark thread through the uneven pattern of her life. They were a recurrent theme, a seeming solution. After her mother's death; on her expulsion from Africa; with Augustin and his wife, at some particularly black moment where she notes, "a collective suicide would be no solution" . . . or later, with Slimène at Ténès, where they were involved in the scandal of the elections and its mud-slinging, and had not the money to pay even the rent of their one room. Here her miseries reached culmination, and the suicide was to be no impetuous gesture, but a premeditated, voluptuous withdrawal, a suicide pact. She left Slimène a note, and went ahead to the fatal rendezvous. "Let us kill ourselves tonight, outside the town. Bring your revolver and some absinthe." The passive, already consumptive Slimène offered no resistance. They kept the rendezvous, but not the pact. After finishing the absinthe and reciting Arab poetry they fell asleep. In the morning light the revolver seemed too dramatic, and they renewed their daily round which was, in fact, hardly less so.

But, exiled to Marseilles, in a small back room, life was worth nothing. Between Russian and French lawyers Isabelle Eberhardt had lost the last of her mother's legacy. From her Russian stronghold of married propriety Trophimowsky's widow claimed the Geneva villa in the name of her late husband, regardless of the fact it was the wronged General de Moërder's money which had originally purchased this melancholy abode of free love and higher thought. When at last the legal machinations were done, Isabelle Eberhardt's share was reduced to a deficit of sixty francs.

She was steeped in misery now: misery without end: no hope, no ray of light: she wallowed, misery for misery's sake. "One must never look for happiness: one meets it by the way—but it is always going in the opposite direction." She was never one to go out after happiness, as an end in itself. On the contrary—"When I suffer, I begin to live."

"The most miserable outcast among the miserable outcasts of this world, a homeless exile, without country, destitute and orphaned writes these lines; they are the truth." Or again, searching obsessively for Truth, *l'Absolue*, "three things can open our eyes to the dazzling morning light of truth; Pain, Faith, and Love—all love." She suffered as simply as she breathed or slept or ate. Even her wildest delights were touched with despair. It was the climate of her soul. She now wrote some of the admirable short stories and sketches later to appear in *L'Akhbar*, the Algerian paper, and more, which were collected and edited so excessively, after her death. Those which were not over-varnished, a fate which befell so much of her simple, sensitive writing, can be compared, in the few stories collected by her biographer, R. L. Doyon, *Au Pays du Sables*, with those handled by M. Barrucand in *Dans l'ombre chaude d'Islam*. Her notes and *Mes journaliers* give further examples of her own style: above all, her absence of those pseudo-poetic fancies grafted on, pretentiously, by other hands. She has certain tricks, Loti-esque touches, the clichéd Oriental melancholies of her epoch, but she penetrated the country and was one with the people as few other Europeans have ever been. Although she herself posed, she never presented herself, in her writings, in Loti's manner of romanticized wishful thinking. She was far more objective. It is not how she writes, but of what she writes which is her strength. She wrote organically, naturally, as she spoke and lived. There was little craft and no technique. She was quite undisciplined. When she felt like it, she wrote, and it was good. If she was lazy, which she often was, or not in the mood, she remained idle for weeks. She was, in fact, an amateur.

In a letter to M. Abd-ul-Wahab, she writes of her work in these terms: "The ambition to make a name, a position for myself by my pen (something in which I have little confidence, and do not hope to achieve) is for me on the second plane. I write because I like the 'Processus' of literary creation: I write like I love, because it is my destiny, probably. It is my only true consolation." She speaks, too, of "that great Unknown which is the only refuge of tormented souls." One wonders what it was, precisely, which made Si Mahmoud such a tormented soul, and one falls back on *l'âme slave*, which obligingly covers such a multitude of obscure neurasthenias.

While rotting and raging in Marseilles, she was corresponding with Brieux, who admired her work, but could not persuade any Parisian editors to publish it. She was writing, too, to anyone whom she thought could help her rejoin Slimène: her projected marriage was now an obsession, an obstinate craving for the unattainable—for Islam, perhaps, rather than Slimène. But her feminist friend Lydia Paschkoff became bored and disillusioned by Si Mahmoud's apparently domestic goal. Was it for this the nomad had ranged abroad? Was the Mazeppa of the desert to rock a cradle? Their friendship cooled, and there are no more letters of advice. Isabelle Eberhardt was now penniless, and worked as a docker. She was in a mood to savor any form of misery, even rupturing herself on the Quai Joliotte. Parts of her novel *Le Trimardeur* are autobiographical and belong to this moment of her life.

But suddenly her luck seemed to change. The good offices of Colonel Rancogne obtained Slimène's transfer. On October 17, 1901, they were married in Marseilles and Si Mahmoud laid aside her burnous for the day, to wear an odd assembly of borrowed female clothing. Since her Moslem fervors had led her to shave her head, leaving only the ritual topknot by which to be transported to Mahommed's Paradise, European woman's dress now implied false hair as well as furbelows, and Isabelle favored a jetty black wig.

But married life in a slum room behind the port was not for Isabelle and Slimène. There is squalor and squalor. They craved the *fondouks* and kasbahs, even if there were flies and filth. They returned to the "âpre et splendide Mahgreb." As Mme Si Ehnni, wife of a French citizen, Isabelle was no longer an expatriate Slav, and she could not be refused entry. Slimène had left the army and looked for work. During these last months, Isabelle had been working on his education with remorseless zeal. He was to be dragged up the intellectual heights, somehow. Besides the more conventional classic authors, Isabelle considered Zola of great sociological importance. Slimène plowed on, dutifully.

Having no resources, they were now obliged to lodge with Slimène's family. The claustrophobic atmosphere was almost as bad as Marseilles. Their burning heyday of love declined, imperceptibly. Si Mahmoud was stifled. Soon, she was off again, heading south for the M'zab for those enclosed, sly, and holy cities lying beyond the black wastes of the Chebka. Slimène, now nominated Khodja or secretary to the Commune

Mixte of Ténès, a small provincial town near Algiers, awaited her return.

On July 7, 1902, this odd couple arrived at Ténès, on the coach from Orléansville. They rented a modest room on the outskirts of the town. An inkpot, some straw mats for beds, a casserole, and some rickety bookshelves were all their household goods. But there were Isabelle's books. Dostoevsky, Nadson, the poet of her adolescence, Turgeniev, Zola, the Goncourts, and, of course, Loti. A rather morbid lot.

Robert Randau has left a portrait of her at this time: elegant and slim, dressed *à la cavalier*, in an immaculate white burnous, and the high red boots of the Spahis, she had black eyes of a striking brilliance, a livid face, high cheekbones, and reddish hair. Under the turban, near the ears, and round the discolored lips, the skin had a yellowish, parchment tinge. Robert Randau was much intrigued by his strange caller. He goes on to say she had a discordant, nasal voice (this seems to have struck everyone who knew her), swore vigorously, but had a curious dignity, and absolutely no sex appeal. Elsewhere, he speaks of her gentleness, "Her face, very soft, was that of an adolescent, and she had the smile of a child."

Robert Randau was an outstanding personality in Algiers, a writer and civil servant, cultivated, generous, and loyal. He and his wife came to love and understand Si Mahmoud, and they stood by her later, when the storm broke. Settled at Ténès, Isabelle Eberhardt began writing intermittently for *L'Akhbar*. Its mildly pro-Arab tone, its sympathy with "*La Ligue des Droits de l'Homme,*" whose ideals were so often quoted by aspiring Arabs, agreed with her own. Séverine, the woman writer who always snubbed her during her lifetime, summed her up posthumously as a disciple of Bakunin: but she was far too fatalistic to make real revolutionary stock. Her sympathies were with the underdog; she believed romantically in justice and equality, and found much to criticize in the anti-Semitic, anti-Arabic policies of many Algerian officials. Basically, however, she was too lazy to participate in any active political movements. Her revolts always took the form of evasions.

The old ways of childhood, the nights of talk centered round the samovar had left their mark. She transposed them to the *cafés maures,* where, cross-legged on a mat, beside a pipe of *kif*, or hashish, rolling her cigarettes, or drinking anisette, she talked wildly or morbidly, or gaily, or any way she felt, all through the hot African nights. Now she was becoming a legendary figure, though there was always a good deal of cold-shouldering by more conventional, perhaps envious, ladies. She had an audience wherever she appeared. Journalists, writers, painters, Arab chiefs: Si Mahmoud was like no one else, and they hung on her words. In the cafés round the harbor, in Algiers, she would sometimes quit a group of her European friends for the long, stylized exchange of Arab courtesies and veiled allusions which are the formal, traditional conversational opening among Arabs: she would stand, reverently bowed, before some bearded patriarchal figure, and return to the European group visibly moved by the encounter. She was indifferent to public opinion, European opinion, that is, and rather liked to flutter the dovecotes with her adventures, or to hurl a bombshell, such as one which stilled the tinkle of coffee cups at a word, when she plunged into a dissertation on the *volupté* of submission, citing an adventure in the Sud-Oranais where she had been living in camp, and on the march, with the Légionnaires: a romantic, brutal adventure of sadistic flavor and erotic inference. An episode where, rebelling against an order to remain in camp during some desert skirmish, a young Lieutenant had punished her disobedience as he would one of his troops, and she was dragged for a day's forced march across the grilling sands, chained to the stirrup of a guard. And how, having survived the terrible hours uncomplaining, all was as before between them with campfire confidences, cognac and that sort of voluptuous camaraderie which was her delight.

She was as superstitious as any unlettered Bedouin; all Trophimowsky's upbringing was for nothing: all those early years of his rationalism, iconoclasm and erudition were set aside. She once burst in on the Randaus in a state of collapse. Her days were numbered! She had seen a vision! Her forbears, some wild Asiatic hordes had appeared, to claim her! Sobbing with terror, she recounted how, riding at night through a ravine, she had stopped to drink, and water her horse at a spring. Her Arab companions fled, warning her the spring was cursed, and gave second sight to the drinker. As she rode after them, her horse suddenly reared and shied, throwing her. Isabelle described how she picked herself up, to see looming over her, out of a mist, the sinister figure of a warrior in chain mail, some far distant ancestor from the Steppes, one of the hordes who had overrun North Africa, perhaps, or one of those giants of the Slav *skazki*, a legendary Bogatyri. He fixed her with a pale stare and beckoned. Across the ages, she recognized him. He was her ancestor, he had come to claim her . . . she knew it all. She must follow: her days were numbered. It was written—*Mektoub!* All the cups of tea and comfort lavished on her by the Randaus were unavailing. Si Mahmoud the adventurer, who galloped over the wild mountains of the Ouled Naïl into the stony deserts of the Chebka, who risked dangers and disease every hour of her life, now trembled like a terrified child.

She must have been a difficult guest. Sometimes she spent the evening sobbing, overcome with absinthe, and *Weltschmerz*, and perhaps, deeper, more bitter than all else, her perpetual craving for the Absolute, the unattainable mystical peace of Sūfism. Far horizons, the Infinite, the Absolute—they were all one. She had the true mystic's unappeased hunger. Sometimes there were luxuriant monologues of misery and self-pity. Riding back from a moonlight picnic outside Ténès, last of the cavalcade, she turned abruptly to Robert Randau. "Ah! if you only knew how I abominate this country. It drives me to excesses. . . . I detest cultivated green country full of crops. Why do I have this morbid craving for a barren land and desert wastes? [What she calls *"la phantasmagorie de pierre, en pleine vie minerale."*] Why do I prefer nomads to villagers, beggars to rich people? *Aie yie yie!* for me, unhappiness is a sort of spice. Oh, yes! I'm very Russian at heart. I love the knout! And I love to be pitied when I'm knouted, too. . . . I don't hate my enemies [here she refers to the animosity which was centering round her in Ténès] any more than I hate the madman who tried to kill me at Béhima,—nor would I hate the executioner who was preparing the rope with which to hang me. I have no hatred for them, because, thanks to them, through them, perhaps, I may arouse compassion in others. Yet all my friends in Algiers—you, too, and everyone here, you are *hard*. You don't understand me, and you never will, since I'm not of your blood. *How many fields of wheat, how many vineyards there are, be-*

*tween you and me!* I hate the Law—yes, chiefly because of its indifference. I want to feel—to make others feel—— And anyhow, I've drunk too much absinthe to-night. . . . I'm drunk, drunk to my soul." Here is the Russian soul, *l'âme slave* in full cry.

Poor pathetic Si Mahmoud; so muddled, so maddening. She was by fits and starts childish and complicated, dignified and unstable, wildly optimistic and absurdly pessimistic. Yet, with all her excesses she retained a style—a breeding. Often she seemed too lazy to live. She neglected her work, herself; letters and bills and messages remained unanswered. She abandoned herself to poverty and inertia. Her diseases multiplied: such freedoms had their price. She made no efforts to be cured. Her teeth began to rot. On her journeys she carried a revolver (well hidden) but no toothbrush. With her high domed forehead, and Kalmuck face, above all, her irritating nasal voice, she cannot have been an engaging figure. Yet she inspired some people with a profound affection which nothing could shake. Among the Arabs she was increasingly respected; indeed she was venerated. By her many acts of piety and kindness she had earned her title of *La Bonne Nomade*.

But at Ténès she was given no quarter. The colony, censorious and sour, turned on her unctuously. When the whole dirty business of local elections came to a head, she and Slimène were accused of buying Arab votes, even accepting bribes, among other equally false inventions. Isabelle Eberhardt defended herself from the charges, and both she and her husband were cleared: indeed, the cunning by which they had been used as scapegoats was revealed; but the mud stuck, and she felt it bitterly. Not that sort of mud, for her. The whole squalid series of political and local intrigues are too involved to recount here. It is sufficient to say that several candidates for the local elections and both pro- and anti-Arab factions were involved, as well as many influential citizens of Algiers, who did much long-range condemnation.

One day, the Soviets will remember that Isabelle Eberhardt was Russian by birth, and it will be easy to make her a dramatic martyr figure; one of them, ideologically. The *moujik* beneath the burnous, little sister of the oppressed. The Cossack of the desert, off on her mission of universal brotherhood, persecuted by the degenerate West, so cynical in their exploitation of the wretched Arab. They have something there, but not enough; and Si Mahmoud's conduct will require a lot of explanation, before it can be brought into Party line, from the viewpoint of purposeful living.

Her persecutions were very real, very cruel; and she did champion the Arabs, yet she remained convinced of the basic advantages of French administration. She was always the first to influence the Arabs to profit by French medicine and education. She belonged to that generation of free-thinking liberal Slavs who looked, from Siberia, from everywhere, towards France as the focal point of all true liberalism.

But to return to Ténès. The scandal had assumed such proportions that apart from the effect which it had on Arab opinion, Administrative investigations were made, and presently, new appointments cleared the air. However, life had become increasingly disagreeable for Si Mahmoud and Slimène. Once again, it was obvious that she was a center of disturbance and had better go: at any rate, till after the elections. When Victor Barrucand, in Algiers, offered her board and lodging (it seems a minimum wage) in return for her services on his newspaper *L'Akhbar*, she accepted eagerly. The grocer's store remained as far away as ever, but newspaper work interested her. It promised opportunities—excuses, perhaps, for further vagabond journeys in the desert. Soon, the *Dépêche Algérienne* commissioned her to make a reportage in the Sud-Oranais, on the borders of Morocco, where the then Colonel Lyautey was subduing the hostile tribes and organizing the new French policy of peace. She was enraptured. This was the work she was born to do, to which all her life had led her. The shabby intrigues of Ténès were forgotten. In a state of exaltation she saw herself exploring the central Sahara, or penetrating the mysterious Hoggar: once again, she was indulging her *goût d'espace*.

\*     \*     \*

In the autumn of 1903 she was in the Sud-Oranais, and there are many people who have left accounts of her at that time. The journalist Rodes, reporting the border skirmishes and hard fighting of the Légionnaires and Goums against the rebel tribes, encountered Isabelle Eberhardt at Beni-Ounif. She moved in on him in his miserable little hotel room, and together, they wrote their dispatches, exchanged experiences, and lived in good companionship. Isabelle Eberhardt preferred to sleep on the floor—she had long lost the habit of beds; she often made the round of the *guinguettes* with the young officers, where she tried to outdrink them with mixtures of kümmel, chartreuse, and cointreau. Sometimes such bravadoes ended in the gutter and her friends would carry her back to the inn, where she would lie groaning on the mat, wailing in her flat nasal tones that she was the most miserable of beings, miserable, wretched outcast. . . . Once, dragging her revolver from her belt, she tried to blow out her brains, and Rodes was nearly shot, taking it from her. Or, overcome with desires, she would rage round the tiny room, "I want a *tirailleur!* I must have a *tirailleur!*" And if any French friends offered themselves, she would repulse them, uncompromisingly. She was known to take only Arab lovers, which was an added irritant to her European detractors. In the words of one who knew her well, "She drank more than a Légionnaire, smoked more *kif* than a hashish addict, and made love for the love of making love."

It is possible that her violent cravings, her need for drink and humiliation, were the heritage of her Asiatic blood. Gorki's *Lower Depths* was peopled with such; a tormented lot. Perhaps, too, she justified her needs by her acquired religious tenets. She may have been influenced, very young, by the opinions of her Turkish suitor, who, in a letter to Trophimowsky, wrote, "I have always thought, according to our revered Prophet, that the only true well-being is here, on earth. . . . Instead of learning, in the manner of bastard Christianity, to despise the earth and Nature's laws, Islam counsels us to love it, and study it, since God has made it all for our delight, and it is only ignorance which brings unhappiness." No one could say that Si Mahmoud held back.

Her perfect command of Arabic impressed all those who knew her. She spoke not only the dialects of the people, but the classic, ritualistic Arabic of tradition, enjoying the savor of such exchanges as she had with the savants and *marabouts*, as much as it was apparent they enjoyed talking with her. After nights of feverish excess, she was able to be in the saddle at dawn, for a punishing ride into the battle areas, to observe, or perhaps to assist at some *pourparler*. Or she could shed all her love of action to live among the most venerated religious brotherhoods, such as the retreat she made, in the summer of 1904, at Kenadza, in the Zaouïa Zianya of the Marabout Sidi Brahim Ould Mohamed. Here, ravaged by her increasingly severe bouts of malaria, she meditated among the other inmates, sharing their religious offices, and left, chalked on the walls of her cell in her graceful Arabic script, a pastel-toned aphorism, "The world moves towards the tomb as the night towards dawn."

The Arabs either accepted, or ignored, the wild side of her character. Probably they recognized the religious mystic behind the libertine's mask. But for Europeans this hidden aspect of Si Mahmoud's true nature was unsuspected until the publication of her journals, many years after her death. Even then, many could not accept that the senses and the spirit could be interdependent manifestations of each other, or that a transmutation from sexual ecstasies to mystic communion was known to most religions.

In Si Mahmoud's own words: "*Et moi, je sais encore des musiques plus étranges et plus fortes, des musiques qui font saigner le cœur en silence, celles que des lèvres ont murmurées, des lèvres absentes qui boiront d'autres souffles que le mien, qui respireront une autre âme que la mienne, parce que mon âme ne pouvait pas se donner, parce qu'elle n'était pas en moi mais dans les choses éternelles, et que je la possède enfin dans la profonde, dans la divine solitude de toute ma chair offerte à la nuit du Sud.*"

I leave this splendidly purple passage in its original. I do not think the Russian soul, expressed in French, would stand yet another transposition.

The Bach-agha Si Moulāi always dismissed any aspersions on Si Mahmoud's character. This distinguished personage was emphatic. "I have never heard it said that Si Mahmoud's conduct lacked dignity," he replied, when questioned, after her death, and furthermore, he caused a street to be named after her in Aïn-Sefra. The Sheik Belaredj of the Zaouïa Zianya of Kenadza, where she was in religious retreat, who died only in 1934, has left a charming picture of her. "Here Si Mahmoud was our guest; during the day he meditated, rested, or wrote, and at twilight he wandered in the garden accompanied by a slave." It will be noticed the Arabs always spoke of her as a man. They accepted or in some cases believed her disguise. "We were told Si Mahmoud was a woman, but we did not believe it," was the reply of one marabout.

From the time that Si Mahmoud was an accredited correspondent, following the military operations round Figuig, or Colomb-Bechar, and the penetration of the Sahara, her true worth began to be recognized. In the eyes of the military she was no longer the suspect of El-Oued, but even a valuable member of their *deuxième bureau.* Though not sufficiently valued. She was often obliged to beg for the advance of a few francs with which to buy fodder for her horse. Then the *bureau* would dole out a meager something, and Isabelle would go on as before, with life reduced to its barest terms. Her horse was her only luxury, her sole possession.

To the colony in Algiers she was still a scandal, but her conduct was much ameliorated by the fact she was now celebrated, a woman war correspondent, and above all—the friend of Lyautey. She was presented to the then Colonel Lyautey in October, 1903. He was, in the words of one who saw them together, "literally enchanted by the strange creature." He protected her and gave her many privileges; above all, a pass, enabling her to roam at will. It is said that he was Si Mahmoud's lover: but then everything was said of both Lyautey and Isabelle Eberhardt. It is certain they spent much time together, "talking Sahara" as General Catroux put it. It is also certain that she enjoyed Lyautey's confidence and that he entrusted her with several delicate missions among the Arab leaders. His trust, before all else, establishes Si Mahmoud's political integrity. It might also be taken to prove that however diseased she may have been, her brain was not affected. *"Dieu connait les choses cachées et la sinceraté des témoignages,"* she wrote in her journal, thinking perhaps, of past injustices.

But she had come into her kingdom too late. At last her life seemed to follow the pattern she had once wished, full of danger and romance and freedom. *Le goût d'espace, le droit du vagabondage,* are recurrent phrases in the journal. Far distances, movement, were always her drug and her stimulus. She speaks of the blessed annihilation of self in the contemplative desert life. *La route vers le lointain inconnu.* Clichés of freedom: but there speaks the last of the romantic nineteenth-century wanderers. The motor age would have killed her, like domesticity. When Robert Randau asked her what she would do if she were to have a child, she replied that she would be a good mother, like all Russian women, but she did not want children.

Her love for Slimène remained, in spite of her many absences and adventures. In her journal she records that she can never thank God enough for the beauty and goodness of Slimène's soul. But she also left it on record that he was the perfect lover. She calls him Rouh, "beloved," and speaks of their meetings in the desert, far from everything, to enjoy their dreams . . . "dreams alternating with hours of madness and pleasure." But now she seldom saw Slimène. He was resigned to her way of life and left her free: maybe he began to find her rather too exhausting. They were together only occasionally, she journeying to the rendezvous from wherever her reportage had led her, and he patiently traveling as much as a thousand kilometers from his post in the north. Her reportages now attracted much attention. They appeared in the *Dépêche Algérienne,* though sometimes she told people she was reporting for the *Journal de Paris.* If this was so, nothing was ever published in its pages. It is probable she was inventing: she whose whole life was wildly romantic, still enjoyed such little flourishes.

But if she sometimes invented or distorted facts about herself, all that she wrote otherwise had the ring of truth. This is one of her greatest charms. She writes about things which are to most people exotic and far removed, and she writes of them objectively, and subjectively too. She saw them, was conscious of them, with the entranced eye of a newcomer, yet she understood and was part of the scene as no ordinary enraptured beholder could be. Thus, for example, she will describe the life in a religious order, in retreat, as it was, as they lived it, and as no European could come to know it, while preserving her detached, European sense of wonder and interest in all about her. She wrote of life in the lonely desert *bordjs,* or forts; of the Légionnaires, the bazaars, foxy lawyers, children, old women, the dramas of everyday life in the verminous villages. Of Oudja, which only grows beautiful at sunset, when, as in a dream one hears the Aissouyiahas praying *"dans la serenité pudique de la nuit, voilant la pourriture des choses, la souffrance et l'abjection des êtres."* Of the songs and banners of a religious procession winding over the hills; of a lizard flicking across a baked-out fountain; of a starry night, a nomad camp; the *bled*, the lovely Algerian countryside. She loved it all. It was hers; she tried to share her treasure. "Only the tomb can take this richness from me. . . . And who can tell? If Fate gives me time to re-create a few fragments, perhaps it will live on, in the minds of others."

Sometimes she would join the troops in their canteen, where she was always welcomed as good company, and very much respected, in spite of everything: even in spite of it being known that, for the price of some hashish, or a bottle of anisette, she would turn pimp, trafficking in Ouled Naïls, supplying comely young creatures to the soldiers.

She talked with the Légionnaires in their various tongues, though it was remarked her Russian was rather rusty. According to Colonel de Loustal, who had known her well, she had reached a state of melancholy which nothing could dispel for long. Her success had come too late. "She did not complain, but one now sensed a bitter disillusion. She was a woman who expected nothing more from life. She was not yet thirty, but all attraction had vanished. She was ravaged by drink. Her voice was raucous. Her head was shaved, and she had no teeth left." Malaria and probably syphilis were gaining on her. There was no future for her, and she must have known it. Slimène was consumptive. What life could there have been for her, growing old and infirm? Was her passivity, her "Mektoubisme," her contemplative side strong enough to accept such an end? Were her religious beliefs growing sufficiently profound to have compensated for the loss of all her violent physical living? She was a tragic figure. Her life had been tragic, a tragicomedy in parts, but her death, generally referred to as a tragedy, was not so, in reality. She was blessed, for she escaped the prison of old age.

The acceleration of her last year was fevered. Did she, perhaps, have some premonition of the approaching end? She ranged the Sud-Oranais; she was at El Moungar, at Aïn-Sefra, and then in Algiers. In May, 1904, she rode out into the *bled* once more, south, across the High Plateaux to Colomb-Bechar. She talked of pushing on, to In'Salah, in Touareg territory. But these vast distances now seemed to exhaust her mortally. When she took leave of her friends in Algiers, in May, she gave them a disordered bundle of papers and manuscripts. "If I don't come back," she said, in the detached, ironic tone she liked to assume, "take care of all these." And she added, "They may be useful for my funeral eulogy."

After her retreat at the Zaouïa of Kenadza, at the end of the summer, her bouts of malaria became so severe she decided to go to the hospital at Aïn-Sefra, the little town on the edge of the Sahara, which she regarded as her base in the south, and which was a last outpost of the Colonial administration and the Foreign Legion. There Lyautey had built the barracks and offices, and the hospital on the high ground. Below, in the *oued* or bed of the ravine beside the dried-up stream, was the poorer part of the town—mud huts, or *gourbi*, the school, and the brothels, with their pensionnaires. It was here Isabelle Eberhardt had rented a little shack. Here, Slimène, arrived from the north, was awaiting her homecoming.

On the morning of October 21, Si Mahmoud was chafing to leave the hospital. She did not wait to see the doctor, who had advised her to stay longer. She left very early, about nine o'clock. If she had listened to the doctor, or even left later in the day, she would have escaped her death. But would she have wished to escape? With her suicidal tendencies, her growing melancholia, could she have foreseen, I believe she would have still chosen to go. She had a rendezvous with Slimène. They would make it a festival. There would be drink, and *kif*, and love; and drunk with all that, they would gallop off into the desert once more, into the far horizons. It was a heavy, thunderous morning, and already the yellowish waters of the *oued* were rising, boiling down through the narrow ravine, as they often did at this time of the year. Suddenly, around eleven o'clock, a roaring torrent broke loose from the mountains, flooding the *oued,* carrying with it houses, cattle, trees, people. Si Mahmoud had reached the shack, and was seen on the rickety balcony, very still, watching the tide of disaster as it swept round. She was never seen again, alive. The waters roared higher with furious impact. The little clay houses literally melted as they collapsed. On the high ground the garrison watched, powerless. Hours later the flood abated and a temporary bridge was contrived. The rescue parties searched for the living, for the dead. There were many lives lost; whole families of Arabs, school children, and the inmates of the brothels. Slimène seemed stunned. It was rumored Isabelle had been washed down stream and was safe: it was also rumored, and the ugly implications were to linger on, that Slimène had deliberately left her to perish.

No one had seen her. Lyautey ordered the search to continue. In icy water, by lantern light, his soldiers hunted in vain. Two days later her body was found, pinned beneath a fallen beam. She had been drowned in the desert. Lyautey thought that she had made no effort to escape, and that in a sort of passive exaltation, she had allowed death to overtake her; the long-sought suicide at last.

Lyautey detailed troops to sift through the rubble and ruins, to search for all her missing papers and manuscripts, which were collected in sodden fragments and later sent, sealed, by special messenger to Barracaund, in Algiers. Lyautey ordered her burial in the Moslem cemetery of Aïn-Sefra, and chose a simple marble stone, with her name, Si Mahmoud, in Arabic, and the rest in French. She lies there, a little removed from the other graves, and facing the desert she loved. Slimène seems to have been absent from the funeral; her few possessions left in Ténès were auctioned by his orders. In a last gesture of pride for his wife's European background, he published one of those black-bordered funeral announcements, so floridly griefstricken, so eloquent of *pompe funèbre.*

It is an extraordinary mixture of people, races, and classes who mourn *"leur épouse, sœur, belle-sœur, alliée et tante, décédée dans la Catastrophe d'Aïn-Sefra . . ."* an odd mixture of names all united on the formal card. Humble Arab clerks or interpreters, high military officials in Warsaw, and Poltava; others in the Ministry of Foreign Affairs, at St. Petersburg. Augustin, listed as *"Professeur d'Allemand à Marseilles."* Geneva tradespeople, more Arabs. . . .

Apart from Slimène, it was probably only Augustin, of all these relatives, who truly mourned Isabelle Eberhardt.

But for her friends she left an aching sense of loss. Lyautey mourned her not only as a friend, but as a valuable collaborator, though he expressed the view that she had attained the sum of her life, and was already on the eve of decline. "Poor Mahmoud!" he wrote. "I loved her for what she was, and for what she was not. I loved her prodigious artistic temperament. . . . She was truly herself; a rebel." There was a spate of lyrical funeral eulogies, mostly by people who had not known her, and several intense women writers seized the opportunity to interpret her life as a feminist crusade. In a fit of belated municipal pride, a street was named after her in Algiers, though as Robert Randau has pointed out, there is a sad symbolism in the fact that it begins in an inhabited quarter, and peters out into a waste land.

The posthumous exploitation of her work, and the deliberate distortion of her style by Victor Barrucand and others, was something which none of her friends forgave. Yet, for all their public indignation, they could not intervene. Si Mahmoud had become a legendary figure: besides, Barrucand had possession of most of her manuscripts. He considered that as he had been her editor, he could continue to present her work as he thought fit. Those who had seen Si Mahmoud's talents neglected during most of her life, saw her, in death, vulgarized, and both her work and her person exploited.

To anyone who has lived in North Africa, Isabelle Eberhardt's writings,—in particular her journals, and *Notes de routes*—are of profound interest. They do not date. I have barely touched the fringes of Arab life, but whenever I re-read her, I am struck, afresh, by her marvelous powers of evocation. The sour and spicy smell of Africa rises round me again: I see again the lumbering, groaning camels, "with their strange heads, half-bird, half-serpent." I hear the harsh, guttural cries of the nomads as they strike camp in the pale greenish light before sunrise. I hear the endless melancholy chants, and watch the far distances lift under the rising sun. These are the simple scenes that Isabelle Eberhardt knew and loved, as well as the dark dramatic histories of the people. She called them *"Les petits décors de vie."* She could evoke many landscapes: the harsh and splendid beauty of the Sud-Oranais, just as she could evoke the mortal boredom of the Légionnaires in *Dimanche au village;* or the *Portrait de l'ouled naïl,* where she describes one of these fabulous prostitutes, both her outward mask, and her inward nature. "A haunting face, the face of an idol . . . the face of a bird of prey." She writes of the passion and subjection and fatalism of the Oriental woman in an admirably unemotional style.

How vividly she conjures all the tumbling, spinning frenzies of the dancers, in *Fête Soudanaise.* And she adds—"there is always something Negroid in these leaping dances. The moorish dance—called *danse du ventre,* on the contrary, acquires, by certain languorous, slow poses, the significance of those sacred dances which stem from a more metaphysical East."

A collection of her writings which Barrucand presented, much adulterated, under the highly colored title *Dans l'ombre chaude d'Islam,* and, moreover, under his name alone, was an immediate success. Only some time later, in subsequent editions, was the name Isabelle Eberhardt added. The book went into many editions. *La Bonne Nomade* had become good business—for others. Barrucand continued to rework her originals into florid travesties, which, while acceptable to the public of that moment are far removed from Isabelle Eberhardt's own writing. It is interesting to compare *Dans l'ombre chaude d'Islam* with *Contes et paysages,* published in 1925, the fruits of subsequently found and untouched manuscripts.

In the years immediately after her death Barrucand ignored all the protests of her friends. Robert Randau, in company with Noiré the painter, cornered him on the matter. They had been speaking of the curious variations of Isabelle Eberhardt's style: how she could write a purely mechanical reportage, good descriptive stuff, but photographic, rather than personal, and then suddenly produce impressive passages, particularly those of a starkly autobiographical nature. To which Barrucand replied that Isabelle Eberhardt was a mediocre writer, incapable of anything more than a reportage, and that all these revealing passages were his work, which he had deliberately inserted into her texts, so as to present her objectively. It was for this reason, he said, he had claimed joint authorship. But he was confounded, years later, with the publication of her notes and journals which had been discovered by chance, and were presented by René-Louis Doyon. These authentic manuscripts proved to be full of just such passages as Barrucand had claimed she was incapable of writing.

But before the real Isabelle Eberhardt was to emerge there were others, besides Barrucand, who exploited her shamefully. And still the half-known, ambiguous personality and writer remained to be truly assessed.

The manner in which *Mes journaliers,* and with them the real woman, was discovered, is as strange as all the rest. In 1914 Mme Chloë Bulliod, a cousin of M. Gaillard, *doyen* of the Algerian press, was offered a sack full of Isabelle Eberhardt's papers, which had escaped the catastrophe of Aïn-Sefra. One of Slimène's family had hawked it round Algiers, only vaguely sensing its value. It had been offered to Barrucand years before, but he had refused to buy it, insisting it should have been his by rights—by what rights it is difficult to imagine. At any rate, he had refused it, preferring, perhaps not unnaturally, to profit by his own versions than to be faced by new, authentic material. Admitting his point of view, it seems odd, all the same, that he did not acquire the manuscripts, if only to have avoided any awkward confrontations later. Madame Bulliod seems to have done nothing with the papers; but when, in 1921, René-Louis Doyon was passing through Bône, on a lecture tour, he learned of their existence. M. Doyon had been passionately interested in the Si Mahmoud legend for years, and the papers passed into his possession.

They were a chaotic collection of letters, journals, notes, bills, manuscripts in Arabic and Russian, legal documents from the High Courts of Moscow; maps, caricatures, verses, and the rather weak but graphic little sketches Si Mahmoud liked to make of the African scene. Most important, most revealing of all, her journals. From these, as wild and disordered as their owner had been, her true image emerged. René-Louis

Doyon published *Mes journaliers,* and worked out a new biography, settling many questions of her origin and background which had puzzled even her closest friends. He established authoritatively the real Isabelle Eberhardt.

But biographies, however exact, do not affect legendary auras. Isabelle Eberhardt has passed into legend: so good, so bad, so weak, so strong: so simple, yet so complicated . . . poor Si Mahmoud, *La Bonne Nomade,* maligned and persecuted—yet free—free of all the little deadly fetters of everyday life: the petty spites too: cavorting off into the desert, sleeping where she fell, racked with fever, consumed with passions. Longing for a little grocer's shop: seeing herself as a maraboute, a pious and venerated priestess. Writing of extraordinary things with banality. Writing with simplicity of spiritual problems and her own tormented *âme slave.* She was a legend in her lifetime, and she has remained one.

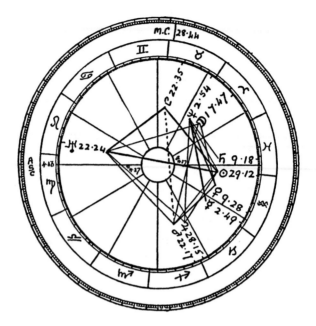

# AN ASTROLOGICAL POSTSCRIPT

## HOROSCOPE OF
## ISABELLE EBERHARDT
### (BY EQUAL HOUSE SYSTEM)
*Born Geneva, 6.0 p.m., 17.2.1877*
*Ascendant, 4° 56′ Virgo M.C., 28° 44′ Taurus. Sun 29° 12′ Aquarius.*
*Mercury, ruler of Ascendant in Aquarius. Uranus, ruler of Sun-sign*
*in Leo.*

As I wandered about North Africa tracking down the Eberhardt legend, I used to watch the *deguez*, or fortunetellers, crouched in the dust,
mumbling their incantations, trapping Destiny in a tray of sand. I remembered how Isabelle Eberhardt had embraced that aspect of Islam,
too. She had become as superstitious as any illiterate Bedouin. She often
consulted these *deguez*. In her journal she writes of visiting *"un sorcier*

*de la rue du Diable.*". . . "Acquired the certain proof of the *reality* of this incomprehensible and mysterious science of magic. . . ."

I know nothing about astrology but I feel an instinctive respect for it. Not for the fatuities of the Sunday newspapers but rather for its age-old traditions. I cannot dismiss it as mumbo-jumbo because its terms are incomprehensible to me. I accept that it can be a charting of a moment of time. Jung, speaking of basic archetypes, has said "whatever is born or done at this moment of time has the qualities of this moment of time."

I have always thought Isabelle Eberhardt would be a remarkable subject. I decided to have her horoscope cast, and obtained the name of Mrs. M. E. Hone, Director of Studies of the Faculty of Astrological Studies. I wrote to her from Switzerland where I was then living, asking if she would undertake to do a horoscope "blind." That is, without knowing anything of the subject concerned, as I thought this would be more interesting—and more of a test, cynics might add. I wrote, calling my subject "Miss E." I gave the necessary data of time and place and I added that the life seemed to be rich material for a horoscope. Nothing more.

Mrs. Hone replied that she did not much care to do "blind" horoscopes, for although the basic chart did not alter, the interpretation or reading could seem inaccurate, by lack of any facts on which to base the interpretation. But, in the same letter, she continued that since beginning her reply she had become curious, cast the horoscope, and found it of such exceptional interest that she would go on. There was, she wrote, some incertitude over a technical question of the time used at Geneva in 1877. (The present zone standard was adopted in 1894.) Meanwhile, she sent me her first "blind" analysis of the character and general pattern of Isabelle Eberhardt's life, as well as listing, precisely, certain dates and outstanding events. Later, on my arrival in London, Mrs. Hone showed me the completed birth chart with its "progressions" for later years and we discussed the way in which the life and the charts dovetailed together.

I think it of interest to publish this horoscope here, together with the first "blind" reading. Skeptics will be irritated and unmoved, no doubt. But there it is. For those who have studied astrology it will be just one more illustration of astrological accuracy. For all the rest of us, uninitiated but open-minded, this reading of Isabelle Eberhardt's life and nature is curiously impressive.

L. B.

The following notes are taken from the first "blind" interpretation, shorn of most technical terms. The italicized comments are my own:

"Here is a person of abundant creative force, with much sympathy, yet always a rebel, who must go her own way. A strongly individualistic nature.

"There should be something odd, or unusual, in her appearance. Her relations with others are odd, too. She devotes herself to them and their 'causes' with pugnacious intensity, yet she seems to be denied complete fulfillment herself. She has great idealism and humanitarian instincts. An overflowing, restless energy in an unusual way, connected with others. Yet, a mystical nature. While full of heart, she seems to have brought some strain into her life, or suffered strain through over-sudden ridding herself of things and people she did not want.

"She is a pioneer in foreign lands.

"She should have achieved some prominence. If denied actual creativity in children, or a cause, she could be a remarkable actress. She may have taken the stage in some other way.

"There should be some special fragility of mind, of the nervous system, even though with a strong physique.

"A person of alternate moods and much pride. A life, in a way, in the hands of, or for, others. A very marked preoccupation with sex, death, and the afterlife."

According to Mrs. Hone, three years stand out:

"Her tenth year. There would have been something in the nature of a loss, a tragedy, or a setback." *Her elder sister's flight from the Villa Neuve?*

"Her twentieth year. A great falling in love or a uniting happiness. A consummation, of fulfillment." *The year of her removal to North Africa, her turning Mohammedan, and her first decisive living among, and with, Arabs.*

"Her twenty-fourth year. One of sudden changes, a crowded, dramatic year of many events and dangers. Of climax. Much to do with others; possibly marriage too." *The year she was initiated into the Kadryas: the year of her attempted assassination; of her meeting with Barrucand. The year of her sentence of exile from North Africa; of her marriage, and her final break with Europe, by returning to Africa as an Arab wife.*

The astrological terms are precise: "The Sun by progression comes to exact aspect with no less than three planets which are themselves in precise aspect to each other in the horoscope. Thus it is indicated that this year must be one of climax.

"The twenty-fifth year shows that the life, which had been withdrawn, or artistic, but not materialistic, may now have begun to be more active, more canalized. It should have come into its full force about six years later, had she lived.

"Her death, apparently sudden, seems to have been more the fault of others than herself." *Slimène leaving her to perish in the flood?*

# BIBLIOGRAPHY

Andréossy, Comte A. F. *Constantinople et la Bosphore*. Paris, 1820.
About, Edmond. *La Grèce contemporaine*. Paris, Hachette, 1854.
Arbuthnot, Mrs. *Journals*, 1820–1831. London, Macmillan and Co. Ltd., 1950. Edited in 2 vol. by F. Bamford and the Duke of Wellington.
Balzac, Honoré de. *Le Lys dans la vallée*. Paris, 1836.
——. Correspondence.
La Barte, Jules. *Le Palais Impérial de Constantinople*. Paris, 1861.
Berlioz, Hector. *Les Années romantiques*, 1819. 42nd. Edited by Julien Tierset. Paris, 1904.
——. Autobiographie, 1803–1865.
Blunt, Lady Anne. *Bedouin Tribes of the Euphrates*. London, J. Murray, 1879.
——. *Pilgrimage to the Nedj*. London, J. Murray, 1881.
Blunt, Wilfred Scawen. *My Diaries*. London, M. Secker, 1919.
Blunt, Wilfred. *Desert Hawk: Abd El Kadir*. London, Methuen, 1947.
Bordeaux, Henry. *Balzac amoureux*. Paris, 1899.
Burckhardt, J. T. *Travels in Arabia*. London, J. Murray, 1822.
Burton, Jean. *Sir Richard Burton's Wife*. New York, Alfred Knopf, 1941.
Burton, Isabel. *A.E.I. (Arabia, Egypt, India)*. London, W. Mullan and Son, 1879.
——. *The Inner Life of Syria, Palestine and the Holy Land*. London, H. S. King & Co., 1875.
——. *The Life of Captain Sir Richard F. Burton, KC., MG., FR., GS.* London, Chapman & Hall, 1893.
Burton, Richard Francis. *Scinde or the Unhappy Valley*. London, R. Bentley, 1851.

——. *Goa and the Blue Mountains.* London, R. Bentley, 1851.

——. *Falconry in the Valley of the Indus.* London, J. van Voorst, 1852.

——. *Personal Narrative of a Pilgrimage to El-Medinah and Meccah.* London, Longman, Brown, Green & Roberts, 1857.

——. *The Lake Regions of Central Africa: a Picture of Exploration.* London, Longman, Brown, Green & Roberts, 1860.

——. *First Footsteps in East Africa: an Exploration of Harar.* London, Longman, Brown, Green & Longman, 1856.

——. *The City of the Saints and Across the Rocky Mountains to California.* London, Longman, Green & Roberts, 1861.

——. *A Mission to Gelele, King of Dahomé.* London, Tinsley Brothers, 1864.

——. *Two Trips to Gorilla Land: the Cataract of the Congo.* London, S. Low, Marston, Low & Searle, 1876.

——. *Exploration of the Highland of the Brazil.* London, Tinsley Brothers, 1869.

——. *The Kasidah: a Lay of the Higher Law.* London, B. Quaritch, 1880.

——. *The Thousand Nights and a Night,* with the Introduction and the Terminal Essay upon the History of the Nights. Printed by the Burton Club, for private subscribers only. London, 1905.

——. Lady Burton's edition of *The Thousand Nights and a Night,* prepared for household reading. London, Waterlow & Sons, 1887.

——. The entire Vol. XXXIII, *Royal Geographical Society,* 1860, and various pamphlets, reviews and notes.

——. *Richard Burton—Selected Papers on Anthropology, Travel and Exploration.* Edited by N. M. Penzer. London, A. M. Philpot, 1924.

Castries, Henry de. *L'Islam.* Paris, Colin, 1896.

Celarier, Henriette. *Lyautey et Isabelle Eberhardt. Le Temps,* 9 Août, 1934.

Channon, Henry. *The Ludwigs of Bavaria.* London, Methuen & Co., 1933.

Cherroll, Sir Valentine. *Fifty Years in a Changing World.* New York, Harcourt Brace & Co., 1928.

Cox, Samuel S. *Diversions of a Diplomat in Turkey.* New York, C. Webster & Co., 1887.

Craven, Lady. *A Journey through the Crimea to Constantinople.* London, 1789.

Creevy, Thomas. *Memoirs, 1793–1838.* Edited by Sir Herbert Maxwell. New York, E. P. Dutton & Co., 1903.

Day, Lillian. *Paganini of Genoa.* New York, The Macauley Co., 1929.

Davey, Richard. *The Sultan and His Subjects.* New York, E. P. Dutton & Co., 1897.

Denais, Joseph. *La Turquie, nouvelle et l'ancien régime.* Paris, 1909.

Dodge, Walter Phelps. *The Real Sir Richard Burton.* London, T. Fisher Unwin, 1907.

Doughty, Charles M. *Travels in Arabia Deserta.* London, Jonathan Cape, 1921.

Dumas, Alexandre. *Mes mémoires, 1852–1854.* Paris, Michel Levy Frères, 1863.

Eberhardt, Isabelle (*avec* Victor Barrucand). *Dans l'ombre chaude de l'Islam.* Paris, Fasquelle, 1905.

——. *Notes de route.* Paris, Fasquelle, 1908.

——. *Pages d'Islam.* Paris, Fasquelle, 1920.

Eberhardt, Isabelle. *Le Trimadeur.* Paris, 1922.

——. *Mes journaliers (précedés de la vie tragique de la Bonne Nomade. René-Louis Doyen).* Paris, La Connaissance, 1923.

——. *Au pays des sables (précedé des infortunes et ivresses d'une errante. René-Louis Doyen).* Paris, Sorlot, 1944.

Ffrench, Yvonne. *Ouida—a Study in Ostentation.* London, Cobden-Sanderson, 1938.

Focqueville, F. C. H. Laurent. *Voyage en Moré à Constantinople.* Paris, 1805.

Friswell, Laura Haine. *In the Sixties and Seventies.* Boston, H. B. Turner & Co., 1906.

Fromentin, Eugène. *Un été dans le Sahara, 1856.* Paris, Plon, 1877.

——. *Une année dans le Sahel, 1853.* Paris, Plon-Nourrit, 1912.

Galton, Francis. *Memories of My Life.* London, Methuen & Co., 1908.

Gautier, E. F. *Figures de conquête Coloniales.* Paris, Payot, 1931.

Gautier, Théophile. *Constantinople.* Paris, 1854.

Gosse, Edmund. *Portraits and Sketches.* London, W. Heinemann, 1912.

Gouffier—Comte C. de Choiseul. *Voyage de la Grèce à Constantinople,* 1782.

Grant, C. P. *The Syrian Desert.* London, A&B Black, Ltd., 1937.

Gribble, Francis. *Balzac, the Man and the Lover.* New York, E. P. Dutton & Co., 1930.

Hallé, Sir Charles. *Life and Letters, 1819–1860.* London, Smith Elder & Co., 1896.

Harris, Frank. *Contemporary Portraits.* New York, M. Kennerley, 1915.

Herskovits, Melville. *Dahomey.* New York, J. J. Augustin, 1938.

Hitchman, Francis. *Richard Burton, His Early, Private and Public Life.* London, S. Low, Marston, Searle and Rivington, 1887.

Janin, Jules. *Galeries des artistes dramatiques.* Paris, 1840.

Jomard, E. F. *Etudes geographique et historiques sur Arabie.* Paris, 1839.

Kenealy, Maurice E. *The Tichborne Tragedy.* London, F. Griffiths, 1913.

Kinglake, William. *Eöthen.* London, G. Bell & Sons, 1898.

Lamartine, Alphonse de. *Histoire de la Turquie.* Paris, 1855.

Lear, Edward. *Journals.* Edited by Herbert van Thal. London, A. Barker, 1952.

Lebel, Roland. *Isabelle Eberhardt.* Paris, Larose, 1925.

——. *Histoire de la littérature Coloniale en France.* Charlot, 1931.

Lee, Elizabeth. *Ouida: a Memoir.* London, T. Fisher Unwin, 1914.

Lenormand, Anne-Marie. *Mémoires historiques et secrets de l'Imperatrice Joséphine.* Paris, 1820.

Lieven, Princess de. *Correspondance, 1820–1826.*

Mackintosh, Mary. *Damascus and Its People.* Connecticut, Seely, Jackson and Halliday, 1883.

Montagu, Lady Mary Wortley. *Letters, 1716–1718.* Philadelphia, Carey, Lea Blanchard, 1837.

Morgan, Lady. *Memoirs.* London, 1832.

Morton, Benjamin A. *The Veiled Empress.* New York, G. P. Putnam's Sons, 1923.

Nerval, Gerard de. *Voyage en Orient.* Paris, 1851.

Nicolson, Harold. *Portrait of a Diplomatist.* Boston, Houghton Mifflin Co., 1930.

Oddie, E. M. *The Odyssey of a Loving Woman.* New York, Harper & Brothers, 1936.

Oliphant, Laurence. *Episodes in a Life of Adventure.* Edinburgh, W. Blackwood & Sons, 1896.

Oliver, G. A. *Travels in the Ottoman Empire.* London, 1801.

Paget Walburga, Lady. *Scenes and Memories.* New York, Charles Scribner, 1912.

——. *In My Tower.* London, Hutchinson & Co., 1924.

——. *Embassies of Other Days.* London. Hutchinson & Co., 1924.

——. *Further Recollections.* London, Hutchinson & Co., 1923.

Palgrave, W. G. *Narrative of a Year's Journey through Arabia.* London, The Macmillan Co., 1865.

Pardoe, Julia. *City of the Sultan.* London, 1837.

Pears, Edwin. *Forty Years in Constantinople.* London, H. Jenkins Ltd., 1916.

Penzer, N. M. *Annotated Bibliography of Sir Richard Francis Burton.* London, A. M. Philpot, Ltd., 1923.

——. *The Harem*. Philadelphia, Lippincott Co.

Poole, Stanley Lane. *Life of Stratford Canning*. London, Longmans, Green & Co., 1888.

Purgstall, J. Hammer. *Histoire de l'Empire Ottomane*. Paris, Bellizand Barthes Dufour et Lowell, 1835–1843.

Randau, Robert. *Isabelle Eberhardt: notes et souvenirs*. Paris, Charlot, 1945.

Redesdale, Lord. *Memories*. London, Hutchinson & Co., 1915.

Russell, Bertrand and Patricia. *The Amberley Papers*. New York, W. E. Norton & Co. Inc., 1937.

Stanley, Dean A. P. *The Eastern Church*. London, 1861.

Stéphan, Raoul. *Isabelle Eberhardt ou la révélation du Sahara*. Paris, Ernest Flammarion, 1930.

Stisted, Georgina M. *The True Life of Capt. Sir Richard F. Burton*. London, H. S. Nichols, 1896.

Slade, Sir Adolphus. *Records of Travel in Turkey, Greece and Albania*. London, 1833.

Symons, A. J. *Dramatis Personae*. Indianapolis, Bobbs-Merrill Co., 1923.

Thiers, Adolphe. *Histoire du Consulate et de l'Empire*. Paris, Furne, Jouvet et Cie., 1883.

Thouvenal, Edouard. *La Grèce du Roi Otho*. Paris, 1880.

Tott, Baron François de. *Mémoires*. Neuchâtel, 1784.

Uzanne, Octave. *Les romantiques inconnus*. Paris, Le Livre, vol. X.

Vambéry, Arminius. *History of Bokhara*. London, H. S. King & Co., 1873.

Weygand, General Maxime. *Histoire militaire de Mohammed Ali et ses fils*. Paris, Imprimerie Nationale, 1936.

Wilkins, W. H. *The Romance of Isabel, Lady Burton*. New York, Dodd Mead & Co. Inc., 1897.

Wright, Thomas. *Life of Sir Richard Burton*. London, Everett & Co., 1906.

Wyndham Horace. *Judicial Dramas*. London, T. F. Unwin, 1927.

Zweig, Stefan. *Balzac*. New York, The Viking Press, 1946.

#### SPECIAL PUBLICATIONS

The Foreign Office Confidential Print 2148, published 1872. Correspondence respecting Consul Burton's Proceedings at Damascus, 1868–1871. Various papers and dispatches addressed to the Foreign Office from the British Embassy at Constantinople, during the years 1809–1826. *Hansard*: Parliamentary Records of the House of Lords and the House of Commons, 1829–1830–1831. *The London Times. The*

*London Morning Post. Le Monde. The Fortnightly Review*, June 1, 1906. Meyer: *Konversations Lexikon.* Burke's *Peerage. The Almanach de Gotha. La Revue des Études Islamic,* 1923. *The Transatlantic Review,* March 1924. *La Connaissance,* June 1920. *Revue des Deux Mondes,* Tome VI, 1921. *Cornhill,* Vol. 51, 1921. *Le Livre,* No. X. *Les Horizons de France,* 1941.

917 – 701 – 0358

Printed in the United States
77606LV00001B/7-9

9 780786 710300